DOING
QUALITATIVE RESEARCH

SECOND
EDITION

DOING
QUALITATIVE RESEARCH

A Practical Handbook

SECOND
EDITION

DAVID SILVERMAN

SAGE Publications
London • Thousand Oaks • New Delhi

104.00

SAGE Publications Ltd
1 Oliver's Yard
55 City Road
London EC1Y 1SP

SAGE Publications Inc.
2455 Teller Road
Thousand Oaks, California 91320

SAGE Publications India Pvt Ltd
B-42, Panchsheel Enclave
Post Box 4109
New Delhi 110 017

British Library Cataloguing in Publication data

A catalogue record for this book is available from the British Library

ISBN 1 4129 0196 0
ISBN 1 4129 0197 9 (pbk)

Library of Congress Control Number 2004095426

Typeset by C&M Digitals (P) Ltd., Chennai, India
Printed in Great Britain by The Cromwell Press Ltd, Trowbridge Wiltshire

For my students

If this stone won't budge at present and is wedged in, move some of the other stones round it first.

All we want to do is to straighten you up on the track if your coach is crooked on the rails. Driving it afterwards we shall leave to you. (Wittgenstein, 1980: 39e)

For my students

Contents

Preface to Second Edition

This edition of *Doing Qualitative Research* has many new features. Six new chapters are included. Chapter 1 provides guidance on how to use this book, Chapter 2 discusses what you can (and cannot) do with qualitative research and the first chapter on the research experience (Chapter 3) is based on entirely different material. Other completely new chapters are on the evaluation of qualitative research (Chapter 15), on making good use of your supervisor (Chapter 18) and on effective qualitative research which serves to summarize the book's themes (Chapter 26). The remaining chapters have all been revised and updated.

I have also tried to make this edition attend to the needs of the range of students from different disciplines who are involved with qualitative research projects. Each chapter also now begins with a list of objectives and ends with a set of key points. The Glossary is greatly expanded and words that appear in it are listed in bold the first time they are used in each chapter.

With these changes, I hope this book will be equally accessible to students of qualitative methods across a wide range of disciplines. Although I cannot escape my own sociological background, I have tried throughout to provide helpful resources for students across the social sciences and throughout the world.

I hope that this book will be used as a basic primer for PhD students, combining 'hands-on' guidance on completing a good qualitative research project with practical advice on the criteria used in oral examinations and in publication. I have also attempted to make the book useful and accessible to the many MA and BA students who now prepare qualitative research dissertations. Although such students will normally be expected to complete their research in months rather than years, they face the same problems of research design, execution and writing up discussed in this book. Even if they do not have an oral examination on their research, the best MA students should be thinking about publishing their work and both BA and MA students should be interested in how higher-level work is evaluated and the significance of 'originality'.

The content of this book derives from my experience over twenty years of teaching introductory workshops for research students, a course in Concepts and Methods of Qualitative Research for MA students and an undergraduate qualitative research course. These courses have convinced me that the only way to learn the craft skills of qualitative research is to apply classroom knowledge about different methodologies to actual data (found here in the case studies and exercises provided in each chapter).

However, my readers should be aware that even textbooks cannot offer purely 'neutral' treatment of the topics they cover. Much will depend upon the material included (and excluded) and upon the particular position of the author – we all have our own 'axes to grind'.

In this book, I argue that doing qualitative research is always a theoretically driven undertaking. This means that 'practical skills' are not the whole of the story, particularly if such skills are (wrongly) seen as sets of arbitrary 'recipes'.

Second, I have long argued that most dichotomies or polarities in social science are highly dangerous. At best, they are pedagogic devices for students to obtain a first grip on a difficult field – they help us to learn the jargon. At worst, they are excuses for not thinking, which assemble groups of researchers into 'armed camps', unwilling to learn from one another.

For instance, unlike some qualitative researchers, I have used quantitative measures where appropriate. This is because, while recognizing the different **models** we often use, I share quantitative researchers' aim to do a 'science' (loosely defined as critical sifting of data, leading to cumulative generalizations which can always be later refuted).

There are pragmatic as well as intellectual reasons for taking this position. As the Introduction to a book I recently co-edited puts it:

> The great conversation that, in practice, is carried out in the world (what researchers like to call "common sense"), assumes tshat facts are 'out there' and can be 'collected' and therefore can constitute 'evidence'. A social research practice that does not go along with this view will, on the whole, fail to enter the world's conversation. (Seale et al., 2004: 6)

Chapter 13 of this book on computer-assisted qualitative data analysis was written (and updated) by Clive Seale. I am most grateful for his skilful exposition of the subject. Anne Ryen kindly made available some of her unpublished data and Anne Murcott allowed me to quote from her unpublished paper on writing a student dissertation. I also want to thank all the students whose work is discussed in Chapter 4 and Moira Kelly, Sally Hunt, Simon Allistone, Seta Waller, Kay Fensom and Vicki Taylor for allowing me to quote from their research diaries. My thanks are due to my editors at Sage: Michael Carmichael for suggesting this second edition and Patrick Brindle for seeing it through to completion. I am particularly grateful for the most helpful suggestions that Lauren Kamada and Aileen Nicholls made about an earlier draft of this second edition.

Introduction

Part One provides a context for thinking about doing qualitative research. A brief introduction to the themes of this book and how best to use it is provided in Chapter 1. Chapter 2 compares qualitative and quantitative research and raises questions about how to decide whether qualitative methods are appropriate for your research topic. Chapters 3 and 4 offer examples of early and late stages of research students' work and show what we can learn from their experiences and ideas. Finally, in Chapter 5, I address (and seek to demystify) the troubling concept of 'originality' in research.

1 How To Use This Book

This is the fifth textbook on methodology which I have written or edited since 1985. Everyone knows that research methods texts often sell well but that is hardly an excuse to write yet another one. So you may properly ask: what has this book to offer?

The brief answer is that, in my view, research students still lack a singly authored, 'hands-on', practical guide to the business of doing qualitative research, writing it up and making use of it. This is what this book sets out to do. Much more than other methodology texts, it aims to teach the skills of qualitative research in the context of the practical problems that face the novice researcher. To this end, it combines telling examples of students' experiences 'in the field', case studies of relevant qualitative research, summaries of key skills and exercises to test your knowledge.

In this short chapter, I outline the structure of this book and provide some suggestions about how to make optimum use of it.

Part One is aimed at the beginning research student. Part Two assumes that you have overcome your initial doubts and now need to deal with the nitty-gritty issues that arise when you start to design a research study. Chapter 6 discusses how to select a topic. Chapters 7 and 8 deal with using theories and choosing a methodology. The tricky question of selecting which case(s) to study is discussed in Chapter 9. The final chapter in Part Two considers how to write a research proposal.

Part Three focuses upon the period when you have begun to gather and analyse data. In Chapter 11, I outline what is to be gained by working early with data sets. Chapter 12 discusses how to develop your early analysis. The next two chapters consider the use of computer-aided qualitative data analysis and validity and reliability. Chapter 15 shows you how to apply what you have learned in Part Three to evaluate qualitative research.

In Part Four, I address ways of keeping in touch with your data, with subjects 'in the field' and with your university department. In four chapters, I discuss record keeping (including a research diary), relations in the field (including ethical issues), making good use of your supervisor and how to get feedback about your research.

Alasuutari describes writing a thesis as rather like learning to ride a bicycle through gradually adjusting your balance:

> Writing is first and foremost analysing, revising and polishing the text. The idea that one can produce ready-made text right away is just about as senseless as the cyclist who has never had to restore his or her balance. (1995: 178)

3

Following Alasuutari, Part Five is concerned with the 'writing-up' stage of research. Its five chapters address the following topics: how to begin your research report; how to write effective literature review and methodology chapters; and how to produce a lively concluding chapter.

For PhD students, the oral or viva is a crucial and much feared part of the process. It also may seem to be shrouded in mystery, like some weird Masonic ritual! Part Six attempts to demystify the PhD examination. While Part Six is only relevant to PhD students, Part Seven offers all readers a discussion of effective qualitative research which provides an overview of the main themes of this book.

The three chapters in Part Eight consider the aftermath of a finished piece of research. Depending on the level of your work, this may involve the possibility of getting your research published and, perhaps, getting a job. Whatever its level, a good research report always is designed for a particular audience.

From Part Two onwards, the order of this book very roughly follows the likely chronological sequence of doing a piece of research. However, I recognize that textbooks are not usually read in the same way as novels. For instance, although you may want to resist the temptation to skip to the final chapter of a whodunnit, no such prohibitions are sensible when using a textbook. So, for example, you may want to consult Chapter 18 on making good use of your supervisor quite early on. Or, if you want a quick summary of the story this book offers, you may turn at once to Chapter 26. Each chapter is more or less self-contained and so there should be no problems in zigzagging through the book in this way, using the glossary provided where appropriate.

Zigzagging also makes sense because qualitative research rarely follows a smooth trajectory from hypothesis to findings. As we shall see, this is less a drawback than an opportunity to refocus your work as new ideas and opportunities arise in the field. Consequently, most readers will want to move backwards and forwards through the book as the occasion arises. Alternatively, you may find it useful to skim-read the book in advance and then work through certain chapters in greater detail to correspond with different stages of your research.

The examples and exercises in this book are designed to allow the novice to emerge with practical skills rather than simply the ability to write good examination answers. The exercises mostly rely upon the stage of your research coinciding with the chapters where they are found. So when you are zigzagging through the book or skimming it, it will usually make sense to return to the exercises at a relevant stage of your work, using your supervisor for feedback and advice.

Ultimately, of course, no book can or should provide for how it will be read. Complete anarchy is nonetheless rarely very useful to anybody. In this spirit, the structure I have provided tries to give you an initial orientation. From then on, it is up to you. As the philosopher Ludwig Wittgenstein wrote:

> All we want to do is to straighten you up on the track if your coach is crooked on the rails. Driving it afterwards we shall leave to you. (1980: 39e)

What You Can (and Can't) Do with Qualitative Research

CHAPTER OBJECTIVES

By the end of this chapter, you will be able to:

- Recognize that there is no simple distinction between 'qualitative' and 'quantitative' research.
- Understand the uses and limitations of both forms of research.
- Work out whether qualitative methods are appropriate to your research topic.

2.1 INTRODUCTION

This chapter offers practical help in answering three very concrete questions that you should consider before you think of beginning a qualitative research study. These are:

- Are qualitative methods always the best?
- Is qualitative research appropriate to the topic in which I am interested?
- If so, how should it influence the way I define my research problem?

In a way, this book as a whole is dedicated to answer these kind of questions. However, some initial answers will help to give you a good sense of the issues involved. As in the rest of the book, I will set out my argument through examples of actual research studies.

2.2 ARE QUALITATIVE METHODS ALWAYS THE BEST?

In the Sociology Department where I used to work, we offered a graduate degree in Qualitative Research. This title was chosen to give a flavour of a course largely taught by **ethnographers** who themselves mainly use qualitative methods.

However, such a title may attract students more in terms of what it promises to avoid rather than by reason of what it offers.

'Qualitative research' seems to promise that we will avoid or downplay statistical techniques and the mechanics of the kinds of quantitative methods used in, say, survey research or epidemiology. In fact, this was indeed the case – although we expected students to take a course in survey methods and to be aware of how the issues of **validity** and **reliability** so often posed by quantitative researchers are relevant to any kind of credible research (albeit in varying ways).

The danger in the title, however, is that it seems to assume a fixed preference or predefined evaluation of what is 'good' or at least 'appropriate' (i.e. qualitative) and 'bad' or 'inappropriate' (i.e. quantitative) research. Yet any good researcher knows that the choice of method should not be predetermined. Rather you should choose a method that is appropriate to what you are trying to find out (see Punch, 1998: 244).

For instance, if you want to discover how people intend to vote, then a quantitative method, like a **social survey**, may be the most appropriate choice. On the other hand, if you are concerned with exploring people's life histories or everyday behaviour, then qualitative methods may be favoured. An insistence that any research worth its salt should follow a purely quantitative logic would simply rule out the study of many interesting phenomena relating to what people actually do in their day-to-day lives, whether in homes, offices or other public and private places. This suggests a purely pragmatic argument ('horses for courses'), according to which our research problem defines the most appropriate method.

So we should never assume that qualitative methods are intrinsically superior. Indeed, a quantitative approach may sometimes be more appropriate to the research problem in which we are interested. So, in choosing a method, everything depends upon what we are trying to find out. No method of research, quantitative or qualitative, is intrinsically better than any other.

Moreover, as we shall see later, research problems are not neutral. How we frame a research problem will inevitably reflect a commitment (explicit or implicit) to a particular model of how the world works. And, in qualitative research, there are multiple, competing **models**.

So when we say that we are committed to qualitative methods, we still need to find answers to at least two further questions:

● Exactly what methods do we have in mind (e.g. interviews, focus groups, observation, texts, audio or video recordings)?
● In what ways are these methods relevant to our research problem and to our model of how the world is put together?

In the next two sections, I will show you how you can begin to think about answering these questions.

TABLE 2.1 SHOULD I USE QUALITATIVE RESEARCH?

1	What exactly am I trying to find out? Different questions require different methods to answer them.
2	What kind of focus on my topic do I want to achieve? Do I want to study this phenomenon or situation in detail? Or am I mainly interested in making standardized and systematic comparisons and in accounting for variance?
3	How have other researchers dealt with this topic? To what extent do I wish to align my project with this literature?
4	What practical considerations should sway my choice? For instance, how long might my study take and do I have the resources to study it this way? Can I get access to the single case I want to study in depth? Are quantitative samples and data readily available?
5	Will we learn more about this topic using quantitative or qualitative methods? What will be the knowledge payoff of each method?
6	What seems to work best for me? Am I committed to a particular research model which implies a particular methodology? Do I have a gut feeling about what a good piece of research looks like?

Source: adapted from Punch (1998: 244–5)

2.3 SHOULD I USE QUALITATIVE METHODS?

Table 2.1 offers some general answers to this question. It shows that qualitative research is not always appropriate to every research problem. You need to think through exactly what you are trying to achieve rather than be guided by some fashion or trivial preference – perhaps you are not comfortable doing statistical calculations. So, following item 2 of Table 2.1, if you are mainly interested in making systematic comparisons in order to account for the variance in some phenomenon (e.g. crime or suicide rates), then quantitative research is indicated. Equally, as a rule of thumb, if it turns out that published research on your topic is largely quantitative (item 3), does it pay to swim against the tide? As I stress several times in this book, if you can align your work with a previous, classic study, this makes a lot of sense. The last thing you want to do is to try to reinvent the wheel!

Let me try to flesh out the broad guidelines provided in this table by using one example which, I believe, shows the issues you need to think about when fitting your choice of **methodology** to your research problem. To concretize the discussion, I will use a research example to help us focus on items 5 and 6 from Table 2.1.

A few months ago, when I was idly reading the job advertisements for university researchers, I came across an advertisement that caught my eye. This was the research question to be tackled:

How is psycho-social adversity related to asthma morbidity and care?

It was explained that this problem would be studied by means of qualitative interviews.

My immediate question was: how can qualitative interviews help to address the topic at hand? The problem is not that people with asthma will be unable to answer questions about their past nor, of course, that they are likely to lie or mislead the interviewer. Rather, like all of us, when faced with an outcome (in this case, a chronic illness), they will document their past in a way which fits it, highlighting certain features and downplaying others. In other words, the interviewer will be inviting a retrospective **rewriting of history** with an unknown bearing on the causal problem with which this research is concerned.

This is not to deny that valuable data may be gathered from such a qualitative study. But rather that it will address an altogether different issue – **narratives** of illness in which 'causes' and 'associations' work as rhetorical moves. By contrast, a quantitative study would seem to be much more appropriate to the research question proposed. Quantitative surveys can be used on much larger samples than qualitative interviews, allowing inferences to be made to wider populations. Moreover, such surveys have standardized, **reliability** measures to ascertain the 'facts' with which this study is concerned.

Indeed, why should a large-scale quantitative study be restricted to surveys or interviews? If I wanted **reliable**, generalizable knowledge about the relation between these two **variables** (psycho-social adversity and asthma morbidity), I would start by looking at hospital records.

I believe this example illustrates the need to fit your research design to your research topic. But, of course, it overplays the opposition between qualitative and quantitative methods.

If resources allow, many research questions can be thoroughly addressed by combining different methods, using qualitative research to document the detail of, say, how people interact in one situation and using quantitative methods to identify variance (see Chapter 8). The fact that simple quantitative measures are a feature of some good qualitative research shows that the whole 'qualitative/quantitative' dichotomy is open to question. In the context of this book, I view many such dichotomies or polarities in social science as highly dangerous. At best, they are pedagogic devices for students to obtain a first grip on a difficult field – they help us to learn the jargon. At worst, they are excuses for not thinking, which assemble groups of researchers into 'armed camps', unwilling to learn from one another.

Of course, as Table 2.1 (item 6) suggests, such armchair debates are of less relevance than the simple test: 'what works for me?' As Becker comments about his use of qualitative data:

> It's the kind of research I've done, but that represents a practical rather than an ideological choice. It's what I knew how to do, and found personal enjoyment in, so I kept on doing it. (1998: 6)

However, Becker adds that his 'choice' has not blinded him to the value of quantitative approaches:

I've always been alive to the possibilities of other methods (so long as they weren't pressed on me as matters of religious conviction) and have found it particularly useful to think about what I did in terms that come from such other ways of working as survey research or mathematical modelling. (ibid.)

Not only does it sometimes pay to think of qualitative research, as Becker suggests, in terms of quantitative frameworks, but also it can be helpful occasionally to combine qualitative and quantitative methods. As I show in Chapter 14, simple tabulations can be a useful tool for identifying **deviant cases**.

In this section, I have used one example to show the importance of thinking through your research problem before committing yourself to a choice of method. But, as I have already hinted, the situation is rather more complicated than this.

2.4 UNDERSTANDING RESEARCH IN TERMS OF DIFFERENT MODELS

We can understand this complication better by returning to item 6 of Table 2.1: that is, am I committed to a particular research model which implies a particular methodology? Models provide an overall framework for viewing reality. They inform the **concepts** we use to define our research problem.

For instance, in the example we have been considering, the problem was defined in terms of the relation between an independent variable ('psycho-social adversity') and two dependent variables ('asthma morbidity' and 'asthma care'). These kinds of concepts appear to derive from a **positivist** model which encourages us to chart the relation between variables which are **operationally defined** by the researcher. Now, although positivism is the most common model used in quantitative research (i.e. the default option), it sits uneasily within most qualitative research designs. This is why I was puzzled by the choice of qualitative data in the design of the asthma study.

Qualitative research designs tend to work with a relatively small number of cases. Generally speaking, qualitative researchers are prepared to sacrifice scope for detail. Moreover, even what counts as 'detail' tends to vary between qualitative and quantitative researchers. The latter typically seek detail in certain aspects of correlations between variables. By contrast, for qualitative researchers, 'detail' is found in the precise particulars of such matters as people's understandings and interactions. This is because qualitative researchers tend to use a non-positivist model of reality.

Note the negative description of a model used in the previous sentence. This was deliberate because, as we shall now see, there is no single agreed model within qualitative research.

Some qualitative researchers believe that qualitative methods can provide a 'deeper' understanding of social phenomena than would be obtained from purely quantitative data. In their editorial introduction to the second edition of their *Handbook of Qualitative Research*, Denzin and Lincoln put it this way:

> Qualitative researchers stress the socially constructed nature of reality, the intimate relationship between the researcher and what is studied, and the situational constraints that shape inquiry. They seek answers to questions that stress *how* social experience is created and given meaning. In contrast, quantitative studies emphasize the measurement and analysis of causal relationships between variables, not processes. Proponents of such studies claim that their work is done from within a value-free framework. (2000: 8, authors' emphasis)

So far, so good. Denzin and Lincoln appear to offer a unitary model which provides a sharp contrast with the model used in quantitative research. Unfortunately, if we dissect the elements that make up their model, all is not so clear. For instance, not all qualitative researchers would agree that, in contrast to quantitative studies, 'values' automatically enter their research (see Chapters 14 and 17).

In addition, there seems to be a tension in the above quotation between a concern with 'social construction' and a focus on 'social experience' and 'meaning'. Why should 'social construction' focus on the concepts of experience and meaning but not involve behaviour and interaction? To use the asthma example again, why would a qualitative study necessarily focus on experience but exclude, say, the organization of clinic interactions in which doctors, patients and patients' families together define 'asthma care'?

A clue to Denzin and Lincoln's real focus is found a little later in their Introduction. They write:

> Both qualitative and quantitative researchers are concerned with *the individual's point of view*. However, qualitative investigators think they can get closer to *the actor's perspective* through detailed interviewing and observation. They argue that quantitative researchers are seldom able to capture their subjects' perspectives because they have to rely on more remote, inferential empirical methods and materials. (2000: 10, my emphasis)

Note the concern evinced here for 'the individual's point of view' and 'the actor's perspective'. This reflects a strong tradition in qualitative research which prioritises the study of perceptions, meanings and emotions. For that reason, we can refer to it as an **emotionalist** model (see Gubrium and Holstein, 1997).

However, as Denzin and Lincoln themselves recognize, qualitative researchers have employed many other models. To simplify, let me pick up the term 'social construction' used in the first Denzin and Lincoln quotation. Opposed to the emotionalist model is a **constructionist** model which prioritises interaction over meaning and, therefore, prefers to look at what people do without any necessary reference to what they are thinking or feeling. The differences between these two models are outlined in Table 2.2.

TABLE 2.2   TWO MODELS COMPARED

	Emotionalism	Constructionism
Focus	Meaning, emotion	Behaviour
Aim	Authentic insights	Studying how phenomena are constructed
Preferred data	Open-ended interviews	Observation; texts; tapes

I discuss the emotionalist position further in Silverman (2004) and the nature and purpose of models is examined in greater depth in Chapter 7. For the moment, I just want to leave you with the thought that 'qualitative research' can mean many different things.

By now, this whole debate may have left you thoroughly confused. As a beginning researcher, you may rightly feel that the last thing you need is to sink into an intractable debate between warring camps.

However, it helps if we treat this less as a war and more as a clarion call to be clear about the issues that animate our work and help to define our research problem. As I argue in Chapter 6, purely theoretical debates are often less than helpful if we want to carry out effective research. The point is to select a model that makes sense to you (and, of course, there are more than the two models relevant to qualitative research – see Chapter 7). The strengths and weaknesses of any model will only be revealed in what you can do with it.)

I will, therefore, conclude this chapter with a single case study which I believe is an inspiring example which shows the value of using a clear-cut model and, thereby, demonstrates the particular explanatory power of qualitative research.

Case study: 'positive thinking'

Wilkinson and Kitzinger (2000) (henceforth WK) were interested in the way in which both laypeople and many medical staff assume that 'positive thinking' helps you cope better with cancer. They point out that most of the evidence for this belief derives from questionnaires in which people tick a box or circle a number.

What alternative can we offer to this kind of quantitative research? The preferred qualitative route has been to analyse what people with cancer say in open-ended interviews. Deriving from what I have called the emotionalist model, such research has generally sought out patients' meanings and emotions and, as WK point out, has broadly supported the findings of quantitative studies. However, there is a problem here:

Cont…

There is a widespread assumption in [both] these literatures that research participants are 'naïve' subjects, intent primarily upon accurately reporting their cognitions to the researcher. (WK, 2000: 801)

By contrast, WK prefer to treat statements about 'thinking positive' as actions and to understand their functions in particular contexts of speaking. So, although they use similar data to the emotionalists (interviews and focus groups), the way they analyse that data is very different. Using what I have called the constructionist model, WK seek to insert 'scare marks' around 'positive thinking' and to examine when and how it is used.

Let us look at one data extract that they use from a focus group of women with breast cancer:

Extract 2.1 [WK, 2000: 805] (see the Appendix for transcript conventions)

Fiona: Life's too short to worry about whether you can af<u>ford</u> or whether you <u>can't</u> afford, or whether you <u>should</u> spend the money or whether you <u>shouldn't</u> spend the money, you know, I think we, we're sort of thinking that towards the back end of next year, we're <u>off</u> on a holiday to Australia. I think you've got to feel like that. If you wanna do it, I think you've gotta go for it, because <u>none</u> of us, I mean, it's all very well, they say, "Oh yeah, you're fine now", you, you know, "Everything's gonna be okay", but none of us <u>know</u> what next <u>week</u>, or next <u>month</u>, or next <u>year</u> has in store. And I, so I think you, you have to be positive.

Fiona ends her comments about spending money now because 'life's too short' by saying 'you have to be positive'. But should we take this to mean that this shows she is a 'positive thinker'?

First, as WK note, Fiona shows that the object of her positive thinking is vague and diverse. She is 'thinking positively neither about the cancer and its effects, nor about [her] possible recovery, but about [her life] apart from the cancer' (2000: 805).

Second, if we inspect closely what Fiona says, we can notice that she uses a multiplicity of different voices to frame what she is saying. 'You' expresses the voice of any reasonable person (e.g. 'if you wanna do it' and 'you have to be positive'). 'They' occurs once to refer to other people who tell you things that may not turn out to be true. 'I' is used to refer to someone who ponders about all this ('I think').

Like many of the women in these focus groups, Fiona frames her references to 'positive thinking' in the voice of 'you'. Used in this way, as what 'you have got to do', 'positive thinking' is used as a kind of maxim.

Cont…

The beauty of maxims is that, because they are supposed to reflect a shared world, their recipients can do little other than agree with them (Sacks, 1992, Vol. 1: 23–5). So, if you say, 'you have to be positive', you are likely to get agreement, in the same way as if you say, 'many hands make light work'. And, interestingly enough, WK report that Fiona's last comment does indeed elicit agreement.

What Fiona is saying turns out to be complex and skilful. A lot of the time we want to obtain the agreement of others and Fiona structures her talk to do just that – notice that she also invokes a maxim ('life's too short') to justify spending money.

This suggests that, at the very least, we should not tear out what Fiona says about 'positive thinking' from the multi-faceted structure of her comments. Let me underline this point with one more extract:

Extract 2.2 [WK, 2000: 807]

Hetty: When I first found out I had cancer, I said to myself, I said right, it's not gonna get me. And that was it. I mean (Yvonne: Yeah) obviously you're devastated because it's a dreadful thing
Yvonne: (overlaps) Yeah, but you've got to have a positive attitude thing, I do
Betty: (overlaps) But then, I was talking to Dr. Purcott and he said to me the most helpful thing that anybody can have with any type of cancer is a positive attitude
Yvonne: a positive outlook, yes
Betty: Because if you decide to fight it, then the rest of your body will st-, will start
Yvonne: Motivate itself, yeah
Betty: to fight it

Once again, on the surface, Extract 2.2 seems to support the idea that 'positive thinking' is an internal, cognitive state of people with cancer. However:

> this overlooks the extent to which these women are discussing 'thinking positive' not as a natural reaction to having cancer (the natural reaction [cited elsewhere in their data] is that, 'obviously you're devastated because it's a dreadful thing'), but rather as a moral imperative: 'you've got to have a positive attitude'. (WK, 2000: 806–7)

So WK's analysis suggests two different ways in which these women formulate their situation:

Positive thinking is presented as a moral imperative, part of a moral order in which they *should* be thinking positive.
Other reactions (including fear and crying) are simply described as what 'I did' not as 'what you have got to do'.

Cont…

This distinction shows the value of looking at how talk is organized and not just treating it 'as providing a transparent "window" on underlying cognitive processes' (WK, 2000: 809). By contrast, WK's constructionist model has allowed us to get a quite different, more processual grasp of the phenomenon.

This has two useful consequences. First, we come to understand the place of 'positive thinking' within a broader range of activities like troubles-telling. In so doing, we move from **substantive theories** to **formal theories** and, thereby, open up the possibility of broader comparisons (see Glaser and Strauss, 1967). Second, rather than simply confirm lay or medical beliefs about the phenomenon, it provides new insights of potential value to both patients and healthworkers.

2.5   CONCLUDING REMARKS

Wilkinson and Kitzinger's study gives a new twist to my earlier comments about the haziness of the distinction between qualitative and quantitative research. Earlier qualitative studies of 'positive thinking' have simply replicated the findings of quantitative surveys but at the cost of precision because of the smaller sample size involved. By contrast, by using a radically different research model, they have come up with new findings that would be difficult to establish through quantitative methods.

Nonetheless, we must not draw too sharp a distinction between quantitative and qualitative research. Qualitative research can mean many different things, involving a wide range of methods and informed by contrasting models.

Ultimately, everything depends on the research problem you are seeking to analyse. I conclude this chapter, therefore, with a statement which shows the absurdity of pushing too far the qualitative/quantitative distinction:

> We are not faced, then, with a stark choice between words and numbers, or even between precise and imprecise data; but rather with a range from more to less precise data. Furthermore, our decisions about what level of precision is appropriate in relation to any particular claim should depend on the nature of what we are trying to describe, on the likely accuracy of our descriptions, on our purposes, and on the resources available to us; not on ideological commitment to one methodological paradigm or another. (Hammersley, 1992: 163)

KEY POINTS

■ 'Qualitative' research involves a variety of quite different approaches.
■ Although some 'quantitative' research can be properly criticized or found insufficient, the same may be said about some 'qualitative' research.
■ In these circumstances it is sensible to make pragmatic choices between research methodologies according to your research problem and model.
■ Doing 'qualitative' research should offer no protection from the rigorous, critical standards that should be applied to any enterprise concerned to sort 'fact' from 'fancy'.

Further Reading

The most useful introductory texts are Alan Bryman's *Quantity and Quality in Social Research* (Unwin Hyman, 1988), Nigel Gilbert's (ed.) *Researching Social Life* (Sage, 1993), Clive Seale's (ed.) *Researching Society and Culture* (Sage, 2004) and Keith Punch's *Introduction to Social Research* (Sage, 1998). More advanced qualitative analysis is offered by David Silverman's *Interpreting Qualitative Data: Methods for Analysing Talk, Text and Interaction* (Sage, 2001), especially Chapter 2; Matthew Miles and Michael Huberman's *Qualitative Data Analysis* (Sage, 1984), Martin Hammersley and Paul Atkinson's *Ethnography: Principles in Practice* (Tavistock, 1983) and Norman Denzin and Yvonna Lincoln's (eds) *Handbook of Qualitative Research* (2nd edn, Sage, 2000). A particularly useful source is 'Inside qualitative research', the introduction to Clive Seale et al.'s edited book *Qualitative Research Practice* (Sage, 2004, 1–11).

In addition to these general texts, readers are urged to familiarize themselves with examples of qualitative and quantitative research. Strong (1979) and Lipset et al. (1962) are good examples of each. Wilkinson elaborates on her work in Wilkinson (2004). Sensible statements about the quantitative position are to be found in Marsh (1982) (on survey research) and Hindess (1973) (on official statistics).

Exercise 2.1

Review any research study with which you are familiar. Then answer the questions below:

1   To what extent are its methods of research (qualitative, quantitative or a combination of both) appropriate to the nature of the research question(s) being asked?

2   How far does its use of these methods meet the criticisms of both qualitative and quantitative research discussed in this chapter?

3   In your view, how could this study have been improved methodologically and conceptually?

Exercise 2.2

In relation to your own possible research topics:

1   Explain why you think a qualitative approach is appropriate.

2   Would quantitative methods be more appropriate? If not, why not?

3   Would it make sense to combine qualitative and quantitative methods? Explain your answer.

The Research Experience I

3.1 INTRODUCTION

Switch on your television and graze through the channels. You will undoubtedly come across a chat show in which people are talking about their rise and fall from grace. Or maybe you will find a sports channel where, more often than not, you will see not a game but interviews with players about their hopes and feelings.

We live in a world in which our yearning for people's 'experiences' is more than satisfied by the popular media. Indeed, very often this pursuit of the 'personal' becomes repetitive and we should resist it (see Atkinson and Silverman, 1997).

However, this is not always the case. Any book which sets out to offer information and advice about doing a piece of research without telling a few personal 'stories' would be in danger of being received as empty and unhelpful. If we can draw out appropriate implications from these stories, moving from the personal to the practical, then we will have achieved something more substantial than merely providing some kind of experiential comfort blanket.

In this spirit, this chapter is devoted to telling the stories of three of my research students. The three students have much in common apart from the fact that I supervized them for a PhD in sociology. Moira Kelly and Sally Hunt began their research many years after their first degrees. Simon Allistone began his PhD at the age of 29. All three were products of the MA in qualitative research at Goldsmiths College and had been supervized by myself on their MA dissertations.

Moira and Sally held down demanding jobs while doing their research. Moira was, in turn, a research nurse, a health promotion research manager and then a health researcher; Sally was a lecturer in nursing. Unlike Moira and Sally, Simon was able to work on his doctorate on a full-time basis thanks to a three-year grant from the British Economic and Social Research Council.

Their work spans a broad range of qualitative methodologies. Moira analysed interviews which she had conducted. Sally carried out an organizational **ethnography** and Simon studied interactions at a school meeting. While all three were registered for a PhD in sociology, their substantive interests crossed into other disciplines: health studies and nursing (Moira and Sally), organization studies (Sally and Simon) and media studies and education (Simon).

However, while the three of them worked with audio-recorded data, their analytic perspectives were rather different. Sally drew on Goffman's (1974) concept of **frames** in her study of decision making by a mental health team (MHT) caring for homeless people. Simon based his study of a Parent–Teachers' Evening on concepts of turn-taking derived from **conversation analysis (CA)**. In her research on interviews with surviving partners of people who had died of cancer, Moira combined CA with an approach familiar to researchers who analyse interview accounts as **narratives**.

I realize that many of my readers will have different interests and backgrounds. Let me assure you at once that you will not need any special knowledge to understand what follows. The approach that my students used is, for my present purposes, of far less significance than the trajectory of their projects. Moreover, as I argue below, there are lessons here to be drawn for anybody who is contemplating writing a research dissertation at any level.

Perhaps more relevant than their common theoretical perspective was the different amount of time that their research took. Working full time, Simon completed his PhD in four years. Reflecting the pressures of demanding jobs, Moira took seven years and Sally finished in ten. As already suggested, these different time-spans were strongly associated with practical contingencies, more or less unrelated to technical issues of research design.

In what follows, the three tell their stories largely in their own words drawn from their research diaries. I have limited myself merely to adding some headings and asides. After each story, I suggest some more general implications. The chapter concludes with a summary in the form of a fifteen-point guide to completing a successful research study.

3.2 MOIRA'S RESEARCH DIARY

3.2.1 Beginnings

The research process began when I took up post as research associate on a study of hospice and hospital care of people with terminal cancer. The aim of that project was to compare hospice and hospital care for people who had died from cancer and their spouses. The project was carried out between October 1994 and September 1995 and was directed by Clive Seale at Goldsmiths College. The main research project included the collection of quantitative and qualitative interview data. I had worked as a research nurse at St Christopher's Hospice (which funded the project) for four years before starting this project. I wanted both to use some of the qualitative data from the project for a PhD and to apply a theoretical approach I had learned during my MA.

I was drawn to the way **ethnomethodology** made it possible to identify the skills and practices ordinary people use to produce social action. The micro-analysis of social interaction seemed to me to be a valuable way of understanding some of the health issues and problems I had encountered in my experience working in clinical health settings as a psychiatric nurse and as a research nurse. Many of these problems appeared to hinge on the interactive practices and skills of the various parties involved (professional and laypeople).

In my post as hospice research nurse, I worked on a range of different topics. In one study I recruited breathless patients to a randomized controlled trial. It was this that got me interested in the (mismatched) relationship between methods of measurement used in research and the actual practices of the people being researched.

In the research trial, breathlessness was treated as a subjective symptom. However, in practice I found that nurses and doctors produced their own assessments of the patient's breathlessness, which sometimes did not correspond, either with each other or with the subjective assessment of patients themselves. This problem formed the basis for my MA dissertation in which I applied Goffman's frame analysis (1974) to patient case note data. This study highlighted the importance of looking at *how* people do things, rather than what they say they do. However, it only went so far in examining **members**' practices.

3.2.2 Theoretical orientations

The experience of doing my MA research, together with my experience as a practitioner, policy-maker and sociologist, led me to believe that social research driven by theoretical concerns (rather than by a defined social problem) can contribute to policy and practice. It can do this through developing knowledge about social issues such as experience of health care but without setting up a rigid definition of the problem at the beginning. This ties in with my experience as a health researcher and practitioner up to that point, where I had observed that problems often appeared to arise around attempts to measure states of health and disease through imposing particular definitions and categorizations.

There seemed to me to be value in taking a step back to get a closer look at the phenomenon. More useful outcomes may be achieved if theoretical impera- tives drive the research in a direction which can offer new perspectives on social problems (see Chapter 15 of this book). Theoretical concerns should steer the analytic conception of the research problem otherwise there is a danger of taking the research problem at face value, and of providing policy-makers and practi- tioners with the answers they require, in *their* terms.

3.2.3 The study data

In the study directed by Clive Seale, seventy interviews were undertaken with bereaved spouses in South London. There were thirty-five interviews with spouses whose husband or wife had died in a hospice, and thirty-five interviews with spouses matched by age and sex, whose husband or wife had died in hospital. The sample was drawn from death certificates of all those who had died from cancer approximately six to nine months beforehand. These were kept at local Departments of Public Health and ethical committee approval was obtained from the three health authorities covered.

Each interviewee received a letter asking them to take part in the study. I called round to their house a couple of days after the letter had been sent and asked to interview them. Written informed consent was gained prior to all the interviews. The main findings from the study were written up, with Clive Seale, for *Palliative Medicine* in 1997.

Sixty-five interviews were tape recorded with the consent of the respondents. The interviews started with an open-ended question, 'tell me the story of what happened'. The intention was that, for this part of the interview, there would be minimal interruption by the interviewer (MK), allowing the respondents to struc- ture their own accounts. The response to this request, the initial 'story', constitutes the data for my PhD study. The rest of the interview followed a semi-structured format involving a series of questions.

Many qualitative research studies set out clear aims and objectives at the start of a project. These may often refer to collecting and analysing data on a particular topic, such as describing the views of patients about a particular type of illness experience. The aims of ethnomethodological studies such as this one tend to be quite general, centring on the examination of some data. When analysis starts, this form of analysis throws up a whole range of possible research problems that could be examined in detail. Decisions therefore need to be made about objectives for particular pieces of analysis at each stage. Eventual objectives can be quite specific but this will follow a more general exploratory analysis to see what members are doing in the talk under examination (e.g. making assessments). Objectives therefore tend to evolve over the course of the research.

The importance of being flexible about objectives is demonstrated in the way in which the specific topics of 'cancer' and 'bereavement' were not treated as central concerns by the interviewees. I had initially used these labels in early descriptions of the study, and in presentations. However, although these accounts are about cancer, in that the 'story of the death' requested is about cancer, the interviewees do not topicalize cancer. In a similar way, as a researcher I had been referring to the data as 'accounts of bereaved spouses' giving the impression to myself and others that the analysis is about bereavement. However, the interviewees did not make bereavement relevant to their descriptions, i.e. they did not talk about their personal experience of being bereaved. This supports the need to consider the relevance of the local context in the production of meanings.

My initial intention was to explore the character of the moral accounting work members do. This contrasts with most interview studies in which the information provided by the interviewee is usually treated as data about the events and experiences described.

Ethnomethodologists view this as problematic and regard interviews as an unreliable source of information about what actually happens in the situations described. A description of health care produced in an interview cannot be treated as a straightforward report of that care. Treating the data as a primary source in this way can be potentially misleading even if one were to take account of such conventional issues as error and bias.

The emphasis in the first instance was on investigating *how* the interviewees (surviving spouses) are saying what they say (as members of a social world), rather than focusing on *what* they are saying, such as 'bereavement talk'. In other words, this was a study not of bereaved spouses, but of social interaction. Following Baker's (2002) theoretical direction, my analysis was concerned with what kind of social world the speakers make happen in their talk and what kind of social world speakers assume so that they can speak in the way they do.

3.2.4   Getting into the data: doing being reasonable

I began the analysis by reading and rereading the five interview accounts I had initially transcribed, looking for a starting point for my analysis. At this point my main interest was in the talk of the interviewees, partly because they did most of the talking. I followed Sacks's call to examine some (interview) data in terms of 'how it is that the thing comes off' (1992, Vol. 1: 11) but as so much goes on in talk, a decision needed to be made as to what the 'thing' would be. Several interesting issues regarding the activities interviewees were doing in their accounts arose and appeared to warrant further exploration. These included: producing a 'reasonable' account, the use of time to locate events, the constitution of lay and medical competences, criticism, gender and emotion.

Given that there were several possible directions for the data analysis, a decision had to be made about what to look at first. In line with the (ethnomethodological) principle adopted by Baruch (1981), that a feature of all accounts is a display of moral adequacy, a key characteristic of these accounts seemed to be the way in which the interviewees construct their behaviour and that of others as reasonable or unreasonable in their descriptions. This seemed like a productive place to start. I again read and reread all the transcripts, this time extracting sections in which the spouses appeared to be presenting their behaviour and that of others as reasonable or unreasonable, systematically going through the data extracts identifying the use of pairs like husband and wife, and other categories, as well as looking for the description of activities which implied particular categories (see Silverman, 1998).

3.2.5 The research process: criticism, assessments and the interview

I reread the transcriptions of the first five interview accounts, identifying instances where criticisms of health professionals were made. The health professionals referred to specifically were doctors and nurses. Identification of criticism in the accounts was not generally clear cut. Considerable identity work was carried out around criticisms. A number of different 'types' of criticism were distinguished, ranging from 'very cautious' to 'direct'. Ambiguity was used by the account-giver, with the interviewer being drawn into the production of the description as criticism. Even when the interviewee identifies their action as criticism, considerable moral work goes on regarding the roles and responsibilities of those involved, including the interviewee and interviewer.

I had initially intended to undertake separate analyses of instances of criticisms of self (by the interviewee) and of the dead spouse in the accounts also. However, having undertaken the analysis of criticism of health professionals, and following the ethnomethodological principles I had adopted, I decided a more constructive tack would be to conduct a closer analysis of members' practices in producing the accounts. So I took a step back in order to take a closer look.

I had identified criticism as an activity in the talk in a similar way to more traditional qualitative studies, and gone some way to describing how it was produced by interviewees through categorization work. I now wished to examine in more depth how activities such as criticism are constructed in the interview talk. This meant refocusing my analysis to look more closely at how assessment work was carried out by both parties and how the interview accounts were co-operatively produced as 'stories'.

3.2.6 Sampling data

I refer to the data analysed here as interviews, though the analysis is based on the first part of the interview only, up to the end of the story. These stories would constitute my data.

The detailed level of analysis involved in examining participants' practices in the talk has meant that the empirical analyses of criticism of health professionals and assessment work drew on the first five interviews only. Later analysis of the construction of the talk using CA drew on twenty-five interviews, with additional interviews (to the five initially analysed) being selected on the basis of emerging theory.

Decisions about the selection of the **sample** were not pre-set, but have been conceptually driven by the theoretical framework underpinning the research from the start (cf. Curtis et al., 2000). In order to undertake analysis that addresses the adequacy of the underlying theory described by Mitchell (1983), decisions about the **sampling** of data have been made during the research. This has been influenced by the two different ethnomethodological research methods which have been applied to the interview data. Analysis of communicative practices (in the interview accounts) can only be discerned in 'the fine grained detail of talk-in-interaction' (Drew, 2001: 267). I have set out to undertake the fine-grained analysis recommended by Drew and also to make comparisons across cases, using both intensive and extensive analysis where appropriate to my research problem.

3.2.7 Practical relevance

This research study set out to contribute to a body of institutional knowledge, the sociology of health and illness. The examination of how the interviews are produced has highlighted a number of analytic points regarding the status attributed to the accounts by the interviewees. They are set up as 'assessments of health care experience'. Setting up the accounts to be heard in this way has implications for the sociology of health and illness, and health care policy, in particular regarding how 'lay' or 'consumer' evaluations of health care experience are produced.

The increasing emphasis on the consumer in British government policy has led to a search for the best ways to find out about both what consumers want from health services, and how satisfied they are with the services they receive. A great deal of this research is quantitative, but there are frustrations with consumer satisfaction questionnaires and scales, as they tend to show uniformly high levels of satisfaction (Avis et al., 1997). There has consequently been a search for different ways of evaluating satisfaction with health care, and an increase in qualitative research. It has been suggested that increased interest in qualitative research has, in part, been fuelled by the growing demand for research that gives consumers a voice in developing services. My study takes up the issues raised above through an ethnomethodological analysis of data initially collected as a form of lay or consumer evaluation.

3.2.8 Concluding remarks

I have worked as a health researcher for a number of years, and this study has been the first time I have not set out with at least a fairly well-defined problem that needed a solution. This includes qualitative studies in which the goal may be to describe something about which little is known. Even in such studies, however, you do know broadly what you are required to describe. In this instance, however, I was attempting to describe something that I knew was going on but could not see at the start.

The need to refrain from introducing my own categorizations *before* producing the description of members' practices that I was aiming for has not been easy. However, I believe that the fine-grained analysis of the practices engaged in by interview participants has enabled me to contribute the new insights to the sociology of health and illness that I had hoped for at the start. What attracted me to ethnomethodology is how, in its suspension of interest in both external structural factors and assumed 'subjective' states, the skills of participants in producing social action through talk are demonstrated. This is made possible through its focus on 'describing members' viewpoints and definitions as the basis for rational actions, and for their participation in the sites of social life' (Drew, 2001: 267).

3.2.9 Implications of Moira's story

The beginning of Moira's story (1, 2) shows the value of basing a PhD thesis on a substantive area with which you are already familiar. Both her work experience and her MA research were in the health area and it made sense to stay in this familiar realm when choosing a topic for her PhD.

Her MA had shown her the uses and limitations of a particular way of conceptualizing health care interactions (1) and now she wanted to shift slightly her analytic focus (2). But she was never in doubt of the need for such a focus in order to make sense of data. For Moira, theory was not a piece of window-dressing to make research respectable. Instead, 'theory' represented the very practical ways in which she made sense of her data.

Moira had gathered her interview data as part of another study with different objectives (3). Drawing on the fortunate fact that these interviews had been audio recorded, she was able to retranscribe them in order to address her new analytic concerns. Note that this did not mean that the previous transcripts were 'faulty'. Transcripts, like other methods of recording data (e.g. field notes, diaries, memos), can only be judged in relation to a specific research problem and theoretical orientation.

The instant availability of her data meant that Moira, unlike many other PhD students, could begin her data analysis on day 1 of her research! As I argue in Chapter 11, such secondary analysis of existing data can offer a marvellous shortcut to completing a PhD freeing you from the need to collect data – provided that you are not looking for excuses for delay and/or sloppy analysis.

Like many qualitative researchers, Moira worked inductively, avoiding too early categorizations of her data and setting research problems and objectives as she explored (analytically) her transcripts (4). As she puts it, the idea is 'to step back in order to take a closer look' (5). So, for instance, given her analytic orientation, it was not enough simply to report 'criticisms' of the treatment of a spouse. Instead, she wanted to understand how apparently critical comments were contexted in the co-production of 'assessments' and 'stories'.

Clearly, Moira's approach required very careful listening to the details of verbal interaction. So she focused mainly on just five out of her sixty-five interviews. However, this did not mean that her other interviews were completely neglected. A much larger sample of interviews were used in her chapters based on CA. In this way, her study combined intensive and extensive analysis (6).

Moira's approach reveals that there need be no simple polarity between qualitative and quantitative research (see Chapter 2). Unlike much quantitative research, our research problems often require much more detailed analyses of small bodies of data. However, by combining intensive and extensive analysis, we can achieve understanding of a relatively large data set and test emerging hypotheses with a fair degree of **credibility**.

Finally, Moira's story shows that theoretically driven research is far from incompatible with practical relevance. Quite the contrary! It is precisely those many, apparently atheoretical studies, which have little to contribute to practical matters simply because their authors do not have the time or the ability to think laterally about their data. As Moira implies, her own work makes a substantial contribution to current debates regarding lay or consumer evaluation of health care (7). It also complements more 'structural' approaches in the study of health and illness with an understanding of the skills of participants involved in health care interactions (8).

3.3 SALLY'S RESEARCH DIARY

3.3.1 *Gaining access*

When I began this case study, I had little idea of how I might go about it. I had vague notions of exploring how diagnoses are constructed by health professionals. This was based on my past experience of having a psychiatric liaison role in a unit linked with an Accident and Emergency department. Looking at patient admission sheets, I was struck by the number of times I read 'schizo/affective disorder' as the reason for admission to hospital. I concluded that such a cautious descriptor could 'cover' both patient and doctor for almost any clinical or legal eventuality. I also had a long-standing interest in the concept of 'illness careers'.

I anticipated that access to the field would be difficult because of the particularly sensitive ethical nature of mental health practice. I made an initial attempt at negotiating access to an in-patient area but this was not successful. A further difficulty was matching the demands of full-time teaching to the constraints of organizational shift patterns.

Like Silverman's (1987) experience of gaining access to the field of paediatric cardiology, my entry to mental health casework was a chance happening. I met up with a former colleague in a local supermarket. After recounting my difficulty in negotiating access to an in-patient area, he invited me to meet the community team with whom he worked. I was both pleased and relieved to have been given this opportunity but I did not recognize it as advocacy at the time. Upon reflection many years later, I now appreciate that this was indeed the case.

Following two separate meetings with the team's psychiatric consultant and with the team leader (a community psychiatric nurse), I was eventually given permission to audio-record the team's weekly case meetings on the understanding that I destroy the tapes when the study concluded.

The choice of team meetings was a deliberate one. These were 'scheduled events' so I did not waste time waiting to see whether or not relevant data would appear but, rather, would have them to hand (see Chapter 4). Having successfully negotiated access to the field I then became a **participant–observer**.

To undertake a case study of 'single homelessness' in the context of full-time employment makes heavy demands on the researcher in terms of personal resources and operational constraints. The field is so vast and the nature of subjects' lives so dispersed that I elected to observe professional caseworkers rather than service users. For practical reasons then, I became a participant–observer at the mental health team's (MHT's) weekly case conferences.

3.3.2   Keeping a record

Having achieved access to mental health casework, my starting point was to observe and record what **members** were saying and doing in their meetings about clients. I audio recorded meetings and made handwritten field notes of my observations whilst the tape was recording. This enabled me to record visual data that might otherwise be lost or unavailable to me if I relied on the audiotape alone.

A total of fifteen meetings lasting approximately seventy-five minutes each were recorded over eight months. The first meeting was 'lost' owing to problems with the tape recorder. Forty-five client stories were available overall. Of these, thirteen were fully transcribed and four were partially transcribed. The shortest transcript was only three pages long. This later turned out to be a deviant case. The longest ran to eighteen pages. One hour of recorded team interaction took an average of ten hours to transcribe.

A total of forty-five hours was spent on data collection overall. This included twenty hours of recording and twenty-five hours of **participant–observation**. No selection process as such was involved in the transcribing of complete accounts. Accounts were transcribed in chronological order which equated with the time frame of the fieldwork.

I chose to collect data in the way that I did because it was/is appropriate to the study of situated action. Audiotapes provide detailed recorded talk which field notes alone cannot provide, while preparing transcripts is itself a research activity.

The act of producing the transcripts was not a straightforward matter. In the main, they were constructed according to my own commonsense reasoning as

I had no precedent for the process of transcribing. Because of this, transcripts do not always conform to accepted conventions. However, there is no perfect transcript and what I have adequately serve my analytic purposes.

The practicalities of audio recording multiple voices in a less–than–soundproof environment exerted certain constraints. It was not possible to denote overlapping voices, for example. Neither was it possible to decipher the simultaneous secondary interactions which frequently occurred alongside the main action. I tried to transcribe what I heard as faithfully as possible using standard spelling and punctuation so that members' accounts would not appear 'unnecessarily odd' to the reader. I did not attempt to represent accented talk and lengths of pauses were not timed exactly.

Fieldwork observation demonstrated that the talk was generally unhurried, even 'leisurely', and that it was frequently punctuated by laughter. I approximated the duration of pauses as being in the range of 1 second for the shortest 'um', to almost 4 seconds for the longest [long pause].

The transcripts, then, cannot be perfect. However, for case study research analysis, they serve the purposes at hand. They capture sufficient detail of the MHT's practice for the kind of analysis I carried out.

With hindsight, I might use more conventional transcription devices if I were to do the transcripts again. This would save the 'creative' work of devising my own. However, lacking the quality of recording more commonly associated with CA, it remains a matter of debate as to whether this could have been a practical option. From a methodological perspective, I did not need the fine detail required by those working with the CA method.

3.3.3 Analysing my data

At the outset I made my own broad descriptive headings for each case account. These were based on the member's introduction to the case which invoked both age and gender. An example of such a heading was: 'Fifty year old woman who has just been accepted by a hostel in the local area'.

I tried to make the description as 'flat' as possible, but found on later inspection that in many instances I had provided my own summary of the opening presentation. The heading was intended to be an identification device for differentiating the transcripts and for matching them to the accompanying field notes. This demonstrates quite clearly that even in the role of note-taker, my recording skills as a fieldworker are influenced by my practitioner past.

I had other surprises. One heading read: 'Surveillance of a twenty nine year old man in a hostel who is preoccupied with religious tapes'. Listening to the tape again and rereading field notes at a later date demonstrated that the word 'surveillance' was not actually used by the narrator of that account. The heading represents my own, broad, descriptive category.

I attempted to transcribe as much as I could of what was said and to record in field notes the setting in which this social activity took place. After transcribing a total of six accounts in full, I began to identify recurring instances in the raw data. These broad, analytic categories are listed, crudely, as follows:

● client vulnerability
● deviancy and commonsense reasoning
● character work
● distancing of other professionals and agencies
● bending the rules
● interchangeable roles.

'Client vulnerability' and 'deviancy' appeared to be topics of concern for MHT members. The remainder of the list was generated after noting instances of the first two categories when they emerged in the transcripts. No computer software package was used in this process. This had advantages as well as disadvantages in that the initial categories remained very flexible. For example, the last category was set aside as it served no immediate analytic purpose.

I had audiotapes, transcripts and field notes which gave me limitless opportunities to return to my original data and redefine the categories as the analysis progressed. Through such means, I was able to test out emerging hypotheses about members' commonsense reasoning generated by fieldwork. It was at this point that I attempted to construct a model which I later rejected because it was too rigid to explain the complexity of members' social action.

I was also able to consider instances in the data which contradicted the emerging **hypotheses** (see Chapter 14). One such instance was an account in which the client was not directly taken on by the team.

Statistical measures were not used in the analysis overall. However, counting the number of times 'family history' was invoked in members' accounts threw new light on gender as an interpretive frame. Hammersley and Atkinson (1983) suggest that with the help of the discriminate use of numbers, quantification can be used as an aid to precision (see Chapter 14). In *this* study, counting was used to examine a hunch.

My focus on members' activities generated initial questions about what they had to know to do their work. It also built on my original interest in diagnostic construction. It was only after the first two phases of fieldwork were complete, and I had constructed the broad categories upon which my preliminary analysis was based, that I began to examine extracts rather than whole transcripts. In this sense, my work differed from research which appears to be based on the use of 'favourable' extracts only.

3.3.4   *Generating a research problem analytically*

By using extracts in this way, I attempted to find 'the sense' of what members were saying, and what was *made* of what they were saying. I then shifted my emphasis to the **discourse**-based question: 'How do participants do things?' My desire to pose such a question derived from my reading of other **ethnographic** work as I strove to define my research problem.

While my early observations provided a descriptive background for my research, I still needed to focus on clear questions to ask about my data and to use these questions to shape the very act of data collection itself.

The earliest influence on my study was Goffman's *Frame Analysis* (1974). It explores the relational dimension of meaning. For Goffman, a **frame** is defined by its *use* rather than by its content. Events are seen in terms of 'primary frameworks'. The particular frame used provides a means of interpreting the event to which it is applied.

For Goffman, frames are both structural *and* flexible as they are susceptible to change by interacting participants. Indeed, they are highly vulnerable, being continually subject to dispute. In the event, much of my study used Goffman's concept of frame to demonstrate how understandings emerged among the MHT.

Data analysis and reading are mutually informing. In a sense, there is no end to updating one's knowledge. In this research, the literature was used as a continuing opportunity to make connections with the MHT data. For instance, half-way through the research the analysis began to lose focus. Reading Holstein's (1992) work on descriptive practice and Loseke's (1989) study of a shelter for battered women provided new knowledge about the accomplishment of social problems work. Similarly, towards the end of my research, fresh material from Kitzinger and Wilkinson (1997) helped me construct a chapter on 'gender' which arose from my reading of Holstein (1992).

3.3.5 Reflections on participant – observation

I was now a participant–observer in a field where members were health care professionals like myself. Although I no longer practise directly, what effect this might have on the data is an important issue.

To suppose that *any* researcher enters a **field** without past experience or some pre-existing ideas is unrealistic. To suppose that their presence will not exert an influence on the data is equally unrealistic (cf. Strong, 1979: 229). In my own case, I accepted that my presence in the field would influence what I saw, but I could not predict 'how' or to what extent. In this sense, data produced by the team were a mutual production which also involved myself as researcher (cf. Emerson et al., 1995: 106).

Unlike Strong's (1979) experience of researching in paediatric settings, I cannot admit to being treated 'as part of the furniture' (1979: 229) by the team members I was observing – possibly because of my practitioner background. However, I *was* aware of feeling more accepted as the fieldwork progressed.

I was initially incorporated into the MHT's practical frame. Members were intolerant of my chosen position at the side of the room during fieldwork and 'ordered' rather than invited me to sit with them in their discussion circle even though I maintained a non-speaking role.

In the team leader's words, this was to 'close the circle'. As Peräkylä surmises about his own role as researcher, maybe this was the best way of collecting data and relating to members in the field (1989: 131). Certainly it was of practical use in that I knew the tape was recording data so I was left free to observe and write notes (cf. Silverman, 2001: 68). However, as Hammersley warns: 'when a setting is familiar the danger of misunderstanding is especially great' (1990: 8).

I was aware that I might become too 'comfortable' with the team but, upon reflection, this did not happen. Speculatively speaking, constructing a democratic atmosphere was possibly also functional to the team in that it positioned me where I could be involved and seen.

Nonetheless, the danger of 'over-rapport' with members of the team was a continuing issue for me. Despite my similar professional background to team members, I had to treat their perspectives as problematic.

3.3.6   *Ethical considerations*

Gaining ethical approval for the study was in no sense 'plain sailing'. In the early months of 1992, I put forward my proposal to the ethical committee of the Trust hospital to which the team was attached. Apart from stressing the qualitative nature of my research intentions and the fact that staff, rather than clients, would be my proposed subjects, I could only state with certainty that I wished to audio-record the team's weekly case conference.

In addition, I found the form I was required to complete somewhat prob-lematic. It conformed to the standard type for purely *clinical* research involving human subjects rather than to any proposed sociological research. Predictably, it was very 'physically' orientated.

One question asked for 'potential hazards' and the precautions I might take to meet them. The possible contravening of confidentiality was my written response to this enquiry. I undertook to use pseudonyms for the names of staff, clients and care areas throughout the research to preserve anonymity and to safeguard confidentiality.

In the event, even references to months or seasons of the year in the transcripts were changed as the work got underway. Dates of legislation were retained as were dates of fieldwork and any reference to clients' ages as such data were necessary to the analysis. In addition, I undertook to write a report on the progress of the study for the ethical committee, should this be required at any stage of the work. I was not given permission to interview clients or to access their case records.

I guaranteed to keep all audiotapes at home under lock and key and to do all my own transcribing rather than eliciting secretarial assistance. I also promised to destroy the tapes at the end of the study. I did not expect to see or interview clients. Finally, I undertook not to proceed without the permission of all team members following a full explanation of what I proposed to do.

Several months later, I received written consent to proceed with my project from the chairman of the ethics committee. I also discussed my proposal with the chairman of the Trust's Mental Health Board, a practising consultant psychiatrist. He voiced no objection in principle and recommended that I contact the team's consultant and team leader to seek their individual permission, which I did.

However, being a participant–observer raises a number of ethical issues which extend beyond formal consent to the research. Before the research began, I decided that the best way to carry out participant–observation both morally and practically was to be as open as possible with the team.

My rationale for making this decision was that this would permit me to be free to ask questions as the fieldwork progressed without creating too much suspicion. Being open would also permit audio recording of data. To a certain extent this strategy worked, although my insider knowledge of professional practice always made me conscious that what I was being offered of the team's world would be partially restricted.

I was aware that my presence in the field might affect the behaviour of those being observed, especially as the team was aware of my health professional background. I entered the field in the knowledge that a certain amount of professional self-consciousness would be inevitable but I accepted this as a necessary 'trade-off' in terms of access. It was a tacit assumption on my part and possibly on theirs, but on the basis of it, both I and they were able to proceed.

In this sense, my past experience as a practitioner is in no way disadvantageous to my present role as researcher. As a case study researcher, it became useful to me as a source of data.

For example, there were almost certainly times in this study when members responded to my presence in terms of what might be called 'ethical correctness'. I sensed that there were some occasions when members overtly displayed their moral adequacy as a consequence of being observed. My general *impression* was that members responded to me as a more senior member of staff, i.e. as an older, experienced professional now working in higher education. I felt that the team's display of moral adequacy in my presence was particularly marked, especially where ethical dilemmas were prominent.

3.3.7 Some implications of Sally's story

Research problems rarely come out of the blue. Sometimes, we may be the more or less fortunate recipient of a topic 'given' to us by a supervisor. In Sally's case, her own work experience combined with previous academic study to suggest an interesting topic. Her previous job as a nurse had underlined what she had read about illness 'careers' and the functions for staff of labelling patients and the intended and unintended consequences of such labels once applied (1).

Now Sally needed a setting in which to explore this issue. She made use of a chance encounter to gain access to a relevant health care context (1). The demands of her full-time work now influenced the data she sought from this setting. Like many part-time researchers, she avoided a time-consuming ethnography of everything that the MHT did, in favour of a focus upon scheduled meetings. This meant that her focus was necessarily on one side of the coin: not on how staff and clients perceived each other but on how staff categorized their homeless clients in order to make decisions about whether (and how) to help them (1).

Three points emerge for beginning researchers. First, a research study can offer an opportunity to pursue a topic that intrigues you personally. Where your own experience seems to support an approach or a study that you have come across, a good research problem may be lying on your lap.

Second, where access to a setting is difficult, draw upon your own contacts and experience as Sally did. Third, as I argue in Chapter 6, research topics and data generally need to be narrowed down in order to be workable. Sometimes, this narrowing down will arise for quite mundane, practical reasons – for example, as in Sally's case, the amount of time you have available. Providing that you thoroughly analyse the data you have, this need not be a problem. Indeed, it can be an advantage by giving your research a direction.

As Sally argues, it was a great advantage to have audiotapes as her core data to complement her field notes (2). Indeed, on one occasion, listening to a tape revealed a crucial error in a note (3).

She was satisfied that her way of transcribing her tapes was appropriate to her research topic. However, on reflection, she realized that it might have been simpler to have used an existing transcription method, like CA notation, rather than to have started from scratch (2).

This illustrates a general point to which I return several times in this book. When you are faced with a new task (e.g. finding data, coming up with a researchable problem, transcribing your data), look around for some already existing model. Nothing is gained (and a lot lost) by wasting time reinventing the wheel!

When she began to analyse her data, Sally, like Moira, worked inductively. She identified recurring instances of some activity in one meeting and then extended her search to several cases 'to examine a hunch' (3). Crucially, she sought contrary as well as confirming evidence to test out her hunches (3).

Throughout her research, Sally was aware that even the most inductive approach depends upon some theoretical orientation. In her case, Goffman's account of 'framing' gave direction to her research (4). However, she kept on reading other work as she analysed her data and showed a welcome readiness to modify direction as she came up with new findings and concepts (4).

Finally, Sally's diary discusses familiar issues in participant–observation: how your own preconceptions may enter into your research; how being observed may affect people's behaviour (towards you and in relation to their own normally routine activities); ethical issues in relation to obtaining informed consent and to what you reveal to the people you are studying (5, 6). As Sally shows, it is wise to reflect on these issues but also to treat them as valuable data. Indeed, she was able to use her core concept of 'frame' to depict the MHT's categorization of herself – and thereby to understand more about how it dealt with others.

3.4 SIMON'S RESEARCH DIARY

3.4.1 Beginnings

My first degree was a BSc in sociology and media studies, chosen partly on account of some spurious advice I had received concerning the 'higher status' of a joint honours degree. I also felt that the media studies component meant that the course would necessarily focus on those cultural products invested with meaning, and therefore relevant to most people on a day-to-day basis. It is not necessary to go into explicit detail regarding the development of my thought during this time, for the purposes of this brief biographical outline. However, it is important to note that, by the end of my period of undergraduate study, I was greatly vexed by issues surrounding the tendency within the various schools of sociology towards using **social structure** too loosely as a way of accounting for data.

The basis for this concern can be broadly represented by examining the focus of my final-year project at City University, which took as a general theme the role of the media as 'moral entrepreneurs' (cf. Becker, 1963; also Cohen and Young, 1973; Cohen, 1980) in the creation and imposition of labels and stereotypes on a societal level. The project consisted of a comparative study of the reporting, by two contemporaneous newspapers, of two similar crime stories from the 1950s and the 1990s. Unfortunately, my experience of travelling to The British Library's Newspaper Library and reading the various original newspaper sources archived there left me with a sense of detachment from the materials I was studying. I had serious doubts as to the veracity of my own reading of the print and claims made regarding it, based mainly on the realization that I had little idea how contemporary readers may or may not have engaged with the texts.

It was in this frame of mind that I decided to broaden my knowledge of research methodologies, and gain some practical research experience in the meantime, by undertaking an MA in sociology with special reference to qualitative research at Goldsmiths College, University of London, in 1997.

3.4.2 Learning about conversation analysis

Whilst the course acquainted with me a wide range of research methodologies, it was my introduction to **conversation analysis (CA)** during this period that most caught my imagination. As the course began to contextualize more clearly my previous misgivings as part of the ongoing debate within sociology regarding the 'theory relative' activity of defining social structure (cf. Silverman, 2001), I was taken by ten Have's statement that 'CA refuses to use available "theories" of human conduct to ground or organize its arguments, or even to construct a "theory" of its own' (1998: 27).

In setting forward 'a different conception of how to theorize about social life', CA also moves away from invoking 'obvious' social–structural factors when explaining social phenomena. While the concept of social structure is an important element in sociological enquiry in general, 'the problem becomes one of not allowing it to take on an analytic life of its own' (Boden and Zimmerman, 1991: 5). The way in which many sociological analyses allow social structure to 'take on a life of its own' is memorably summed up by Sacks in his analogy of society being viewed by the social sciences as a piece of machinery where much of what takes place is random, and it is worth quoting at length:

> Such a view suggests that there are a few places where, if we can find them, we will be able to attack the problem of order. If we do not find them, we will not. So we can have an image of a machine with a couple of holes in the front. It spews out some nice stuff from those holes, and at the back it spews out garbage. There is, then, a concern among social scientists for finding "good problems," that is, those data generated by the machine which are orderly, and then attempt to construct the apparatus necessary to give those results. (1984b: 21–2)

The search for 'good problems' not only is carried out mainly in terms of reference to 'big issues' regarding large-scale institutions, but also necessarily imposes order on the phenomena being studied. Rather than search for an order based on the analyst's conception of what this order might be, CA proposes an examination of how individuals orient to (and therefore display) that order themselves: 'whatever humans can do can be examined to discover some way they do it, and that way will be stably describable. That is, we may alternatively take it that there is order at all points' (Sacks, 1984b: 22).

Not only did I find the movement away from fruitless theoretical debates between opposing theories refreshing, but I was also impressed by the methodological focus that CA afforded. In focusing on the order found at all points within 'what humans do', CA delineated its field of study, since, as Sacks pointed out, it is possible that 'detailed study of small phenomena may give an enormous understanding of the way humans do things and the kinds of objects they use to construct and order their affairs' (1984b: 24). Indeed, this focus meant that the question of social structure took on a new relevance for me, since in examining the ways in which interactional parties display their identities relative to one another, *and* how it matters to them, CA necessarily deals with the 'senses of "who they are" that connect directly to what is ordinarily meant by "social structure"' (Schegloff, 1991: 48).

3.4.3   Hoping to be relevant

Although the need for some theoretical formulation of what should be studied was no longer an overriding consideration, I still inclined towards research that could be said to be of practical relevance. On one level, this was due to my own lack of confidence in my ability to add anything of worth or interest to the cumulative fund of interactional knowledge that ten Have has typified as the aim of 'pure CA' (1998: 8). But it was equally due to a reaction against the ongoing dismissive view within the British media towards sociological research, claiming it is irrelevant and badly conducted.[1] Fortunately, I found that both concerns were addressed within CA.

Not only does the primacy of mundane conversation provide the 'richest available research domain' (Heritage, 1984: 240), but it also 'uses the practices found in ordinary conversation as a baseline from which to analyse institutional talk' (Silverman, 2001: 172). Added to this, Silverman (2001), in his discussion of the contribution social science could make to wider society, highlights CA's role in offering a new perspective to participants within institutional settings. He states that 'researchers ought not to begin from normative standards of "good" and "bad" communication' (2001: 278), but should focus instead upon understanding 'the *skills* that participants deploy and the *functions* of the communication patterns that are discovered' (ibid., – original emphasis).

3.4.4   Finding a topic

It was with these issues in mind that I happened across the parents' evening data. At the time my partner was a relatively new primary school teacher, and her exposure to the realities of parents' evening led to her assertion that such meetings had not been directly addressed within her teacher-training course. This difficulty with parents' evening from the teacher's perspective chimed with further anecdotal information from my own parents, whose experience of such meetings tallied with the 'public relations exercise' view outlined by Baker and Keogh:

> [Parents' evenings] are understood and talked about as ritual or ceremonial encounters, in which teachers go through routine expressions of interest and academic diagnosis, and which parents attend in order to show their 'interest' in their children's schooling. (1995: 264)

Part of this characterization involves the view that parents' evening meetings are events in which 'nothing much was accomplished' (cf. Baker and Keogh, 1995, and above), which as Baker and Keogh point out 'is an invitation, if not provocation, to ethnomethodological inquiry' (1995: 265). It should equally be remembered, however, that Baker and Keogh's characterization of such meetings stems from their understanding of 'educational folklore' (1995: 264). Indeed, some parents find these occasions very helpful opportunities to review their child's academic progress. But this in itself provides further justification for examining the meetings.

Handy and Aitken, in their study of the organization of the primary school, point out that whilst there exists for all schools 'a bond between them and the families and communities they serve' (1994: 246), in practice the situation is not that simple. As they note:

> Some parents are over-anxious and expect more from the school for their child than is realistic. But sadly too many other parents abdicate once their child is at school. Teachers know that the parents whom they really want to see, to know, and to help are often the ones who never come to school. (Handy and Aitken, 1994: 246)

Given both this variation in parents' attitudes to their childrens' schooling in general, and teachers' views of parents' evening meetings in particular, it is perhaps unsurprising that the assorted sections of the school community, be they teachers, parents or children, regard parents' evening in such different ways. With the question of what parents' evening 'means' being such a contentious one, the need to examine what goes on during them seemed to me to be particularly relevant.

3.4.5   Obtaining access

Having had these meetings drawn to my attention in this way, I began to consider their use as the basis for my dissertation. My ongoing unofficial pastoral role at my partner's school meant that I had already built up a rapport with the head teacher, so approaching him with a proposal to record some parents' evening meetings was straightforward enough. Once the process of the research was explained and agreed upon, he was happy for the recording taking place, with one stipulation: my access was restricted to the recording of only one teacher in the school, namely my partner. Not wanting to risk what rights to conduct the research I had already gained, I decided not to make any representations regarding the recording of any of the other Year 6 teachers. This did not unduly worry me at the time, since this restriction sat well with the time frame within which I could gather, transcribe and analyse the data for my MA dissertation. As it transpired, I only used a single meeting for the dissertation, leaving me (so I thought) with a surfeit of data.

3.4.6   Worrying about sample size

Focusing upon a single teacher has certain limitations in terms of generalizing the findings of this research to a wider population. It can be argued that the conversational techniques utilized by the teacher in this research are unique to her, and therefore not easily extrapolated to the parents' evening practice of other teachers. Equally, the fact that the teacher in the data was a class teacher rather than a set teacher could have been an important influential factor. Perhaps set teachers do things differently in such meetings by dint of the fact that they are dealing with the specificities of their curriculum area. Furthermore, the entire format of the meetings might have been different at another stage of the academic year, even if carried out by the same teacher studied in this research. In short, various permutations in the actual accomplishment of parents' evening could be hidden by the fact that the data sample consists of a single teacher on a single parents' evening.

How, then, should this research be seen in terms of both **sampling** variety and external **validity**? Indeed, given the tension between the specific difficulties associated with the gathering of the data and the ideal research design outlined above, can this study say anything useful about the phenomenon that has been studied?

I believe the answer lies in seeing this research not as an attempt to provide categorical 'truths' about all parents' evenings in general, but as an attempt to raise questions about such meetings by looking at a single case in detail (see Chapter 9 of this book). To some extent, raising questions in this way relies upon the perspective within CA that '*social practices that are possible*, that is, *possibilities of language use*, are the central objects of all conversation analytic case studies on interaction institutional settings' (Peräkylä, 2004: 297, original emphasis).

This element of *possibility* can be taken too far in terms of ascribing a certain level of universality to the findings of studies into conversational and interactional phenomena, but as Seale points out, 'readers must always make their own judgements about the relevance of findings for their own situations' (1999: 108). The corrective, he suggests, is simple: 'threats to such transferability are dealt with most adequately if details, or "thick" descriptions of the "sending" context (or the "sample"), are provided' (ibid.). This study can therefore be seen as being *exploratory* rather than *definitive*, examining the achievement of routine by a single individual in a specific setting in such a way that further analytical possibilities are opened up.

3.4.7   Narrowing down my research problem

Although I subsequently came to realize the deficiencies in my MA thesis, and sought to correct them during my doctoral research, the findings of the MA (such as they were) formed the basis for my research proposal to a major British research council (the ESRC). Although the majority of the proposal focused upon CA's methodological relevance to my funding agency's thematic area of communication and learning, it did include the following research problem:

> Whilst these meetings would seem to fall distinctly into the category of professional-lay interactions, with the attendant problems associated with the differential exercise of power by the interactants, in this situation both the parents and the teacher can claim a level of 'expert' knowledge with regard to the subject of the interaction, namely the child. The research problem to be addressed is that of what impact this dual claim to competency has upon the joint construction of context by the parents and teacher as the two most powerful interactants.

Aside from some of the more obvious difficulties related to the unproblematic application of concepts such as 'power' and 'claims to expert knowledge', this research proposal conflicted with CA's stated aim that analysis should always begin with what Psathas (1990: 45) has called 'unmotivated looking' (see Moira's discussion above). This is summed up by Sacks's assertion that 'when we start out with a piece of data, the question of what we are going to end up with, what kind of findings it will give, should not be a consideration' (1984b: 27). So, despite the stated aims (however limited) of the research proposal, at the start of the PhD course I struggled to come to the data 'anew', without the constraint of wondering where I was going to 'end up'.

Of course, the central issue of this struggle is one of discipline, not only in terms of focusing on one or two analytic concepts at a time, but also with regard to allowing the details of the talk to go where they will. As Sacks has pointed out, 'it ought never to be a matter of concern to anybody who's doing a piece of description which way it comes out, as long as it comes out some way' (1992: Vol. 1, 472).

Discipline was imposed by moving away from the consideration of individually interesting features, framing them instead with regard to the overall structural organization of the meetings. CA deals with and explicates 'patterns of stable, recurrent structural features' (Heritage, 1984: 241, and above) within talk. By examining the trajectory of the reportings on the child, fitted to both the search for parental response by the teacher and how the form of the response shaped the unfolding trajectory, a framework for the research began to become clearer.

3.4.8   Some implications of Simon's story

The experience of writing an undergraduate dissertation had given Simon an understanding of the uses and limits of a key concept: 'social structure' (1). Once again, this underlines the point that true understanding comes by applying ideas one has learned in the library to new topics.

However, being aware of the deficiencies of a concept is not sufficient. One also needs to learn an analytic approach to data and then discover how to use it. Conversation analysis (CA) turned out to be Simon's key to the social world (2). Of course, ultimately such approaches cannot be true or false but only more or less useful (see my discussion of **models** in Chapter 7). For Simon, the usefulness of CA seemed to be twofold. First, it gave him a clear idea of what kind of data he wanted and of how to analyse it. Second, it made personal sense to him by according with his previous research experience and also, perhaps, by being aesthetically pleasing.

Yet the appeal of theory can be double edged. Aesthetic satisfaction can sometimes mean that you never can extricate yourself from the charms of the library to confront the external world (see my discussion of 'grand theory' in Chapter 6). Simon was aware of this danger from the outset and was determined to combine his theoretical 'narrowness' with a concern for practical relevance (3).

At this point, like Sally, Simon had a lucky break. His partner was a primary school teacher prepared to give him access to her work. A Parent–Teachers' Evening was looming and this appeared to be a setting which was problematic to its participants and under-researched (4). Needing to tape his data (a requirement of CA), Simon drew upon his own fortuitous association with the school and received permission from the head teacher.

However, achieving access brought its own worry. Simon was now troubled about the small size of his sample. While studying one teacher's work seemed to be enough for his MA thesis, would it be sufficient for a PhD? As it turned out, Simon came to the conclusion that a small sample will do if you have thought through its limitations (5) and if the quality of the analysis is sufficient.

Indeed, when it came to the stage of data analysis, Simon was confronted by multiple, emergent research problems. This created an initial tension between the inductive approach he was using and his funding body's demand for an initial hypothesis. For a while, he could not see the wood for the trees. Fortunately, in time, an overall unifying theme became clearer as his various observations revealed a sequential structure to the parents' meetings (6). So Simon's thesis became organized around the trajectory of reportings of 'news' to parents by their class teacher.

3.5 CONCLUDING REMARKS

Obviously, there are many different stories that research students can tell about their experience and I do not pretend that what you have read was typical or representative. Nonetheless, there are several clear messages in these stories that are worth listening to.

I set these out below as a *fifteen-point guide*. Obviously, like any recipe, you will, of course, need to apply it to your own circumstances. Nevertheless, I believe the points below apply to *all levels* of student research from BA and MA dissertations through to the PhD.

1 *Begin in familiar territory*: if you can, work with data that is close to hand and readily accessible. For instance, if, as in Moira's case, you have data from another study which you can (re)analyse, grab the opportunity. There are no 'brownie points' to be obtained for gathering your data in difficult circumstances. Make it easy on yourself at this stage so that you can concentrate your energies on the infinitely more important task of data analysis.

2 *Find a settled theoretical orientation*: as I stress throughout this book, research is never just about techniques. All three stories refer to finding a theoretical approach which made sense to them and then could provide a settled basis for inference and data analysis.

3   *Narrow down your topic*: strive to find a topic that is appropriate to your theory and data and is workable (this issue is discussed at length in Chapter 6). Later, if you wish, like Moira, Sally and Simon, you can use your research to make contributions to a substantive area (e.g. health and illness, education), to a methodology (e.g. interview research, ethnography, CA) and to reflect upon issues of social policy.

4   *Don't try to reinvent the wheel*: in Chapter 5, I discuss what 'originality' might mean in research. For the moment, it is worth recalling that Moira used an earlier study as a model for her research and that both she and Simon used a well-established method of transcribing their audiotapes. So, at the outset, look at previous successful dissertations in your university library or departmental files and, where possible, focus on work directed by your supervisor.

5   *Keep writing*: commit your ideas to paper. Don't worry how short or draft your papers are. Indeed, in some way, it makes more sense, initially at least, to submit 500-word pieces so that you can be guided in the right direction before you have expended too much time and effort.

6   *Begin data analysis early*: don't be deflected away from early data analysis by literature reviews and the exigencies of data gathering. If you haven't got any data yourself at an early stage, try analysing someone else's data–published data, your supervisor's data, etc. (see Chapter 11).

7   *Think critically about data*: when you start to identify a pattern in your data, don't rush to conclusions. See how robust this pattern is by working comparatively with different parts of your data (as Moira did) and by trying to identify deviant cases (like Sally).

8   *Use your supervisor*: to test out your ideas and give you confidence.

9   *Use other resources and opportunities*: graduate students should take every opportunity to attend relevant conferences and, better still, to give conference papers, and to take appropriate training courses. Find out if there are study groups of research students working on similar topics. If not, try to establish such a group.

10 *Do not expect a steady learning curve*: be prepared for the sequence of highs and lows that will inevitably happen. For instance, Sally found that her early ideas about how her MHT made decisions were too simplistic and Simon puzzled over how to integrate his apparently diverse findings. Treat setbacks as opportunities: Sally came up with a better explanatory model and Simon eventually saw an overall pattern.

11 *Keep a research diary*: Moira, Sally and Simon kept a file of their current ideas, hopes and worries. This file is an invaluable resource which, as I suggest in Chapter 22, can be used, in edited form, in your methodology chapter.

12 *Earmark blocks of working time*:[2] if you are researching part time, it is crucial to find blocks of time in which you can focus solely on your research. Use this time for intensive data analysis and writing.

13 *Do not reproach yourself*: if you experience a setback, it may be best to take some time out to relax before you return to your research.

14 *Treat field relations as data*: how others treat you in the field is never just a technical matter. Like Moira and Sally, reflect upon how your interaction with your subjects is shaping your data.

15 *Understand that there is no 'perfect' model of research design*: practical contingencies (e.g. access or the lack of it; the time you have available) are always going to affect any piece of research. Don't be afraid of working with what data you happen to have. Your examiners will not be comparing your research with some 'perfect' model but they will expect you to have thought through the limitations of your data and your analysis (see Chapter 5).

KEY POINTS

- It helps to begin your research in familiar territory.
- Find a settled theoretical orientation that works for you.
- Once you get a feel of your field, narrow down your topic as soon as you can.
- Don't try to reinvent the wheel – find what has worked for others and follow them.
- Keep writing.
- Begin data analysis immediately.
- Think critically about your data – don't rush to conclusions.
- Test out your ideas with your supervisor – don't worry if, in the early stages, you are often wide of the mark.
- Use other resources and opportunities inside and outside your own department.
- Do not expect a steady learning curve – no research study is without some disasters.
- Keep a research diary.
- Earmark blocks of working time to complete different activities.
- Do not reproach yourself about setbacks.
- Treat your relations within the field as data.
- Understand that there is no perfect model of research design.

NOTES

1 Although many examples could be cited, this brief quotation from an article by Will Buckley in the *Observer* newspaper of 30 May 1999 serves as a case in point:

Here we go again. Yet more supposed research (this time from the sociology department at Edinburgh University) claiming that men are lousy parents, incapable of spending more than

15 minutes a day with their children … . Crap dads are back on the agenda because yet another bored sociologist has made a few phone calls and cobbled together some stats.

2   Items 12 and 13 were suggested by Vicki Taylor after reading an earlier draft of this chapter.

Further reading

The best place to look for similar research histories is in the writings of students at your own university. BA students should seek to obtain past successful undergraduate dissertations from their department. Graduate students should study MA and PhD theses in the library, focusing particularly on the work of people who had the same supervisor as you. If the methodology chapter does not include an autobiographical account, try to contact their authors and discuss what lessons they draw from their experience.

Judith Bell's *Doing Your Research Project* (2nd edn, Open University Press, 1993) is a good introduction to research at the undergraduate level. Estelle Phillips and Derek Pugh's *How to Get a PhD* (2nd edn, Open University Press, 1994) is the best British account of the practical issues involved in writing a PhD. For an American guide, see Kjell Rudestam and Rae Newton's *Surviving Your Dissertation* (Sage, 1992).

Exercise 3.1

Keep a research diary for a given period (one month for an undergraduate dissertation, three months for an MA project, at least six months for a PhD). Record:

- changes in your ideas about topic, data, theory and method
- new ideas from the literature or from lectures and talk
- meetings with your supervisor and their consequences
- life-events and their consequences for your work.

At the end of your chosen period, reread your research diary and assess:

- What you have achieved in that period.
- What would be required for you to do better in future.
- Your achievement targets for the next equivalent period.

4 The Research Experience II

4.1 INTRODUCTION

In this part of the book, I have been attempting to set out the context in which qualitative research dissertations are written. We began with a brief overview of qualitative research. Then, in Chapter 3, we considered the lessons that could be drawn from three completed research dissertations.

Yet, for many readers of this book, their own completed graduate or undergraduate dissertation is a distant, desired object. So, in this chapter, we draw upon the accounts of research students at an early stage of their research. Through these accounts, we examine the analytical, methodological and practical problems that confront the beginning researcher.

In some senses, the beginning researcher has far less to prove than established scholars. If you imagine a sliding scale of levels of achievement, then journal articles, as the stock in trade of established scholars, are (or should be) at the pinnacle of scholarly accomplishment. Somewhat surprisingly, books are a little further down the scale since they do not depend on the same degree of independent review. Further down the scale are completed research dissertations which, I suggest, are properly viewed as displays of successful apprenticeship.

However, my sense of a sliding scale in research is intended simply to mark a stage of a research career – it is not a moral category. Although it is more than thirty years since I was at that stage, I do not look down upon the work of first-year research students. Indeed, frankly, I sometimes come across more exciting ideas in a first-year graduate seminar than in many journal articles!

What follows is by no means a representative survey of qualitative research at its early stages. Instead, the material below has been drawn from research students in my own department and in various social science and humanities departments of Finnish universities.[1]

While the range of research covered below is limited, I hope you will eventually agree that it is not narrow. In other words, I hope and expect that readers will find at least some echo of their own ideas and interests represented below.

In collating these presentations for this chapter, I had to decide upon an organizing principle. In particular, I had to choose whether to organize the material by topic, theory or methodology. I reasoned that grouping by topic would be lively but might appear to exclude readers working on different topics. By contrast, a theory grouping might be too abstract and, perhaps, confusing for an audience coming from a disparate range of disciplines. By taking a methodological perspective, I hope to be more inclusive by encompassing many of the methods used (and contemplated) by qualitative researchers.

The discussion below is thus organized by method, with sections on interview studies, **ethnographies**, textual analysis, work with video- and audiotapes, and multiple methods. However, such a focus on method is not narrowly technical. As I make clear below, methods only acquire meaning and vitality by their embeddedness in particular theoretical perspectives.

As in Chapter 3, I will proceed case by case, offering some comments with each example and then summarizing the points that emerge from each methodology. The chapter concludes with some suggestions about managing the early stages of research.

After each topic below, I have noted the social science discipline in which the student is working as well as the student's name.

4.2 INTERVIEWS

4.2.1 *Living and coping in a community of elderly people*

(Information Studies/Sociology) [Tippi]
Tippi writes about her joint research: 'We wanted to ask how the inhabitants feel about living in the community where they have lived for many years.' Her study is based upon thematic interviews with a random sample of eight elderly people from the community. As she puts it, the aim of this study 'is to (clarify) ... the basic meaning of living (in this community)'. This is how she describes her interviews: 'the elderly people were asked about their daily schedules, their attitudes to relatives, services, neighborhood and environment, their interests and their opinions about society today compared with their earlier life-experiences'.

Preliminary findings suggest two things. First, members of the community told the same kinds of lifestories. Second, such people described themselves as more independent than she had thought. They described 'coping' by attempting to keep control of four issues: financial, social, health-related and security.

An analytic issue potentially arises in such studies where interviews are used to elicit respondents' perceptions. How far is it appropriate to think that people attach a single meaning to their experiences? In this case, may not there be multiple meanings of living in the community, represented by what people say to the researcher, to each other, to carers and so on (Gubrium, 1997)?

This raises the important methodological issue about whether interview responses are to be treated as giving direct access to 'experience' or as actively constructed **narratives** (Holstein and Gubrium, 1995). Both positions are entirely legitimate but the position taken will need to be justified and explained.

4.2.2   Students' views of evaluation and feedback

(Behavioural Sciences) [Laura]
Laura is examining students' responses to the assessment of their Distance Education essays. Her research question is: 'does it deliver the feedback that is needed and when it is needed?'. Her data is derived from thematic interviews with eleven students chosen from four different localities. Her preliminary findings suggest that students want more detailed, critical feedback on their essays so that they can know what are the gaps in their knowledge and what they can do about them.

Laura describes the theoretical basis of her research as a **hermeneutic** method based on how researcher and subjects interpret the world and attempt to merge their horizons of meaning. This is ambitious and its value will need to be demonstrated in the data analysis. Indeed, it might be simpler to settle on presenting her research as a descriptive study based upon a clear social problem. Either way, the issues about the status of interview data, also raised in Tippi's project, will need to be engaged.

4.2.3   Football and masculinity

(Sociology) [Steven]
Steven's approach is based upon theories of masculinity within the general area of gender studies. More specifically, his work is concerned with football supporters and masculinity. He is particularly interested in understanding the experience of football supporters as opposed to the way in which their behaviour is represented (for instance, in the media).

Care needs to be taken in how such appeals to 'experience' are described. This is one way of 'slicing the cake' and other approaches (e.g. studies of media representations of sport), using other forms of data, are not directly competitive.

The data he is using derives from interviews with football supporters. As Steven acknowledges, he still needs to sort out tricky methodological issues relating to his sampling procedure, his involvement with his interviewees and how he analyses his data. A possible resource is Cornwell's study of health, gender and poverty, *Hard Earned Lives* (1981), an interview study which shares some of his ambitions.

It is always sensible, in this situation, to familiarize yourself more deeply with the methodological literature on analysing interview data. Even if you choose to take a position opposed to such texts, you will need to be able to justify it. Without doing this, you are in danger of trying to reinvent the wheel.

4.2.4 Text processing in foreign-language classrooms

(English) [Pia]
In Finland, foreign languages are primarily taught through textbooks. Yet textbook-based learning is often defined as monotonous or boring by students. Pia's topic is whether there are different ways of talking about foreign-language teaching and is there a conflict between them? Her broader concern is with what hinders change in classroom practices.

Her data consists of twelve interviews (half with teachers and half with students). She also has five 'think aloud' sessions in which students were asked to do an exercise from a text and think aloud at the same time. This is an interesting idea because it attempts to relate what people say to a particular task they are doing – although it has to cope with the likelihood that people's practical skills are far more complicated than they could tell you in so many words (Garfinkel, 1967).

Pia describes her analytical approach as **discourse analysis** (DA). This implies that she is more interested in identifying different ways of *talking* about foreign-language reading than in addressing the actual experiences of learning a foreign language through a textbook. Given that the latter can be seen as a social problem, there may be a mismatch between DA, which assumes that issues of social definition are paramount, and a direct address of social problems. This might suggest either dropping DA or reconceptualizing the problem.

If we are interested in what happens in the classroom, there is a further issue about the appropriateness of interview data. Shouldn't we observe what people do there instead of asking them what they think about it? Is how we talk about schooling directly related to what happens in schooling?

4.2.5 The family grief and recovery process as narratives

(Psychiatry) [Katarin]
Katarin is analysing interviews with couples after the loss of their baby. She is interested in how family members construct stories about their grief and recovery processes after such a loss. She has identified three discourses at work here:

- a religious discourse ('everything is clear ... I think my faith is strengthened')
- a medical discourse ('our baby did not have a chance to live, this is better, the lungs were undeveloped')
- a protest discourse ('who can decide who is allowed to live and who isn't?').

Katarin calls her work narrative analysis. By treating her respondents' accounts as skilfully structured stories, she gets a lively, theoretically informed grip on her data.

Only two cautions are appropriate here. First, the mere identification of different discourses in respondents' talk can lead to a simple, reductive list. At some stage, it is analytically productive to move beyond such a list in order to attempt to map the skilful way in which such discourses are laminated on one another (see Silverman, 2001; 198–202).

Second, the assembly of **narratives** in interviews (or conversations) is always a two-way process. Therefore, we must treat the interviewer's questions not as (possibly distorted) gateways to the authentic account but as part of the process through which a narrative is collectively assembled (see Holstein and Gubrium, 1995).

4.2.6   Narratives by bereaved relatives

(Sociology) [Moira]
We first came across Moira's research in Chapter 3. Here I describe her early thoughts on her project in a presentation at a graduate workshop. Using interview data drawn from an earlier study, Moira, like Katarin, is concerned with how bereaved relatives organize their initial stories of their bereavement. Moira's approach is drawn from **ethnomethodology**'s concern with how people demonstrate the rationality and moral accountability of their talk. In their stories, people show that they hear (and pre-emptively manage) possible charges against them. By doing this, the analysis can fully show how people are not 'judgemental dopes' but rather display a lively concern for the maintenance and repair of the moral order.

Her method derives from Sacks's **membership categorization analysis**, using Baruch's work on the 'moral tales' of mothers of handicapped children as an example. As we saw in the previous chapter, basing your work on an earlier study deriving from a clear-cut theoretical approach can be a shortcut to a successful research dissertation (see also Chapter 6).

In her presentation, Moira showed how she had started to analyse five data extracts using this method. At a later point, in line with her theoretical approach, the analysis can be deepened by working more intensively with small pieces of data to delineate precisely how particular descriptions serve to support particular activities like 'doing a complaint', 'excusing oneself' and so on. In this way, like Katarin, she can avoid the temptation simply to *list* different categories.

4.2.7   Interviews: summary

Common themes have emerged from our six interview studies which I summarize below. For the sake of simplicity, I present this summary in the form of a list of questions that you need to think about if you are planning to do an interview study.

It should be apparent that here, as elsewhere, I am concerned with data *analysis* rather than the mechanics of data gathering. I strongly believe that to provide recipes for data gathering is to risk either gross oversimplification or utter triteness. Moreover, in qualitative research, what happens in the **field** as you attempt to gather your data is itself a source of data rather than just a technical problem in need of a solution (see Chapter 17).

What status do you attach to your data?

Many interview studies are used to elicit respondents' perceptions. How far is it appropriate to think that people attach a single meaning to their experiences? May there not be multiple meanings of a situation (e.g. living in a community home) or of an activity (e.g. being a male football fan) represented by what people say to the researcher, to each other, to carers and so on (Gubrium, 1997)?

This raises the important methodological issue about whether interview responses are to be treated as giving direct access to 'experience' or as actively constructed 'narratives' involving activities which themselves demand analysis (Silverman, 2001; Holstein and Gubrium, 1995). Both positions are entirely legitimate but the position you take will need to be justified and explained.

Is your analytic position appropriate to your practical concerns?

Some ambitious analytic positions (e.g. hermeneutics, discourse analysis) may actually cloud the issue if your aim is simply to respond to a given social problem (e.g. living and coping in a community of elderly people, students' views of evaluation and feedback). If so, it might be simpler to acknowledge that there are more complex ways of addressing your data but to settle on presenting your research as a *descriptive* study based upon a clear social problem.

Does interview data really help in addressing your topic?

If you are interested in, say, what happens in school classrooms, should you be using interviews as your major source of data? Think about exactly why you have settled on an interview study. Certainly, it can be relatively quick to gather interview data but not as quick as, say, texts and documents. How far are you being influenced by the prominence of interviews in the media (see Atkinson and Silverman, 1997)?

In the case of the classroom, couldn't you observe what people *do* there instead of asking them what they *think* about it? Or gather documents that routinely arise in schools, e.g. pupils' reports, mission statements and so on?

Of course, you may still want to do an interview study. But, whatever your method you will need to justify it and show you have thought through the practical and analytical issues involved in your choice.

Are you making too large claims about your research?

It always helps to make limited claims about your own research. Grandiose claims about originality, scope or applicability to social problems are all hostages to fortune. Be careful in how you specify the claims of your approach. Show that you understand that it constitutes one way of 'slicing the cake' and that other approaches, using other forms of data, may not be directly competitive.

Proper analysis goes beyond a list

Identifying the main elements in your data according to some theoretical scheme should only be the first stage of your data analysis. By examining how these elements are linked together, you can bring out the active work of both interviewer and interviewee and, like them, say something lively and original.

We now turn to **ethnographic** studies that involve some element of observation. As we shall see, these kinds of studies also raise complex methodological and analytic issues.

4.3 ETHNOGRAPHIES

Ethnographies are based on observational work in particular settings. The initial thrust in favour of ethnography was anthropological. Anthropologists argue that, if one is really to understand a group of people, one must engage in an extended period of observation. Anthropological fieldwork routinely involves immersion in a **culture** over a period of years, based on learning the language and participating in social events with them.

By contrast, non-anthropologists are more likely to study particular milieux or **sub-cultures** in their own society. We will see examples of this latter approach in the studies discussed below where activities in classrooms, hospitals and the Internet become objects of research observation.

4.3.1 The analysis of communicative functions of peer interaction during small-group learning

(Education) [Caroline]
Working in small groups has become a common feature of modern education. The exact nature of such 'learning' presents a clear and apparently under-researched topic tied to a recognizable social problem. As Caroline remarks: 'the ways in which knowledge is constructed in children's verbal interactions during small group work learning without direct teacher control has not yet been fully researched'.

Caroline has gathered data from children aged from 10 to 12 in small classroom groups working on mathematics, science and language. Her focus is on 'the socio-cognitive and interpersonal dynamics of peer interaction' using categories 'based on the communicative functions identified in the interactions'.

This is a theoretically defined topic which nonetheless might have a clear practical input. It uses a clearly defined method derived from certain forms of discourse analysis. However, Caroline's study also raises a more general issue about how a researcher goes about identifying features in the data.

Caroline's use of the passive voice in her reference to 'the communicative functions *identified* in the interactions' draws attention to a neglected issue in social research: that is, how does the analyst go about 'identifying features' in the data? One common answer is to claim to follow proper procedural rules. For instance, coders of data are usually trained in procedures with the aim of ensuring a uniform approach.

This is a tried and trusted method designed to improve the **reliability** of a research method. However, it is sensible to be conscious that **coding** is not the preserve of research scientists. In some sense, these students, like all of us, 'code' what they hear and see in the world around them. Moreover, this 'coding' has been shown to be mutual and interactive (Sacks, 1992; Silverman, 1998).

Of course, as I said earlier, the research 'cake' can be legitimately sliced in many ways. So I am *not* suggesting that the vast mass of researchers who treat 'coding' as purely an analyst's problem abandon their work. Instead, my minimalist suggestion is that they mention and respond to this well-established critique (for an example, see Clavarino et al., 1995).

4.3.2 *Analysing how radiologists work*

(Information Processing Science) [Julia]
Radiology, like many health professions, has recently experienced a sea change of technologies with the conventional X-ray image being complemented by computer-based, digitized images. As Julia points out, any new technology creates new constraints as well as new possibilities. Her focus is on such technologically mediated interaction in workplace settings.

Using videotapes, observation and interviews, Julia has gathered data about radiological image interpretation conferences. By examining actual workplace interaction she hopes to contribute to the growing body of knowledge about human–computer interaction and to inform future technological design (see Suchman, 1987; Heath, 2004).

I hope you will agree with me that this is an exciting combination of a theoretically defined approach with clear practical relevance. However, Julia writes that she is concerned about what is *missing* from both her interviews and videos. As she puts it:

Thus far in my research it has become clear that there are aspects of work which I can't 'reach' through interviews (people can't readily articulate aspects that are so familiar to them as to be unremarkable) or through observation and interactional analysis of video recordings (those aspects of work that are not evident in what people can actually be seen to do).

In a sophisticated way, Julia raises a problem that often troubles research students: the necessarily 'partial' character of any data source. I believe this problem is potentially huge yet, in a practical sense, easily resolved. One simply avoids trying to find the 'whole picture'. Instead, one analyses different kinds of data separately, aware that all the data is partial.

So make do with what you have and understand that there are multiple phenomena available in any research setting. If you must go beyond any particular data set, save that until you have completed smaller-scale analyses. Worrying about the 'whole picture' at the outset is, in my view, a recipe for stalling your research (see Silverman and Gubrium, 1994).

4.3.3   Newsgroups on the Internet

(Sociology) [Danny]

Danny's topic is the Internet. He is concerned with how people assemble themselves as a community via the Net, without recourse to speech inflections or body language. Broader issues relate to how the Net is regulated, how it developed and what is exchanged on it. He proposes to focus on newsgroups on the Net since their messages are publicly available and offer an interesting way to look at how a 'community' is assembled and develops.

Danny's approach derives from his interest in the Net as a possible new locus of power and, to this end, he plans to draw upon the German critical theorist Jurgen Habermas's conception of distorted communication. In this way, he will compare how people actually communicate with Habermas's **normative** theory.

Danny's study shows the implications of making theoretical choices. Using Habermas's concept of 'distorted communication' will give a particular thrust to his study very different from other kinds of theory.

Even if you decide to eschew such grand theories, that itself is a theoretical choice! In this sense, there is no escape (nor should there be) from theory. At the same time, however, there is nothing wrong with a descriptive study providing that the researcher is conscious about the choice that is being made.

4.3.4   Ethnographies: summary

Once more, I have been concerned with how you analyse your data. I deal below with three issues that have arisen above.

What is involved in coding data?

As we have seen, coders of data are usually trained in procedures with the aim of ensuring a uniform approach. Later in this book, we examine how computer-aided qualitative data analysis can help in such coding (see Chapter 13).

However, as I pointed out, it is sensible to be conscious that 'coding' is not the preserve of research scientists. All of us 'code' what we hear and see in the world around us.

One response is to make this everyday 'coding' (or 'interpretive practice') the object of enquiry. Alternatively, we can proceed in a more conventional manner but mention and respond to this well-established critique.

Is my data 'partial'?

Of course it is. But this is not a problem – unless you make the impossible claim to give 'the whole picture'. So celebrate the partiality of your data and delight in the particular phenomena that it allows you to inspect (hopefully in detail).

Is my theory appropriate?

Your theory must be appropriate to the research questions in which you are interested. Indeed, rather than being a constraint, a theory should generate a series of directions for your research.

4.4 TEXTS

To introduce a separate section on 'texts' can look a little artificial. After all, aren't people on the Internet constructing texts? Again, if we treat an interview as a narrative, this can mean looking for the same textual features as researchers working with printed material. Indeed, the mere act of transcription of an interview turns it into a written text.

In this section, I use 'text' as a heuristic device to identify data consisting of words and images which have become recorded without the intervention of a researcher (e.g. through an interview). Below I examine five studies of texts.

4.4.1   Analysing classroom religious textbooks

(Teacher Education) [Pertti]
Since 1985 Finnish schools have had a religious instruction syllabus mainly based on three textbooks deriving from the Finnish Lutheran Church. Pertti's approach treats such textbooks as a form of literary genre (see Silverman, 2001: 198–200) which filters certain values into the school. He is examining such features as tables of contents in order to ask 'how is otherness constructed in these texts through particular methods of classification?' His analysis derives from Michel Foucault's (1977, 1979) discussion of the construction of subjects and disciplines.

This study benefits from a manageable body of data – three textbooks are more than enough to carry out the analysis Pertti proposes. The analysis derives from a clearly defined theoretical approach, although it may be uneconomical to work with both Foucauldian ideas and writers on literary genre. In particular, from a Foucauldian position, one would want to study education in its own right, not in terms of ideas developed to study literature.

4.4.2 The form of Japanese 'modernity'

(Sociology) [Yoji]

Yoji is interested in how far Japanese modernity depends upon concepts and practices deriving from the West (e.g. the assumption that history involves 'progress') and how far it is a feature of Western colonialization. His data will be drawn from representations of urban space in Tokyo. Although a major focus will be on the family, Yoji is also interested in other institutions including prisons, the police, the hospital, the school and the factory.

Yoji's approach derives from Foucault's (1977) account of the micropolitics of space. From this perspective, he is concerned with how space is racialized, colonized and gendered. It also leads to a concern with how space constructs 'modern' subjects (e.g. 'us' and 'them') and the 'inside' and 'outside' (for instance, the inner city, the ghetto, etc.).

Like Pertti, Yoji is working with a clear analytic approach. However, he might learn from Pertti's limited database by focusing on one archive or body of data. He is currently working with historical data from around the Meiji Restoration and it may be fruitful just to focus on one such period and/or to limit the material to visual images or certain texts.

4.4.3 The medicalization of the middle-aged female body in the twentieth century

(Sociology) [Greta]

Greta is interested in the way in which middle-aged women have become a topic for medicine and the 'psy' sciences. Like Pertti and Yoji, Greta's analysis is based upon a Foucauldian discourse analytic approach, concerned with the construction of subjects within various forms of power/knowledge. Using this approach, she is able to chart how the medical gaze has moved from a biomedical model to medico-psy models and, most recently, a medico-psycho-social model.

Her data derives from the *British Medical Journal*, medical textbooks and a history of menopause clinics in the 1970s. Simple keyword analysis has proved fruitful in the early stages of her research, illustrating for instance how the clinical type of 'the chronic pelvic woman' emerged into discourse.

As Greta's research develops, like Katarin and Moira's interview studies (discussed above), she will want to map how different discourses are laminated on each other. She will also have to decide whether to look for yet more sources of data (e.g. articles and letters on advice pages in women's magazines) or to narrow down the amount of data she has already collected.

4.4.4   *The representation of 'crime' in local newspapers*

(Sociology) [Kay]
Analysis of newspapers in the UK has usually focused on the mass circulation press and has used theoretical models deriving from either Marxism or literary studies. Kay's work is distinctive in that it uses data drawn from small, local newspapers and draws on the small corpus of newspaper studies using Sacks's membership categorization analysis (see Silverman, 1998: Chapters 5 and 7). The research incorporates a nice comparative perspective as the two newspapers Kay is studying derive from different geographical locations: suburban London and a Northern Ireland city. The value of this comparison can be explored by examining the local categories that the newspapers use in their descriptions of crime (e.g. national and local boundaries).

Like Pertti, Kay has a manageable body of data. By limiting her data simply to two newspapers' headlines on 'crime' stories she is in a good position to say 'a lot about a little'. Like Greta, her clear analytic approach will pay off when used as more than a simple listing device in order to reveal the precise sets of relationships locally constructed in her data.

4.4.5   *'Enterprise discourse' in higher education*

(Sociology) [Neil]
Neil's research is concerned with strategic development documents from a higher education college arising from recent changes in the tertiary sector. He is focusing on what he calls 'enterprise discourse' and how it constitutes the professional's conception of identity.

Like Kay, Neil's original approach derives from **ethnomethodology** and was based on Sacks's membership categorization analysis. However, Neil acknowledges the attraction of the Foucauldian approach and aims to recast his concerns in terms of Foucault's conception of the 'architecture of the text'.

Neil's problem is that Foucault provides no clear methodology (but see Kendall and Wickham, 1998). He is attempting to find a usable method from the 'critical linguistics' of Norman Fairclough and from semiotics' concern with **syntagmatic** and **paradigmatic** relations (see Silverman, 2001: 198–200). Using these approaches, the aim is to analyse whole texts rather than a few extracts. The value of these approaches will be clearer when Neil presents an extensive piece of data analysis.

However, I feel there is less to worry about in relation to Neil's concerns that working on a single case might mean that he has too little data. As Mitchell (1983) shows, the **validity** of qualitative analysis depends more on the quality of the analysis than on the size of the sample. Moreover, the comparative method can be used on a single case by isolating and comparing different elements.

4.4.6   Texts: summary

Limit your data

Like many other qualitative approaches, textual analysis depends upon very detailed data analysis. To make such analysis effective, it is imperative to have a limited body of data with which to work. So, while it may be useful initially to explore different kinds of data (e.g. newspaper reports, scientific textbooks, magazine advice pages), this should usually only be done to establish the data set with which you can most effectively work. Having chosen your data set, you should limit your material further by only taking a few texts or parts of texts (e.g. headlines).

Have a clear analytic approach

All the textual studies discussed above have recognized the value of working with a clearly defined approach. Even Neil who was unsure which approach to use was convinced that such a choice is crucial. Having chosen your approach (e.g. Foucauldian discourse analysis, Saussurian **semiotics**, Sacks's analysis of membership categorizations), treat it as a 'toolbox' providing a set of concepts and methods to select your data and to illuminate your analysis.

Recognize that proper analysis goes beyond a list

I make no apology for repeating a point that I made above in my discussion of interview studies. It seems to me that the distinctive contribution qualitative research can make is by utilizing its theoretical resources in the deep analysis of small bodies of publicly shareable data. This means that, unlike much quantitative research, we are not satisfied with a simple coding of data. Instead, we have to show how the (theoretically defined) elements identified are assembled or mutually laminated.

4.5   AUDIOTAPES

The three types of qualitative data discussed so far all end up in the form of some kind of text. For instance, in interviews, researchers usually work with written transcripts and in ethnographies one often records and analyses written field notes.

In the same way, audiotapes of **naturally occurring** interaction are usually transcribed prior to (and as part of) the analysis. The two main social science traditions which inform the analysis of transcripts of tapes are **conversation analysis (CA)** and **discourse analysis (DA)**. For an introduction to CA, see ten Have (1998); for DA, see Potter and Wetherell (1987) and Potter (2004). Both examples below involve the use of CA (a further example is found in Simon's research, discussed in Chapter 2).

4.5.1   Team meetings at a hospice

(Sociology) [Anthony]
While studying for his MA, Anthony started to do voluntary work at a hospice in a London suburb. Staff at the hospice were later happy to grant him access to tape-record some of their work. He chose team meetings for two reasons. First, focusing on such data meant that he did not need to trouble patients. Second, team meetings in which patients were discussed were scheduled events so Anthony did not have to waste time waiting for 'relevant' data to appear. Moreover, another researcher had already tape recorded some team meetings at the hospice and was happy to lend him her good-quality tapes.

Anthony had used conversation analytic methods for his MA dissertation and applied the Jeffersonian CA transcription method to his new data (see the Appendix to this book). He then inspected his transcripts informed by CA's focus on the sequential organization of talk. After an initial series of discrete observations, he selected a number of sequences in which disagreements emerged and were resolved by team members. The management of agreements and disagreements has been extensively analysed within CA through the concept of **preference organization** (Heritage, 1984: 265–9). However, Anthony now realizes that his data allowed a new twist to be given to such analyses by looking at how 'third parties' manage disagreements by others. This looks likely to be both analytically interesting and practically relevant to medical staff concerned with effective decision making.

4.5.2   Asymmetry in interactions between native
and non-native speakers of English

(English) [Marla]
Marla is working with taped naturally occurring conversations in English between native speakers of English and Finnish (both informal conversations and professional/client encounters). As she notes:

> Research in pragmatics and sociolinguistics has shown that various forms of communicative trouble may arise where the linguistic and sociocultural resources of the participants are not shared.

However, she is taking a different approach. Rather than treat asymmetries as a 'trouble', her initial idea is to examine how the participants 'use emerging asymmetries as a resource through which they can renegotiate the current context of discourse and their interpersonal relationship'.

Like much good research, this is based on a nicely counter-intuitive idea which derives from a clear theoretical perspective (CA suggests that participants can treat apparent troubles as local resources). As in Anthony's case, Marla's data, method and analytical approach are elegantly intertwined.

4.5.3 Audiotapes: summary

Choose a single concept or problem

Choosing a clear analytic approach is a help but is not everything. The danger is that you seek to apply too many findings or concepts deriving from that approach. This can make your analysis both confused and thin or a naive listing of observations consonant with each of these concepts. By narrowing down to a single issue (e.g. preference organization or troubles as a local resource), you may begin to make novel observations.

Give a problem a new twist

As the data analysis proceeds, you should aim to give your chosen concept or issue a new twist. In the studies above, we have seen this done by pursuing a counter-intuitive idea and by noting an additional feature little addressed in the literature.

Make data collection as easy as possible

There are no 'brownie points' given by most disciplines for having gathered your own data – perhaps with the exception of anthropology's expectation that most researchers will have spent their statutory year with their 'tribe'. Indeed, by choosing 'difficult' situations to gather data (either because nothing 'relevant' may happen or even because background noise may mean you have a poor-quality tape), you may condemn yourself to have less time to engage in the much more important activity of data analysis.

Marla and Anthony found practical ways of efficiently gathering data. Both chose to study scheduled encounters and Anthony was able to supplement his own data with tapes collected by somebody else. As I pointed out in the previous chapter, secondary analysis of other people's data is to be commended rather than condemned.

4.6 VIDEOTAPES

When people interact face to face, they do not use merely verbal cues – except if they are on the telephone. Researchers who work with videos have access to many of these cues. However, as we shall see, complicated data can often mean complicated analysis!

4.6.1 Talk, text and visual communication
in desktop video-conferencing environments

(English) [Erkki]

Erkki is studying a one-month teaching experiment in which a university course was given on the Internet in two places in Finland and Sweden. Ideas and papers were regularly exchanged and weekly presentations and feedback sessions were held through video conferencing (Internet seminars). Recordings of the video-mediated sessions between the two centres were obtained and transcribed (see Heath, 2004).

Erkki is combining CA with ideas from Goffman (1974) about 'participation frameworks' adopted in particular settings. This setting is, of course, pretty unusual in that participants' sharing of time and space is technologically mediated. In some sessions, the camera positions were fixed. In others, the camera zoomed in and out on the participants. This is allowing Erkki to get a hold on how different use of video-conferencing technology affects interaction.

Erkki's work combines a manageable body of data and a clear theoretical approach ('participation frameworks') with a likely practical input for systems design. As she recognizes, however, it is very complex to work with video data since both transcription and analysis are more complex than is the case with audio data. Fortunately, there is a growing body of CA-inspired work on technologically mediated interaction which Erkki can use as a model (see Heath, 2004).

4.6.2 The early interaction between a mother
and a baby aged under 1

(Finnish) [Suzanne]

This is a study of interaction between Suzanne's own baby, Sara, and others based on 9.5 hours of videos of twenty-two episodes up till Sara's first birthday. Suzanne's initial interest was at what age a baby begins to imitate other people. Consequently, she is attempting to describe what (and how) she says to her baby at different ages and what linguistic elements begin to emerge in the baby's vocalizations.

Like Erkki, she is using transcription methods and analytic ideas from CA. Based on this approach, she is treating mother–baby talk as interactional, e.g. how does the mother interpret the baby's utterances and behaviour in concrete situations and how does she act in response to them?

At the time of her presentation, Suzanne submitted a set of written questions which I set out below with my answers:

● *Is one baby (my own) enough data?* For qualitative work, one case study is sufficient. Obviously, there are issues to be thought through where you are yourself a principal actor. However, from a CA point of view, the complexity of what all of us do is so great that we are unable to grasp it or indeed to change it significantly at the time.

- *Is one videocamera enough particularly as you don't always see mother and baby together?* This is not a major objection. Once you recognize that there can be no 'perfect' recording of interaction, it is always a case of making do with what you have.
- *How far can you reconstruct all aspects of the interaction between a baby and her family from ten hours of videotape?* Never attempt to reconstruct *everything* about an interaction! Not only is this an impossible task but it is likely to deflect you from establishing a clear focus on one manageable topic.
- *Does an analysis of interactional situations give any hints as to how the baby reciprocally interprets her mother's actions?* Who knows what baby (and mother) are thinking? CA instructs us to look at what each party does without speculating about what they are thinking.
- *Should imitations associated with gestures and expressions be analysed separately from vocal imitations?* No! Use your rich video data to examine the interweaving of talk, gesture and expression.
- *Should more approaches be used (e.g. **hermeneutics**)?* Don't even think about it! Once you have found an approach which suits you, stick with it. Using multiple approaches is uneconomical and likely to delay completion of your research.
- *How do we distinguish 'imitation' from other activities such as 'repetition'?* Look at how baby's utterances are treated by mother, e.g. praise. But be prepared to change topic. 'Imitation' may give you an early hold on the topic but detailed description may lead in different directions.

4.6.3 The construction of ethnic identity among Spanish immigrants in London

(Sociology) [Viviana]

Viviana's work focuses on styles of cultural consumption in relation to inter-generational differences within families of first- and second-generation immigrants. She has moved from an interview-based study to one based largely on observation and videotaping of Spanish families watching television together.

Viviana's research involves two overlapping areas – media studies and nationality. It is important for her to think through whether her main focus is on media reception or, as I think, on national identity, using the media as a case study. Again, although video data is potentially exciting material, it is notoriously difficult to analyse. Even though the analysis of interview data has all kinds of difficulties attached to it (see above), it may be more suited to her focus on ethnic identity. With a video, you have to infer identities. Through interviews, you can ask people to speak about their identity.

4.6.4 How 'female experience' is presented and problematized on television

(Sociology) [Nora]

Nora's research is concerned with 'confessional' television as represented by Oprah Winfrey and other 'chat' shows. She has a particular interest in how 'psychological health' is invoked in such programmes.

She argues that most existing research focuses on audience participation in terms of issues relating to democracy and resistance. As she points out, the problem with such studies is that they simply posit general structures of power, class and gender. Instead, Nora, following Foucault, wants to problematize subjectivity. In particular, she is interested in the productivity of power in relation to what it means to be a woman, the kind of ethical agent who might adopt this subject position and the forms of knowledge that have helped to construct it.

By its focus on media products from a Foucauldian perspective, her research promises to break new ground. Her major difficulty is the lack of any detailed direction for empirical work on media products within Foucault's work. Given this absence, I suggest that she speedily review methodologies deriving from other traditions to see if there are any useful points to be derived. In particular, CA offers a detailed way of transcribing video material and is beginning to address issues of **validity** and **reliability** in relation to single case studies (see Peräkylä, 2004).

4.6.5 Videotapes: summary

All the points made above about audio data apply here, so I limit myself to a few additional observations arising from our four video studies.

Beware of complexity

Although video data is very attractive, it is very complex to work with since both transcription and analysis are more difficult than is the case with audio data. So think very carefully about whether you need video data for your research. For instance, unlike CA, neither Foucault nor theories of identity provide a clear template for video analysis.

Keep it simple

You are not making a feature film! One video camera is fine for most purposes. When you have your data, maintain a clear focus. Never attempt to reconstruct all aspects of the interaction from the videotape.

Stick with one approach

By all means test out different ways of analysing your data but always settle on one clear analytic approach. Draw on other approaches only for particular technical skills (e.g. in transcribing video data).

4.7 MULTIPLE METHODS

Researchers are often tempted to use multiple methods. For instance, ethnographers often seek to combine observation with the interviewing of 'key informants'. In the section below, I consider four examples of ethnographic work involving methods additional to observation.

4.7.1 How texts are reconstructed

(Sociology) [Anne]
Anne's research is concerned with how a text changes as it moves from a book to television or radio. She is also concerned with the effects of mediation on performance.

Her approach derives from an extensive literature on theories of mediation dealing with literary products, film, sound/music and art. This seems to form a good basis for her research, although perhaps more work needs to be done on distinguishing these theories from our everyday assumption that something is 'lost' when books are turned into mass media products.

Anne intends to study media practices during the process of production as well as to interview translators, scriptwriters and actors to try to understand the principles that inform mediators. This looks like an interesting project working with accessible data but I wonder if her data analysis might be simplified by focusing on media practice and products and leaving out any reference to the 'intentions' of those involved in the process and/or by just following through the transformation of one text.

4.7.2 Botswana women in public life (from 1800)

(Sociology) [Mercy]
This study is a development of Mercy's earlier research. It centres around questions of women, power and politics in the context of Botswana society and culture. Her research derives from a feminist focus on the factors limiting women's political influence in Botswana. This means concentrating on forms of patriarchy as expressed in the *kgotla* system and in women's fragile citizenship rights. The research questions that flow from this concern women's changing experiences, the limits to women's participation in political life and the role of outside influences.

To answer these questions, Mercy proposes to use three methods: interviews, **focus groups** and the analysis of archive material perhaps using ideas from Foucault. However, she may be limited by the need to obtain government approval for her research.

This is an ambitious project which may be made more manageable by considering using only one data set and not pursuing her reading of Foucault unless she decides to make the textual data her primary focus. However, as in all field research, it makes sense to treat her dealings with official authorities as data rather than as a technical difficulty prior to data gathering (see Chapter 17).

4.7.3 American 'concert dance' in the post-war era

(Sociology) [Rita]

Rita's background is in dance studies and, more recently, sociology. After the Second World War, Rita found that the US government was building a new relationship with the dance community through sending out cultural 'ambassadors'. The period also coincided with the development of an American dance 'style' eschewing expressionism in favour of formalism.

Rita wants to explain both the politics of US support for dance and the emergence of a style which avoided seeking to express the 'self' or 'inner emotions'. She will focus on two groups of dance companies, as well as examining performances and texts by dance theorists.

Rita describes her approach as deriving from the work of Pierre Bourdieu, drawing upon his account of the body as a site in which agents struggle for domination. Bourdieu's work should help her achieve her ambitious aim to bring together history and social theory.

It remains to be seen whether it will be possible effectively to combine data deriving from different methods. Not only does this increase the scope of the research, but also it raises complicated issues about how to 'map' one set of data upon another (see my critique of **triangulation** in Chapter 14).

4.7.4 How women experience depression

(Sociology) [Philippa]

Philippa's research is concerned with how women, as user communities of psychiatry, experience depression, self and identity. Her interest in this topic arose partly from family and work experience and partly because of her curiosity about the statistics which seem to show that women are twice as likely as men to be diagnosed as 'depressives'.

Her approach derives from Foucauldian **genealogical** analysis and hence leads to a focus on how 'depression' is discursively constituted. This approach differs from feminist concerns with patriarchy and misogyny and from an interactionist focus on labelling by psychiatrists. The research questions that arise for her from this approach are: how do women speak of themselves as subjects who are 'depressed'? How do women position/speak about themselves compared to 'normal' gendered subjects? And how far do we find traces of a 'pharmacological culture' in how depression is constituted and treated?

Her data is drawn from women whom she meets through her work as a counsellor. Unusually, given her approach, Philippa has opted initially at least for a questionnaire (partly this reflects her lack of confidence in interviewing women she also counsels). A pilot of this questionnaire showed a high rate of non-response. She is currently revising her questionnaire as well as planning to do some archive analysis.

Philippa is aware that there might be more fruitful research designs. In particular, the use of focus groups or of open-ended interviews based on a single question (such as, 'tell me your story') might overcome the problem of using leading or incomprehensible questions. Nonetheless, her project is ambitious and she might consider working entirely with available archives in the usual Foucauldian manner.

4.7.5 Multiple methods: summary

Keep it simple I

Like videotapes, multiple methods are tempting because they seem to give you a fuller picture. However, you need to be aware that multiple sources of data mean that you will have to learn many more data-analysis skills. You will need to avoid the temptation to move to another data set when you are having difficulties in analysing one set of material.

Keep it simple II

Often the desire to use multiple methods arises because you want to get at many different aspects of a phenomenon. However, this may mean that you have not yet sufficiently narrowed down your topic. Sometimes a better approach is to treat the analysis of different kinds of data as a 'dry run' for your main study. As such, it is a useful test of the kind of data which you can most easily gather and analyse.

Keep it simple III

'Mapping' one set of data upon another is a more or less complicated task depending on your analytic framework. In particular, if you treat social reality as constructed in different ways in different contexts, then you cannot appeal to a single 'phenomenon' which all your data apparently represents.

Research design should involve careful thought rather than seeking the most immediately attractive option. However, none of the points above exclude the possibility of using multiple means of gathering data. Ultimately, everything will depend on the quality of your data analysis rather than upon the quality of your data.

4.8 CONCLUDING REMARKS

In this chapter, we have examined the early stage of student research projects. The following suggestions have been made:

- Define your research problem analytically.
- Limit your data.

- Demonstrate that your data analysis goes beyond a list.
- Limit the claims you make about your study.
- Think about the relevance of your research for other scholars and for 'society'.

These points are explained below.

Define your problem

1 Research 'problems' do not arise out of a clear blue sky! Sometimes, their source is a scholarly debate; sometimes a pressing social problem. In any event, you will need to think through the *analytic basis* of your way of defining your research problem. Having chosen an approach, treat it as a 'toolbox' providing a set of concepts and methods to select your data and to illuminate your analysis.

2 Your approach must be appropriate to the research questions in which you are interested. Indeed, rather than being a constraint, a theory should generate a series of directions for your research (see Chapter 6). It will influence what status you attach to your data – for instance, as a true or false representation of reality – and how you code it.

Limit your data

1 Decide which data to use by asking yourself which data is most appropriate to your research problem – for instance, are you more interested in what people are thinking or feeling or in what they are doing?

2 To make your analysis effective, it is imperative to have a limited body of data with which to work. So, while it may be useful initially to explore different kinds of data, this should usually only be done to establish the data set with which you can most effectively work (see Chapter 8).

3 Make data collection as easy as possible. There are no 'brownie points' given by most disciplines for having gathered your own data. Indeed, by choosing 'difficult' situations to gather data (either because nothing 'relevant' may happen or even because background noise may mean you have a poor-quality tape), you may condemn yourself to have less time to engage in the much more important activity of data analysis.

4 Beware of complexity. For instance, as we have seen, although video data is very attractive, it is very complex to work with. So keep data gathering simple. Go for material that is easy to collect. Do not worry if it only gives you one 'angle' on your problem. That is a gain as well as a loss!

Data analysis goes beyond a list

1 Choosing a clear analytic approach is a help but is not everything. The danger is that you seek to apply too many findings or concepts deriving from that

approach. This can make your analysis both confused and thin or a naive listing of observations consonant with each of these concepts. By narrowing down to a single issue, you may begin to make novel observations.

2 Identifying the main elements in your data according to some theoretical scheme should only be the first stage of your data analysis. Go on to examine how these elements are linked together (see Chapters 11 and 12).

3 As your data analysis proceeds, you should aim to give your chosen concept or issue a new twist, perhaps by pursuing a counter-intuitive idea or by noting an additional feature little addressed in the literature.

Limit the claims you make about your research

It always helps to make limited claims about your own research. Grandiose claims about originality, scope or applicability to social problems are all hostages to fortune. Be careful in how you specify the claims of your approach. Show that you understand that it constitutes one way of 'slicing the cake' and that other approaches, using other forms of data, may not be directly competitive.

Issues of relevance

1 When you have finished, reflect upon the contribution that your research makes to contemporary scholarly debates. How does it add to knowledge or change our sense of the role of particular methods or concepts? (See Chapter 24.)

2 Is your analytic position appropriate to any practical concerns you have? For instance, many contemporary social theories look at the world quite differently from respondents, policy-makers or practitioners. If you use such an approach, you will need to think carefully about what you can offer such groups – although, it may well turn out that you can offer them more interesting findings than rather more conventional research (see Chapters 24 and 28).

KEY POINTS

In this chapter, we have examined the early stage of student research projects. The following suggestions have been made:

▬ Define your research problem analytically.
▬ Limit your data.
▬ Demonstrate that your data analysis goes beyond a list.
▬ Limit the claims you make about your study.
▬ Think about the relevance of your research for other scholars and for 'society'.

NOTE

1   These research ideas derive from presentations during graduate workshops I co-ordinated at Goldsmiths College and at Oulu University, Finland. In the Finnish material, I have been able to draw upon research abstracts written by the students prior to the workshop. I was dependent upon my contemporary notes for the Goldsmiths material and apologize for any inaccuracies present. In any event, it should be borne in mind that this is an account of the early stages of research studies which, no doubt, have developed and changed. For this reason, students' names have been anonymized.

Further reading

An excellent practical guide to the business of writing a dissertation is Pat Cryer's *The Research Student's Guide to Success* (Open University Press, 1996). Judith Bell's *Doing Your Research Project* (Open University Press, 2nd edn, 1993) is a much more basic treatment, mainly aimed at undergraduate dissertations. If you plan to do qualitative interviews, a useful website is:
http://www.andrle.org.uk

Exercise 4.1

The following exercise is meant to help you think through the issues raised in this chapter about the value and implications of different ways of gathering and analysing qualitative data. Please go through the following steps, ideally with another student:

1   Define your research topic in no more than two sentences.

2   Explain which method you propose to use to gather data. Why that method?

3   Why would other methods not be possible or appropriate?

4   How big a data sample do you intend to collect? Could you manage with less data? Might you need more?

5   What theoretical approach do you favour? How will it help or hinder you in the analysis of your data?

6   What other approaches might be appropriate/inappropriate? Why?

7   Is there anything about your theory/method/data that could be simplified to make a more effective study?

What Counts as 'Originality'?

5.1   INTRODUCTION

All students speculate about the standards through which they will be assessed. Many students beginning a research study crave to be 'original'. Whether the research is for a PhD, MA or only a humble BA dissertation, 'originality' is, for many, both a goal and a perceived critical standard which will be used by your examiners to beat you with!

Such fears are associated with a lack of knowledge about what is expected at a new, 'higher' level of your education. In this respect, we are talking about a common experience when we reach the next step on any ladder.

Many social transitions are associated with rites of passage and educational careers are no exception. In English secondary schools, after the age of 16, one enters the sixth form where one is expected to specialize narrowly and to become more self-reliant and less spoonfed. At my own school, boys just out of short trousers suddenly found themselves addressed by their sixth-form teacher as 'gentlemen'. We looked round the room but, weirdly, the appellation was directed at us.

The process is repeated in some form all over the world when you begin a BA at a university. Now, it seems, you are truly on your own, having to meet strange new criteria of achievement without any obvious means of support. Your time tends to be much more your own and you have to decide how much time to allocate to the library, computer centre – or, at British universities, the Students' Union bar.

How much worse, then, when you register to do an MA or PhD. Suddenly, everything you could count on in the past now seems to amount to nothing. You are no longer the outstanding undergraduate but just one of many students, all of whom, presumably, achieved good first degrees. In the past, university examinations were mysteries that you had cracked. Now, although some further written examinations may await, you know that this is not how you are going to be mainly judged.

To some extent, this transition from BA to PhD is eased by the provision of taught courses for first-year research students, many of whom will have already taken an MA. However, a nagging doubt is still likely to torment many beginning PhD students. Are you 'up to it'? Above all, do you have the capacity to be 'original'? Or is 'originality', like so many things these days, something you can learn?

5.2 ORIGINALITY

Original: not derived, copied, imitated or translated from anything else; novel; creative; independent in invention. (*Chambers English Dictionary*, 1990)

Consulting a dictionary about 'originality' brings mixed blessings. You are not planning to plagiarize anybody else and so should have no problem in meeting the 'negative' definition of 'originality' given above: your dissertation is unlikely to be 'derived, copied, imitated or translated from anything else'.

But how about the 'positive' components of 'originality'? Can you be 'novel; creative; independent in invention'? Moreover, since 'imaginativeness' is linked to 'originality' by Roget's *Thesaurus*, have you the talent to be 'imaginative'?

However you answer these questions, you are going to be in trouble! Obviously, if you don't feel that your intellect is especially 'novel', 'creative', 'inventive' and 'imaginative', then you are going to worry yourself sick about whether you are up to doing a worthwhile piece of research. Conversely, if you are full of confidence about these matters, it is very likely that you are underestimating what is required to be granted these epithets.

If you doubt me, scan the book review pages in a journal in your field. My guess is that you will not find such words thrown around freely. And, remember, many of the books reviewed will be authored by established scholars, well past their own PhDs.

If the work of established scholars is not regularly judged to be 'novel', 'creative', 'inventive' or 'imaginative', what chance do you have? The answer is surprising – you have no problem.

Such epithets are rarely used by the examiners of successful PhD dissertations. Most dissertations are no more than solid and competent. Indeed, it would cheapen the currency of academic description to use the vocabulary of 'originality' too frequently. Even Nobel Prize laureates never fail to cast doubt on their own supposed 'genius'. Instead, they regularly refer to the support of their research teams and to the old metaphor: 'one per cent inspiration, ninety-nine per cent perspiration' (see Mulkay, 1984).

As Phillips and Pugh point out, in the context of a PhD, 'an original contribution to knowledge' is a very shaded term: 'it does not mean an enormous breakthrough which has the subject rocking on its foundations' (1994: 34). Following Kuhn (1970), PhD research is unlikely to involve a **paradigm** shift in your discipline. Instead, Phillips and Pugh suggest, it demonstrates that you have a good grasp of how research is normally done in your field (i.e. that you can do what Kuhn calls 'normal science'). What does this mean in practice?

Among other things, it can mean:

> making a synthesis that hasn't been made before; using already known material but with a new interpretation, bringing new evidence to bear on an old issue … (and) adding to knowledge in a way that hasn't been done before. (Phillips and Pugh, 1994: 61–2)

So Phillips and Pugh suggest that a PhD is less to do with 'originality' and is more about displaying that you are 'a fully professional researcher' (19). In turn, this means showing:

- that you have something to say to which your peers will want to listen
- that you are 'aware of what is being discovered, argued about, written and published by your academic community across the world' (Phillips and Pugh, 1994: 19).

The upshot of this is that a PhD is best viewed as an apprenticeship prior to the admission to a community of scholars. This implies that:

> you are not doing research in order to do research; you are doing research in order to demonstrate that you have learned *how* to do research to fully professional standards. (Phillips and Pugh, 1994: 20)

5.3 BEING A PROFESSIONAL

'Originality' is only one of four criteria upon which examiners of the University of London PhD must report. To get a London PhD, the examiners must report:

- that the thesis is genuinely the work of the candidate
- that the thesis forms a distinct contribution to the knowledge of the subject, and affords evidence of originality by *the discovery of new facts* and/or *the exercise of independent critical power* (my emphasis)

● that the thesis is satisfactory as regards literary presentation
● that the thesis is suitable for publication … as submitted or in abridged or modified form.

Despite the passing reference to 'originality' in the second item, all these criteria are really about professionality. We only need to concern ourselves about the second criterion: the discovery of new facts and the exercise of independent critical thought.

Considered on its own, 'the discovery of new facts' is rarely an important or even challenging criterion in most of the social sciences. In the natural sciences, perhaps, a PhD researcher may discover a new substance or process and be applauded. But, in my experience, it is much more rare for qualitative social science PhDs to argue that they have found new 'facts'. Indeed, if they did so, they would most likely be greeted with the riposte: 'So what?'

For example, say such a dissertation claims that it has discovered that a particular group has beliefs or displays behaviours that were previously unknown. Any examiner worth their salt would then want to ask: 'Why, on earth, should it matter that this is the case?' In other words, what analytical or practical significance are we being asked to attach to this 'finding'?

Such a line of questioning is *not* a case of the examiner being difficult. As I argue in Chapter 7, any scientific finding is always to be assessed in relation to the theoretical perspective from which it derives and to which it may contribute.

This means that, while 'facts' are never unimportant, they derive their relevance from the theoretical perspectives from which they stem and to which they contribute. The clear implication is that 'the exercise of independent critical thought' is the major criterion through which your dissertation will be assessed.

How can you satisfy this criterion? If professionality consists in the display of independent critical thought, what is the secret of being independent, critical and professional?

5.4   INDEPENDENT CRITICAL THOUGHT

In fact, as is the usual case in research, there is no secret or magic process to be revealed. In Chapter 3, we saw how Moira, Sally and Simon went about their research as solid craftpersons. Although, occasionally, they may have jumped out of their bath shouting 'Eureka', most of their time they just plodded along, building a competent analysis in the face of setbacks and opportunities.

Using their experience and the work of other students I have supervized, I outline below four procedures which contribute to the successful display of 'independent critical thought':

● developing a concept or a methodology
● thinking critically about your approach

- building on an existing study
- being prepared to change direction.

5.4.1 Develop a concept and/or a methodology

In 1997, Acourt completed a theoretical dissertation on the emergence and apparent disappearance of discussion of 'progress' in the social science literature. Armed with a well-supported argument about the analytical and practical relevance of such a concept, he was able to convince his examiners of his 'independent critical thought'.

Many social science dissertations have a more empirical content. Sally used Goffman's (1974) concept of **frames** to understand how a mental health team made decisions about what services to offer to homeless people. Moira and Simon employed the concepts and methodology that the sociologist Harvey Sacks used to study the descriptive process.

Moira applied **membership categorization device** analysis (MCDA) and **conversation analysis (CA)** to interviews with the partners of people who had recently died in hospital. Simon used CA to study the sequential organization of talk at parent–teacher meetings.

Twenty years earlier, Baruch (1981) had used one of these approaches (MCDA) to analyse transcripts of interviews with parents of handicapped children. Like Moira and Simon, he showed the ability to work with and to advance Sacks's specialist approach. Indeed, Moira used Baruch's thesis as a baseline for her own research and showed how his analysis of interviews as 'moral tales' could be developed.

In the normal way, Moira, Simon and Baruch were influenced by the interests and skills of their supervisor. In my case, I had a long-standing interest in making Sacks's work more widely known (see Silverman, 1998) and four of my other successful PhD students have used the concepts and methodology of the subdiscipline Sacks founded.

Of course, social science has a broad and rich stream of concepts and methodologies and my students' work has expressed this breadth while reflecting my interests in processes of language and representation. So Kobena Mercer used some ideas from the French tradition of semiotics in his research on the speeches of an English politician, Enoch Powell (Mercer, 1990). The related concepts of Foucauldian discourse analysis were used by Mary Fraser in her study of representations of children in a British nursing journal (Fraser, 1995).

In all these cases, because the approach was theoretically informed, the dissertation could justifiably argue that it had contributed to conceptual development.

5.4.2 Think critically about your approach

As we saw in Chapter 3, your prior experience usually has an important bearing on how you approach your data. For instance, Sally was constantly aware of how her own nursing experience might be influencing how her health professionals related to her and how she might be taking for granted certain aspects of their behaviour.

Sometimes, doubts about an overall approach can have far-reaching consequences for how you think about your data. So Moira became dissatisfied with the conventional version of open-ended interviews as a potential window into people's experiences. Instead of using brief extracts from her interviews to illustrate particular categories, she started to analyse the sequential devias through which her interviewees told recognizable 'stories'. Similarly, Simon was determined not to treat his parents' evenings as mere 'products' of familiar social structural **variables** (e.g. class and ethnicity of the parents, measured ability of the child).

Fifteen years earlier, another of my students, Gill Chapman, had devised an unusual way of demonstrating her independent critical thought. Having discussed a range of possible ways of analysing her audiotapes of nurses' meetings, she decided to experiment with a wide range of concepts and methodologies. Each of the empirical chapters of her dissertation is thus both an analysis of her data and a critical evaluation of the approach used (Chapman, 1987).

5.4.3   Build on an existing study

Don't try to reinvent the wheel! Try to find a previous study that, in some respect, mirrors your own interests and topic. Then model your own research on that study and develop some aspect of it.

Of course, with limited resources, you are unlikely to be able to offer a complete 'test' of the findings of that study. But by careful analysis of your limited data, you can reflect on its approach and conclusions in an informed way.

Sometimes a more realistic model is a previous PhD thesis. It is worth recalling that Moira used an earlier PhD that I had supervized as a model for her research. So, at the outset, look at earlier dissertations in your university library and, where possible, focus on work directed by your supervisor.

5.4.4   Be prepared to change direction

Sometimes students believe that what matters most is showing that their research has followed a logical sequence. Based on how research is sometimes reported, this structure seems to display the following sequence:

Research problem
Hypothesis
Data analysis
Conclusion.

However, anyone who has ever done any research knows that such a rigid sequence is rarely followed. Moreover, it sometimes makes sense to divert from an expected path if you come across new data or a new concept or if your data suggests a different focus (see Chapter 12 for a discussion of how I changed paths in my research on a paediatric cardiology clinic).

So, as I argue in Chapter 25, although your examiners will look for evidence of a logical structure to your research, they will also want to see that you have been prepared to be flexible and to change direction when appropriate. After all, originality is not consonant with always following a predetermined plan.

5.5 CONCLUDING REMARKS

The message of this chapter is that a successful dissertation does not require genius. Once one defines the task of the research student in terms of the display of professional competence, then one can abandon those sessions in front of the mirror wondering whether you really look like Einstein, Keynes or Marie Curie!

In any event, you are likely to discover these things after a while through the response of your supervisor to your work. As Phillips and Pugh point out, worrying about the originality of your thought tends to be a concern only during the first few months. After then, this problem tends to disappear.

The case of a PhD examination many years ago makes this point very nicely. The thesis of the philosopher Ludwig Wittgenstein was being examined by two famous professors: Bertrand Russell and G.E. Moore. While these two had no doubt about its merits, there is some evidence that both examiners found Wittgenstein's thesis somewhat beyond them. In their report, Russell and Moore make clear that getting a PhD is different from being a genius. As they put it:

This is a work of genius. It is also up to the standard required for a Cambridge PhD.

KEY POINTS

Students at all levels desire to be original. However, BA and MA students can comfort themselves that even PhDs are rarely awarded for originality. In the context of a research degree, 'originality' is largely about your ability to display 'independent critical thought'. In turn, such thought can be shown by:

- developing a concept or a methodology
- thinking critically about your approach
- building on an existing study
- being prepared to change direction.

Further reading

Estelle Phillips and Derek Pugh's *How To Get a PhD* (Open University Press, 2nd edn, 1994: Chapters 3–6) gives a realistic, supportive account of what is required to achieve a PhD. Another helpful account of what counts as 'originality' in student research is Pat Cryer's *The Research Student's Guide to Success* (Open University Press, 1996: Chapters 15–17).

Exercise 5.1

Cryer has suggested that we can understand originality in research through an analogy with a travel expedition: 'the research student is the explorer and the expedition is the research programme' (1996: 145). Cryer uses the expedition analogy to suggest different senses of 'original research'.

Review each kind of originality below in terms of what you think your research might contribute and decide which kind is most likely to be applicable to your work:

● originality in tools, techniques and procedures

● originality in exploring the unknown

● originality in exploring the unanticipated

● originality in use of data

● originality in outcomes

● originality in by-products (Cryer, 1996: 146–8).

You might return to this exercise at regular intervals to review any changes in how you view your research.

Starting Out

Part One of this book was aimed at the beginning research student. Part Two assumes that you have overcome your initial doubts and now need to deal with the nitty-gritty issues that arise when you start to design a research study. Chapter 6 discusses how to select a topic. Chapters 7 and 8 deal with using theories and choosing a methodology. The tricky question of selecting which case(s) to study is discussed in Chapter 9. The final chapter in Part Two considers how to write a research proposal.

Selecting a Topic

6.1 INTRODUCTION

In this chapter, I discuss the problems that you may find in defining your research topic. I then suggest some strategies you can use to overcome these problems.

People are often impressed when they find out that you are 'doing research'. They may even want to know more. If you have ever been in this situation, you will know how embarrassing it can be if you are unable to explain clearly exactly what you intend to study. Such embarrassment can be multiplied a thousandfold if your interrogator is, say, a smart professor you have never met before. How are you to respond?

The answer to this question becomes easier if you recognize that there are practical as well as social reasons for having a clear research topic. Above all, such clarity can give your research focus as shown in Table 6.1 below.

TABLE 6.1 THE ROLE OF RESEARCH QUESTIONS

1	They organize the project and give it direction and coherence
2	They delimit the project, showing its boundaries
3	They keep the researcher focused
4	They provide a framework when you write up your research
5	They point to the methods and data that will be needed

Source: adapted from Punch (1998: 38)

Unfortunately, many undergraduate social science programmes reward passive knowledge rather than the ability to use ideas for yourself. They often leave students better able to leap the hurdles to pass their assessments than to use their knowledge to formulate a workable research topic.

In qualitative methodology courses, this phenomenon is seen when courses encourage rote learning of critiques of quantitative research and offer minimal practice of alternative methods. By contrast, in quantitative methods courses, one tends to learn by rote recipe knowledge which *is* of practical use in drafting a research proposal (e.g. defining variables and measures).

In this context, selecting a research topic to be studied through qualitative methods is a very risky activity. This is because it involves committing yourself to a particular course of action rather than reiterating spoonfed 'critiques'.

Faced with this risk, students often try to play safe by opting for one of three apparently 'low-risk' strategies:

● simplistic inductivism
● the 'kitchen sink' gambit
● grand theory.

I briefly discuss each below before offering some more satisfactory solutions.

6.2 SIMPLISTIC INDUCTIVISM

In many social sciences, the qualitative tradition was initially characterized by its opposition to the strict research designs demanded in most quantitative work. So anthropologists would select their tribe, take up residence, learn the language and do no more than keep a field diary. Similarly, sociological **ethnographers** would identify an activity, institution or sub-culture and just 'hang out'. In both cases, the idea was to grasp 'reality' in its daily accomplishment.

The hope was that somehow meaning would 'emerge' by itself from such 'in-depth' exposure to the field. It was believed that any prior definitions of topics or concepts would only stand in the way of a sensitive understanding of the slice of the cultural world to which one was being exposed.

In the 1960s, this belief was apparently supported by Glaser and Strauss's (1967) famous idea of theory 'grounded' in data rather than presumed at the outset of a research study. Ironically, but understandably, the idea of qualitative research as unstructured 'exposure' to the world was also supported by quantitative researchers. So we learn, in one quantitative text, that:

> Field research is essentially a matter of immersing oneself in a naturally occurring ... set of events in order to gain firsthand knowledge of the situation. (Singleton et al., 1988: 11)

In common with crude inductivists, Singleton et al., refer to 'the situation' as if 'reality' were a single, static object awaiting observation. Like such qualitative researchers, they emphasize 'immersion' which they implicitly contrast with later, more focused, research. This is underlined in their subsequent identification of qualitative or field research with 'exploration' and 'description' (296) and their approval of the use of field research 'when one knows relatively little about the subject under investigation' (298–9).

This apparent unanimity at both ends of the research spectrum is noted by the authors of one qualitative methodology text: 'The conventional image of field research is one that keeps prestructuring and tight designs to a minimum' (Miles and Huberman, 1984: 27).

Miles and Huberman note two objections to this position and the cosy consensus that supports it: the omnipresence of theory and the need for a research design. I will briefly consider each in turn.

First, 'any researcher, no matter how unstructured or inductive, comes to fieldwork with *some* orienting ideas, foci and tools' (Miles and Huberman, 1984: 27). As Gubrium and Holstein (1997) note, the apparently atheoretical position of some ethnographers itself derives from a theory:

> The directive to "minimize presuppositions" in order to witness subjects' worlds on their own terms is a key to *naturalistic* inquiry. (1997: 34, my emphasis)

So the idea of just 'hanging out' with the aim of 'faithfully representing subjects' worlds' is a convenient myth derived from a theory that Gubrium and Holstein term **naturalism**. Of course, without some conceptual orientation, one would not recognize the **field** one was studying. So the problem is that many closet naturalists fail to come clean about the theory dependence of their research.

A second objection to simply going out into the field and inducing observations is that it can be an excuse for sloppy, unfocused research. Mason (1996: 6) rejects the suggestion that qualitative research can just 'describe' or 'explore' the social world. As Miles and Huberman point out, such unfocused research can be a recipe for disaster:

> the looser the initial design, the less selective the collection of data; *everything* looks important at the outset to someone waiting for the key constructs or regularities to emerge from the site, and that wait can be a long one. (1984: 28)

Moreover, such a purely **inductive** approach can be blind to the need to build cumulative bodies of knowledge. If this is not an intentionally anti-scientific ploy, it can be just naive. In the 1920s and 1930s, research students in Chicago, following Robert Park's injunction to get out of their armchairs into the virgin territory of urban streetlife (see Bulmer: 1984), could justify their inductivist aims. By the 1960s, however, even Glaser and Strauss (1967) were requiring that field researchers think about the **formal theories** that might be developed out of apparently isolated substantive, inductive studies.

At the turn of the century, qualitative research would indeed have been in a sorry state if it had not developed such theories and related cumulative bodies of knowledge. As I commented recently:

> we no longer need to regard qualitative research as provisional or never based on initial hypotheses. This is because qualitative studies have already assembled a usable, cumulative body of knowledge. (Silverman, 1997: 1)

Sometimes, the previous literature or (for experienced researchers) one's own work will suggest a **hypothesis** crying out to be tested or a finding ripe for re-testing. Where this happens, particularly where the earlier study derived from a theoretical approach to which you are sympathetic, an attempt to strike out afresh would be in danger of reinventing the wheel.

Of course, as Chapter 3 shows, this does not mean that you should necessarily be stuck with your original ideas. The beauty of qualitative research is that its rich data can offer the opportunity to change focus as the ongoing analysis suggests. But such changes of direction, like the original research proposal, do not come out of the blue but reflect the subtle interplay between theory, concepts and data.

6.3   THE 'KITCHEN SINK' GAMBIT

Like any piece of advice, you can take too far the suggestion that you should avoid simplistic inductivism. In drafting your first research proposal, it is tempting to select a very broad topic. By including every aspect of a problem that you can think of, you hope to show the breadth of your knowledge and to impress potential supervisors.

Unfortunately, this 'kitchen sink' approach is a recipe for disaster. Unless you have the resources for a big team of researchers, depth rather than breadth is what characterizes a good research proposal. If you define your topic very widely, you will usually be unable to say anything at great depth about it.

As I tell my students, your aim should be to say 'a lot about a little (problem)'. This means avoiding the temptation to say 'a little about a lot'. Indeed, the latter path can be something of a 'cop-out'. Precisely, because the topic is so wide ranging, one can flit from one aspect to another without being forced to refine and test each piece of analysis.

The case study below illustrates how one research student worked to refine and narrow down her problem. Over time, Seta Waller moved from quite a broad psychological interest in the 'alcoholic' to a quite narrow but workable concern with the narrative structure of patients' accounts.

Case study: Seta's process of 'narrowing down' her topic

My interest in developing a research study in the field of alcoholism came about naturally as I had been working in this field for many years. My research experience and training, however, had been exclusively in quantitative socio-medical studies on alcoholism.

Following training in social policy and administration, I joined the Alcohol Treatment Unit (ATU) of a psychiatric hospital. At the ATU I was involved in a set of quantitative studies designed to measure treatment outcome in alcoholic patients.

When I decided to develop a PhD study, my initial interest was to find out what patients thought of their drink problem – how they conceptualized it. This would have been a quantitative study but quite different from the usual measurement of outcome studies. I therefore began designing a quantitative study enquiring into alcoholic patients' concepts of alcoholism. The sample was to be drawn from groups of alcoholics, admitted to a four-week in-patient treatment programme in the alcohol treatment unit where I was employed.

Having developed some rating scales on concepts of alcoholism, following interviews with patients, I carried out a pilot study on a small sample. Patients were asked to complete five-point rating scales consisting of statements, by indicating whether they agreed or not with each statement, responses ranging from 'agree strongly' to 'disagree strongly'.

This whole process took about eight months. However, I was feeling uncomfortable with the results of my pilot study as I tried to make sense of the data. I felt very uncertain about the attitudes and beliefs expressed in the scales; I began to question how one could consider that all patients who, for instance, stated 'agree strongly' on the rating scales, meant the same thing.

I started thinking of a new study with a qualitative methodology which I was introduced to on my MA course in Sociology at Goldsmiths College. On this course, I became aware of the relevance of the status of interview data, how **naturally occurring data** or unstructured interview data can be treated as analysable texts which do not need to be considered as being true or false.

As my main interest in my work had been alcoholism for many years, I decided to look at alcoholic patients' accounts of their experiences by means of open-ended interviews rather than the traditional structured methods. I therefore asked the patients to tell me about their drinking, allowing them to talk with a non-directive approach. I tape recorded some interviews in the beginning, and, when I looked at my transcripts, I knew this was what

Cont…

I ought to do. The qualitative data resulting from this kind of approach was so rich and rewarding that I decided to proceed in this way and carried out forty interviews.

At first my approach to the analysis of the data was to look at 'social meanings', concerned mainly with 'why' certain causes of alcoholism were given as explanations, partly inspired by Douglas's work (1975). I then tried a **frame** analysis following Goffman's methodology (Goffman, 1974). After having applied frame analysis to some patients' interview data, I still was not satisfied with the results as I had no means of knowing if the staff used similar frames. Patients' hospital notes did not reveal sufficient data to study this. I realized that my interest lay in how patients were formulating and presenting their drinking problem and then to attempt to look at 'why' they were presenting in these particular ways.

Adopting a qualitative approach, I was able to look at the **narrative** structure of patients' accounts to see how the texts were accomplished and organized. The structure of the accounts seemed to have a common chronologically organized pattern. Examination of the narratives made me realize that patients were showing their skills in presenting themselves as morally adequate individuals, as Baruch (1981) had found in his sample of parents of children with congenital illness. I also found that patients were displaying considerable insights into their problems and were emerging as well-informed individuals.

My current approach is therefore not simply an analytical shift, but another way of looking at interview data to see how it can help our understanding of alcoholic patients' versions and presentations of their problems.

The case study above illustrates how ideas derived from methodology and theory can help in specifying a research topic. However, some people are more comfortable at working solely at a theoretical level and seek to substitute theoretical syntheses or critiques for data analysis. Following Mills (1959), I call this approach **grand theory**.

6.4 THE GRAND THEORIST

While the kitchen-sinker flits about trying this and that, the grand theorist is kept busy building theoretical empires. Stuck firmly in their armchairs, such theorists need never trifle with mere 'facts'. Instead, they may sometimes spin out cobwebs of verbiage which, as Mills (1959) shows, can be reduced to a few sentences.

Nonetheless, a situation in which you can obtain a research degree without ever leaving your familiar university library is not to be despised. Indeed, I should be the last to criticize grand theory since my own PhD was obtained by this very method!

However, it is usually wise to assume that every 'solution' contains seeds of further problems. In the case of grand theory, these problems include:

- Can you ever get out of the library in order to write your thesis? One book will surely have a list of further 'crucial' references and so on, *ad infinitum*. Anybody who thinks a library PhD is a 'quick fix' would be well advised to ponder whether they have the will-power to stop reading. They would also be wise to consult a short story called 'The Library of Babel' by the Argentinian writer Borges. This tells a chastening tale of scholars who believe that, if they only keep on looking, all knowledge will finally be revealed by yet another book.
- Theoretical fashions change – nowhere more so than in the social sciences. If you commit yourself to a theoretical topic, you must always be looking over your shoulder at the prospect of some change in direction in the theoretical wind from, say, Paris to an obscure location with a school of thought of which you are totally unfamiliar.

If you do grand theory, you may spend so much time constructing elegant accounts of the world that you never touch base with the ground upon which the world rests. Kafka's (1961) wonderful short story 'Investigations of a Dog' creates a marvellous image of 'Airdogs' (*Lufthunde*) who float on cushions above the ground, surveying the world from on high, yet cut off from any contact with it (so cut off that Kafka's doggy investigator wonders how they manage to reproduce). However, readers of this book will be more interested in solutions than in critiques. In response to this, I set out below some practical strategies that may be of use to potential 'simplistic inductivists', 'kitchen-sinkers' and 'grand theorists'.

6.5 STRATEGIES FOR SIMPLISTIC INDUCTIVISTS

If your previous education has equipped you with few research ideas of your own, comfort yourself that your predicament is not unusual and can be resolved.

I outline below three strategies that you can use if you find yourself in this boat. Each seeks to encourage you to use the knowledge you have already gained as a resource in generating a researchable problem. The three strategies I discuss are:

- Using concepts as sensitizing resources.
- Following up findings from other studies.
- Introducing a third variable.

6.5.1 *Using concepts*

Treating the knowledge you have learned as a resource involves thinking about how it can sensitize you to various researchable issues. In an earlier book

(Silverman, 2001: 9–11), I sought to distinguish three types of sensitivity: historical, political and contextual.

Most of this is self-explanatory. Historical sensitivity means that, wherever possible, one should examine the relevant historical evidence when setting up a topic to research. Political sensitivity shows the vested interests behind current media 'scares' and reveals that this way of determining our research topics is just as fallible as designing research in accordance with administrative or managerial interests.

Contextual sensitivity is the least self-explanatory and most contentious category in the present list. A longer explanation is, therefore, set out below. By 'contextual' sensitivity, I mean two things:

- the recognition that apparently uniform institutions like 'the family', 'a tribe' or 'science' take on a variety of meanings in different contexts
- the understanding that participants in social life actively produce a context for what they do and that social researchers should not simply import their own assumptions about what context is relevant in any situation (Silverman, 2001: 10–11).

Such contextual sensitivity would suggest that matters like 'recovery from depression', 'quality care' and 'urban healing' are not uniform phenomena but take on particular meanings in different local contexts and local cultures (Gubrium, 1988), depending, among other things, on who is the audience for the description.[1]

One final point: the three kinds of sensitivity we have been considering offer different, sometimes contradictory, ways of generating research topics. I am not suggesting that all should be used at the beginning of any research study. However, if we are not sensitive to *any* of these issues, then we run the danger of lapsing into a commonsensical way of defining our research topics. This is a topic to which I shall return, particularly in Chapter 7.

6.5.2 Following up other finding

Phillips and Pugh (1994: 49–52) suggest that one aid for the sluggish research imagination is to begin with previously proposed generalizations and then try to find their limits by postulating new conditions.

Since most undergraduate social science teaching places a great deal of emphasis on the 'classic' literature, you can sometimes mobilize your knowledge of 'classical' work in order to generate a research problem. In an earlier book (Silverman, 1985: 10–11), I gave two sociological examples of postulating a new condition for a classical generalization:

- Gouldner (1954) observed that Max Weber's 'ideal type' of bureaucracy was largely based on studies of government bureaucracies. This meant that Weber stressed the role of democratically defined formal rules in obtaining consent. By studying rule following in the private sector, Gouldner was able to identify varying levels and bases of consent by staff to rules.

● Lipset et al. (1962) noted that Robert Michels' 'Iron Law of Oligarchy' had encouraged a focus on the factors that make organizations undemocratic. By studying a highly democratic organization, Lipset et al. identified both anti-democratic and democratic pressures in how organizations operate. By doing so, they were able to question the inevitability of this iron law.

More recently, I became interested in the conditions under which clients were likely to demonstrate uptake of the advice that they were given in interviews with health professionals. In a study of interviews between British health visitors and first-time mothers, Heritage and Sefi (1992) had found that mothers were more likely to acknowledge the relevance of advice which was related to their expressed concerns.

In my own study of HIV-test counselling (Silverman, 1997), I began with Heritage and Sefi's findings as my initial research focus. However, I observed that time constraints in many counselling centres meant that it was very difficult for counsellors to adopt such an apparently 'client-centred' approach. My research question then changed to considering how both parties acted to prevent open disagreements while giving or receiving potentially irrelevant advice (Silverman, 1997: 154–81).

6.5.3   *Introducing a third variable*

As described by Rudestam and Newton (1992: 12–16), introducing a third variable involves adding a focusing factor to your area of research interest. These authors give the example of a student interested in how young people view the elderly. You can make this topic less general, more researchable and interesting by introducing a third variable. For instance, you can ask: does living with a grandparent influence this? Alternatively, you can focus on the effect on young people of media representations of the elderly. Further, using 'contextual sensitivity', as described above, you can limit your focus even more by asking how, when and where young people generate descriptions of elderly people.

If you have a tendency to be a 'simplistic inductivist', you should now attempt Exercise 6.1 at the end of this chapter.

6.6   STRATEGIES FOR KITCHEN-SINKERS

Do less, more thoroughly. (Wolcott, 1990: 62)

Wolcott's advice is sound. Narrowing down is often the most crucial task when drafting a research proposal. Kitchen-sinkers have so many ideas buzzing around in their heads that getting down to a focused piece of research is entirely beyond them.

Every issue seems so fascinating. Each aspect seems interconnected and each piece of reading that you do only adds further ideas (and suggests further readings). So, while you can grasp the value of making a lot out of a little, it is easier said than done. The question remains: how do you go about narrowing your ideas down?

I set out below three practical techniques which help to answer this question:

- Draw a flow chart.
- Find a puzzle.
- Look through a zoom lens.

6.6.1   The flow chart

Dealing with data means moving from passive reading to active analysis. If you have failed to use the early stages of your research to narrow down your topic, data analysis is going to be very difficult:

> having a large number of research questions makes it harder to see emergent links across different parts of the data base and to achieve successful integration of findings. (Miles and Huberman, 1984: 36)

To help you narrow down, it can make sense to do an early flow chart setting out your key concepts and how they might relate. Following Miles and Huberman:

> Conceptual frameworks are best done graphically, rather than in text. Having to get the entire framework on a single page is salutary. (1984: 33)

The single-page flow chart is a useful technique in writing books as well as in doing research. For instance, as I write these words, I regularly move to a second document which houses the outline of this book. This outline was continually revised as I did my preliminary reading. It is still being revised as I write each chapter.

Several attempts will usually be needed to get your flow chart into a state that will be useful to you. Miles and Huberman recommend experimenting with different ways of specifying your research focus. But their basic advice is to 'begin with a foggy research question and then try to defog it' (35).

6.6.2   Find a puzzle

One way to break out of the vicious circle of unending facts and theories is to put your books on one side and to ask yourself: What am I really trying to find out? More specifically, what *puzzle* am I trying to solve?

Think of research as one of many kinds of puzzle solving among a set of activities like doing jigsaws, completing crosswords or solving crimes. Each activity will be associated with its own set of more or less unique activities (but see Alasuutari (1995) on the parallel between the qualitative researcher and Sherlock Holmes). Mason has argued that 'all qualitative research should be formulated around an intellectual puzzle' (Mason, 1996: 6). She distinguishes three kinds of question that may generate the type of intellectual puzzle which qualitative researchers would recognize, namely:

- How or why did X develop? (a developmental puzzle)
- How does X work? (a mechanical puzzle)
- What causes X or what influence does X have on Y? (a causal puzzle). (Mason, 1996: 14)

Let us consider how, following Mason, you might find a puzzle. Say you have a general interest in 'child abuse'. You might narrow down your topic by choosing among the following questions:

- How or why was 'child abuse' first recognized? (a developmental puzzle)
- How (and by whom) is 'child abuse' identified? (a mechanical puzzle)
- What are the characteristics of child-abusers and abused children? What effect does child abuse have on each group? (a causal puzzle)

Once you make a list of this kind, you should see that it is impossible to solve satisfactorily all these puzzles. So which puzzle do you choose? Below are some further questions that are worth asking:

- Which puzzle most interests me?
- Which puzzle might most interest my supervisor/funding body?
- Which puzzle most relates to issues on which I already have some theoretical, substantive or practical background?
- Which puzzle would generate questions that could be answered using my own resources and with readily available data?

6.6.3 The zoom lens

Wolcott (1990) gives the example of one PhD student who never finished his study of classroom behaviour. The true 'kitchen-sinker', this poor student was always reading more or gathering yet more data.

Wolcott uses the analogy of a zoom lens to suggest a practical solution. Say you want to take some photographs of a holiday resort. You could find some suitably high place, say a nearby hill, and try to take a picture of the whole resort. Then, as Wolcott points out: 'if you want to take in more of the picture, you must sacrifice closeness of detail' (1990: 63).

Alternatively, you can zoom in on one small image. What you lose in breadth, you may well gain in telling detail – say a particular dish that you enjoyed or the interaction between two local people.

Now apply the zoom lens analogy to defining your own research task. Wolcott suggests 'taking some manageable "unit of one" as a focus' (1990: 69). So if, like his student, you are interested in classroom behaviour, focus on one student, one day, one lesson or one critical event.

The beauty of this narrowing of focus is that it will produce a manageable and achievable research task. Moreover, you are not locked for ever in this close-up picture. Just like the photographer you can:

> zoom in progressively closer and closer until your descriptive task is manageable, then zoom back out again to regain perspective. (Wolcott, 1990: 69)

Following Wolcott, later on you can always attempt to broaden your generalizations through more data at different levels of 'reality'. But your initial 'zooming in' will have got you going – out of the library and into dealing with data.

If you have a tendency to be a 'kitchen-sinker', you should now attempt Exercise 6.2 below.

6.6.4   A caution: avoid reductionism

One of the advantages of introducing a third variable is that it guards against the tendency to try to explain complex social processes in terms of a single cause. Such reductionism is regularly demanded in both legal cross-examinations ('answer yes or no'!) and in media interviews (where the demand for simplification sometimes makes research scientists seem like incoherent babblers).

So my diagnosis of 'kitchen sinking' and my recommendations for specifying a research problem should not be confused with attempts to reduce the complexities of the social world to a single **variable**. Just as doctors talk about meeting patients who make their hearts sink, there is nothing worse when a detailed seminar on one's research is greeted by some bright spark with a version of: 'that's all very interesting. But surely what you've described is all to do with power/gender/ post-modernity etc.'

What a nice, simple world it would be if everything reduced to one factor! For the moment, however, we should leave the pursuit of this kind of simplicity to bigots and to those theoretical physicists who valiantly are seeking a single theory of matter.

So narrowing down a research problem should not be confused with this kind of reductionism. I can only echo the arguments of the authors of a fairly recent qualitative methodology textbook:

Such reductive arguments are always distressing, given the variety and complex organization of social worlds. They reflect mentalities that cannot cope with the uncertainties and ambiguities of social research. (Coffey and Atkinson, 1996: 15)

6.7 STRATEGIES FOR GRAND THEORISTS

Reducing 'reality' to ungrounded sets of categories is an obvious potential failing of grand theorists. However, the minority of readers who feel they have the flair and temperament for theorizing will not, I suspect, be dissuaded by anything I might write. Indeed, sometimes, as I have already remarked, library-based work can be a quick way to write an acceptable thesis.

In this situation, all I can usefully do is wish you luck and offer you a couple of suggestions to speed you on your way. First, try to ignore fashions. Second, think about how some data may actually help you to theorize better. I set out these suggestions below.

6.7.1 Ignore fashions

Having found the corner of the intellectual garden which suits you, stick with it. Don't worry about those smart alecs who have always read a 'crucial' book by some new author – nine times out of ten, it will just distract you. Guided by your supervisor, work out the set of readings that will be your central material and stay with them. When you have written most of your thesis, you may then have the luxury of reading more widely and using that reading to reflect on the implications and limitations of your position – perhaps for your final chapter. Till then, don't be distracted.

6.7.2 Find some data

Even the most active minds can become a little stilted when confined to their armchairs. So think about examining some empirical materials of some kind. Even though these may not be central to your thesis, they may work as an aid to the sluggish imagination.

Take the case of two students in my own department who wrote 'theoretical' PhDs. Nick was interested in what he calls 'the refusal of work' which he linked to theoretical ideas about 'the ontology of desire'. Despite this highly complex theory, Nick still felt it worthwhile to gather material on the history of *Autonomia* – an Italian movement to refuse work – and the organization of unemployment benefit in the UK.

Jake was interested in a critique of existing theories of the community. In this context, he attempted what he described as largely a philosophical exercise.

Nonetheless, to aid his thinking, he observed and interviewed homeless people, beggars and the mainstream community. Attempting what he called 'a situated phenomenology of the moral encounter', his data was intended to be only illustrative.

6.8 STRATEGIES FOR ALL RESEARCHERS

Whether you tend to be this kind of a grand theorist or you are a kitchen-sinker or simplistic inductivist, there are certain general issues that apply to everybody who wants to select a research topic. I call these issues:

- finding a workable (not just narrow) research topic
- recognizing 'feedback loops' between topic(s) and data analysis
- understanding that your categories (or variables) are always theoretically saturated.

I deal with each issue below.

6.8.1 *Find a workable research topic*

'Narrowing down' is necessary but not sufficient for a good research project. It is possible to have a narrowly defined, clear and unambiguous research topic (using concepts which clearly connect to data indicators) which is simply not workable. For instance, there may be no way you could obtain appropriate data or the topic may simply not be very interesting or important. Table 6.2 lists three features of workable research questions.

TABLE 6.2 WORKABLE RESEARCH QUESTIONS

1 *Answerability*: we can see what data is required to answer them and how the data will be obtained

2 *Interconnectedness*: the questions are related to each other in some meaningful way, rather than being unconnected

3 *Substantively relevant*: the questions are interesting and worthwhile so justifying the investment of research effort

Source: adapted from Punch (1998: 49)

6.8.2 *Recognize feedback loops*

Good research rarely moves smoothly from A (research topic) to B (findings). As Seta's case (discussed above) shows, alert researchers are always prepared to change their focus as they learn new things from others and from their own data. Wield has called this to and fro between data and topic a 'feedback loop' (2002: 42). This is how he addresses the issue of research focus in the context of such feedback:

Each stage of the research work will result in challenging a project's focus and lead to some re-evaluation. At all times, you will find that you have to maintain a careful balancing act between the desirable and the practical. Too strong a focus early on may lead to you ignoring what actually are more important issues than the ones you have chosen. Too weak a focus results in following up each side issue as it emerges and not getting anywhere! So focus needs to remain an issue as the research progresses in order to avoid the pitfall of these extremes. (ibid.)

6.8.3 *Recognize the theoretical saturation of categories*

Seta's case, above, nicely illustrates that the categories we use to formulate our research problem are not neutral but, inevitably, theoretically saturated. In her case, the issue revolved around the status which she should attach to her interviewees' accounts. To take two extreme formulations: were these the raw experiences of alcoholics or provoked narratives in which a drinking story was constructed?

These kinds of issues have already been discussed in Chapter 4 when I examined several interview studies. They are considered at greater length in Silverman (2001: 83–118). The interdependence between research design and such analytical issues is examined in the next chapter of this book.

6.9 CONCLUDING REMARKS

Like most dispositions, whether you tend to be a simplistic inductivist, kitchen-sinker or grand theorist is likely to arise from a combination of temperament and experience. As such, you are unlikely to be deflected by anything I write. So this chapter will have succeeded not by converting you, but if it helps you to speed along your ordained path.

On the other hand, it may be overreductionist to view these three tendencies as personal dispositions. Jay Gubrium (personal correspondence) has suggested to me that simplistic inductivism, kitchen-sinkism and grand theory are occupational hazards of all social science enquiry. In this sense, they are tendencies present in all of us and we need to be constantly wary of them if our enterprise is going to be theoretically informed *and* empirically grounded.

KEY POINTS

Selecting a research topic can be made easier if you resist three temptations:

1 *Simplistic inductivism* assumes that we need make no assumptions in studying the world. Instead, hypotheses will somehow just emerge if we just

---

'hang out' with the aim of 'faithfully representing subjects' worlds'. Simplistic inductivism is at best a convenient myth which ignores the theory-saturated nature of any observation and can be an excuse for sloppy, unfocused research. It is best countered by:

- using concepts as sensitizing resources
- using other people's generalizations
- introducing a third variable.

2 *The kitchen sink gambit* seeks to include every aspect of a problem that you can think of in order to show the breadth of your knowledge and to impress potential supervisors. However, if you define your topic very widely, you will usually be unable to say anything at great depth about it. Depth rather than breadth is what characterizes a good research proposal. It can be countered by:

- drawing a flow chart
- finding a puzzle
- looking through a zoom lens.

3 *Grand theorists* build theoretical empires. Stuck firmly in their armchairs, such theorists need never trifle with mere 'facts'. The consequence may not be enlightenment but merely cobwebs of verbiage. This tendency can be countered by:

- ignoring the latest fashions
- finding some data.

NOTE

1 See Chapter 15 for further discussion of studies of these topics in relation to evaluating the 'quality' of qualitative research.

Further reading

To help you think some more about defining your research, I recommend three basic texts: Amanda Coffey and Paul Atkinson's *Making Sense of Qualitative Data* (Sage,1996), Chapter 1; Jennifer Mason's *Qualitative Researching* (Sage, 2nd edn, 2002), Chapters 1–2, and David Silverman's *Interpreting Qualitative Data: Methods for Analysing Talk, Text and Interaction* (Sage, 2001), Chapter 1. Useful but more specialist texts are: Pertti Alasuutari's *Researching Culture* (Sage, 1995), Chapter 13; Martyn Hammersley and Paul Atkinson's *Ethnography: Principles in Practice* (Tavistock, 1983), Chapter 2; and Anselm Strauss and Juliet Corbin's *Basics of Qualitative Research* (Sage, 1990), Chapters 1–4.

Exercise 6.1 Strategies for 'simplistic inductivists'

1 Attempt to relate your research ideas to *one* or *all* of the types of 'sensitivity' discussed above:

● historical

● political

● contextual.

How might this lead you to reformulate your research interest?

2 Review any theoretical or research study with which you are familiar. Try to postulate new conditions which might allow you to develop a new but related research topic.

3 Try adding a few extra variables into your area of research interest. Now work out which of these variables would add most depth to your project and/or be most simply researched (e.g. is the data available and can it be relatively easily gathered?)

Exercise 6.2 Strategies for 'kitchen-sinkers'

1 Draw a flow chart of no more than one page setting out your key concepts and how they relate.

2 Review your area of research interest in terms of the following questions and formulate your research problem in terms of *one* kind of puzzle:

● How or why did X develop? (a developmental puzzle)

● How does X work? (a mechanical puzzle)

● What causes X or what influence does X have on Y? (a causal puzzle)
  (Mason, 1996: 14)

3 Use the zoom lens technique to focus in on some manageable 'unit of one' which might serve as an initial data set to resolve your puzzle.

Exercise 6.3 A trick from Howard Becker

Howard Becker is the author of a very useful book for research students called *Tricks of the Trade* (1998). One trick he mentions, suggests the following exercise:

1   Ask your supervisor (or a fellow student who knows your work reasonably well) to offer a snap characterization of what you are trying to find out.

2   Now respond to this characterization of your work (e.g. by denying it or modifying it).

This exercise, says Becker, should help you to get a better understanding of what you *are* trying to do.

Using Theories

CHAPTER OBJECTIVES

By the end of this chapter, you will be able to:

- Know what a **theory** is.
- Distinguish between a theory, a **model** and a **concept**.
- Think about ways of building theories from your data.

7.1 INTRODUCTION

Some people become qualitative researchers for rather negative reasons. Perhaps they are not very good at statistics (or think they are not) and so are not tempted by quantitative research. Or perhaps they have not shone at library work and so are not tempted to write a purely theoretical dissertation.

However, the latter disposition begs the question of the relevance of **theory** to research. In part, this varies between social science disciplines. For, at least until recently, the different social sciences seemed to vary in the importance that they attached to theory. To take just two examples, psychologists and anthropologists, for all their differences, seemed to downplay theory.

In psychology, the benchmark was the laboratory study. For psychologists, the motto seemed to be: 'demonstrate the facts through a controlled experiment and the theories will take care of themselves'. Anthropologists were just as interested in 'the facts'. However, their most important facts were revealed in observational case studies of groups or tribes usually found in faraway lands. Nonetheless, until recently, most English-speaking anthropologists followed psychologists in elevating 'facts' above 'theories'.

By contrast, generations of British sociology students have been made very aware of the primary importance attached to theory in their discipline. For instance, although undergraduate sociology courses tend to be split into three main areas (the 'holy trinity' of social theory, **social structure** and research methods), it is the course in social theory which is usually given the most prestige. Moreover, theory has recently become much more important in psychology and anthropology, as battles have commenced between traditionalists and qualitative **discourse analysts** (in psychology) and **post–modern** and gender theorists (in anthropology).

The social sciences' concern with theory is reflected in how PhD dissertations are assessed. As we saw in Chapter 5, 'the discovery of new facts' is rarely an important or even challenging criterion in the assessment of most qualitative research. Any scientific finding is usually to be assessed in relation to the theoretical perspective from which it derives and to which it may contribute. This means that, while 'facts' are never unimportant, they are always subsidiary to theories. Successful dissertations display 'independent critical thought' (in the words of the University of London PhD regulations) by engaging with theory.

However, this begs an important question. What is 'theory'? In the section below, I show why, for qualitative researchers, theory is altogether more interesting than the dry pages of theory textbooks. Later sections deal with the differences between theories, models and **hypotheses** and the role of generalizations in building theories. The chapter concludes with some tips about how to theorize with your data.

7.2   WHAT IS THEORY?

O'Brien has used the example of a kaleidoscope to answer this question. As he explains:

> a kaleidoscope … (is) the child's toy consisting of a tube, a number of lenses and fragments of translucent, coloured glass or plastic. When you turn the tube and look down the lens of the kaleidoscope the shapes and colours, visible at the bottom, change. As the tube is turned, different lenses come into play and the combinations of colour and shape shift from one pattern to another. In a similar way, we can see social theory as a sort of kaleidoscope – by shifting theoretical perspective the world under investigation also changes shape. (1993: 10–11)

How theory works as a kaleidoscope can be vividly seen in a concrete example taken from Livingston (1987). He asks us to imagine that we have been told to carry out some social research on city streets. Where should we begin? Some alternatives are set out in Table 7.1.

As Livingston points out, each of these different ways of looking involves basic theoretical as well as methodological decisions. Very crudely, if we are attached to social theories which see the world in terms of correlations between social facts (think of demography or macroeconomics), we are most likely to consider gathering official statistics (option 1 in Table 7.1). By contrast, if we think that social meanings or perceptions are important (as in certain varieties of sociology and

TABLE 7.1 VIEWING A STREET: DATA POSSIBILITIES

1 Official statistics (traffic flow, accidents)
2 Interviews (how people cope with rush hours)
3 Observation from a tower (viewing geometric shapes)
4 Observation/video at street level (how people queue/organize their movements)

Source: adapted from Livingston (1987: 21–7)

psychology), we may be tempted by the interview study (option 2). Or if we are anthropologists or those kinds of sociologists who want to observe and/or record what people actually do *in situ*, we might elect options 3 or 4. But note the very different views of people's behaviour we get from looking from on high (3), where people look like ants forming geometrical shapes like wedges, or from street level (4), where behaviour seems much more complex.

The point is that none of this data is more real or more true than the others. For instance, people are not really more like ants or complex actors. It all depends on our research question. And research questions are inevitably theoretically informed. Even down to earth policy-oriented research designed to evaluate some social service will, as Livingston implies, embed itself in theoretical issues as soon as it selects a particular evaluation method (see my discussion of HIV counselling research in Chapter 8).

So we *do* need social theories to help us to address even quite basic issues in social research. Howard Becker quotes a famous American social psychologist of the past to make just this point:

> One can see the empirical world only through some scheme or image of it. The *entire* act of scientific study is oriented and shaped by the underlying picture of the empirical world that is used. This picture sets the selection and formulation of problems, the determination of what are data, the kinds of relations sought between data, and the forms in which propositions are cast. (Blumer, 1969: 24–5)

However, O'Brien's analogy of a kaleidoscope and Livingston's example of viewing a city street only take us so far. But what precisely is a 'theory'? And how does it differ from a hypothesis?

Questions like this mean that I can no longer postpone the potentially tiresome business of defining my terms. Once I have completed these definitions, I will, once again, provide a set of concrete examples to clarify what I mean.

7.3   THEORIES, MODELS AND HYPOTHESES

In this section, we shall be discussing models, concepts, theories, hypotheses, methods and methodologies. In Table 7.2, I set out how each term will be used.

As we see from Table 7.2, *models* provide an overall framework for how we look at reality. In short, they tell us what reality is like and the basic elements it

TABLE 7.2   BASIC RESEARCH TERMS

Term	Meaning	Relevance
Model	An overall framework for looking at reality (e.g. behaviouralism, feminism)	Usefulness
Concept	An idea deriving from a given model (e.g. 'stimulus–response', 'oppression')	Usefulness
Theory	A set of concepts used to define and/or explain some phenomenon	Usefulness
Hypothesis	A testable proposition	Validity
Methodology	A general approach to studying research topics	Usefulness
Method	A specific research technique	Good fit with model, theory, hypothesis and methodology

Source: Silverman (2001: 3)

contains ('ontology') and what is the nature and status of knowledge ('epistemology'). In this sense, models roughly correspond to what are more grandly referred to as **paradigms**.

In social research, examples of such models are functionalism (which looks at the functions of social institutions), behaviourism (which defines all behaviour in terms of 'stimulus' and 'response'), **interactionism** (which focuses on how we attach symbolic meanings to interpersonal relations) and **ethnomethodology** (which encourages us to look at people's everyday ways of producing orderly social interaction).

Within the narrower sphere of qualitative research, Gubrium and Holstein (1997) use the term 'idiom' to encompass both the analytical preferences indicated by 'model' and tastes for particular vocabularies, investigatory styles and ways of writing. They distinguish (and criticize) four different 'idioms':

● 'Naturalism': a reluctance to impose meaning and a preference to 'get out and observe the field'.
● 'Ethnomethodology': shares naturalism's attention to detail but looks in detail at people's taken-for-granted ways of creating orderly social interaction.
● 'Emotionalism': desires 'intimate' contact with research subjects and favours the personal biography.
● 'Post-modernism': seeks to deconstruct the concepts of the 'subject' and the 'field'.

Concepts are clearly specified ideas deriving from a particular model. Examples of concepts are 'social function' (deriving from functionalism), 'stimulus/response' (behaviouralism), 'definition of the situation' (interactionism) and 'the documentary method of interpretation' (ethnomethodology). Concepts offer ways of looking at the world which are essential in defining a research problem.

Theories arrange sets of concepts to define and explain some phenomenon. As Strauss and Corbin put it: 'Theory consists of plausible relationships produced among concepts and sets of concepts' (1994: 278).

Without a theory, such phenomena as 'death', 'tribes' and families' cannot be understood. In this sense, without a theory there is nothing to research. So theory provides a footing for considering the world, separate from, yet about, that world. In this way, theory provides both:

- a framework for critically understanding phenomena and
- a basis for considering how what is unknown might be organized (Jay Gubrium, personal correspondence).

By provoking ideas about the presently unknown, theories provide the impetus for research. As living entities, they are also developed and modified by good research. However, as used here, models, concepts and theories are self-confirming in the sense that they instruct us to look at phenomena in particular ways. This means that they can never be disproved but only found to be more or less useful.

This last feature distinguishes theories from hypotheses. Unlike theories, *hypotheses* are tested in research. Examples of hypotheses, discussed in Silverman (2001), are:

- how we receive advice is linked to how advice is given
- responses to an illegal drug depend upon what one learns from others
- voting in union elections is related to non–work links between union members.

In many qualitative research studies, there is no specific hypothesis at the outset. Instead, hypotheses are produced (or induced) during the early stages of research. In any event, unlike theories, hypotheses can, and should, be tested. Therefore, we assess a hypothesis by its validity or truth.

A *methodology* refers to the choices we make about cases to study, methods of data gathering, forms of data analysis, etc., in planning and executing a research study. So our methodology defines how one will go about studying any phenomenon. In social research, methodologies may be defined very broadly (e.g. qualitative or quantitative) or more narrowly (e.g. **grounded theory** or **conversation analysis**). Like theories, methodologies cannot be true or false, only more or less useful.

Finally, *methods* are specific research techniques. These include quantitative techniques, like statistical correlations, as well as techniques like observation, interviewing and audiorecording. Once again, in themselves, techniques are not true or false. They are more or less useful, depending on their fit with the theories and methodologies being used and the hypothesis being tested and/or the research topic that is selected. So, for instance, behaviouralists may favour quantitative methods and interactionists often prefer to gather their data by observation. But,

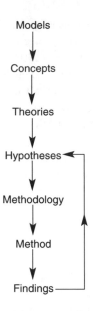

FIGURE 7.1   LEVELS OF ANALYSIS

depending upon the hypothesis being tested, behaviouralists may sometimes use qualitative methods – for instance, in the exploratory stage of research. Equally, interactionists may sometimes use simple quantitative methods, particularly when they want to find an overall pattern in their data.

The relation between models, concepts, theories, hypotheses, methodology and methods can be set out schematically as in Figure 7.1.

Reading Figure 7.1 downwards, each concept reflects a lower level of generality and abstraction. The arrows from 'findings' to 'hypotheses' indicate a feedback mechanism through which hypotheses are modified in the light of findings.

7.4   SOME EXAMPLES

Let me now try to put flesh on the skeleton set out in Figure 7.1 through the use of some concrete examples. Imagine that we have a general interest in the gloomy topic of 'death' in society. How are we to research this topic?

Before we can even define a research problem, let alone develop a hypothesis, we need to think through some very basic issues. Assume that we are the kind of social scientist that prefers to see the world in terms of how **social structures** determine behaviour, following the sociologist Emile Durkheim's (1951) injunction to treat social facts as real 'things'. Such a model of social life will suggest concepts that we can use in our research on death. Using such a model, we will tend to see death in terms of statistics relating to rates of death (or 'mortality').

And we will want to explain such statistics in terms of other social facts such as age or social class.

Armed with our concepts, we might then construct a theory about one or other aspect of our topic. For instance, working with our assumption that death is a social fact, determined by other social facts, we might develop a theory that the rate of early death among children, or 'infant mortality', is related to some social fact about their parents, say their social class. From this theory, it is a quick step to the hypothesis that the higher the social class of its parents, the lower the likelihood of a child dying within the first year of its life. This hypothesis is sometimes expressed as saying that there is an 'inverse' relationship between social class and infant mortality.

As already implied, a model concerned with social facts will tend to favour a quantitative methodology, using methods such as the analysis of official statistics or the use of large-scale social surveys based on apparently reliable fixed-choice questionnaires. In interpreting the findings of such research, one will need to ensure that due account is taken of factors that may be concealed in simple correlations. For instance, social class may be associated with quality of housing and the latter factor (here called an **intervening variable**) may be the real cause of variations in the rates of infant mortality.

This overall approach to death is set out schematically in Figure 7.2.

Figure 7.3 below sets out a very different way of conceiving death. For certain sociologists, social institutions are created and/or stabilized by the actions of participants. A central idea of this model is that how we label phenomena defines their character. This, in turn, is associated with the concept of 'definitions of the situation' which tells us to look for social phenomena in how meaning gets defined by people in different contexts. The overall message of this approach is that 'death' should be put in inverted commas and hence leads to a theory in which 'death' is treated as a social construct.

Of course, this is very different from the 'social fact' model and, therefore, nicely illustrates the importance of theories in defining research problems. Its immediate drawback, however, may be that it appears to be counter-intuitive. After all, you may feel, death is surely an obvious fact. Either we are dead or not dead and, if so, where does this leave **constructionism**?

Let me cite two cases which put the counter-argument. First, in 1963, after President Kennedy was shot, he was taken to a Dallas hospital with, according to contemporary accounts, half of his head shot away. My hunch is that if you or I were to arrive in a casualty department in this state, we would be given a cursory examination and then recorded as 'dead on arrival' (DOA). Precisely because they were dealing with a president, the staff had to do more than this. So they worked on Kennedy for almost an hour, demonstrating thereby that they had done their best for such an important patient (cf. Sudnow, 1968a).

Now think of contemporary debates about whether or when severely injured people should have life-support systems turned off. Once again, acts of definition

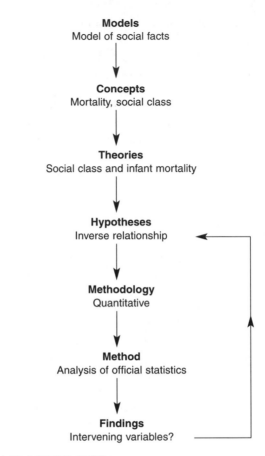

FIGURE 7.2   DEATH AS A SOCIAL FACT

constitute whether somebody is alive or dead. And note that such definitions have real effects.

Of course, such a way of looking at how death is socially constructed (sometimes called 'social constructionism') is just one way of theorizing this phenomenon, not intrinsically better or worse than the 'social fact' approach. But, once we adopt one or another model, it starts to have a big influence upon how our research proceeds. For instance, as we have seen, if 'DOA' can be a label applied in different ways to different people, we might develop a hypothesis about how the label 'dead on arrival' is applied to different hospital patients.

Because of our model, we would then probably try to collect research data that arose in such **naturally occurring** (or non-research-generated) contexts as actual hospitals, using methods like observation and/or audio or video recording. Note, however, that this would not rule out the collection of quantitative data (say from hospital records). Rather, it would mean that our main body of data would probably be qualitative. Following earlier research (e.g. Jeffery, 1979; Dingwall and

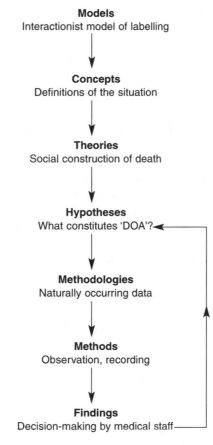

FIGURE 7.3 DEATH AS A SOCIAL CONSTRUCTION

Murray, 1983), our findings might show how age and presumed moral status are relevant to such medical decision making as well as social class. In turn, as shown in Figure 7.3, these findings would help us to refine our initial hypothesis.

7.5 GENERALIZATIONS AND THEORY BUILDING

Theorizing about data does not stop with the refinement of hypotheses. In this section, I will show how we can develop generalizations out of successfully tested hypotheses and, thereby, contribute to *building* theories. Further discussion of theory building, in the context of **grounded theory** (Strauss and Corbin, 1990) is found in Chapters 12 and 13.

First, we need to recognize that case studies, limited to a particular set of interactions, still allow one to examine how particular sayings and doings are embedded in particular patterns of social organization.

A classic case of an anthropologist using a case study to make broader generalizations is found in Douglas's (1975) work on a Central African tribe, the Lele. Douglas noticed that an anteater, that Western zoologists call a 'pangolin', was very important to the Lele's ritual life. For the Lele, the pangolin was both a cult animal and an anomaly. It was perceived to have both animal and human characteristics – for instance, it tended only to have one offspring at a time, unlike most other animals. It also did not readily fit into the Lele's classification of land and water creatures, spending some of its time on land and some time in the water. Curiously, among animals that were hunted, the pangolin seemed to the Lele to be unique in not trying to escape but almost offering itself up to its hunter.

Fortunately, Douglas resisted what might be called a 'tourist' response, moving beyond curiosity to systematic analysis. She noted that many groups who perceive anomalous entities in their environment reject them out of hand. To take an anomalous entity seriously might cast doubt on the 'natural' status of your group's system of classification.

The classic example of the rejection of anomaly is found in the Old Testament. Douglas points out that the reason why the pig is unclean, according to the Old Testament, is that it is anomalous. It has a cloven hoof which, following the Old Testament, makes it clean but it does not chew the cud – which makes it dirty. So it turns out that the pig is particularly unclean precisely because it is anomalous. Similarly, the Old Testament teachings on intermarriage work in relation to anomaly. Although you are not expected to marry somebody of another tribe, to marry the offspring of a marriage between a member of your tribe and an outsider is even more frowned upon. In both examples, anomaly is shunned.

However, the Lele are an exception: they celebrate the anomalous pangolin. What this suggests to Douglas is that there may be no *universal* propensity to frown upon anomaly. If there is variability from community to community, then this must say something about their social organization.

Sure enough, there is something special about the Lele's social life. Their experience of relations with other tribes has been very successful. They exchange goods with them and have little experience of war.

What is involved in relating well with other tribes? It means successfully crossing a frontier or boundary. But what do anomalous entities do? They cut across boundaries. Here is the answer to the puzzle about why the Lele are different.

Douglas is suggesting that the Lele's response to anomaly derives from experiences grounded in their social organization. They perceive the pangolin favourably because it crosses boundaries just as they themselves do. Conversely, the Ancient Israelites regarded anomalies unfavourably because their own experience of crossing boundaries was profoundly unfavourable. Indeed, the Old Testament reads as a series of disastrous exchanges between the Israelites and other tribes.

By means of this historical comparison, Douglas has moved from a single-case explanation to a far more general theory of the relation between social exchange and response to anomaly. Glaser and Strauss (1968) have described this movement towards greater generality as a move from **substantive** to **formal theory**. In their own research on hospital wards caring for terminally ill patients, they show how, by using the comparative method, we can develop accounts of people's own awareness of their impending death (i.e. a substantive theory) to accounts of a whole range of 'awareness contexts' (formal theory).

Douglas's account of the relation between responses to anomaly and experiences of boundary crossing can also be applied elsewhere. Perhaps bad experiences of exchanges with other groups explains why some Israeli Jews and Palestinian Muslims are so concerned to mark their own identity on the 'holy places' in Jerusalem and reject (as a hateful anomaly) multiple use of the same holy sites?

In any event, Douglas's study of the Lele exemplifies the need to locate how individual elements are embedded in forms of social organization. In her case, this is done in an explicitly Durkheimian manner which sees behaviour as the expression of a 'society' which works as a 'hidden hand' constraining and forming human action. Alternatively, Moerman (1974) indicates how, by using a constructionist framework, one can look at the fine detail of people's activities without treating social organization as a purely external force. In the latter case, people cease to be 'cultural dopes' (Garfinkel, 1967) and skilfully reproduce the moral order.

7.6 HOW TO THEORIZE ABOUT DATA

Unlike Moerman or Douglas, most readers will not bring to their research any very well-defined set of theoretical ideas. If you are in this position, your problem will be how you can use data to think in theoretical terms. The list below is intended merely as a set of suggestions. Although it cannot be exhaustive, it should serve as an initial guide to theorizing about data. It can also be read in conjunction with my discussion of the three kinds of research sensitivity in Chapter 6.

In carrying out your research, it is suggested that you think about the following six issues:

1 *'What'* and *'how'* questions: avoid the temptation to rush to explanations of your data. Don't begin with 'Why?' questions. Instead ask yourself 'what' verbal and behavioural and contextual resources are being used here and look for the detail of 'how' they are being used (and with what consequences).
2 *Chronology*: look at the timing of people's behaviour or their use of time in their accounts. Alternatively, gather data over time in order to look at processes of change. If appropriate, try searching out historical evidence which may at least suggest how your research problem came into being.
3 *Context*: how is your data contextualized in particular organizational settings, social processes or sets of experiences? For instance, as Moerman shows, answering an interviewer's question may be different from engaging in the

activity which is the topic of the interview. Therefore, think about how there may be many versions of your phenomenon.

4   *Comparison*: like Douglas, who generated her theory by comparing how different groups treated anomalies, always try to compare your data with other relevant data. Even if you cannot find a comparative case, try to find ways of dividing your data into different sets and compare each one. Remember that the comparative method is the basic scientific method.

5   *Implications*: when you are reporting your research, think about how what you have discovered may relate to broader issues than your original research topic. In this way, a very narrow topic (e.g. how the Lele perceive the pangolin) may be related to much broader social processes (e.g. how societies respond to anomalous entities).

6   *Lateral thinking*: be like the Lele. Don't erect strong boundaries between concepts but explore the relations between apparently diverse models, theories and methodologies. Celebrate anomaly!

7.7   CONCLUDING REMARKS

The philosopher of science Thomas Kuhn (1970) has described some social sciences as lacking a single, agreed set of concepts. In Kuhn's terms, this makes social research 'pre-paradigmatic' or at least in a state of competing **paradigms**. As I have already implied, the problem is that this has generated a whole series of social science courses which pose different social science approaches in terms of either/or questions.

Such courses are much appreciated by some students. They learn about the paradigmatic oppositions in question, choose A rather than B and report back, parrot fashion, all the advantages of A and the drawbacks of B. It is hardly surprising that such courses produce very little evidence that such students have ever thought about anything – even their choice of A is likely to be based on their teacher's implicit or explicit preferences. This may, in part, explain why so many undergraduate social science courses actually provide a learned incapacity to go out and do research.

Learning about rival 'armed camps' in no way allows you to confront research data. In the field, material is much more messy than the different camps would suggest. Perhaps there is something to be learned from both sides, or, more constructively, perhaps we start to ask interesting questions when we reject the polarities that such a course markets?

Even when we decide to use qualitative and/or quantitative methods, we involve ourselves in theoretical as well as methodological decisions. These decisions relate not only to how we conceptualize the world but also to our theory of how our research subjects think about things.

But theory only becomes worthwhile when it is used to explain something. Becker (1998:1) reports that the great founder of the Chicago School, Everett

Hughes, responded grumpily when students asked what he thought about theory. 'Theory of what?', he would reply. For Hughes, as for me, theory without some observation to work upon is like a tractor without a field.

Theory, then, should be neither a status symbol nor an optional extra in a research study. Without theory, research is impossibly narrow. Without research, theory is mere armchair contemplation.

KEY POINTS

Research questions are inevitably theoretically informed. So we do need social theories to help us to address even quite basic issues in social research. But theories need to be distinguished from models and concepts:

Models provide an overall framework for how we look at reality.

Concepts are clearly specified ideas deriving from a particular model.

Theories arrange sets of concepts to define and explain some phenomenon.

Methodologies define how one will go about studying any phenomenon.

Methods are specific research techniques.

You can improve your ability to theorize about data by thinking about:

- *'What'* and *'how'* questions.
- *Chronology*: gathering data over time in order to look at processes of change.
- *Context*: considering how your data is contextualized in particular organizational settings, social processes or sets of experiences.
- *Comparison*: trying to find ways of dividing your data into different sets and comparing each one.
- *Implications*: thinking about how what you have discovered may relate to broader issues than your original research topic.
- *Lateral thinking*: exploring the relations between apparently diverse models, theories and methodologies.

Further Reading

Clive Seale et al.'s edited book *Qualitative Research Practice* (2004) contains seven chapters which show the relevance of seven contemporary theories to qualitative research (Part 2 'Analytic frameworks': 107–213). Becker's (1998) book, *Tricks of the Trade*, contains two chapters which are highly relevant to learning how to theorize about your data (Chapter 2 on 'Imagery' and Chapter 4 on 'Concepts'). Jaber Gubrium and James Holstein's (1997) text *The New Language of Qualitative Method* is an invaluable, thought-provoking guide to the vocabularies, investigatory styles and ways of writing of different theoretical 'idioms'.

Exercise 7.1

Howard Becker reports that his colleague Bernard Beck responded to students seeking to theorize about their data by instructing them: 'Tell me what you've found out, but without using any of the identifying characteristics of the actual case' (Becker, 1998: 126).

Becker gives the example of his own research on Chicago teachers which seemed to show that these teachers sought to improve their situation by moving to different schools rather than trying to get promoted in their present school. Using his data but forbidden to talk about 'teachers' or 'schools', how might Becker have generated an account of his research that would have satisfied Beck?

Choosing a Methodology

8.1 INTRODUCTION

As we saw in Chapter 7, decisions about **methodology** are always theoretically loaded. In this chapter, I provide more specific advice about the role of methodological issues in the way you design your research study. First, I introduce the concept of 'research strategy'. This is then illustrated by a case study. Next I discuss the contentious topic of whether naturally occurring data has a special place in qualitative research design. Finally, I examine whether it makes sense to use multiple research methods.

8.2 YOUR RESEARCH STRATEGY

In Chapter 7, I defined 'methodology' as 'a general approach to studying research topics'. In this sense, your choice of method should reflect an 'overall research strategy' (Mason, 1996: 19) as your methodology shapes which methods are used and how each method is used.

Four issues arise when you decide that strategy:

● Making an early decision about which methods to use.
● Understanding the link between methods, methodologies and society.

- Appreciating how models shape the meaning and use of different methods.
- Choosing method(s) appropriate to your research topic.

8.2.1 An early decision

> Knowing what you want to find out leads inexorably to the question of *how* you
> will get that information. (Miles and Huberman, 1984: 42)

In quantitative research, it is expected that you begin by establishing a set of
variables and methods (often using already existing, proven measures). However,
when you are at the start of a piece of qualitative research, how far are you forced
to choose between different methods?

This question is raised by Miles and Huberman (1984) who suggest that qualitative researchers have a range of options in how far they use what the authors
call 'prior instrumentation' (i.e. predefined methods and measures):

- *No prior instrumentation*: fieldwork must be open to unsuspected phenomena
  which may be concealed by 'prior instrumentation'; all you really need are
  'some orienting questions, some headings for observations (and) a rough and
  ready document analysis form' (Miles and Huberman, 1984: 42).
- *Considerable prior instrumentation*: if the research is not focused, you will gather
  superfluous data; using measures from earlier studies allows for comparability.
- *An open question*: exploratory studies need to be far less structured than con-
  firmatory studies; if your sample size is very small then cross-case comparison
  will be more limited and, therefore, the need for standardized research instruments will be less.

Miles and Huberman show that, although prior structuring of a research design
is more common in quantitative studies, such structuring is worth considering in
more qualitative work. Thus, there have to be good reasons for any decision to
begin a study with 'no prior instrumentation'. Qualitative research can be highly
structured and what Miles and Huberman call 'no prior instrumentation' should
not be regarded as the default option for non-quantitative research. An early
decision about your preferred methods is therefore preferable.

8.2.2 Methods are linked to methodologies and to society

Most research methods can be used in research based on either qualitative or
quantitative methodologies. This is shown in Table 8.1. The table underlines my
earlier point that methods are techniques which take on a specific meaning
according to the methodology in which they are used. All this means is that we
need to resist treating research methods as mere *techniques*.

To take just one example, although there are quantifiable, standardized observation schedules, observation is not generally seen as a very important method of

TABLE 8.1 DIFFERENT USES FOR FOUR METHODS

Method	Methodology	
	Quantitative research	Qualitative research
Observation	Preliminary work, e.g. prior to framing questionnaire	Fundamental to understanding another culture
Textual analysis	Content analysis, i.e. counting in terms of researchers' categories	Understanding participants' categories
Interviews	'Survey research': mainly fixed-choice questions to random samples	'Open-ended' questions to small samples
Transcripts	Used infrequently to check the accuracy of interview records	Used to understand how participants organize their talk and body movements

Source: Silverman (2001: 12)

data collection in quantitative research. This is because it is difficult to conduct observational studies on large samples. Quantitative researchers also argue that observation is not a very reliable data-collection method because different observers may record different observations. If used at all, observation is held to be only appropriate at a preliminary or 'exploratory' stage of research.

Conversely, observational studies have been fundamental to much qualitative research. Beginning with the pioneering case studies of non-Western societies by early anthropologists (Malinowski, 1922; Radcliffe-Brown, 1948) and continuing with the work by sociologists in Chicago prior to the Second World War (Hughes, 1984), the observational method has often been the chosen method to understand another **culture** or **sub-culture**.

But there is a broader, societal context in which methods are located and deployed. As a crude example, texts depended upon the invention of the printing press or, in the case of television or audio recordings, upon modern communication technologies.

Moreover, such activities as observation and interviewing are not unique to social researchers. For instance, as Foucault (1977) has noted, the observation of the prisoner has been at the heart of modern prison reform, while the method of questioning used in the interview reproduces many of the features of the Catholic confessional or the psycho-analytic consultation. Its pervasiveness is reflected by the centrality of the interview study in so much contemporary social research. Think, for instance, of how much interviews are a central (and popular) feature of mass media products, from 'talk shows' to 'celebrity interviews'. Perhaps, we all live in what might be called an **interview society** in which interviews seem central to making sense of our lives (see Atkinson and Silverman, 1997).

This broader societal context may explain qualitative researchers' temptation to use methods such as the interview. Of course, such a link between culture and

TABLE 8.2 METHODS AND MODELS OF QUALITATIVE RESEARCH

Method	Model I	Model II
Observation	'Background' material	Understanding of 'sub-cultures'
Texts and documents	'Background' material	Understanding of language and other sign systems
Interviews	Understanding 'experience'	Narrative construction
Audio and video recording	Little used	Understanding how interaction is organized

method should be an opportunity to question ourselves about our methodological preferences. However, such self-questioning (sometimes, mistakenly, I think, referred to as **reflexivity**) does not itself provide a warrant for the choices we make. As I argue in Chapters 14 and 15, such a warrant depends on the robustness and credibility of our research design.

8.2.3   *Models shape the meaning of methods*

Many qualitative researchers believe that they can provide a 'deeper' understanding of social phenomena than would be obtained from purely quantitative data. However, such purportedly 'deep' understanding arises in qualitative researchers' claims to have entered and mapped very different territories such as 'inner experiences', 'language', 'narratives', 'sign systems' or 'forms of social interaction'. Some of these claims, associated with different qualitative models are set out in Table 8.2.

Each activity shown in Table 8.2 is not neutral but depends upon an implied model of how social reality works. In this table, I have simplified different approaches into just two models. However, in terms of Gubrium and Holstein's (1997) four **idioms** discussed in Chapter 7, **naturalists** give priority to understanding 'sub-cultures', **emotionalists** favour understanding 'experience' and focus on the open-ended interview, **ethnomethodologists** prefer to understand 'interaction' and **post-modern theorists** prioritize sign systems.

Such idioms or models are a necessary but not sufficient warrant for a claim that any given research method has been properly used. So a purely theoretical warrant does not guarantee that a method will be appropriately used in a particular data analysis.

8.2.4   *Choosing an appropriate method*

There are no right or wrong methods. There are only methods that are appropriate to your research topic and the model with which you are working.

Let us take two contrasting examples from Chapter 4. Tippi was interested in the experience of living in a community of elderly people. Her concept of 'experience' clearly derives from an emotionalist model. This makes her choice of open-ended interviews entirely appropriate. By contrast, if she were interested instead in how people *behave* in such a community, this naturalist topic might have suggested that she should use observational methods.

Anne's research was concerned with how a narrative changes as it is moved from book to television or radio. Her intention to observe what happens during the process of production sounds like a highly appropriate method for this topic. However, she also wanted to interview the participants to understand their motivation.

The problem here is the potential conflict within her research design between emotionalist and naturalist models. If she primarily wants to understand behaviours, then the naturalist stress on observation makes most sense. By contrast, if 'experience' and 'motivation' are really her thing, then she should stick with the interview method. This argument is developed in my discussion of 'multiple methods' below.

Of course, sometimes it does make sense to think laterally and to combine methods and models. But the safest option for most apprentice researchers is to keep it simple and to have a straightforward fit between the topic, method and model.

What follows next is an extended discussion of one case. It shows how I encountered these issues in designing a study of HIV-test counselling (Silverman, 1997).

8.3   CHOOSING A METHODOLOGY: A CASE STUDY

8.3.1   *Studying counselling*

The counselling study discussed here emerged out of my work as a medical sociologist. Between 1979 and 1985, I worked on data from British outpatient consultations which involved parents and children. At the same time, I also conducted a small study of adult oncology clinics, comparing National Health Service (NHS) and private consultations conducted by the same doctor. This research was reported in a number of papers (Silverman, 1981, 1983, 1984; Silverman and Bloor, 1989) and brought together in a book (Silverman, 1987). In that book, I focused on how apparently 'patient-centred' medicine can work in many different directions.

In 1987, I was given permission to sit in at a weekly clinic held at the Genito-Urinary Department of an English inner-city hospital (Silverman, 1989). The clinic's purpose was to monitor the progress of HIV-positive patients who were taking the drug AZT (Retrovir). AZT, which seems able to slow down the rate at which the virus reproduces itself, was then at an experimental stage of its development.

Like any observational study, the aim was to gather first-hand information about social processes in a naturally occurring context. No attempt was made to interview the individuals concerned because the focus was upon what they actually did in the clinic rather than upon what they thought about what they did. The researcher was present in the consulting room at a side-angle to both doctors and patient.

Patients' consent for the researcher's presence was obtained by the senior doctor. Given the presumed sensitivity of the occasion, tape recording was not attempted. Instead, detailed handwritten notes were kept, using a separate sheet for each consultation. The sample was small (fifteen male patients seen in thirty-seven consultations over seven clinic sessions) and no claims were made about its representativeness. Because observational methods were rare in this area, the study was essentially exploratory. However, as we shall see, an attempt was made to link the findings to other social research about doctor–patient relations.

As Sontag (1979) has noted, illness is often taken as a moral or psychological metaphor. The major finding of this early study was the moral baggage attached to being HIV-positive. For instance, many patients used a buzzer to remind them to take their medication during the night. As one commented, 'It's a dead give-away. Everybody knows what you've got.'

However, despite the social climate in which HIV infection is viewed, there was considerable variation in how people presented themselves to the medical team. Four styles of 'self-presentation' (Goffman, 1959) were identified which I called 'cool', 'anxious', 'objective' and 'theatrical' (Silverman, 1989). But there was no simple correspondence between each patient and a particular 'style' of self-presentation. Rather, each way of presenting oneself was available to each patient within any one consultation, where it might have a particular social function. So the focus was on social processes rather than on psychological states.

Along the way, I also discovered how an ethos of 'positive thinking' was central to many patients' accounts and how doctors systematically concentrated on the 'bodies' rather than the 'minds' of their patients. This led on to some practical questions about the division of labour between doctors and counsellors.

About the time I was writing up this research, Kaye Wellings, who then was working for the publicly funded Health Education Authority (HEA), approached me about the possibility of extending my research to HIV counselling. Until that time, the HEA had been funding research on the effectiveness of 'safer sex' messages carried in the mass media. In the light of the explosion in the number of HIV tests in the UK in the late 1980s, Kaye thought it might be useful to take a longer look at the effectiveness of the health promotion messages being delivered in counselling people around the HIV antibody test.

I was interested in such a study for two reasons. First, it was the logical development of my study of medical interviews with AIDS patients. Second, it offered the opportunity to pursue my interest in looking at how communication between professionals and their clients worked out in practice – as opposed to the injunctions of textbooks and training manuals. Consequently, I submitted a research proposal and received funding from the HEA for thirty months beginning in late 1988.

8.3.2 The quantitative bias

McLeod has reminded us that 'almost all counselling and psychotherapy research has been carried out from the discipline of psychology' (1994: 190). One consequence has been a focus on quantitative studies concerned with the attributes of individuals. This has meant that linguistic and sociological issues, such as language use and social context, have been downplayed (see Heaton, 1979).

Such a psychological focus has also had an impact on research design, leading to the dominance of experimental and/or statistical methods favoured in psychology. Of course, no research method is intrinsically better than any other; everything will depend upon one's research objectives. So it is only a question of restoring a balance between different ways of conceiving counselling research.

In designing my research proposal, I therefore needed to balance two competing objectives:

- my desire to examine how HIV counselling worked in actual counsellor–client interviews
- having to adjust to a context in which most counselling research had been informed by either a quantitative methodology or **normative** assumptions about what constitutes 'good' counselling.

8.3.3 Designing a methodology: three familiar options

Quantitative or normative approaches suggest three obvious ways of researching counselling all of which appear to take seriously the demands of **validity** and **reliability**. These three methodologies are set out in Table 8.3.

TABLE 8.3 THREE METHODOLOGIES FOR COUNSELLING RESEARCH

1 Measuring clients' response to counselling by means of research interviews which elicit their knowledge and reported behaviour. This would involve a longitudinal study, following a cohort of patients. The study could have either an experimental or non-experimental design
2 Measuring clients' response to counselling by means of objective behavioural indicators. This also would involve a longitudinal study, following a cohort of patients
3 Measuring the degree of fit between actual counselling practice and certain agreed normative standards of 'good counselling'

Source: Silverman (1997: 16)

In order to underline the methodological options that arise in the early stages of research design, I review each strategy below. In doing so, we will see that each raises both methodological and analytic questions. I shall suggest that, in terms of either or both of these questions, none of these three strategies is entirely satisfactory.

The Research Interview

As already noted, this might have either an experimental or non-experimental design.

In the experimental design, we might randomly assign clients to two groups. In group 1, clients are counselled, while in group 2, the control group, no counselling is provided. Both groups are then interviewed about their knowledge of AIDS and how they intend to protect themselves against the disease. This interview is followed up, some months later, with a further interview examining their present behaviour compared with their reported behaviour prior to the experiment.

In the non-experimental design, existing counselling procedures are evaluated by a cohort of patients. Again, we might follow up a cohort some time later.

The advantage of such research designs is that they permit large-scale studies which generate apparently 'hard' data, seemingly based on unequivocal measures. However, a number of difficulties present themselves. Of course, I recognize that these problems are recognized by researchers who use such research instruments. In turn, they have ingenious methods for dealing with them. Let me list a few:

1 How seriously are we to take patients' accounts of their behaviour? Isn't it likely that clients will tend to provide answers which they think the counsellors and researchers will want to hear (see McLeod, 1994: 124–6)?

2 Doesn't study (1) ignore the *organizational* context in which health care is delivered (e.g. relations between physicians and other staff, tacit theories of 'good counselling', resources available, staff turnover, etc.)? Such contexts may shape the nature and effectiveness of counselling in non-laboratory situations.

3 Even if we can overcome the practical and ethical problems of not providing, say, pre-test counselling to a control group, may not the experience of being allocated to a control group affect the reliability of our measures and the validity of our findings (see McLeod, 1994: 124)?

4 Don't both studies treat subjects as 'an aggregation of disparate individuals' who have no social interaction with one another (Bryman, 1988: 39)? As such, they give us little hold on how counselling is organized as a local, step-by-step social process and, consequently, we may suspect that we are little wiser about how counselling works in practice.

The non-experimental study may have either a quantitative or qualitative design. In the latter case, we might expect to carry out a relatively small number of open-ended interviews in order 'to enter, in an empathic way, the lived experience of the person or group being studied'. (McLeod, 1994: 89)

This pursuit of 'lived experience' means that many qualitative researchers favour the open-ended interview (see Chapter 15). Unfortunately, both the 'in-depth' accounts apparently provided by the 'open-ended' interview and the apparently unequivocal measures of information retention, attitude and behaviour that we obtain via laboratory or questionnaire methods have a tenuous basis in what people may be saying and doing in their everyday lives. Moreover, if our interest is in the relation of counselling to health-related behaviour, do such studies tell us how people actually talk with professionals and with each other as opposed to via responses to researchers' questions?

An example makes the point very well. At a recent meeting of social scientists working on AIDS, much concern was expressed about the difficulty of recruiting a **sample** of the population prepared to answer researchers' questions about their sexual behaviour. As a result, it was suggested that a subsequent meeting should be convened at which we could swap tips about how to recruit such a sample.

Now, of course, this issue of recruiting a sample is basic to survey research. And, for potentially 'delicate' matters, like the elicitation of accounts of sexual behaviour, survey researchers are quite properly concerned about finding willing respondents.

At the same time, it is generally acknowledged that the best chance of limiting the spread of HIV may be by encouraging people to discuss their sexual practices with their partners. This implies something about the limits of interview-based research in this area. Such research necessarily focuses on finding people prepared to talk about their sexuality in an interview. However, it can say nothing about how talk about sexuality is organized in 'naturally occurring' environments such as talk between partners or, indeed, talk about sexuality in the context of real-time counselling interviews.

Behavioural indicators

This method seeks to elicit behavioural measures which reliably report the effectiveness of counselling. Its advantage is that, unlike the research interview, it does not depend upon potentially unreliable client perceptions and self-reports of behaviour and behavioural change. Moreover, by eliminating a concern with the information that clients may acquire from counselling, it takes on board the research that shows that acquired knowledge does not have any direct link with behavioural change.

In relation to HIV-test counselling, it was suggested to me by a senior physician at an AIDS unit in Sweden that an appropriate behavioural indicator is seroconversion (developing antibodies to the HIV virus). Presumably, then, we would need to study a cohort of patients who test seronegative and are counselled. We could then retest them after a further period, say twelve months, to establish what proportions from different counselling centres and with different counsellors have seroconverted. In this way, it would be claimed, we could measure the effectiveness of counselling in relation to promoting safer behaviour.

As already noted, the advantage of this approach is that it generates quantitative measures of behaviour which are apparently objective. However, like the research interview, its **reliability** also has serious shortcomings:

1   How do we know that the counselling alone is the variable that has produced the reported behaviour? Although we may be able to **control** for some gross **intervening variables** (like gender, age, sexual preference, drug use, etc.), it is likely that some non-measured variables may be associated with the reported behaviour (e.g. access to other sources of information, availability of condoms or clean injecting equipment, etc.).

2   *Ad hoc* decisions are often made about which part of a counselling interview should be assessed. The scope extends from one whole interview (or even several interviews with the same client) down to a microsegment of one interview. The latter approach gains precision but with a loss of context. Such context is provided by studying whole interviews but at a likely loss of precision.

3   Even if such measures are reliable and precise, the result 'assesses only the presence or absence of a mode, and not the skilfulness with which it is delivered' (McLeod, 1994: 151).

Such problems in attempts to use internal, normative standards of evaluation look even worse when viewed in the context of studies which seek to relate such measures to particular outcomes. As McLeod (1994) notes, one such study (Hill et al., 1988) found that only 1 per cent of variance in client responses was related to observed measures of counsellor behaviour!

8.3.4   The methodology chosen

It is now time to lay my cards on the table and to offer the alternative approach on which my research was based – **conversation analysis** (henceforth CA). CA, as we saw in the studies discussed in Chapters 3 and 4, is centrally concerned with the organization of talk, although its concern with social organization leads it to describe its subject matter as 'talk-in-interaction'.

Equally, counsellors, by definition, treat talk as a non-trivial matter. However, even if we concede the centrality of talk to social life, why should counselling researchers give priority to recording and transcribing talk? Given the usefulness of other kinds of data derived, say, from observations of behavioural change or interviews with clients, what is the special value of transcripts of tape recordings of conversation?

One way to start to discuss this question is to think about how research based upon data which arises in subjects' day-to-day activities can seek to preserve the 'phenomenon' of interactions like counselling interviews. Although such **naturally occurring data** is never uncontaminated (for instance, it may need to be recorded and transcribed), it usually gives us a very good clue about what participants usually do outside a research setting.

Conversely, in research interviews, as Heritage puts it: 'the verbal formulations of subjects are treated as an appropriate substitute for the observation of actual behaviour' (Heritage, 1984: 236). The temptation here is to treat respondents' formulations as reflections of some pre-existing social or psychological world.

However, even when counselling researchers contemplate tape recording actual interactions, they sometimes become easily deflected away from the counselling session itself. For instance, although McLeod (1994) calls for a study of 'the interior of therapy', he also cites favourably attempts at 'interpersonal process recall' where participants are played back the tape 'to restimulate the actual experience the person had during the session' (1994: 147). Thus, in common with many qualitative researchers, what matters for McLeod is what people think and feel rather than what they do.

However, if we follow this temptation in designing a study of counselling, then we deny something that all counsellors recognize: that talk is itself an activity. Although this is recognized in many **normative** versions of counselling, to base our research on such versions would be to narrow our focus to those activities which we already know about.

An alternative is to investigate how counselling interviews actually proceed without being shackled by normative standards of 'good' communication. In this way, we might discover previously unnoticed skills of both counsellors and clients as well as the communicational 'functions' of apparently 'dysfunctional' counsellor behaviour.

8.3.5   Summary and implications

In this section, I have used the case of a study of HIV counselling to illustrate several options that are available in designing a qualitative study. I did not want to imply that a CA study of counselling interviews is the 'one right method'. Instead, I wanted to demonstrate that choosing a particular method always has more implications than you might think. I have shown here how those implications encompass preferred analytical models, questions of reliability and validity and, in this particular case, relevance for professional practice. To follow up this point, you should attempt Exercise 8.1 now.

In developing my research design in this study, I took a position on two issues that need further discussion: I chose to study behaviour *in situ* (i.e. naturally occurring data) and I rejected combining multiple methods. This reflected my own preferences. Since other choices can (rightfully) be made by others, it is worth reviewing both issues.

8.4   NATURALLY OCCURRING DATA?

Some qualitative researchers prefer to avoid creating data through setting up particular 'artificial' research environments like interviews, experiments, **focus groups** or survey questionnaires. They argue that, since so much data occurs 'naturally' (i.e. without the intervention of a researcher), why not study that and, thereby, access what people are routinely up to without, say, being asked by a researcher? To those who argue that such access can be difficult, the answer is that lateral thinking can move you into areas which *are* accessible.

For instance, to use an example raised by someone at a recent talk I gave, we might think that how couples negotiate the consequences of their different sleeping patterns can only be elicited by interviewing those involved. However, if indeed this is a real problem to members of society, it should crop up say in the advice or letters pages of certain magazines. Why not try looking for actual instances first, before resorting to interviews?

Moreover, the problem with methods like interviews and (to some extent) focus groups is that the researcher has to set things up by asking questions of respondents. By contrast, the beauty of naturally occurring data is that it may show us things we could never imagine. As Sacks once put it: 'Thus we can start with things that are not currently imaginable, by showing that they happened' (Sacks, 1992, Vol. 2: 420).

Although I am highly sympathetic to this argument, it also has limitations (see Speer, 2002). For instance:

● Data cannot be intrinsically unsatisfactory; it all depends on what you want to do with the data.
● No data can be 'untouched by human hands' (e.g. recording equipment is sometimes present and this has to be positioned by a researcher).
● The difference between what is 'natural' and 'non-natural' should be investigated rather than used as a tacit research resource.

These are powerful arguments. However, rather than abandon my preference, I prefer to take a non-dogmatic position. This involves the following two elements:

● Everything depends on your research topic. So, as Speer notes, if you want to study how counselling gets done, it may not make sense to seek retrospective accounts from clients and practitioners or to use a laboratory study.
● We need to consider how far any research setting is *consequential* for our research topic. For instance, in one lab study, limitations were placed on who could speak. This made the experimental setting consequential for its topic (of 'self-repair') and undercut its conclusions (Schegloff, 1991: 54). Without such limitations, the study would have been sound.

To conclude: choosing any method, based on any kind of data, can never be intrinsically right or wrong. However, as a non-emotionalist, I am sympathetic to Potter's argument that, given the (unthought?) dominance of open-ended interviews in qualitative research:

the justificatory boot might be better placed on the other foot. The question is not why should we study natural materials, but why should we not?' (J. Potter, 2002: 540)

8.5   MULTIPLE METHODS?

So far I have been assuming that you will always want to choose just one method. However, the methods presented in Table 8.2 are often combined. For instance, many qualitative case studies combine observation with interviewing. This may be because you have several research questions or 'because you want to use different methods or sources to corroborate each other so that you are using some form of methodological **triangulation**' (Mason, 1996: 25).

For instance, Miles and Huberman (1984: 42) give the example of research on how police suspects are arrested and booked. You might think here of combining several methods, e.g.:

- interviews (with suspects, police and lawyers)
- observation (of arrests and bookings)
- collecting documents (produced by this process)
- recording (of arrests and bookings).

If you are a pure **empiricist**, uninterested in the theoretical bases of research design, multiple methods may look like a good idea. By having a cumulative view of data drawn from different contexts, we may, as in trigonometry, be able to triangulate the 'true' state of affairs by examining where the different data intersect. In this way, some qualitative researchers believe that triangulation may improve the reliability of a single method. But do multiple methods always make analytical sense?

As I remarked in Chapter 4, 'mapping' one set of data upon another is a more or less complicated task depending on your analytic framework. In particular, if you treat social reality as constructed in different ways in different contexts, then you cannot appeal to a single 'phenomenon' which all your data apparently represents (see Chapter 14).

Mason (1996: 27) gives the example of the mistaken attempt to combine (say) interview data on individuals' perceptions with **discourse analysis** (DA) of particular texts. The mistake arises because DA treats all accounts as socially constructed and, therefore, cannot treat interview accounts as providing a definitive version of reality.

Such triangulation of data seeks to overcome the context-boundedness of our materials at the cost of analysing their sense in context. For purposes of social research, it may simply not be useful to conceive of an overarching reality to which data, gathered in different contexts, approximates.

At the very least, we need to note Fielding and Fielding's (1986) suggestion that the use of triangulation should operate according to ground rules, set out below:

- always begin from a theoretical perspective or model
- choose methods and data which will give you an account of structure and meaning from within that perspective (e.g. by showing the structural contexts of the interactions studied).

Many theoretical perspectives in sociology and elsewhere suggest we cannot simply aggregate data in order to arrive at an overall 'truth'. This implies that we should receive with caution the clarion calls for multiple methods in areas like nursing, family medicine and elsewhere. As Hammersley and Atkinson point out:

> one should not adopt a naively 'optimistic' view that the aggregation of data from different sources will unproblematically add up to produce a more complete picture. (1983: 199)

As already noted in Chapter 4, multiple methods are often adopted in the mistaken hope that they will reveal 'the whole picture'. But this 'whole picture' is an illusion which speedily leads to scrappy research based on under-analysed data and an imprecise or theoretically indigestible research problem. For instance, multiple methods may tempt novice researchers to move to another data set when they are having difficulties in analysing one set of material. It is usually far better to celebrate the partiality of your data and delight in the particular phenomena that it allows you to inspect (hopefully in detail).

8.6 CONCLUDING REMARKS

The debate about multiple methods and naturally occurring data illustrates the theoretically laden environment in which we make methodological choices. It underlines the fact that many apparently technical choices are saturated with theoretical import.

Of course, to some extent this complicates the picture when you are attempting to design a research study. However, a concern at this stage with theoretical issues also helps in at least two ways. First, it may allow you to simplify your research design as you realize that it is often misleading to attempt to research 'the whole picture'. Second, thereby, it may add theoretical consistency and even some elegance to the research design. As I remarked in Part One, often the best research says 'a lot about a little'.

KEY POINTS

▬ Your choice of method should reflect both your research topic and your overall research strategy as your methodology shapes which methods are used and how each method is used.

- Although most research methods can be used in either qualitative or quantitative studies, research methods are more than mere *techniques*. Different theoretical idioms or models provide different justifications for using particular research methods.
- Methods do not just belong to social researchers. Before choosing a method, you should reflect upon the broader, societal context in which this method is located and deployed.
- Think carefully before you generate data through research instruments like interviews and focus groups. Sometimes such methods may indeed be appropriate to your topic and model. Sometimes, however, you may be neglecting to study illuminating, naturally occurring data.
- Think carefully before adopting multiple methods. Many models suggest that we cannot simply aggregate data in order to arrive at an overall 'truth'. Choose simplicity and rigour rather than the often illusory search for the 'full picture'.

Further reading

David Silverman's (ed.) *Qualitative Research: Theory, Method and Practice* (2nd edn, Sage, 2004) provides state-of-the-art accounts by leading scholars of the uses of interviews, observations, texts, Internet data, and audio and visual data. Other useful books on methodology are: Amanda Coffey and Paul Atkinson's *Making Sense of Qualitative Data* (Sage, 1996), Jennifer Mason's *Qualitative Researching* (2nd edn, Sage, 2002), Pertti Alasuutari's *Researching Culture* (Sage, 1995) and David Silverman's *Interpreting Qualitative Data: Methods for Analysing Talk, Text and Interaction* (2nd edn, Sage, 2001).

Exercise 8.1

Mason (1996: 19) notes that your choice of a methodology is likely to reflect your own biography and the knowledge and training your education has given you. As she comments: 'Whilst practical issues to do with training and skill are ... relevant in your choice of method ... they should not govern your choice' (ibid.). She suggests instead making a list of possible research methods and data source options and to think through why you are accepting or rejecting each one.

1 Follow Mason's suggestion about making a list of possible research methods and data source options. Explain why you are accepting or rejecting each one.

2 Answer the following questions (adapted from Mason, 1996: 20–1):

   ● What data sources and methods of data generation are potentially available or appropriate?

   ● What can these methods and sources feasibly tell me?

   ● Which phenomena and components or properties of social 'reality' might these data sources and methods potentially help me to address?

   ● Which of my research questions could they help me to address?

Selecting a Case

CHAPTER OBJECTIVES

By the end of this chapter, you will be able to:

- Understand what a case study is.
- Know the main types of case study.
- Understand how to generalize from a single case.

9.1 INTRODUCTION

I concluded the previous chapter with my favourite research maxim: 'make a lot out of a little'. If you take me seriously, you will have every chance of producing a thorough, analytically interesting research study. However, at least three nagging doubts may well remain. I list them below together with some soothing words about each:

- *'My case may not be important'* Here you are worried that the case you are studying may be seen by others as 'trivial' or 'not a real problem'. The famous ethnographer Howard Becker remarks that such criticisms have been made of his own work on several occasions. As he puts it: 'Just as some people think tragedy is more important than comedy … some problems are seen as inherently serious and worthy of grownup attention, others as trivial, flyspecks on the wallpaper of life … mere exotica' (Becker, 1998: 92). There is a very good response to this kind of complaint: what seems to be important is usually governed by little more than current fashions; who knows what might become important? Apparently trivial cases may, through good analysis, turn out to have far-reaching implications.
- *'I can only study the (part of the) case to which I have access'* This is a more serious issue. When we are studying an organization, we are dependent on the whims of gatekeepers. Such people will usually seek to limit what we can study, assuring us that, if we need to know more, they can tell us about it (Becker, 1998: 90).

How do we get round this problem? Becker suggests two answers. First, 'doubt everything anyone in power tells you'. Second, look for other opinions (1998: 91). Like Dalton (1959), in his classic study of middle managers, case study researchers should systematically attempt to assess the likely linkages between opinions, activities and interests.

● '*I have so little data, just one case*' This is a serious problem. As we shall see below, even in qualitative research it is important to consider what kind of generalizations can be made from a single case.

The rest of this chapter will be devoted to the issue of generalizability in case study research. First, however, we need to define both terms.

9.2   WHAT IS A CASE STUDY?

This question has a relatively simple answer. As Punch puts it:

> The basic idea is that one case (or perhaps a small number of cases) will be studied in detail, using whatever methods seem appropriate. While there may be a variety of specific purposes and research questions, the general objective is to develop as full an understanding of that case as possible. (1998: 150)

There are, of course, an endless variety of possible 'cases'. If, like Becker, we are interested in occupations, cases to study may range from dancehall musicians to student physicians. By contrast, if you are interested in childhood, a case may be a single child, a classroom or clinic, or a charity or other organization concerned with the welfare of children. So, as Stake suggests:

> A case may be simple or complex … (but) it is one among others. In any given study, we will concentrate on the one'. (2000: 436)

All this is purely descriptive. Table 9.1 identifies three analytic features of case study research.

9.3   GENERALIZING FROM CASES

Generalizability is a standard aim in quantitative research and is normally achieved by statistical sampling procedures. Such sampling has two functions. First, it allows you to feel confident about the representativeness of your sample: 'if the population characteristics are known, the degree of representativeness of a sample can be checked' (Arber, 1993: 70). Second, such representativeness allows you to make broader inferences:

TABLE 9.1   CASE STUDY RESEARCH

1   Each case has boundaries which must be identified at an early stage of the research (e.g. if you are studying a school, does this include classroom behaviour, staff meetings, parent–teacher meetings, etc.?)
2   Each case will be a case of something in which the researcher is interested. So the unit of analysis must be defined at the outset in order to clarify the research strategy
3   Case studies seek to preserve the wholeness and integrity of the case. However, in order to achieve some focus, a limited research problem must be established geared to specific features of the case

Source: adapted from Punch (1998: 153)

> The purpose of sampling is usually to study a representative subsection of a precisely defined population in order to make inferences about the whole population. (1993: 38)

Such sampling procedures are, however, usually unavailable in qualitative research. In such studies, our data is often derived from one or more cases and it is unlikely that these cases will have been selected on a random basis. Very often a case will be chosen simply because it allows access. Moreover, even if you were able to construct a representative sample of cases, the sample size would be likely to be so large as to preclude the kind of intensive analysis usually preferred in qualitative research (Mason, 1996: 91).

This gives rise to a problem, familiar to users of quantitative methods: 'How do we know … how representative case study findings are of all members of the population from which the case was selected?' (Bryman, 1988: 88).

9.4   TYPES OF CASE STUDIES

Stake (2000: 437–8) has identified three different types of case study:

1   The *intrinsic case study* where 'this case is of interest … in all its particularity and ordinariness'. In the intrinsic case study, according to Stake, no attempt is made to generalize beyond the single case or even to build theories.
2   The *instrumental case study* in which a case is examined mainly to provide insight into an issue or to revise a generalization. Although the case selected is studied in depth, the main focus is on something else.
3   The *collective case study* where a number of cases are studied in order to investigate some general phenomenon.

The idea of a purely *intrinsic case study* is resisted by many qualitative researchers. If all you aim to do is simply to 'describe a case', you may rightly get the response: 'so what?' Description itself is a tricky activity which is inevitably theoretically laden. If you doubt this, you might look back at Table 7.1 in Chapter 7.

In this context, most supervisors of student qualitative research would expect your study of a case to be based upon some **concept**(s) which are developed as a result of your study. For examples of concept development through case study research, see Chapter 3.

Furthermore, empirical issues arise in case studies just as much as theoretical concerns. It is reasonable to ask what knowledge your case study has produced. If you are to answer this question, you must consider the degree of generalizability of your research. As Mason puts it:

> I do not think qualitative researchers should be satisfied with producing explanations which are idiosyncratic or particular to the limited empirical parameters of their study …. Qualitative research should (therefore) produce explanations which are *generalizable* in some way, or which have a wider resonance' (1996: 6)

So description of a case for description's sake (the *intrinsic* case study) is a weak position. Quite rightly, the problem of 'representativeness' is a perennial worry of many qualitative or case study researchers. How do they attempt to address it? Can we generalize from cases to populations without following a purely statistical logic?

In the rest of this chapter, I will discuss four different but positive answers to this question of how we can obtain generalizability:

- combining qualitative research with quantitative measures of populations
- purposive sampling guided by time and resources
- theoretical sampling
- using an analytic model which assumes that generalizability is present in the existence of *any* case.

9.5 COMBINING QUALITATIVE RESEARCH WITH QUANTITATIVE MEASURES OF POPULATIONS

Quantitative measures may sometimes be used to infer from one case to a larger population. Hammersley (1992) suggests three methods through which we can attempt to generalize from the analysis of a single case:

- obtaining information about relevant aspects of the population of cases and comparing our case to them
- using survey research on a random sample of cases
- co-ordinating several ethnographic studies.

Hammersley argues that such comparisons with a larger sample may allow us to establish some sense of the representativeness of our single case.

However, two of Hammersley's methods are very ambitious for the student researcher. For instance, you are unlikely to have the funds for even a small piece of survey research while the co-ordination of several ethnographic studies requires substantial resources of time and personnel as well as good contacts with other researchers. Such contacts allowed Miller and Silverman (1995) to apply the comparative approach in describing talk about troubles in two counselling settings: a British haemophilia centre counselling patients who are HIV-positive and a family therapy centre in the USA. In this study, we focused on similarities in three types of discursive practices in these settings: those concerned with trouble definitions, trouble remedies, and the social contexts of the clients' troubles (see also Gubrium, 1992).

Without such contacts and resources, the student researcher is left with Hammersley's first method: obtaining information about relevant aspects of the population of cases and comparing our case to them. This is more useful because, at its simplest, this method only involves reading about other cognate studies and comparing our case to them. For instance, in my study of HIV counselling (Silverman, 1997), I compared my counsellor–client interviews with Heritage and Sefi's (1992) data on interviews between health visitors and first-time mothers. Although this had little to do with establishing the representativeness of my sample, it gave a firmer basis to my generalizations about advice-sequences in my data (Silverman, 1997: 124–8). The comparative method used here allows you to make larger claims about your analysis without leaving your library. As Peräkylä puts it:

> The comparative approach directly tackles the question of generalizability by demonstrating the similarities and differences across a number of settings. (2004: 296)

In this sense, your literature review (see Chapter 17) has as much to do with the issue of **generalizability** as with displaying your academic credentials.

9.6 PURPOSIVE SAMPLING

Before we can contemplate comparing our case to others, we need to have selected our case. Are there any grounds other than convenience or accessibility to guide us in this selection?

Purposive sampling allows us to choose a case because it illustrates some feature or process in which we are interested. However, this does not provide a simple approval to any case we happen to choose. Rather, purposive sampling demands that we think critically about the parameters of the population we are studying and choose our sample case carefully on this basis.

As Denzin and Lincoln put it:

> Many qualitative researchers employ ... purposive, and not random, sampling methods. They seek out groups, settings and individuals where ... the processes being studied are most likely to occur. (2000: 370)

TABLE 9.2 A TYPOLOGY OF CHILDREN'S MUSEUMS

	Type of museum		
Programme type	**Art**	**Science**	**History**
Exhibitory	1	2	3
Participative	4	5	6

Source: adapted from Stake (2000: 446–7)

Stake (2000: 446–7) gives the example of a study of interactive displays in children's museums. He assumes that you only have resources to study four such museums. How should you proceed?

He suggests setting up a *typology* which would establish a matrix of museum types as in Table 9.2.

The typology set out in Table 9.2 yields six cases which could be increased further by, say, distinguishing between museums located in small and big cities – bringing up the cases to twelve. Which cases should you select?

You will be constrained by two main factors. First, there may not be examples to fit every cell. Second, your resources will not allow you to research every existing unit. So you have to make a practical decision. For instance, if you can cover only two cases, do you choose two participatory museums in different locations or in different subjects? Or do you compare such a museum with a more conventional exhibit-based museum?

Provided you have thought through the options, it is unlikely that your selection will be criticized. Moreover, as we see below, how you set up your typology and make your choice should be grounded in the theoretical apparatus you are using. Sampling in qualitative research is neither statistical nor purely personal: it is, or should be, theoretically grounded. To improve your understanding of this point, you could now attempt Exercise 9.1.

9.7 THEORETICAL SAMPLING

Theoretical and purposive sampling are often treated as synonyms. Indeed, the only difference between the two procedures applies when the 'purpose' behind 'purposive' sampling is not theoretically defined.

Bryman argues that qualitative research follows a theoretical, rather than a statistical, logic: 'the issue should be couched in terms of the generalizability of cases to *theoretical* propositions rather than to *populations* or universes' (1988: 90, my emphasis).[1]

The nature of this link between sampling and theory is set out by Mason:

theoretical sampling means selecting groups or categories to study on the basis of their relevance to your research questions, your theoretical position … and most importantly the explanation or account which you are developing. Theoretical sampling is concerned with constructing a sample ... which is meaningful theoretically, because it builds in certain characteristics or criteria which help to develop and test your theory and explanation. (1996: 93–4)

Theoretical sampling has three features which I discuss below:

- choosing cases in terms of your theory
- choosing 'deviant' cases
- changing the size of your sample during the research.

9.7.1 Choosing cases in terms of your theory

Mason writes about 'the wider universe of social explanations in relation to which you have constructed your research questions' (1996: 85). This theoretically defined universe 'will make some sampling choices more sensible and meaningful than others'. Mason describes choosing a kind of sample which can represent a wider population. Here we select a sample of particular 'processes, types, categories or examples which are relevant to or appear within the wider universe' (Mason, 1996: 92). Mason suggests that examples of these would include single units such as 'an organization, a location, a document ... (or) a conversation'.

Mason gives the example of a **discourse analysis** of gender relation as discourses which construct subjects of gender relations. In this approach, as she puts it: 'you are ... unlikely to perceive the social world in terms of a large set of gender relations from which you can simply draw a representative sample of people by gender' (Mason, 1996: 85).

So in qualitative research the relevant or 'sampleable' units are often seen as theoretically defined. This means that it is inappropriate to sample populations by such attributes as 'gender', 'ethnicity' or even age because how such attributes are routinely defined is itself the *topic* of your research.

As an example of theoretically defined sampling, Bryman uses Glaser and Strauss's discussion of 'awareness contexts' in relation to dying in hospital:

> The issue of whether the particular hospital studied is 'typical' is not the critical issue; what is important is whether the experiences of dying patients are typical of the broad class of phenomena ... to which the theory refers. Subsequent research would then focus on the validity of the proposition in other milieux (e.g. doctors' surgeries). (Bryman, 1988: 91)

We can understand better the theoretical logic behind choice of a sample in a further example of a study of policework. Say you are interested in the arrest and booking of suspects (see Miles and Huberman, 1984: 37–8). You are now confronted with a series of choices which relate to:

- the particular setting to be studied
- the elements or processes on which you will focus
- how you might generalize further.

Let us look at each of these in turn.

Settings

In independent, unfunded research, you are likely to choose any setting which, while demonstrating the phenomenon in which you are interested, is accessible and will provide appropriate data reasonably readily and quickly. In the police study, this might well lead you to study the police station rather than a squad car, the scene of the crime, the suspect's residence or hangout. In the police station, at the very least, you will keep warm and dry, you will be safe and you can expect several arrests and bookings on any visit. However, so far you are being guided by quite practical influences.

The research focus

In focusing your research, you necessarily are making a theoretically guided choice. By opting to focus on particular individuals, events or processes, you are electing particular theoretical frameworks. For instance, a focus on differential behaviour between police officers and suspects with different characteristics may draw on some version of the structural determinants of action. Conversely, a focus on how laws are interpreted in practice (cf. Sudnow, 1968b) may derive from a concern with the creative power of commonsense interpretive procedures.

Generalizing further

When wedded to other studies which share your theoretical orientation, a single police station may provide enough data to develop all the generalizations you want about, say, how commonsense reasoning works. However, if you have a more 'structural' bent, it may now be necessary to widen your sample in two ways. First, to add more observations of arrests in this police station and, second, to compare it with other stations, perhaps in a range of areas.

In all these cases, the sample is not random but theoretical. It is:

> designed to provide a close-up, detailed or meticulous view of particular units which may constitute … cases which are relevant to or appear within the wider universe. (Mason, 1996: 92)

9.7.2 Choosing 'deviant' cases

Mason notes that you must overcome any tendency to select a case which is likely to support your argument. Instead, it makes sense to seek out negative instances as defined by the theory with which you are working.

One of Becker's 'tricks of the trade' is:

> Just to insist that nothing that can be imagined is impossible, so we should look for the most unlikely things that we can think of and incorporate their existence, or the possibility of their existence, into our thinking. (1998: 85–6)

For instance, in a study of the forces that may make trade unions undemocratic, Lipset et al. (1962) deliberately chose to study a US printing union. Because this union had unusually strong democratic institutions, it constituted a vital deviant case compared with most American unions of the period. Lipset et al.'s union was also deviant in terms of a highly respected theory which postulated an irresistible tendency towards 'oligarchy' in all formal organizations.

So Lipset et al. chose a deviant case because it offered a crucial test of a theory. As our understanding of social processes improves, we are increasingly able to choose cases on such theoretical grounds.

9.7.3 Changing the size of your sample during the research

So far we have been discussing theoretical sampling as an issue at the *start* of a research study. However, we can also apply such sampling during the course of a piece of research. Indeed, one of the strengths of qualitative research design is that it often allows for far greater (theoretically informed) flexibility than in most quantitative research designs. As Mason puts it:

> Theoretical or purposive sampling is a set of procedures where the researcher manipulates their analysis, theory, and sampling activities *interactively* during the research process, to a much greater extent than in statistical sampling. (1996: 100)

Such flexibility may be appropriate in the following cases:

- As new factors emerge you may want to increase your sample in order to say more about them (for instance, a **gatekeeper** has given you an explanation that you doubt on principle).
- You may want to focus on a small part of your sample in the early stages, using the wider sample for later tests of emerging generalizations.
- Unexpected generalizations in the course of data analysis lead you to seek out new deviant cases.

Alasuutari has described this process using the analogy of an hourglass:

> a narrow case-analysis is broadened ... through the search for contrary and parallel cases, into an example of a broader entity. Thus the research process advances, in its final stages, towards a discussion of broader entities. We end up on the bottom of the hourglass. (1995: 156)

Alasuutari (1995: 155) illustrates this hourglass metaphor through his own study of the social consequences of Finnish urbanization in the 1970s. He chose local pubs as a site to observe these effects and eventually focused upon male 'regulars'. This led to a second study even more narrowly focused on a group where drinking was heavier and where many of the men were divorced. As he puts it: 'Ethnographic research of this kind is not so much generalization as extrapolation … the results are related to broader entities' (Alasuutari, 1995: 155).

9.8 GENERALIZABILITY IS PRESENT IN A SINGLE CASE

The fourth and final way of thinking about how we generalize in qualitative research is far more radical than our earlier alternatives. According to this approach, since the basic structures of social order are to be found anywhere, it does not matter where we begin our research. Look at *any* case and you will find the same order.

For this linguistically inspired approach, the possibility that something exists is enough. As Peräkylä suggests:

> Social practices that are possible, i.e., *possibilities of language use*, are the central objects of all conversation analytical case studies on interaction in particular institutional settings. The possibility of various practices can be considered generalizable even if the practices are not actualized in similar ways across different settings. (2004: 297)

Peräkylä illustrates his argument by the example of his own study of AIDS counselling in a London teaching hospital (Peräkylä, 1995). This study focused on specific questioning practices used by counsellors and their clients. As he puts it:

> As possibilities, the practices that I analysed are very likely to be generalizable. There is no reason to think that they could not be made possible by any competent member of (at least any Western) society. In this sense, this study produced generalizable results. The results were not generalizable as descriptions of what other counsellors or other professionals do with their clients; but they were generalizable as descriptions of what any counsellor or other professional, with his or her clients, *can* do, given that he or she has the same array of interactional competencies as the participants of the AIDS counselling sessions have. (Peräkylä, 2004: 297)

As the most cogent proponent of this view once put it: 'tap into whomsoever, wheresoever and we get much the same things' (Sacks, 1984b: 22).

Sacks had a strategy of working with any data that crossed his path. This clearly conflicts both with the standard approach of quantitative social scientists, who usually work with random samples from particular populations, and with the common defensiveness of their qualitative brethren about the representativeness of the cases that they study.

Sacks's lack of defensiveness on this issue stems from his argument about the obvious pervasiveness of the social forms (or what he calls the 'machinery') with which he is concerned. For example, Sacks notes the ability of a child to learn a culture from very limited contacts and of the sociolinguist Whorf to build a Navajo grammar from talking to just one person (Sacks, 1992, Vol. 1: 485).

The pervasiveness of structures which these examples suggest imply to Sacks that it does not matter what data you select. As he argues:

> Now if one figures that that's the way things are … then it really wouldn't matter very much what it is you look at – if you look at it carefully enough. And you may well find that you [have] got an enormous generalizability because things are so arranged that you *could* get them; given that for a **member** encountering a very limited environment, he has to be able to do that, and things are so arranged as to permit him to. (Sacks, 1992, Vol. 1: 485, bold added)

However, apprentice researchers have to be very cautious about simply parroting Sacks's 'solution' to the problem of the generalizability of research findings. This solution is really only appropriate to the most basic research on social order guided by theoretically sophisticated positions like Sacks's own **conversation analytic** (CA) approach (or, perhaps, French **structuralism**). If you are interested in this sort of research, you should now attempt Exercise 9.2.

Within CA, following Sacks:

> the baseline assumption is that the results are or should be generalizable to the whole domain of ordinary conversations, and to a certain extent even across linguistic and cultural boundaries. (Peräkylä, 1995: 214)

However, even Peräkylä notes that this depends on the type of CA research:

> Even though the most primordial conversational practices and structures – such as **turn-taking** or **adjacency pairs** – are almost universal, there are others, such as openings of telephone calls (see Schegloff, 1986; Houtkoop-Steenstra, 1991; Lindström, 1994), which show considerable variation in different cultures. This variation can only be tackled through gradual accumulation of studies on ordinary conversation in different cultures and social milieux. (1995: 156–7, bold added)

Peräkylä's observation about the need for comparative work shows that even the most potentially radical approach, like CA, has to take seriously the issue of the empirical generalizability of its findings. Sometimes, an appeal to 'possibilities' will be sufficient. Often, however, other examples will be required.

9.9 CONCLUDING REMARKS

In this chapter, I have set out various strategies which you can use to defend your research against the charge that it 'merely' depends upon a single case. My overall message is that there is usually no need to be defensive about the claims of qualitative research. As Becker argues:

> Sampling is a major problem for any kind of research. We can't study every case of whatever we're interested in, nor should we want to. Every scientific enterprise tries to find out something that will apply to *everything* of a certain kind by studying a *few examples*, the results of the study being, as we say "generalizable" to all members of that class of stuff. We need the sample to persuade people that we know something about the whole class. (1998: 67)

Following Becker, **sampling** is not a simple matter even for quantitative researchers. Indeed, as we have seen, the relative flexibility of qualitative research can improve the generalizability of our findings by allowing us to include new cases after initial findings are established.

The crucial issue here seems to be thinking through one's theoretical priorities. Providing that you have done that and can demonstrate a research design driven by those priorities, nobody should have cause for complaint.

So the secret seems to be to substitute theoretical cogency for the statistical language of quantitative research. In this sense, as Alasuutari has suggested, perhaps 'generalizability' is the wrong word to describe what we attempt to achieve in qualitative research. As he puts it:

> Generalization is ... (a) word ... that should be reserved for surveys only. What can be analyzed instead is how the researcher demonstrates that the analysis relates to things beyond the material at hand ... *extrapolation* better captures the typical procedure in qualitative research. (Alasuutari, 1995: 156–7)

KEY POINTS

There are four positive answers to the question of how we can generalize from qualitative data:

- combining qualitative research with quantitative measures of populations
- purposive sampling guided by time and resources
- theoretical sampling
- using an analytic model which assumes that generalizability is present in the existence of *any* case.

NOTE

1   As Clive Seale (personal correspondence) has pointed out, theoretical sampling may have more to do with generating theories than with empirical generalization. I take up Seale's point at the end of this chapter in relation to Alasuutari's argument that the idea of empirical generalization 'should be reserved for surveys only' (Alasuutari, 1995: 156).

Further reading

Clive Seale et al.'s edited book *Qualitative Research Practice* (Sage, 2004: 420–72) contains three very useful chapters on case studies by Flyvberg, Gobo and Emerson. The most thorough book on this topic is Clive Seale's *The Quality of Qualitative Research* (Sage, 1999). Other useful discussions are: Jennifer Mason's *Qualitative Researching* (2nd edn, Sage, 2002); Pertti Alasuutari's *Researching Culture* (Sage, 1995), Chapter 12 ('Generalization') and Howard Becker's *Tricks of the Trade* (1998), Chapter 3 ('Sampling'). Robert Stake's chapter 'Case studies' is a good account of the conventional qualitative methods position on generalizability (in N. Denzin and Y. Lincoln's edited *Handbook of Qualitative Research*, 2nd edn, Sage, 2000) and Anssi Peräkylä's chapter 'Reliability and validity in research based upon transcripts' is an excellent, more specialist treatment (in David Silverman's (ed.) *Qualitative Research*, 2nd edn, Sage, 2004).

Exercise 9.1

Assume that you are studying a single case. On what basis do you think you might generalize from your findings? Distinguish your possible empirical contribution from any potential development of concepts.

Exercise 9.2

Imagine that you have the resources to study *four* cases of the phenomenon in which you are interested. Following my discussion of Stake (Table 9.2), draw up a typology to indicate the universe of cases potentially available. This typology should include between six and twelve possible cases.

Now explain why you propose to select your four cases in terms of the logic of purposive sampling.

Exercise 9.3

Using conversation analysis, Harvey Sacks has argued: 'tap into whomsoever, wheresoever and we get much the same things' (Sacks, 1984b: 22).

Consider how far your own theoretical model might allow you to use Sacks's argument to justify working with a very small data set.

Writing a Research Proposal

CHAPTER OBJECTIVES

By the end of this chapter, you will be able to:

- Understand the key components of a qualitative research proposal.
- Recognize the importance of clarity, planning and persuasiveness in writing a proposal.
- Understand that writing of any kind must be **recipient designed** for a particular audience.

10.1 INTRODUCTION

Before you can set out on your research, you will usually need to submit a research proposal for approval. Although this is, in one sense, a bureaucratic hurdle, it is also an opportunity for you to make sure that you are perfectly clear about the direction which you want your research to take.

Writing a research proposal allows you to clarify in your own mind that you have fully grasped the issues we have been discussing in Part Two of this book. Moreover, it adds a useful discipline. Now it is not just a matter of convincing yourself but of convincing a potentially sceptical audience who will expect you to answer briefly and clearly a set of difficult questions. These questions are set out in Table 10.1.

The best way to answer these questions with brevity and clarity is to follow a standard format. Table 10.2 indicates a basic structure for a qualitative research proposal.

In preparing your proposal, it is worth bearing in mind the special difficulties qualitative researchers can face in achieving credibility. Particularly if you are within a university department where quantitative research is the mainstream, bear in mind that your proposal is likely to receive highly sceptical reviews.

TABLE 10.1 QUESTIONS ANSWERED BY A RESEARCH PROPOSAL

1 *What*? What is the purpose of my research? What am I trying to find out?
2 *How*? How will the proposed research answer these questions?
3 *Why*? Why is the research worth doing (and/or funding)? What will we learn and why is it worth knowing?

Source: adapted from Punch (1998: 268)

TABLE 10.2 A STRUCTURE FOR A QUALITATIVE RESEARCH PROPOSAL

1 Title
2 Abstract (further advice on titles and abstracts is found in Chapter 20)
3 Background or introduction, e.g. contemporary debates in social policy/social science
4 Statement of purpose or aims: the research question ('The intellectual problem(s) I may help solve through this research is (are)...')
5 Review of the relevant literature (showing the importance of the project in the context of the classic or definitive pieces of research in this area)
6 Methods (description of cases(s) chosen, procedures for data collection and data analysis in terms of (a) their appropriateness to your theoretical orientation and (b) how they satisfy criteria of **validity** and **reliability** (see Chapters 8 and 14)
7 Ethical issues (see Chapter 17)
8 Dissemination and policy relevance: explain how you will communicate your findings (see Chapters 17, 27 and 28)
9 A timetable indicating the length of time to be devoted to each stage of the research
10 References – use a standard system like Harvard[1]

Source: adapted from Morse (1994: 228), Kelly (1998: 115–21) and Rudestam and Newton (1992: 18)

Such sceptics may make the following assumptions:

● qualitative research is unstructured
● the results of qualitative research are unpredictable
● the outcome is uncertain (Morse, 1994: 227).

Moreover, most experienced qualitative researchers will expect their potential students to be aware of such concerns and to have thought about how to respond to them. How, then, can one convince a potential university supervisor to support your research proposal?

Of course, following the format set out in Table 10.2 should help. But how should you frame your proposal in a way likely to maximize acceptance?

The following suggestions form the rest of this chapter:

● Aim for crystal clarity.
● Plan before you write.
● Be persuasive.

- Be practical.
- Make broader links.

10.2   AIM FOR CRYSTAL CLARITY

> The proposal should use language and terminology that is understandable to an
> intelligent lay person as well as to a subject expert. (Cryer, 1996: 15)

Although it is tempting to seek to display your newly acquired technical jargon,
bear in mind that your proposal is likely to be read, in the first instance, by a
faculty member who is unlikely to be a specialist in your area of the discipline. So
never be content by a proposal which can look like a stream of (perhaps undi-
gested) theories or concepts. Always aim for clear language that describes your
research in a way that non-specialists can comprehend.

As Morse suggests, this means that you should resist the temptation to lapse
into pure jargon: 'because some of the reviewers will be from other disciplines, the
proposal writer should assume nothing and explain everything' (Morse, 1994: 227).

By explaining everything, you will have demonstrated the ability to think (and
write) clearly. Not only is this the way to write a research proposal, but also it is the
best indicator that your research itself will be organized in a clear and logical way:

> A sloppily prepared proposal will, at best, send a message to the agency that if it funds
> the proposal, the research may also be sloppy. (Morse, 1994: 226–7)

For instance, your objectives: 'should be clear and it should be easy to decide
whether they have been achieved or not' (Kelly, 1998: 117). The ways to achieve
this are:

- be concise (there is no reason why a proposal for a piece of student research
  should be more than 500 words)
- use short, simple sentences
- use headings as in Table 10.2.

10.3   PLAN BEFORE YOU WRITE

> The writer must show that the design is the result of a series of decisions that
> she made because of knowledge gained from the … literature. (Marshall and
> Rossman, 1989: 13)

Not only must the proposal demonstrate that it is based on an intelligent understanding of the existing literature, but also it must show that you have thought
about the time you will need to conduct each stage of the research from obtaining

access to writing up your data analysis. So, as Arber notes, your research proposal will partly be judged by how you state you are going to use your time:

> You need to adopt a systematic and logical approach to research, the key to which is the planning and management of your time. (1993: 33)

Kelly (1998: 120-1, adapted here) offers an example from an interview study planned to last thirty-two weeks:

Week 2   Submit proposal to University Ethical Committee
Week 6   Draw up sample
Week 8   Begin interviews
Week 15   End interviews
Week 23   Complete data analysis
Week 26   First draft sent out for comments
Week 32   Submission of final report

We are not born with a natural ability to prepare research timetables! To help you plan such a timetable, seek the assistance of a trusted teacher in your department. Failing that, seek out an existing research student. With their help, make a list of all the options available in relation to your research problem, method and case(s) to be studied. Now you are in a better position to write a reasoned research proposal that explains the actual choices you have made.

10.4   BE PERSUASIVE

> It is easy to get very wrapped up in the subject and think that, because we are convinced of the particular value of our research, others will be too. The way in which the proposal is presented can enable the reader to appreciate what you are planning to do. (Kelly, 1998: 121)

Kelly is reminding us that, in framing a research proposal, one must think first of the audience who is going to read it (and judge it). This means that it should set out to convince such readers that this is something worth supporting:

> The first principle of grantsmanship is to recognize that a good proposal is an argument ... for the researcher's project. The proposal must make a case to the granting agency that the research question is interesting (and) that the study is important ... Thus the proposal must be written persuasively. (Morse, 1994: 226)

Morse is suggesting that you try to 'sell' your proposal. This means that you must recognize that the craft of selling (your proposal, yourself) is not incongruent with working in a university. 'Ivory towers' were never so isolated as the term suggests!

However, this persuasiveness must be balanced with a realistic understanding about what you can achieve within a few years as a single researcher. Like any good salesperson, do not oversell your goods!

10.5   BE PRACTICAL

One way to persuade non-specialists, Morse suggests, is to show the specific ways that your research can address a social problem or solve an organizational trouble (e.g. staff turnover).

Such a concern with practical problems cannot be shrugged off even if you are proposing to do a purely academic piece of research with no expectation that it will be read outside the university. Academic funding bodies are increasingly demanding practical payoffs as well as analytic insights. For instance, Kelly (1998: 112) quotes a policy statement by the body that funds social science PhDs in the UK:

> Any lingering public perception of social science as a source of irrelevant, introverted and incoherent output is set for radical alteration …. In future, research which makes a difference to the health and wealth of the population, rather than merely supports 'ivory tower' academic excellence will be the ESRC's priority. (Economic and Social Research Council, 1996)

The issue of *audiences* for your research is discussed further in Chapter 28. However, if what you are proposing is 'basic research', i.e. a study deriving from debates and concepts internal to social science, then all is not lost. You can strengthen the persuasiveness of your case by showing non-specialists why they ought to take your ideas seriously. One way to do this is to try to make broader links between your (very narrow) research proposal and wider issues.

10.6   MAKE BROADER LINKS

Realism need not mean that you must present your research as a narrow, anaemic exercise. Even if you cannot cover every aspect of the field yourself, you should demonstrate your understanding of the broader implications of your proposed research.

One way to do that is to hint at a wider context:

> place the problem in context to show, for instance, that "when we understand this, we will be able to work on that". (Morse, 1994: 227)

Of course, you will be studying very few cases or maybe only a single case. Be positive about the gains as well as the losses of this! Show how a relatively small database will enable you to conduct an in-depth analysis (see Chapters 8 and 13). And argue that your case can indicate far larger phenomena:

> The writer must show how, in examining a specific setting or group of individuals, she is studying a case of a larger phenomenon. (Marshall and Rossman, 1989: 12)

10.7 CONCLUDING REMARKS

If you eventually submit a research proposal with the kind of logical structure I have been suggesting, you may be plagued by a horrible thought. Will you actually have to follow, word for word, every idea you have suggested? If things turn out differently to the way you now expect, will your supervisor insist that you follow your self-prescribed route?

Fortunately, the answer to these kinds of questions is 'generally no'. Your research proposal should not be regarded as some kind of contract which, if approved, is legally enforceable. Every practitioner recognizes that all researchers may, at some stage, find it worthwhile to divert from an initial path. This is particularly true of qualitative research where analysis of **field** data often leads in unexpected but fruitful directions (see Chapter 12).

Of course, this does not mean that you may not be asked to justify any diversion. But any research proposal should not be set in stone for all time.

What, then, is the point of having to write an initial proposal? Let me suggest two answers to this reasonable question.

First, having had to work out a clear, persuasive research proposal is a wonderful discipline which will help you work out exactly what it is you want to do. As such, it can guide you in the initial stages of your research. Second, such a proposal helps others. In particular, it allows your potential supervisors to see if you are the kind of student who is able to think critically and, just as important, to move outside your own inner world in order to work out what others may be looking for.

This means that ultimately a research proposal should not be regarded as a legal contract but as a way of responding to the potential questions experienced researchers may ask about your plans. These questions are summarized in Table 10.3.

TABLE 10.3 QUESTIONS A RESEARCH PROPOSAL MUST ANSWER

1   Why should anyone be interested in the research?
2   Is the research design credible, achievable and carefully explained?
3   Is the researcher capable of doing the research?

Source: adapted from Marshall and Rossman (1989: 2)

KEY POINTS

When preparing a research proposal, try to find answers to *three* questions suggested by Punch (1998: 268):

1 *What?* What is the purpose of my research? What am I trying to find out?
2 *How?* How will the proposed research answer these questions?
3 *Why?* Why is the research worth doing (and/or funding)? What will we learn and why is it worth knowing?

You can answer these questions better by following *five* principles:

- Aim for crystal clarity.
- Plan before you write.
- Be persuasive.
- Be practical.
- Aim for broader links.

NOTE

1 The Harvard system presents references in this order:

In the main body of your text (not in footnotes): surname of author, followed by date and page reference. In your references: author (with initials), date, title, place of publication, publisher and page references (for articles or chapters).

Further reading

A research proposal is crafted according to the level of your research. Beginning researchers should turn to: Moira Kelly's 'Writing a research proposal' (in C. Seale (ed.), *Researching Society and Culture,* Sage, 1998: 111–22). At PhD level, useful references are: Pat Cryer's *The Research Student's Guide to Success* (Open University Press, 1996), Chapter 2, and Keith Punch's *Developing Effective Research Proposals.* (Sage, 2000) (a much shorter version is contained in Punch's book *Introduction to Social Research,* Sage, 1998: 268–79). Beyond the PhD, you should consult Janice Morse's 'Designing funded qualitative research' (in N. Denzin and Y. Lincoln (eds), *Handbook of Qualitative Research,* Sage, 1994: 220–35).

Exercise 10.1

Prepare a draft proposal about your research (no more than 1500 words) covering the following elements:

1 Title

2 Abstract

3 Background or introduction

4 Statement of purpose or aims

5 Review of the relevant literature

6 Methods (description of case(s) chosen, procedures for data collection and data analysis)

7 Ethical issues

8 Practical relevance

9 A timetable

10 A set of preliminary references.

Analysing your data

Part Three moves you on to issues in data analysis. In Chapter 11, I outline what is to be gained by working early with data sets. Chapter 12 discusses how to develop your early analysis. The next two chapters in this part of the book consider the use of computer-aided qualitative data analysis and validity and reliability. Chapter 15 shows you how to apply what you have learned in Part Three to evaluate qualitative research.

Beginning Data Analysis

11.1 INTRODUCTION

After their first year of research, people have varying degrees of certainty about the future. As Coffey and Atkinson (1996) put it, the end of year 1 sees two kinds of researcher. The uncertain one feels she is drowning in data and asks: 'I've collected all this data, now what should I do?' The other, more confident, researcher states: 'I've collected all my data, now I'm going to analyse it and write it up'.

The temptation might be to find merit in both positions. After all, self-questioning and self-confidence both seem to be worthy qualities in a researcher. In fact, *neither* position is satisfactory and both reflect a more or less wasted first year of research:

> Both positions imply a woeful lack of appreciation of what is and can be meant by analysis … . [Such analysis] is a *pervasive* activity throughout the life of a research project. Analysis is not simply one of the later stages of research, to be followed by an equally separate phase of 'writing up results'. (Coffey and Atkinson, 1996: 10–11, my emphasis)

Research designs which devote the first year solely to a literature review and/or data gathering may look excellent on paper. Indeed, they may be just the thing in quantitative studies more concerned with implementing pre-designed 'measures' rather than employing a theoretical imagination. But in most qualitative research, unless you are *analysing* data more or less from day 1 you will always have to play 'catch up'.

All very well, you might respond, but where on earth am I going to get my data from on day 1? Surely, most of my first year is going to be spent on getting access to some research site or set of respondents and then, if successful, gathering my data. How is it going to be possible to start data analysis so quickly?

In the rest of this chapter, I show you how to kick-start your data analysis very early on. I then discuss ways to begin data analysis on many different kinds of qualitative data: interviews, field notes, texts, visual data and transcripts of conversation.

11.2   KICK-STARTING DATA ANALYSIS

As already noted, you might well ask: where am I going to get my data on day 1? There are five very practical, complementary solutions to this puzzle:

● analyse data already in the public sphere
● beg or borrow other people's data
● seek advice from your supervisor
● analyse your own data as you gather it
● ask key questions about your data.

I briefly discuss each strategy below.

11.2.1   *Analyse data already in the public sphere*

Some types of naturally occurring materials are already waiting for you. For instance, when undergraduate students doing a dissertation at my London college used to approach me with their concerns about gathering and analysing data in, say, a three-month time-slot, I usually gave the following advice. Hop on a train to Colindale in North London. Turn right out of the station and you will come to a big building marked British Museum Newspaper Library. Now select a few newspapers which covered a particular story (e.g. Princess Diana's death, the O.J. Simpson trial or the trial of the British nanny, Louise Woodward). Of course, you still lack a research problem and a method of analysis and you will need to think long and hard about both. But you have your data, so go to it!

Needless to say, the public sphere contains much more than newspapers. There are all the other kinds of written texts from novels to the contents of different web sites on the Internet. There are the products of the broadcast media, radio and TV programmes, from phone-ins to soap operas and news broadcasts. Then there are those rare qualitative studies which reproduce large portions of data, making them available for your own reanalysis perhaps following up different questions from those originally asked.

Even if you intend, in due course, to gather your own data, these materials are immediately available. As such, they provide a marvellous opportunity to refine your methods and to get a feel of the joys (and torments) of 'hands-on' data analysis.

11.2.2 Beg or borrow other people's data

Perhaps your research interests cannot be accommodated by data in the public sphere. If so, it is always worth making enquiries in your department about relevant data that other people may be willing to share with you.

Your supervisor is an obvious person to turn to. Having agreed to supervise you and thereby acknowledged a common research interest, it is probable that your supervisor will have already gathered data that may be relevant to your project. Don't be shy to ask if you might have access to it. This was exactly the strategy that my student Vicki Taylor followed. I was delighted to pass on my data to her so she could explore a research problem which was different to mine.

Of course, there may be ethical or other reasons why such access is not always possible. But most supervisors will be delighted, perhaps even flattered, if you are interested in their own data. After all, your research may lead to new ideas which will help them in their own work.

If your supervisor cannot deliver the goods, explore your various peer groups. Fellow research students in your department, perhaps two or three years into their research, may, like your supervisor, welcome passing on some of their own data. Or perhaps you can turn to members of study groups in your area or even to visiting speakers talking on a relevant topic.

Above all, you must remember that, in most disciplines, no 'brownie points' are usually given for having your own data. It is the quality of your data *analysis* that will matter, not whether you can show how clever you were to access your data. Perhaps only in anthropology may the display of how, in pursuit of your 'tribe', you have travelled thousands of miles, learnt a foreign language and endured endless hardships count for something – but not much I suspect.

Even if you feel happier to have your own data, remember that this does not exclude the first two strategies. In the early stages, analysis of other people's data or public data may still give you the impetus you need for research 'lift-off' when you are ready to analyse your own materials.

You should now attempt Exercise 11.1.

11.2.3 Seek advice from your supervisor

As an undergraduate, your main face-to-face contact with a faculty member may have been when you submitted a term-paper or, occasionally, when you got some feedback after such a submission. However, this model of a student-staff relationship is totally inappropriate when you are doing your own research.

Supervisors are there to offer support when you most need it (see Chapter 18). If you feel that you are 'drowning in data', that is a prime time to ask for help.

One way they can help you gain focus is to suggest a small and hence achievable task. Two examples of such tasks from Becker and Wolcott are given below:

● Offering a snap characterization of what seems to be happening in your data and asking you to respond to it. It really doesn't matter how wide of the mark this idea is if it can get you to start working with your data (Becker, 1998).
● Asking you to take 'some manageable *unit of one* as a focus' (Wolcott, 1990: 69, discussed at greater length in Chapter 5). In this way, instead of confronting your data as one large, threatening mass, you can narrow down and achieve a focus on one topic, one activity or one day (or one minute).

These kinds of tasks should help you overcome the kind of mental blocks we all too readily erect for ourselves when first confronting data. If we are set a small task, we are more likely to succeed and to gain confidence. Moreover, through such small tasks, we can start to see subtleties in our data which may be hidden if we ask big questions at the outset. As Becker (1998) reminds us, don't over-theorize early on in data analysis. Instead, begin from a situation or a piece of data and then build theories out of this limited material.

11.2.4   *Analyse your own data as you gather it*

Data analysis should not only happen after all your data has been safely gathered. If you only have one interview or recording or set of field notes, go to it! Where appropriate, start transcribing. In all cases, start reviewing your data in the light of your research questions.

Now is the time to test out methods, findings and concepts. Here are some good questions to ask yourself:

● Do I feel comfortable with my preferred method of data analysis (e.g. **grounded theory, narrative, conversation** or **discourse analysis**)?
● Is my data-analysis method suggesting interesting questions?
● Is it giving me a strong grip on my data that looks like it might generate interesting generalizations?
● Do previous research findings seem to apply to my data? If not, why not? If so, how can I use my data to develop these findings?
● How do particular concepts from my preferred model of social research apply to my data? Which concepts work best and hence look likely to be most productive?

None of these questions can be properly answered from the armchair or drawing board. No matter how elegant your original research proposal, its application to your first batch of data is always salutary. In most qualitative research, sticking with your original research design can be a sign of inadequate data analysis rather than demonstrating a welcome consistency.

None of this will you know until you begin analysing your data. Of course, this will mean committing yourself to writing up your analysis at a very early stage. As Wolcott (1990: 20) argues: 'You cannot begin writing early enough.' Even a 200-word shot at data analysis will give your supervisor something to go on. And even if your understandable initial hesitancy means that you are not 'off and running', at least you will have started.

You should now attempt Exercise 11.2.

11.2.5   Ask key questions about your data

Of course, what is a 'key' question will depend upon your research topic and your preferred model of qualitative research. Although this means that there are few if any 'free-floating' key questions, the following list has worked with my own students and is worth posing about your own research:

- What are the main units in your data and how do they relate to one another? Remember, that no meaning resides in a single unit and so everything depends on how your units fit together. This is an issue of *articulation*.
- Which categories are actually used by the people you are studying? Remember that, unlike quantitative researchers, we do not want to begin with our own categories at the outset. This is an issue of *definition*.
- What are the contexts and consequences of your subjects' use of categories? Remember that it is rarely right to ask 'why?' questions before you have identified the local phenomena involved. This is an issue of *hows?* and *whats?*.
- How do your difficulties in the field over, say, access and how you are defined by your research subjects provide you with further research topics? Remember that the beauty of qualitative research is that it offers the potential for us to topicalize such difficulties rather than just treat them as methodological constraints. This is an issue of the creative use of *troubles*.

So far I have been discussing ways to 'kick-start' your data analysis. However, my attempt to offer useful tips for any kind of study has meant that I have had to talk about qualitative research in general. I now want to move to a lower level of generality and to examine how you may begin to analyse different kinds of qualitative data. I will consider five different kinds of data:

- interviews
- field notes

- texts
- visual data
- transcripts.

For each data source, I will offer an example of how, in a particular study, data analysis took off.

11.3   INTERVIEWS

In Chapter 4, I examined the various ways that researchers can read sense into answers that respondents give to open-ended interviews. The most popular approach is to treat respondents' answers as describing some external reality (e.g. facts, events) or internal experience (e.g. feelings, meanings). Following this approach, it is appropriate to build into the research design various devices to ensure the accuracy of your interpretation, so you can check the accuracy of what your respondents tell you by other observations (see Chapter 14 on the method of **triangulation**). And you can treat such measures as inter-coder agreement (see Chapter 14) and computer-assisted qualitative data programmes (see Chapter 13) as a means of securing a fit between your interpretations and some external reality. Let us call this a realist approach to interview data.

As Clive Seale has pointed out (personal correspondence), realism is here used in the sense of the literary genre whose aim is to describe the 'gritty' reality of people's lives. In this approach, typical of tabloid journalism, 'confessional' stories are gathered and presented to the reader as new 'facts' about personalities. This form of realism has had much influence on qualitative research (see Atkinson and Silverman, 1997).

An alternative approach treats interview data as accessing various stories or narratives through which people describe their world (see Holstein and Gubrium, 2004). This approach claims that, by abandoning the attempt to treat respondents' accounts as potentially 'true' pictures of 'reality', we open up for analysis the culturally rich methods through which interviewers and interviewees, in concert, generate plausible accounts of the world. Although this second approach may use similar measures to achieve 'quality control' (e.g. group data sessions to ensure agreement about the researchers' reading of a transcript), these measures are used in pursuit of a different, 'narrated' reality in which the 'situated', or locally produced, nature of accounts is to the fore.

I am aware that many readers of this volume will favour the former approach. At the same time, I do not want to neglect the latter, **narrative** approach – particularly as it is closer to my own theoretical orientation. Fortunately, there are examples available which show how you can kick-start a piece of interview research using both these approaches.

Miller and Glassner (2004) describe a study involving in-depth, open-ended interviews with young women (aged 13 to 18) who claim affiliation with youth gangs in their communities (Miller, 1996). These interviews follow the completion of a survey interview administered by the same researcher.

Here is how the authors describe the purposes of each form of data:

> While the survey interview gathers information about a wide range of topics, including the individual, her school, friends, family, neighborhood, delinquent involvement, arrest history, sexual history, and victimization, in addition to information about the gang, the in-depth interview is concerned exclusively with the roles and activities of young women in youth gangs, and the meanings they describe as emerging from their gang affiliation. (Miller and Glassner, 2004: 131)

Let us focus on the data that Miller obtained from her in-depth interviews. This is one example:

> Describing why she joined her gang, one young woman told Miller, "well, I didn't get any respect at home. I wanted to get some love and respect from somebody somewhere else". (Miller and Glassner, 1997: 107)

Here is another respondent's explanation of why she joined a gang: 'I didn't have no family ... I had nothin' else' (1997: 107).

Another young woman, when asked to speculate on why young people join gangs, suggested:

> Some of 'em are like me, don't have, don't really have a basic home or steady home to go to, you know, and they don't have as much love and respect in the home so they want to get it elsewhere. And, and, like we get, have family members in gangs or that were in gangs, stuff like that. (1997: 107)

Let us assume that you have gathered this data and now want to begin analysis. Put at its starkest, what are you to do with it?

In line with the realist approach, using software programs such as ETHNO-GRAPH or NUD•IST (see Chapter 13), you may start by coding respondents' answers into the different sets of reasons that they give for participation in gangs. From this data, two reasons seem to predominate: 'push' factors (unsupportive families) and 'pull' factors (supportive gangs).

Moreover, given the availability of survey data on the same respondents, you are now in a position to correlate each factor with various background characteristics that they have. This seems to set up your research in good shape. Not only can you search for the 'subjective' meanings of adolescent gangs, but also you can relate these meanings to 'objective' **social structures**.

The 'realist' approach thus has a high degree of plausibility to social scientists who theorize about the world in terms of the impact of (objective) social structures upon (subjective) dispositions. Moreover, the kind of research outputs that it seeks to deliver are precisely those demanded by 'users' in the community, seeking immediate practical payoffs from social science research.

However, say we are not entirely satisfied by the apparent plausibility of realism? How can the narrative approach kick-start data analysis?

Miller and Glassner (2004: 134–5) suggest that one way to begin is to think about how respondents are using culturally available resources in order to construct their stories. They refer to Richardson's suggestion that:

> Participation in a culture includes participation in the narratives of that culture, a general understanding of the stock of meanings and their relationships to each other. (Richardson, 1990: 24)

How, then, can the data above be read in these terms? The idea is to see respondents' answers as *cultural stories*. This means examining the rhetorical force of what interviewees say as:

> interviewees deploy these narratives to make their actions explainable and understandable to those who otherwise may not understand. (Miller and Glassner, 1997: 107)

In the data already presented, Miller and Glassner note that respondents make their actions understandable in two ways. First, they do not attempt to challenge public views of gangs as bad. But, second, they do challenge the notion that the interviewee herself is bad.

However, Miller and Glassner note that not all their respondents glibly recycle conventional cultural stories. As they put it:

> Some of the young women go farther and describe their gang involvement in ways that directly challenge prevailing stereotypes about gangs as groups that are inherently bad or antisocial and about females roles within gangs. (1997: 108)

This is some of the respondents' accounts that they have in mind:

> It was really, it was just normal life, the only difference was, is, that we had meetings.

> [We] play cards, smoke bud, play dominoes, play video games. That's basically all we do is play. You would be surprised. This is a bunch of big kids. It's a bunch of big old kids in my set. (1997: 109)

In accounts like these, Miller and Glassner argue that there is an explicit challenge to what the interviewees know to be popular beliefs about youth gangs. Instead of accepting the conventional definition of their behaviour as 'deviant', the girls attempt to convey the normalcy of their activities.

These narratives directly challenge stereotypical cultural stories of the gang. Following Richardson, Miller and Glassner refer to such accounts as 'collective stories' which: 'resist the cultural narratives about groups of people and tell alternative stories' (Richardson, 1990: 25).

Miller's research on adolescent gang culture follows an earlier study of American adolescents' perception and use of illegal drugs. In this study, Glassner and Loughlin (1987) treat interview responses as *both* culturally defined narratives and as possibly factually correct statements. So, for instance, when someone says she uses marijuana because her friends do, Glassner and Loughlin (1987: 35) take this to suggest *two* findings:

> She has made use of a culturally prevalent way of understanding and talking about these topics [identifying a narrative].

> We now have evidence that marijuana smoking is part of peer gatherings [the realist version].

Glassner and Loughlin argue that narrative analysis works through examining the nature and sources of the 'frame of explanation' used by the interviewee. However, the character of what the interviewee is saying can also be treated, through a realist approach, as a factual statement and validated by observation (e.g. of the series of interactions through which her friends' use comes to affect her own).

If we treat interviewees' responses as factual statements, then it becomes crucial to ask: 'Can we believe the kids?' Clearly, the authors take this to be a serious question, arguing that, indeed, we should trust (their report of) what the kids are saying. They base this assertion on a set of claims about how 'rapport' was established with subjects: interviewers were accepted as peer-group members, showed 'genuine interest' in understanding the interviewee's experiences and guaranteed confidentiality (1987: 35).

Calling their approach a 'methodology for listening', Glassner and Loughlin are thus centrally concerned with 'seeing the world from the perspective of our subjects' (1987: 37). In this respect, they share the same assumptions about the 'authenticity' of 'experience' as do other realists and **emotionalists**. However, their sensitive address of the narrative forms from which perspectives arise suggests an alternative path for interview analysis (for a more developed version of the narrative approach, see Gubrium and Holstein, 1997).

11.4 FIELD NOTES

Tape-recorded interviews, like texts and tapes of **naturally occurring** interaction, allow you to return to your data in its original form as often as you wish. The problem with field notes is that you are stuck with the form in which you made them at the time and that your readers will only have access to how you recorded events.

There are two partial solutions to this problem: following strict conventions in writing field notes and adhering to a consistent theoretical orientation. The issue of field note conventions will be discussed in Chapter 12. In this chapter, I discuss an observational research study which began from a well-defined theory.

In the early 1980s, I obtained access to a number of clinics treating cancer patients in a British National Health Service (NHS) hospital. Following Strong's (1979) account of the 'ceremonial order of the clinic', I was interested in how doctors and patients presented themselves to each other. For instance, Strong had noted that NHS doctors would adhere to the rule 'politeness is all' and rarely criticize patients to their faces.

While at the hospital, I noticed that one of the doctors regularly seem to 'go missing' after his morning clinics. My curiosity aroused, I made enquiries. I discovered that most afternoons he was conducting his 'private' practice at consulting rooms in a salubrious area of London's West End. Nothing ventured, nothing gained, so I tried asking this doctor if I could 'sit in' on his private practice. To my great surprise, he consented on condition that I did not tape record. I happily agreed, even though this meant that my data was reduced to (what I saw as) relatively unreliable field notes.

Obviously, in making field notes, one is not simply recording data but also analysing it. The categories you use will inevitably be theoretically saturated – whether or not you realize it! Given my interest in Strong's use of Goffman's (1974) concept of frames, I tried to note down the activities through which the participants managed their identities. For instance, I noted how long the doctor and patient spent on social 'small talk' and how subsequent appointments were arranged.

However, if the researcher is physically present, two different kinds of issues should never be neglected:

● what you can see (as well as hear)
● how you are behaving/being treated.

11.4.1 What you can see

Both NHS clinics were held in functional rooms, with unadorned white walls, no carpets, simple furniture (a small desk, one substantial chair for the doctor and a number of stacking chairs for patients, families and students). Like most NHS hospitals, heating pipes and radiators were very obtrusive.

To enter the consulting rooms of the private clinic is to enter a different world. The main room has the air of an elegant study, perhaps not unlike the kind of room in a private house where a wealthy patient might have been visited by an eighteenth-century doctor. The walls are tastefully painted and adorned with prints and paintings. The floor has a fine carpet. The furniture is reproduction antique and includes a large, leather-topped desk, several comfortable armchairs, a sofa, a low table covered with coffee table books and magazines, and a bookcase which holds ivory figures as well as medical texts. Plants are placed on several surfaces and the room is lit by an elegant central light and a table lamp. To add an executive touch, there are three phones on the desk, as well as a pen in a holder.

This room establishes an air of privacy as well as luxury. At the NHS clinics, patients are nearly always examined in curtained-off areas. Here, however, the examination couch is in a separate room which can only be entered through the consulting room. Although more functional than the latter, it is nonetheless carpeted and kept at a high temperature to keep patients warm. Even the doctor himself may knock before entering this examination room while the patient is dressing or undressing.

11.4.2 *How you are being treated*

The emphasis on privacy in British 'private' medicine creates a special problem for the researcher. While at the NHS clinics I sheltered happily behind a name-tag, at the private clinic my presence was always explained, if ambiguously ('Dr. Silverman is sitting in with me today if that's alright?'). Although identified and accepted by the patient, I remained uncomfortable in my role in this setting. Its air of quiet seclusion made me feel like an intruder.

Like the doctor, I found myself dressing formally and would always stand up and shake hands with the patient. I could no longer merge into the background as at the NHS clinics. I regularly experienced a sense of intruding on some private ceremony.

My impression was that the private clinic encouraged a more 'personalized' service and allowed patients to orchestrate their care, control the agenda, and obtain some 'territorial' control of the setting. In my discussion of the data, like Strong, I cite extracts from consultations to support these points, while referring to deviant cases and to the continuum of forms found in the NHS clinics.

My interest in how observers are treated in medical settings is nicely demonstrated in Peräkylä's (1989) study of a hospital ward for terminally ill people. Peräkylä shows how staff use a 'psychological' frame to define themselves as objective surveyors of the emotional reactions of such patients. The psychological frame is a powerful means of resolving the identity disturbances found in other frames – when a patient resists practical or medical framing, staff can explain this in terms of the patient's psychological state.

However, the psychological frame also turns out to be highly relevant to understand staff's response to Peräkylä himself. By seeing him as a researcher principally interested in patients' feelings, the staff had a ready-made explanation of his presence to give to patients and also were able to guess which of their own activities might need explaining to him.

Like Peräkylä, by examining my own involvement in the 'framing' of the interaction, and using my eyes as well as my ears, I had kick-started my analysis. However, were there other ways in which I could systematically compare the two NHS clinics with the private clinic? In Chapter 12, I discuss some simple quantitative measures I used in order to respond to this problem.

11.5 TEXTS

Quantitative researchers try to analyse written material in a way which will produce reliable evidence about a large sample. Their favoured method is content analysis in which the researchers establish a set of categories and then count the number of instances that fall into each category. The crucial requirement is that the categories are sufficiently precise to enable different coders to arrive at the same results when the same body of material (e.g. newspaper headlines) is examined (see Berelson, 1952).

In qualitative research, small numbers of texts and documents may be analysed for a very different purpose. The aim is to understand the participants' categories and to see how these are used in concrete activities like telling stories (Propp, 1968; Sacks, 1974), assembling files (Cicourel, 1968; Gubrium and Buckholdt, 1982) or describing 'family life' (Gubrium, 1992).

The constructionist orientation of many qualitative researchers thus means that they are more concerned with the processes through which texts depict 'reality' rather than with whether such texts contain true or false statements. As Atkinson and Coffey put it:

> In paying due attention to such materials, however, one must be quite clear about what they can and cannot be used for. They are 'social facts', in that they are produced, shared and used in socially organized ways. They are not, however, transparent representations of organizational routines, decision-making processes, or professional diagnoses. They construct particular kinds of representations with their own conventions. (2004: 58)

The implications of this are clear:

> Documentary sources are not surrogates for other kinds of data. We cannot, for instance, learn through written records how an organization actually operates day-by-day. Equally, we cannot treat records – however 'official' – as firm evidence of what they report … . This recognition on reservation does not mean that we should ignore or downgrade documentary data. On the contrary, our recognition of their existence as social facts (on constructions) alerts us to the necessity to treat them very seriously indeed. We have to approach documents for what they are and what they are used to accomplish. (2004: 58)

What does it mean to approach texts 'for what they are'? Let us take a concrete example. In two of Sacks's lectures, he refers to a *New York Times* story about an interview with a navy pilot about his missions in the Vietnam War (Sacks, 1992, Vol. 1: 205–22, 306–11). Sacks is specially interested in the story's report of the navy pilot's reported answer to a question in the extract below.

11.5.1   *The navy pilot story*

> How did he feel about knowing that even with all the care he took in aiming
> only at military targets someone was probably being killed by his bombs?
>
> 'I certainly don't like the idea that I might be killing anybody,' he replied. 'But
> I don't lose any sleep over it. You have to be impersonal in this business. Over
> North Vietnam I condition myself to think that I'm a military man being shot
> at by another military man like myself.' (Sacks, 1992, Vol. 1: 205)

Sacks invites us to see how the pilot's immediate reply ('I certainly don't like the
idea…') shows his commitment to the evaluational scheme offered by the journalist's question. For instance, if the pilot had instead said 'Why do you ask?', he
would have shown that he did not necessarily subscribe to the same moral universe
as the reporter (and, by implication, the readers of the article).

Having accepted this moral schema, Sacks shows how the pilot now builds an
answer which helps us to see him in a favourable light. The category 'military
man' works to defend his bombing as a category-bound activity which reminds
us that this is, after all, what military pilots do. The effect of this is magnified by
the pilot's identification of his co-participant as 'another military man like myself'.
In this way, the pilot creates a pair (military man/military man) with recognizable
mutual obligations (bombing/shooting at the other). In terms of this pair, the
other party cannot properly complain or, as Sacks puts it:

> there are no complaints to be offered on their part about the error of his ways, except
> if he happens to violate the norms that, given the device used, are operative. (1992,
> Vol. 1: 206)

Notice also that the pilot suggests 'you have to be impersonal in this business'.
Note how the category 'this business' sets up the terrain on which the specific pair
of military men will shortly be used. So this account could be offered by either
pair-part.

However, as Sacks argues, the implication is that 'this business' is one of many
where impersonality is required. For:

> if it were the case that, that you had to be impersonal in this business held only for
> this business, then it might be that doing this business would be wrong in the first
> instance. (1992, Vol. 1: 206)

Moreover, the impersonality involved is of a special sort. Sacks points out that we
hear the pilot as saying not that it is unfortunate that he cannot kill 'personally'
but rather that being involved in this 'business' means that one must not consider
that one is killing persons (1992, Vol. 1: 209).

However, the pilot is only *proposing* a pair of military man–military man. In that sense, he is inviting the North Vietnamese to 'play the game' in the same way as a child might say to another 'I'll be third base'. However, as Sacks notes, in children's baseball, such proposals can be rejected:

> if you say 'I'll be third base', unless someone else says 'and I'll be …' another position, and the others say they'll be the other positions, then you're not that thing. You can't play. (1992, Vol. 1: 307)

Of course, the North Vietnamese indeed did reject the pilot's proposal. Instead, they proposed the identification of the pilot as a 'criminal' and defined themselves as 'doing police action'.

As Sacks notes, these competing definitions had implications which went beyond mere propaganda. For instance, if the navy pilot were shot down then the Geneva Conventions about his subsequent treatment would only properly be applied if he indeed were a 'military man' rather than a 'criminal' (1992, Vol. 1: 307).

Sacks's analysis derives from his particular way of treating texts (like Atkinson and Coffey) as representations. Like Garfinkel (1967), Sacks wanted to avoid treating people as 'cultural dopes', representing the world in ways that some culture demanded. Instead, Sacks approached **culture** as an 'inference-making machine': a descriptive apparatus, administered and used in specific contexts. The issue for Sacks was not to second-guess societal members but to try to work out:

> how it is that people can produce sets of actions that provide that others can see such things … [as] persons doing intimacy … persons lying, etc. (1992, Vol. 1: 119)

Given that many categories can be used to describe the same person or act, Sacks's task was:

> to find out how they [members] go about choosing among the available sets of categories for grasping some event. (1992, Vol. 1: 41)

So Sacks does not mean to imply that 'society' determines which category one chooses. Instead, he wants to show the active interpretive work involved in rendering any description and the local implications of choosing any particular category. Whether or not we choose to use Sacks's precise method, he offers an inspiring way to begin to analyse the productivities of any text.

11.6 VISUAL DATA

Visual data is a very broad category which can encompass anything from videos to photographs to naturally occurring observational data like that discussed in

Section 11.4 above and to such aspects of our environment like street signs and advertisements (see Emmison and Smith, 2000).

The analysis of visual data can be very complicated and, in some hands, can be so over-theorized that one feels that the theoretical tail is wagging the empirical dog! To simplify matters for the beginning researcher, I will use as an example a relatively straightforward study and illustrate how data analysis took off.

Sharples et al. (2003) had the interesting idea of studying the kinds of photographs made by children. A total of 180 children of three different ages (7, 11 and 15) were given single-use cameras and asked to use them in any way they pleased over a weekend. Over 4300 photographs were generated by this means.

Data analysis took off through using a form of **content analysis** which produced a kind of 'radar screen ... a two-dimensional scatterplot showing the principal axes of variability' (Sharples et al.: 311). This data was set up in this way in order to answer some early, key research questions:

- What is the content of each photograph?
- Are the people or objects shown posed?
- Who are the people shown?
- How do each of these features vary by the age of the photographer?

The analysis showed significant variation by the age of the child. For instance 7-year-old children were more likely to take photographs of toys and other possessions. They also took more photographs of their home and family. By contrast, the 11-year-olds concentrated on outdoor and/or animal photographs (usually their pets), while the 15-year-olds mainly took photographs of their friends, usually of the same sex and often in 'informal and striking poses' (316–17).

This study shows that an apparently simple count of such apparently basic features can raise a number of interesting issues. In this case, the researchers sought to pursue these issues by qualitative interviews with their child photographers.

Following Section 11.2.5 above, this study took off by beginning with descriptive questions of 'what?' and 'how?'. This generated 'why?' questions which they later sought to answer through interviews with subjects. The interviews also allowed the comparison of the categories that the researchers used with those used by the children themselves.

11.7 TRANSCRIPTS

Like any kind of data, the analysis of tapes and transcripts depends upon the generation of some research problem out of a particular theoretical orientation. As with the writing of field notes, the preparation of a transcript from an audio- or videotape is a theoretically saturated activity. Where there is more than one researcher, debate about what you are seeing and hearing is never just about collating data – it is data *analysis*. But how do you push the analysis beyond an agreed transcript?

The temptation is to start at line 1 of your transcript and to work your way down the page making observations as you go. However, the danger of proceeding in this way is that your observations are likely to be *ad hoc* and commonsensical. Moreover, if you are committed to an approach (like CA or DA) which looks at how the participants co-produce some meaning, then beginning with a single utterance gets you off on the wrong foot. How else can you proceed?

In Chapter 6, we came across Mason's (1996) idea of formulating a research topic in terms of different kinds of puzzles. Identifying a puzzle can also be the way to kick-start the analysis of a transcript. Once you have found your puzzle, the best method is often to *work back and forth* through your transcript to see how the puzzle arises and is resolved.

As in the other sections, let me take a concrete example. I was working on some transcripts of parent–teacher interviews gathered in Australian schools by Carolyn Baker and Jayne Keogh. The following examples involve a student, Donna (S), her parents (F and M) and her teacher (T). In Extracts 11.1 and 11.2 there are no audible responses from Donna or Donna's parents to a piece of advice from the teacher (> indicates turn-slots where receipts are absent):

Extract 11.1

T: that's the only way I can really (1.0) really help at the moment and (.) for Donna herself to um do a little bit more in class and not chat so much down the back with Nicky and (.) Joanne?
> (1.0)
T: um(2.0)

Extract 11.2

T: Or we maybe, if- our next unit of work, Donna? if it's (.) another group do you think you- you'd perform better not working with the same girls?
> (1.0)
T: work with a different, with someone different in the class?
> (2.0)
T: you'd prefer to work with the same girls

In Extract 11.3 below, Donna's father eventually responds after a pause in a turn-slot in which Donna might have spoken:

Extract 11.3

T: I- don't- know it's really the <u>three</u> of you got to pull up your socks sort of thing or (.) or you sit somewhere <u>different</u> but
> (2.0)
T: [( )
F: [I think you should sit somewhere different

Finally, in Extract 11.4, Donna does not respond to her father's advice:

Extract 11.4

F: I think you should sit somewhere different
M: Mm?
F: well think of your marks it's just (4.0) it's pretty rubbishy

The absence of (spoken) responses by students to their teacher's or parents' advice in Extracts 11.1–11.4 gave us the puzzle which kick-started our analysis (Silverman et al., 1997). Such silence is a puzzle because it does not appear to fit with what we know about conversation where the absence of a response by someone selected for next turn is remarkable and accountable (Sacks et al., 1974).

To try to solve this puzzle, we searched other data for comparable findings. In over sixty advice sequences in pre-HIV-test counselling, I have only one example of such a silent response to advice (Silverman, 1997). This is shown below [C = counsellor, P = patient]:

Extract 11.5 [Silverman, 1997: 118]

```
 1   C:   this is why we say hh if you don't know the person that
 2        you're with (0.6) and you're going to have sex with them hh
 3        it's important that you tell them to (0.3) use a condom
 4   >    (0.8)
 5   C:   or to practice safe sex that's what using a condom means.
 6   >    (1.5)
 7   C:   okay?
 8        (0.3)
 9   P:   uhum
10        (0.4)
11   C:   has your partner ever used a condom with you?
```

Notice the 1.5 second pause at the second >. Since this follows a possible turn-completion point as C concludes her advice, the pause can be heard as P's pause. Moreover, C demonstrates that she monitors it this way by using 'okay' to go in pursuit of some utterance to indicate that at least P is listening. When, after a further pause, she obtains 'uhum', C can now continue.

However, it is also worth noting C's explanation (or gloss) which follows 'use a condom'. Since that phrase could also have been heard as terminating C's advice, she seems to have inspected the 0.8 second pause that follows as representing an absent **continuer** and, therefore, a possible lack of understanding. So she provides her gloss in order, unsuccessfully as it turns out, to create a stronger environment in which to get a continuer.

Extract 11.5 shares one further similarity with the teacher–pupil advice sequences. Here the patient is a 16-year-old person, by far the youngest of all the clients in our HIV counselling extracts.

On a non-analytic level, what we seem to be dealing with here is the social problem well known to both professionals and parents: that is, the common non-response of adolescents when told what to do by adults (or even when asked questions). This social problem is seen massively in hospital clinics run for adolescents and evokes continual, unsuccessful attempts to get the child to speak (see Silverman, 1987). In Extracts 11.6–11.8 below, taken from such clinics, we also find non-response to advice [D = doctor, P = patient and M = mother]:

Extract 11.6 [Diabetic clinic 1 (NH:17.7)]

D: What should we do about your diabetes? Because you've not
        been doing your testing (untimed pause)
D: I know at the moment your feeling sod all this altogether
P: Don't know
D: Would it help if we got off your back?
        (untimed pause)

Extract 11.7 [Diabetic clinic 2 (S:12.2)]

D: The blood sugar is really too high
        (untimed pause) [P is looking miserable]
M: We have to fight this all the way
D: One or two units, does this really upset you?
        (untimed pause) [P is looking down and fiddling with her coat]

Extract 11.8 [Cleft-palate clinic (14.32-3)]

D: Um (2.0) but you're satisfied with your lip, are you, we don't want
        anything done to that?
M: She doesn't (1.0) it doesn't seem to worry her
D: Heh heh don't want anything done about any[thing?
M: [heh heh
D: Not your nose?
        (3.0)

Throughout Extracts 11.5–11.8, adolescents fail to respond in the second-turn position to advice and questions. In Extracts 11.5 and 11.6, they eventually offer a minimal response after a second prompt. By contrast, in Extracts 11.7 and 11.8, when these young patients fail to take a turn when nominated as next speaker, their mothers speak for them, offering a commentary on their child's behaviour or feelings. Finally, in Extract 11.8, when D once more renominates the patient as next speaker, nothing is heard.

However, if we had stopped at the observation of a congruence between professional–client encounters involving young people in both medical and educational settings, we would only be restating a social problem well known to parents and professionals dealing with young people. I work on the assumption that the skills of social scientists arise precisely in their ability to look at the world afresh and hence hold out the possibility of offering insights to practitioners. The question is, then, how can we move from our commonplace observation to a social science analysis?

Earlier in this book I suggested that qualitative research is at its strongest in answering questions like 'how?' and 'what?' rather than 'why?'. So our initial response was to shift the focus away from *explaining* our observation towards locating its interactional *achievement*. Thus we asked: how is questioning and advice giving interactionally managed, turn by turn, where the ostensible answerer or advice recipient is apparently non-responsive?

In multi-party professional–client settings, the recipient of a particular turn is not given by some institutional rule but is actively 'worked at' by the participants. Extract 11.8 is a very nice example of this and is given here again:

Extract 11.8 [Cleft-palate clinic (14.32–3)]

D: Um (2.0) but you're satisfied with your lip, are you, we don't want anything
        done to that?
M: She doesn't (1.0) it doesn't seem to worry her
D: Heh heh don't want anything done about any[thing?
M: [heh heh
D: Not your nose?
        (3.0)

As I have already remarked, in line 1, D appears to nominate as next speaker someone who might appropriately make an assessment about their 'lip'. However, although next speaker orients to this nomination (talking about 'she' and 'her' rather than 'I' and 'me' in line 3), she is not the next speaker so nominated. Moreover, when D appears to renominate M's daughter as next speaker (lines 4 and 6), although she is silent, M claims recipiency via her laughter at line 5.

Extract 11.8 shows that recipiency is constructed on a turn-by-turn basis. Moreover, even within a single turn, the recipient may be redefined. Notice, for instance, how D switches from the voice of 'you' to 'we' within line 1.

Such a switch is interactionally ambiguous. First, 'we' may be heard as no more than the patronizing way of referring to organizational clients quite common in England (and, sometimes, the object of a sarcastic response, e.g. 'me and who else?'). Second, in this local context, it creates the possibility that D's question about 'lip-satisfaction' is addressed to both or either mother and daughter. Indeed, it may be this very possibility that allows a parent to respond without a pause (in line 3) in a slot in which the child might have been expected to answer a question.

Extract 11.8, from a cleft-palate clinic, shows how the parties play with the ambiguity about who is the recipient of a particular question. Rather than treating ambiguity as a communication *problem*, the analysis has begun to show how the interactants can use ambiguity as a *resource*.

The same interpretation may be attached to the child's silence. Instead of treating this silence as indicating some *deficiency* on the part of the child, we argue that, faced with the ambivalence built into such questions and comments by teachers (and parents), silence can be treated as a display of interactional *competence*. Finally moving on to the 'why?' question, we can speculate that this is because silence (or at least lack of verbal response) allows children to avoid implication in the collaboratively accomplished adult moral universe and, thus, enables them to resist the way in which an institutional discourse serves to frame and constrain their social competencies.

11.8   CONCLUDING REMARKS

In this chapter, I have shown how, using the four main kinds of qualitative data, you can begin data analysis. By generating a puzzle by early inspection of some data, whether your own or borrowed, you can kick-start any research project. In Chapter 12, we examine how data analysis can be developed after these first stages.

KEY POINTS

Avoid spending the first period of your research without analysing any data. There are several ways to kick-start data analysis:

- analyse data already in the public sphere
- beg or borrow other people's data
- seek advice from your supervisor
- analyse your own data as you gather it
- ask key questions about your data

When analysing different kinds of qualitative data, the following issues arise:

Interviews: is your aim to describe the 'gritty' reality of people's lives (realism) or to access the stories or narratives through which people describe their worlds (constructionism)?

Field notes: you need to note what you can see (as well as hear) as well as how you are behaving and being treated.

Texts and visual material: is your goal precise content analysis in which you establish a set of categories and then count the number of instances that fall into each category? Or is your aim to understand the participants'

---

categories and to see how these are used in concrete activities like telling stories, assembling files or taking photographs?

Transcripts: the preparation of a transcript from an audio- or videotape is a theoretically saturated activity. Where there is more than one researcher, sorting out what you are seeing and hearing is never just about collating data – it is data *analysis*.

Further reading

Harry Wolcott's little book, *Writing Up Qualitative Research* (Sage Qualitative Research Methods Series, Number 20,1990), especially Chapter 2, is a helpful, informal guide to beginning data analysis. Other relevant sources are: Amanda Coffey and Paul Atkinson's *Making Sense of Qualitative Data* (Sage, 1996), Chapter Two, and Jennifer Mason's *Qualitative Researching* (2nd edn, Sage, 2002). For further details of the case studies discussed in this chapter, see: Jody Miller and Barry Glassner's 'The inside and the outside: finding realities in interviews', in my edited collection *Qualitative Research* (2nd edn, Sage, 2004); my two monographs *Communication in the Clinic* (Sage, 1987); and *Discourses of Counselling* (Sage, 1997); and Harvey Sacks's *Lectures on Conversation* (Vol. 1, Blackwell, 1992), 205–22 and 306–11. If you are interested in using Internet data, consult Annette Markham's chapter 'Internet communication as a tool for qualitative research' in my book *Qualitative Research* (2004).

Exercise 11.1

This gives you the opportunity to think about relevant data sets to which you may have early access.

1 Review relevant data already in the public sphere, for instance on the media (from newspapers to television and radio to the Internet). Select a data set and begin to analyse it.

2 Ask your supervisor and/or fellow students about any relevant data that they might have which you could borrow either as a preliminary exercise or possibly to develop long-term collaboration. Do a brief analysis of some of it.

Exercise 11.2

This gives you an opportunity to analyse your own data as soon as you obtain it.

1 Which questions does your preferred method of data analysis suggest? What interesting generalizations can you start to pull out of your data?

2 Do previous research findings seem to apply to your data? If not, why not? If so, how can you use your data to develop these findings?

3 How do particular concepts from your preferred model of social research apply to your data? Which concepts work best and hence look likely to be most productive?

Developing Data Analysis

CHAPTER OBJECTIVES

By the end of this chapter, you will be able to:

- Systematize and analyse field notes.
- Know what to look for in audiotapes.
- Feel confident about developing good data analysis.

12.1 INTRODUCTION

Chapter 11 stressed the importance of early data analysis and showed how to kick-start such analysis. In this chapter, we will examine how you can develop your research after these beginnings. Although we will focus here just on observational and tape-recorded data, many of the suggestions equally apply to other kinds of qualitative data. For the analysis of interview data, see Moira Kelly's account of her research on pp. 19–25.

However, a checklist of 'suggestions' can appear somewhat anaemic and without substance. This chapter begins, therefore, with an account of how data analysis developed in one qualitative study. The beauty of qualitative research is that it gives you access to the nitty-gritty reality of everyday life viewed through a new analytic lens. Through the example that follows, you will learn how to take advantage of that access in order to focus and then refocus your data analysis.

12.2 A CASE STUDY

In the early 1980s (see Silverman, 1987: Chapters 1–6) I was directing a group of researchers studying a paediatric cardiology (child heart) unit. Much of our data derived from tape recordings of an outpatient clinic that was held every Wednesday.

It was not a coincidence that we decided to focus on this clinic rather than upon, say, interaction on the wards. Pragmatically, we knew that the clinic, as a scheduled and focused event lasting between two and four hours and tied to particular outcomes, would be likely to give us a body of good-quality data. By contrast, on the ward, tape recording would be much more intrusive and produce tapes of poorer quality because of multiple conversations and background noise. Even if these technical problems could be overcome, the (apparently) unfocused character of ward life meant that it would be far harder to see order than in the outpatient clinic. For instance, unlike the latter, there would be no obvious repetitive structures like scheduled meetings by appointment, physical examinations and announcements of diagnosis and prognosis.

Of course, this does not mean that a researcher should never study apparently unfocused encounters – from the hospital ward to the street corner. But it does mean that, if you do, you must be prepared for long vigils and apparently unpromising data before researchable ideas start to gel.

At our hospital clinic, we became interested in how decisions (or 'disposals') were organized and announced. It seemed likely that the doctor's way of announcing decisions was systematically related not only to clinical factors (like the child's heart condition) but to social factors (such as what parents would be told at various stages of treatment). For instance, at a first outpatients' consultation, doctors would not normally announce to parents the discovery of a major heart abnormality and the necessity for life-threatening surgery. Instead, they would suggest the need for more tests and only hint that major surgery might be needed. They would also collaborate with parents who produced examples of their child's apparent 'wellness'. This step-by-step method of information giving was avoided in only two cases. If a child was diagnosed as 'healthy' by the cardiologist, the doctor would give all the information in one go and would engage in what we called a 'search and destroy' operation, based on eliciting any remaining worries of the parent(s) and proving that they were mistaken.

In the case of a group of children with the additional handicap of Down's syndrome, as well as suspected cardiac disease, the doctor would present all the clinical information at one sitting, avoiding a step-by-step method. Moreover, atypically, the doctor would allow parents to make the choice about further treatment, while encouraging them to dwell on non-clinical matters like their child's 'enjoyment of life' or friendly personality.

We then narrowed our focus to examine how doctors talked to parents about the decision to have a small diagnostic test on their children. In most cases, the doctor would say something like:

What we propose to do, if you agree, is a small test.

No parent disagreed with an offer which appeared to be purely formal – like the formal right (never exercised) of the Queen not to sign legislation passed by the

TABLE 12.1 FOUR WAYS TO DEVELOP DATA ANALYSIS

- Focus on data which is of high quality and is easiest to collect (tape recordings of clinics)
- Look at one process within that data (how medical 'disposals' are organized)
- Narrow down to one part of that process (announcing a small diagnostic test)
- Compare different sub-samples of the population (Down's syndrome children and the rest)

British Parliament. For Down's syndrome children, however, the parents right to choose was far from formal. The doctor would say things to them like the following:

I think what we would do now depends a little bit on parents' feelings.

Now it depends a little bit of what you think.

It depends very much on your own personal views as to whether we should proceed.

Moreover, these consultations were longer and apparently more democratic than elsewhere. A view of the patient in a family context was encouraged and parents were given every opportunity to voice their concerns and to participate in decision making.

In this sub-sample, unlike the larger sample, when given a real choice, parents refused the test – with only one exception. Yet this served to reinforce rather than to challenge the medical policy in the unit concerned. This policy was to discourage surgery, all things being equal, on such children. So the democratic form co-existed with (and was indeed sustained by) the maintenance of an autocratic policy.

The research thus discovered the mechanics whereby a particular medical policy was enacted. The availability of tape-recordings of large numbers of consultations, together with a research method that sought to develop hypotheses inductively, meant that we were able to develop our data analysis by discovering a phenomenon for which we had not originally been looking.

The lessons to be drawn from this study are summarized in Table 12.1.

In the second half of this chapter, I discuss the more general research strategies available to you when your data, as here, is in the form of tape recordings of **naturally occurring data**. But perhaps you do not possess your data on tape. Does this mean that everything is lost?

In the next section, I attempt to show how you can shore up the quality of your field notes. Even if, in the final analysis, field notes can never rival the **reliability** of a good-quality tape and transcript, thoughtfully constructed field notes can provide the impetus for advanced data analysis.

TABLE 12.2 FUNCTIONS OF DETAILED FIELD NOTES

- To identify and follow *processes* in witnessed events
- To understand how members themselves *characterize* and *describe* particular activities, events and groups
- To convey members' *explanations* for when, why or how particular things happen and, thereby, to elicit members' theories of the *causes* of particular happenings
- To identify the *practical concerns*, *conditions* and constraints that people confront and deal with in their everyday lives and actions

Source: adapted from Emerson et al. (1995)

12.3 FIELD NOTES AND DATA ANALYSIS

12.3.1 *Why detail matters*

> Field researchers seek to get close to others in order to understand their way of life. To preserve and convey that closeness, they must describe situations and events of interest in detail. (Emerson, et al., 1995: 14)

By preserving the details of interaction, you are in a better position to analyse the issues set out in Table 12.2.

Like any set of animating questions, the kind of issues set out in Table 12.2 reflect a particular **model** of the social world. As in my study of heart clinics, Emerson et al. assume a **constructionist** or **ethnomethodological** model in which the meaning of events is not transparent but is actively constructed by the participants (**members**).

Two methodological imperatives flow from this model. First, a concern with what participants take to be *routine* or obvious. Second, a recognition that what is routine is best established through watching and listening to what people do rather than asking them directly. So, unlike much **ethnographic** fieldwork, the interview is not regarded as a major research tool. Instead:

> the distinctive procedure is to observe and record naturally occurring talk and inter-action ... [while] it may be useful or essential to interview members about the use and meaning of specific local terms and phrases ... the researcher's deeper concern lies in the actual, situated use of those terms in ordinary interaction. (Emerson et al., 1995: 140)

Such a concern with what participants take to be ordinary and unexceptional gives a clear focus to making and analysing field notes. Data analysis can then develop through asking the sort of questions set out in Table 12.3.

TABLE 12.3   SIX GROUPS OF QUESTIONS FOR FIELD NOTE ANALYSIS

1	What are people doing? What are they trying to accomplish?
2	How exactly do they do this? What specific means and/or strategies do they use?
3	How do members talk about, characterize and understand what is going on?
4	What assumptions are they making?
5	What do I see going on here? What did I learn from these notes?
6	Why did I include them?

Source: Emerson et al. (1995: 146)

12.3.2   Two ways of developing field note analysis

Two practical rules have been suggested for developing ethnographic work beyond the initial questions shown in Table 12.3:

- thinking about what we can see as well as what we hear
- expanding field notes beyond immediate observations.

Using your eyes

In a study of the social organization of a restaurant, Whyte (1949) reaped rich rewards by using his eyes to observe the spatial organization of activities. More recently, in a study of interaction in hospital wards, Anssi Peräkylä (personal correspondence) notes how spatial arrangements differentiate groups of people. There are the wards and patient rooms, which staff may enter anytime they need to. Then there are patient lounges and the like, which are a kind of public space. Both areas are quite different from areas like the nurses' room and doctors' offices where patients enter only by invitation. Finally, if there is a staff coffee room, you never see a patient there.

As Peräkylä points out, one way to produce different categories of human beings in a hospital is the allocation of space according to categories. At the same time, this allocation is reproduced in the activities of the participants. For instance, the perceptive observer might note the demeanour of patients as they approach the nurses' room. Even if the door is open, they may stand outside and just put their heads round the door. In doing so, they mark out that they are encroaching on foreign territory.

Unfortunately, we have all become a little reluctant to use our eyes as well as our ears when doing observational work. However, these are exceptions. Stimson (1986) has noted how 'photographs and diagrams are virtually absent from sociological journals, and rare in sociological books' (641). He then discusses a room set out for hearings of a disciplinary organization responsible for British doctors. The Professional Conduct Committee of the General Medical Council sits in a high-ceilinged, oak-panelled room reached by an imposing staircase. There are stained-glass windows, picturing sixteen crests and a woman in a classical Greek pose. As Stimson comments:

> This is a room in which serious matters are discussed: the room has a presence that is forced on our consciousness … speech is formal, carefully spoken and a matter for the public record. Visitors in the gallery speak only, if at all, in hushed whispers, for their speech is not part of the proceedings. (1986: 643–4)

In such a room, as Stimson suggests, even without anything needed to be said, we know that what goes on must be taken seriously. Stimson aptly contrasts this room with a McDonald's hamburger restaurant:

> Consider the decorations and materials – plastic, paper, vinyl and polystyrene, and the bright primary colours. [Everything] signifies transience. This temporary character is further articulated in the casual dress of customers, the institutionally casualized dress of staff and the seating that is constructed to make lengthy stays uncomfortable. (1986: 649–50)

Stimson and Peräkylä show that ethnographers who fail to use their eyes as well as their ears are neglecting a crucial source of data. This lesson is most readily learnt if you imagine a sighted person being forced to make sense of the world while blindfolded!

Expanded field notes

> Fieldwork is so fascinating and coding usually so energy-absorbing, that you can get preoccupied and overwhelmed with the flood of particulars – the poignant quote, the appealing personality of a key informant. You forget to *think*, to make deeper and more general sense of what is happening, to begin to explain it in a conceptually coherent way. (Miles and Huberman, 1984: 69)

In order to make 'deeper and more general sense of what is happening', Spradley (1979) suggests that observers keep four separate sets of notes:

1. Short notes made at the time.
2. Expanded notes made as soon as possible after each field session.
3. A field work journal to record problems and ideas that arise during each stage of field work.
4. A provisional running record of analysis and interpretation (discussed by Kirk and Miller, 1986: 53).

Spradley's suggestions help to systematize field notes and thus improve their reliability (see Chapter 14). Like Spradley, Miles and Huberman offer systematic ways

TABLE 12.4   QUESTIONS FOR CONTACT SUMMARY SHEETS

- What people, events or situations were involved?
- What were the main themes or issues in the contact?
- Which research questions did the contact bear most centrally on?
- What new hypotheses, speculations or guesses about the field situations were suggested by the contact?
- Where should the fieldworker place most energy during the next contact, and what sorts of information should be sought?

Source: Miles and Huberman (1984: 50)

of expanding what gets recorded in field notes. They suggest writing 'contact summary sheets' or extended memos after each observation (Miles and Huberman, 1984: 50–1, 69–71).

An example of how to use a contact summary sheet to encourage analytic thinking is set out in Table 12.4.

Miles and Huberman suggest five reasons why such contact sheets are valuable:

1   to guide planning for the next contact
2   to suggest new or revised codes
3   to co-ordinate several fieldworkers' work
4   to serve as a reminder of the contact at a later stage
5   to serve as the basis for data analysis (adapted from Miles and Huberman, 1984: 51).

How we record data is important because it is directly linked to the quality of data analysis. In this sense, field notes and contact sheets are, of course, only a means to an end – developing the analysis.

12.3.3   *Developing analysis of field data*

> The move from coding to interpretation is a crucial one … . Interpretation involves the transcendance of 'factual' data and cautious analysis of what is to be made of them. (Coffey and Atkinson, 1996: 46)

As Miles and Huberman (1984) point out, qualitative data comes in the form of words rather than in numbers. The issue, then, is how we move from these words to data analysis.

They suggest that data analysis consists of: three concurrent flows of activity: data reduction, data display and conclusion drawing/verification (Miles and Huberman, 1984: 21):

- *Data reduction* 'refers to the process of selecting, focusing, simplifying, abstracting, and transforming … "raw" data' (ibid.). Data reduction involves making decisions about which data chunks will provide your initial focus.
- *Data display* is 'an organized assembly of information that permits conclusion drawing and action taking' (ibid.). It involves assembling your data into displays such as matrices, graphs, networks and charts which clarify the main direction (and missing links) of your analysis.
- *Conclusion drawing* means 'beginning to decide what things mean, noting regularities, patterns, explanations, possible configurations, causal flows and propositions' (1984: 22).
- *Verification* means testing the provisional conclusions for 'their plausibility, their sturdiness, their "confirmability" – that is, their validity' (ibid.).

Miles and Huberman demonstrate that in **field** studies, unlike much quantitative research, we are not satisfied with a simple coding of data. As I argued in Chapter 4, this means that qualitative researchers have to show how the (theoretically defined) elements that they have identified are assembled or mutually laminated. The distinctive contribution qualitative research can make is by utilizing its theoretical resources in the deep analysis of usually small bodies of publicly shareable data.

This means that coding your data according to some theoretical scheme should only be the first stage of your data analysis. You will then need to go on to examine how these elements are linked together. At this second stage, lateral thinking can help. For instance, you can attempt to give your chosen concept or issue a new twist, perhaps by pursuing a counter-intuitive idea or by noting an additional feature little addressed in the literature. In any event, as I show below, one way of achieving better data analysis is by a steadily more narrow focus.

12.3.4   *Progressive focusing in fieldwork*

We only come to look at things in certain ways because we have adopted, either tacitly or explicitly, certain ways of seeing. This means that, in observational research, data collection, hypothesis construction and theory building are not three separate things but are interwoven with one another.

This process is well described by using an analogy with a funnel:

Ethnographic research has a characteristic 'funnel' structure, being progressively focused over its course. Progressive focusing has two analytically distinct components. First, over time the research problem is developed or transformed, and eventually its scope is clarified and delimited and its internal structure explored. In this sense, it is frequently only over the course of the research that one discovers what the research is really 'about', and it is not uncommon for it to turn out to be about something quite remote from the initially foreshadowed problems. (Hammersley and Atkinson, 1983: 175)

Atkinson (1992) gives an example of such a redefinition of a research problem. Many years after completing his PhD, Atkinson returned to his original field notes on medical education. He shows how the original data can be reread in a quite different way. Atkinson's earlier method had been to fragment his field notes into relatively small segments, each with its own category. For instance, a surgeon's description of post-operative complications to a surgical team was originally categorized under such headings as 'unpredictability', 'uncertainty', 'patient career' and 'trajectory'. When Atkinson returns to it, it becomes an overall narrative which sets up an enigma ('unexpected complications') which is resolved in the form of a 'moral tale' ('beware, unexpected things can always happen'). Viewed in this way, the surgeon's story becomes a text with many resemblances to a fairy tale!

Two studies of British medical clinics that I carried out in the 1980s also nicely illustrate Hammersley and Atkinson's funnel. As I showed above, my observation of a paediatric cardiology unit moved unpredictably in the direction of an analysis of disposal decisions with a small group of Down's syndrome children Similarly, my research on cancer clinics, discussed in Chapter 9, unexpectedly led into a comparison of fee-for-service and state-provided medicine (Silverman, 1981, 1987).

These two cases had three features in common:

1 The switch of focus – through the 'funnel' – as a more defined topic arose.
2 The use of the comparative method as an invaluable tool of theory building and testing.
3 The generation of topics with a scope outside the substantive area of the research. Thus, the 'ceremonial orders' found in the cancer clinics are not confined to medicine, while the 'democratic' decision making found with the Down's children had unexpected effects of power with a significance far beyond medical encounters.

As I have noted elsewhere (Silverman, 2001), working this way parallels Glaser and Strauss's (1967) famous account of **grounded theory**. A simplified model of this involves these stages:

● an initial attempt to develop categories which illuminate the data
● an attempt to 'saturate' these categories with many appropriate cases in order to demonstrate their relevance
● developing these categories into more general analytic frameworks with relevance outside the setting.

Glaser and Strauss use their research on death and dying as an example. They show how they developed the category of 'awareness contexts' to refer to the kinds of situations in which people were informed of their likely fate. The category was then saturated and finally related to non-medical settings where people learn about how others define them (e.g. schools).

'Grounded theory' has been criticized for its failure to acknowledge implicit theories which guide work at an early stage. It also is more clear about the generation of theories than about their test. Used unintelligently, it can also degenerate into a fairly empty building of categories or into a mere smokescreen used to legitimize purely empiricist research (see my critique of four qualitative studies in Chapter 15 and Bryman, 1988: 83–7). At best, 'grounded theory' offers an approximation of the creative activity of theory building found in good observational work, compared to the dire abstracted empiricism present in the most wooden statistical studies.

However, quantification should not be seen as the enemy of good field research. In the section below, I discuss one example of how simple tabulations were used to test an emergent hypothesis in the study of cancer clinics.

12.3.5 *Using tabulations in testing fieldwork hypotheses*

In the cancer study, I used a coding form which enabled me to collate a number of crude measures of doctor and patient interactions (Silverman, 1984). The aim was to demonstrate that the qualitative analysis was reasonably representative of the data as a whole. Occasionally, the figures revealed that the reality was not in line with my overall impressions. Consequently, the analysis was tightened and the characterizations of clinic behaviour were specified more carefully.

The crude quantitative data I had recorded did not allow any real test of the major thrust of this argument. Nonetheless, it did offer a summary measure of the characteristics of the total sample which allowed closer specification of features of private and NHS clinics. In order to illustrate this, let me briefly show you the kind of quantitative data I gathered on topics like consultation length, patient participation and the scope of the consultation.

My overall impression was that private consultations lasted considerably longer than those held in the NHS clinics. When examined, the data indeed did show that the former were almost twice as long as the latter (20 minutes as against 11 minutes) and that the difference was statistically highly significant. However, I recalled that for special reasons, one of the NHS clinics had abnormally short consultations. I felt a fairer comparison of consultations in the two sectors should exclude this clinic and should only compare consultations taken by a single doctor in both sectors. This sub-sample of cases revealed that the difference in length between NHS and private consultations was now reduced to an average of under 3 minutes. This was still statistically significant, although the significance was reduced. Finally, however, if I compared only *new* patients seen by the same doctor, NHS patients got 4 minutes more on average – 34 minutes as against 30 minutes in the private clinic. This last finding was not suspected and had interesting implications for the overall assessment of the individual's costs and benefits from 'going private'. It is possible, for instance, that the tighter scheduling of appointments at the private clinic may limit the amount of time that can be given to new patients.

TABLE 12.5 PRIVATE AND NHS CLINICS: CEREMONIAL ORDERS

	Private clinics ($n = 42$)	NHS clinics ($n = 104$)
	(% in all such clinics)	
Treatment or attendance fixed at patients' convenience	15 (36%)	10 (10%)
Social elicitation	25 (60%)	31 (30%)

Source: adapted from Silverman (2001: 243)

As a further aid to comparative analysis, I measured patient participation in the form of questions and unelicited statements. Once again, a highly significant difference was found: on this measure, private patients participated much more in the consultation. However, once more taking only patients seen by the same doctor, the difference between the clinics became very small and was *not* significant. Finally, no significant difference was found in the degree to which non-medical matters (e.g. patient's work or home circumstances) were discussed in the clinics.

This quantitative data was a useful check on over-enthusiastic claims about the degree of difference between the NHS and private clinics. However, as I argued in Chapter 10, my major concern was with the 'ceremonial order' of the three clinics. I had amassed a considerable number of exchanges in which doctors and patients appeared to behave in the private clinic in a manner deviant from what we know about NHS hospital consultations. The question was: would the quantitative data offer any support to my observations?

The answer was, to some extent, positive. Two quantitative measures were helpful in relation to the ceremonial order. One dealt with the extent to which the doctor fixed treatment or attendance at the patient's convenience. The second measured whether patients or doctor engaged in polite small talk with one another about their personal or professional lives. (I called this 'social elicitation'.) As Table 12.5 shows, both these measures revealed significant differences, in the expected direction, according to the mode of payment.

Now, of course, such data could not offer proof of my claims about the different interactional forms. However, coupled with the qualitative data, the data provided strong evidence of the direction of difference, as well as giving me a simple measure of the sample as a whole which contexted the few extracts of talk I was able to use. I do not deny that counting can be as arbitrary as qualitative interpretation of a few fragments of data. However, providing researchers resist the temptation to try to count everything, and base their analysis on a sound conceptual basis linked to actors' own methods of ordering the world, then both types of data can inform the analysis of the other.

In Chapter 14, I return to the role of counting as an aid to **validity** in qualitative research. In the case of observational studies, such counting will often be based on the prior coding of field notes. I now, therefore, turn to the issues that arise in such coding.

12.3.6   Limits in coding field notes

The tabulations used in the cancer study derived from:

> that well-established style of work whereby the data are inspected for categories and instances. It is an approach that disaggregates the text (notes or transcripts) into a series of fragments, which are then regrouped under a series of thematic headings. (Atkinson, 1992: 455)

Such coding by thematic headings has recently been aided by computer-aided qualitative data analysis systems as discussed in Chapter 13. In larger projects, the reliability of coding is also buttressed by training coders of data in procedures which aim to ensure a uniform approach.

However, there remain two problems with coding field notes. The first, and more obvious, problem is that every way of seeing is also a way of not seeing. As Atkinson points out, one of the disadvantages of coding schemes is that, because they are based upon a given set of categories, they furnish 'a powerful conceptual grid' (Atkinson, 1992: 459) from which it is difficult to escape. While this 'grid' is very helpful in organizing the data analysis, it also deflects attention away from uncategorized activities. Therefore, as Clive Seale (personal correspondence) has noted:

> a good coding scheme would reflect a search for 'un-categorized activities' so that they could be accounted for, in a manner similar to searching for deviant cases.

The second, less obvious problem is that, as I pointed out in Chapter 4, 'coding' is not the preserve of research scientists. All of us 'code' what we hear and see in the world around us. This is what Garfinkel (1967) and Sacks (1992) mean when they say that societal members, like social scientists, make the world observable and reportable.

Put at its simplest, this suggests that researchers must be very careful how they use categories. For instance, Sacks quotes from two linguists who appear to have no problem in characterizing particular (invented) utterances as 'simple', 'complex', 'casual' or 'ceremonial'. For Sacks, such rapid characterizations of data assume 'that we can know that [such categories are accurate] without an analysis of what it is [members] are doing' (1992, Vol. 1: 429).

How should we respond to Sacks's radical critique of ethnography? The first point is not to panic! Sacks offers a challenge to conventional observational work of which everybody should be aware. In particular, Sacks's lecture 'Doing "being ordinary"' (Sacks, 1992, Vol. 2: 215–21) is essential reading for every fieldworker.

However, awareness does not mean that everybody has to follow Sacks's radical path. So one response is to state something like 'thanks but no thanks'. For instance, grounded theory is an equally respectable (and much more popular) way of theorizing (about) fieldwork.

To this effective but essentially defensive manoeuvre, we can add two more ambitious responses. First, we can seek to integrate Sacks's questions about 'how' the social world is constituted with more conventional ethnographic questions about the 'whats' and 'whys' of social life (Gubrium and Holstein, 1997). Or, second, as I describe below, we can make this everyday 'coding' (or 'interpretive practice') the object of enquiry by asking 'how' questions about talk-in-interaction.

12.4 TRANSCRIPTS AND DATA ANALYSIS

The two main social science traditions which inform the analysis of transcripts of tapes are **conversation analysis** (CA) and **discourse analysis** (DA). For an introduction to CA, see ten Have (1998); for DA, see Potter and Wetherell (1987) and Potter (2004).

In this book, however, we are, of course, more concerned with the practicalities of doing qualitative research. In the rest of this chapter, I will, therefore, deal with two practical issues:

- the advantages of working with tapes and transcripts
- the elements of how to do analysis of such tapes.

12.4.1 Why work with tapes?

the kind of phenomena I deal with are always transcriptions of actual occurrences in their actual sequence. (Sacks, 1984b: 25)

The earlier ethnographers had generally relied on recording their observations through field notes. Why did Sacks prefer to use an audio recorder?

Sacks's answer is that we cannot rely on our recollections of conversations. Certainly, depending on our memory, we can usually summarize what different people said. But it is simply impossible to remember (or even to note at the time) such matters as pauses, overlaps, inbreaths and the like.

Now whether you think these kinds of things are important will depend upon what you can show with or without them. Indeed, you may not even be convinced that conversation itself is a particularly interesting topic. But, at least by studying tapes of conversations, you are able to focus on the 'actual details' of one aspect of social life. As Sacks put it:

> My research is about conversation only in this incidental way, that we can get the actual happenings of on tape and transcribe them more or less, and therefore have something to begin with. If you can't deal with the actual detail of actual events then you can't have a science of social life. (1992, Vol. 2: 26)

Tapes and transcripts also offer more than just 'something to begin with'. In the first place, they are a public record, available to the scientific community in a way that field notes are not. Second, they can be replayed and transcriptions can be improved and analyses take off on a different tack unlimited by the original transcript. As Sacks told his students:

> I started to play around with tape recorded conversations, for the single virtue that I could replay them; that I could type them out somewhat, and study them extendedly, who knew how long it might take … . It wasn't from any large interest in language, or from some theoretical formulation of what should be studied, but simply by virtue of that; I could get my hands on it, and I could study it again and again. And also, consequentially, others could look at what I had studied, and make of it what they could, if they wanted to disagree with me. (1992, Vol. 1: 622)

A third advantage of detailed transcripts is that, if you want to, you can inspect sequences of utterances without being limited to the extracts chosen by the first researcher. For it is within these sequences, rather than in single turns of talk, that we make sense of conversation. As Sacks points out:

> having available for any given utterance other utterances around it, is extremely important for determining what was said. If you have available only the snatch of talk that you're now transcribing, you're in tough shape for determining what it is. (1992, Vol. 1: 729)

It should not be assumed that the preparation of transcripts is simply a technical detail prior to the main business of the analysis. The convenience of transcripts for presentational purposes is no more than an added bonus.

As Atkinson and Heritage (1984) point out, the production and use of transcripts are essentially 'research activities'. They involve close, repeated listenings to recordings which often reveal previously unnoted recurring features of the organization of talk.

Such listenings can most fruitfully be done in group data sessions. As described by ten Have, work in such groups usually begins by listening to an extract from a tape with a draft transcript and agreeing upon improvements to the transcript. Then:

> the participants are invited to proffer some observations on the data, to select an episode which they find 'interesting' for whatever reason, and formulate their understanding or puzzlement, regarding that episode. Then anyone can come in to react to these remarks, offering alternatives, raising doubts, or whatever. (ten Have, 1998: 124)

However, as ten Have makes clear, such group data sessions should be rather more than an anarchic free for all:

> participants are, on the one hand, *free* to bring in anything they like, but, on the other hand, *required* to ground their observations in the data at hand, although they may also support them with reference to their own data-based findings or those published in the literature. (ibid.)

12.4.2 Analysing tapes

There is a strongly inductive bent to the kind of research that ten Have and Sacks describe. As we have seen, this means that any research claims need to be identified in precise analyses of detailed transcripts. It is therefore necessary to avoid premature theory construction and the 'idealization' of research materials which uses only general, non-detailed characterizations.

Heritage sums up these assumptions as follows:

> Specifically, analysis is strongly 'data-driven' – developed from phenomena which are in various ways evidenced in the data of interaction. Correspondingly, there is a strong bias against *a priori* speculation about the orientations and motives of speakers and in favour of detailed examination of conversationalists' actual actions. Thus the empirical conduct of speakers is treated as the central resource out of which analysis may develop. (1984: 243)

In practice, Heritage adds, this means that it must be demonstrated that the regularities described can be shown to be produced by the participants and attended to by them as grounds for their own inferences and actions. Further, **deviant cases**, in which such regularities are absent, must be identified and analysed.

However, the way in which CA obtains its results is rather different from how we might intuitively try to analyse talk. It may be helpful, therefore, if I conclude this section by offering a crude set of prescriptions about how to do CA. These are set out in Tables 12.6 and 12.7.

If we follow these rules, the analysis of conversations does not require exceptional skills. As Schegloff puts it, in his introduction to Sacks's collected lectures, all we need to do is to:

> begin with some observations, then find the problem for which these observations could serve as ... the solution. (Schegloff in Sacks, 1992, Vol. 1: xlviii)

This means that doing the kind of systematic data analysis that CA demands is not an impossibly difficult activity. As Sacks once pointed out, in doing CA we are only reminding ourselves about things we already know:

> I take it that lots of the results I offer, people can see for themselves. And they needn't be afraid to. And they needn't figure that the results are wrong because they can see

TABLE 12.6   HOW TO DO CA

1   Always try to identify sequences of related talk
2   Try to examine how speakers take on certain roles or identities through their talk (e.g. questioner/answerer or client–professional)
3   Look for particular outcomes in the talk (e.g. a request for clarification, a repair, laughter) and work backwards to trace the trajectory through which a particular outcome was produced

Source: Silverman (2001: 177)

TABLE 12.7   COMMON ERRORS IN CA

1   Explaining a turn at talk by reference to the speaker's intentions
2   Explaining a turn at talk by reference to a speaker's role or status (e.g. as a doctor or as a man or woman)
3   Trying to make sense of a single line of transcript or utterance in isolation from the surrounding talk

Source: Silverman (2001: 177)

them … . [It is] as if we found a new plant. It may have been a plant in your garden, but now you see it's different than something else. And you can look at it to see how it's different, and whether it's different in the way that somebody has said. (1992, Vol. 1: 488)

12.5   CONCLUDING REMARKS

Using the examples of tapes and field notes, we have seen how data analysis can be developed after the first stages. However, as I have implied throughout, good data analysis is never just a matter of using the right methods or techniques but always is based on theorizing about data using a consistent model of social reality. This commitment to theorizing about data makes the best qualitative research far superior to the stilted empiricism of the worst kind of quantitative research.

However, theorization without methodological rigour is a dangerous brew. In Chapter 13, we consider how computer software can aid qualitative research. Then, in Chapter 14, the issues of validity and reliability are discussed.

KEY POINTS

Develop data analysis by:

- Working with data which is easy to collect and reliable.
- Focusing on one process within those data.
- Narrowing down to one part of that process.
- Comparing different sub-samples of the population concerned.

Further reading

Miles and Huberman's book *Qualitative Data Analysis* (Sage, 1984) provides a useful treatment of coding observational data. For a more recent discussion, see Robert Emerson et al.'s *Writing Ethnographic Fieldnotes* (University of Chicago Press, 1995) Martyn Hammersley and Paul Atkinson's *Ethnography: Principles and Practice* (Tavistock, 1983), Chapters 7–8, is a classic discussion of how to analyse ethnographic data. A development of some of these ideas can be found in Martyn Hammersley's *What's Wrong with Ethnography? Methodological Explorations* (Routledge, 1992). A relatively recent treatment of 'grounded theory' is to be found in Anselm Strauss and Juliet Corbin's *Basics of Qualitative Research* (Sage, 1990). Sacks's work on conversation analysis is discussed in my book *Harvey Sacks: Social Science and Conversation Analysis* (Polity, 1998). The case studies of the cancer and heart clinics discussed here are found in my book *Communication and Medical Practice* (Sage, 1987), Chapters 6–7.

Exercise 12.1

This exercise is based on the various ways to develop data analysis discussed in this chapter. With reference to your own data:

1 Focus on one process within that data. Now narrow down your focus to one *part* of that process. Survey your data in terms of this narrow focus. What can you now find?

2 Compare different sub-samples of your data in terms of a single category or process. What does this show?

3 Decide what features of your data may properly be counted and tabulate instances of a particular category. What does this tabulation indicate? Identify 'deviant' cases and explain what you will do with them.

4 Attempt to develop your categories into more general analytic frameworks with relevance outside the setting you are studying.

Using Computers to Analyse Qualitative Data

Clive Seale

CHAPTER OBJECTIVES

By the end of this chapter you will be able to:

- Understand the strengths and limitations of computer software for qualitative data analysis.
- Recognize the key features of some of the main CAQDAS software packages.
- Find the details of CAQDAS software packages on the Internet and evaluate their usefulness for your research project.

13.1 INTRODUCTION

The use of computers for basic **content analysis** of text became popular in the humanities from the 1960s onwards. Scholars of literature, for example, found that they could use the large mainframe computers of the time for counting the number of times particular words occurred in a text. A computer might have been used to count the frequency of Shakespeare's use of a particular word or phrase, to compare this with some other dramatist, or between Shakespeare's late plays and his early ones, or his comedies and tragedies, plays versus poetry and so on. The co-occurrence of particular words, or the incidence of particular phrases characteristic of particular writing genres, could be reported objectively, meaning that literary analysis could be based on apparently more rigorously reported evidence. Computers could do these things because of their capacity for rapidly processing large volumes of text (Miall, 1990).

Social researchers also exploited the advantages of computers for data analysis, but this was largely confined to statistical work until the early 1980s, when qualitative researchers began to catch up. There are several reasons for the delay. Before the widespread availability of personal computers, use of mainframes was expensive and slow, requiring a degree of certainty about the analysis required so that it could be pre-specified accurately. Statistical procedures could be programmed into computers because they were well described. They were planned on one day, often run on data during the night, results being examined the following morning. By contrast, qualitative analysis was (and still is) far less formulaic, often requiring an approach to computing that gives quick feedback on the results of emergent questions, involving an interactive cycle of thinking and innovation only really made possible with the personal computer.

Additionally, qualitative research, as a social movement like many others, emerged as an initially radical response to a dominant orthodoxy: that of quantitative research work. This involved a heartfelt rejection of the technological appearance of statistical work, which smacked of dehumanization, over-control, obsession with technical puzzles rather than engagement with pressing social and political issues of the time. The computer symbolized these things, and many qualitative researchers remain distanced from this technology because of feelings that it may impose an alien logic on their analytic procedures. This, though, can impede a more balanced assessment of the advantages and disadvantages of the computer-assisted analysis of qualitative data (**CAQDAS**), which is, of course, not suitable for all of the things that qualitative researchers wish to do with data, but does offer significant benefits.

In this chapter I propose to show you how CAQDAS can be helpful in doing the kind of qualitative data analysis discussed in the last two chapters – while also pointing out its limitations. I will describe features of programs which have been widely used by qualitative researchers since specialized packages were introduced from the early 1980s onwards. I will also discuss some of the less often used but more advanced features of packages, such as those involved in theory building.

While particular packages will be mentioned, I do not aim to review all of them, or seek to describe the finer details of how particular packages work. Such information would probably become out of date quickly, since software developers continue to release new versions with extra features. At the end of the chapter is a section to help you gain access to the many free demonstration versions of the latest software that exist, so that this type of learning can occur. As in statistical analysis, you will learn best when you have a specific project in mind, and have time to explore how various available techniques might benefit what you want to do.

13.2 ADVANTAGES OF CAQDAS

The advantages of CAQDAS fall into four main categories:

1 Speed at handling large volumes of data, freeing the researcher to explore numerous analytic questions.
2 Improvement of rigour, including the production of counts of phenomena and searching for deviant cases.
3 Facilitation of team research, including the development of consistent coding schemes.
4 Help with **sampling** decisions, be these in the service of representativeness or theory development.

13.2.1 Speed

This advantage is most obvious to the researcher faced with a large amount of word-processed qualitative data, wanting to sort it into categories or coded segments which may then be filed and retrieved easily. For someone in this position, the speed at which programs can carry out sorting procedures on large volumes of data is remarkable. This saves time and effort which might otherwise be expended on boring clerical work, perhaps involving mounds of photocopied paper, colour coded, sorted into piles on the floor, cut up, pasted and so on. In turn, this gives the data analyst more time to think about the meaning of data, enabling rapid feedback on the results of particular analytic ideas so that new ones can be formulated. Qualitative data analysis then becomes more devoted to creative and intellectual tasks, less immersed in routine.

In the initial stages of analysis, the rapidity with which CAQDAS can identify patterns in large volumes of text can be useful. Fisher (1997) gives an example using a feature similar to those used in the Shakespeare example earlier. This was from a project involving 244 interviews with children, parents and social workers about local authority child care procedures. The data had been analysed previously using manual methods. Fisher's analysis was done in order to assess the contribution which different CAQDAS software packages could make. He used a program (SONAR) to search for the word 'discipline' in the interviews and found that different family members appeared to have different meanings for the word, a feature that had been missed in the original manual analysis. This led to some creative thinking about what could have led to this and what it might mean for child care issues. In turn, this thinking led to the development of ideas for **coding** segments of text. Fisher likens this sort of pattern searching to an aerial view of a landscape. Patterns can sometimes be seen from the air which, to the person on the ground, are merely random features.

A further example is a project at the University of Ulm, Germany, by Mergenthaler (1996) in which some 2 million words of transcription from 300 hours of transcribed psychotherapy sessions were searched for the incidence of particular words. It was found that a high incidence of certain words used in sessions, selected because they related to the researcher-generated concepts of 'emotion' and 'abstraction', were associated with particular sessions evaluated by participants as 'good'. Of course, the issue of why there is this connection requires more meaningful analysis of the interactions, perhaps using a coding approach or conversational analysis, but as an initial finding generated by the simple word counting facilities of a CAQDAS program it helped focus the minds of the researchers on particular lines of enquiry rather than others.

13.2.2 Rigour

An additional advantage of CAQDAS is that it can help researchers demonstrate that their conclusions are based on rigorous analysis. This adds to the trust placed in research texts by readers, a matter with which most authors are still concerned in spite of some radical **post–modern** analyses of research texts (e.g. Tyler, 1986; Denzin, 1997). This can involve counting the number of times things occur as well as demonstrating that you have searched for negative instances by examining the whole corpus of data rather than selecting only anecdotes supporting your interpretation. This is made relatively easy by CAQDAS.

Mention of counting is a reminder that the days of a great divide between qualitative and quantitative research work have now largely passed. The argument that each of these methodologies is inextricably linked to separate philosophical or theoretical positions (e.g. Smith and Heshusius, 1986) is less and less convincing to most practising social researchers. The alternative position (e.g. Bryman, 1988; Hammersley, 1992) is that for many purposes the two forms of analysis can be helpfully combined (see also Chapter 14).

CAQDAS helps you to make this combination. First, as already mentioned, events can be counted. These may be word strings in the text, as in the use made by literary scholars described above, or coded segments of text. I can give an example of this from my own work, where I had coded interviews with 163 people who had known elderly people living alone in private households in the year before their deaths. For this project I was using the ETHNOGRAPH program. I wanted to show what the speakers had said about the elderly people's attitudes to receiving help from others and I wrote in the final report:

> It was very common for the people living on their own to be described either as not seeking help for problems that they had (65 instances covering 48 people), or refusing help when offered (144 instances in 83 people). Accounts of this often stressed that this reflected on the character of the person involved, although other associations were also made. In particular, 33 speakers gave 44 instances where they stressed the independence which this indicated:
>
> '[She] never really talked about her problems, was very independent …';
>
> '[She] was just one of those independent people who would struggle on. She wouldn't ask on her own';
>
> 'She used to shout at me because I was doing things for her. She didn't like to be helped. she was very independent.'
>
> Being 'self sufficient', 'would not be beaten', and being said to 'hate to give in' were associated with resisting help. (Seale, 1996: 34)

As you can imagine, the 163 interviews generated a large amount of text. Because I had read through each interview, marking segments of text with code called *Help* to indicate when speakers had discussed the topic of the elderly person's attitude to help, which I had then entered on the computer, I was able to generate a listing of all these coded segments. Reading through this, I was able to code these into sub-categories, distinguishing segments describing elderly people not seeking help in spite of problems, instances where a refusal of help was described, and, within this, those segments that involved explicit reflections on the character of the person. A code called *Indep* marked segments where independence was mentioned. For all these things, the CAQDAS program which I was using allowed me to generate counts, some of which can be seen in the text above. I could then select illustrative quotations that gave good, typical examples of the things I was talking about.

If I had wanted to take this analysis further, I could have asked the computer to show me quotations about women separately from men, or to compare what neighbours as opposed to adult children said about the elderly person's attitude to help. Such an analysis might have been done as part of a more general investigation of the effect of gender on the experience of living alone towards the end of life, or as a part of an investigation into kinship obligations in contemporary society. The computer would have generated lists of quotations separately, which might then have been subjected to more detailed scrutiny (e.g. how do women discuss 'independence' compared with men?) but would also have enabled these to be counted. Such counts help the reader to see how widespread phenomena are, guarding against excessive emphasis on rare things that happen to suit the researcher's preferred arguments.

Durkin (1997) reports these benefits of CAQDAS too, in his study of people's experience of asbestosis litigation. For example, a comparison of interviews done in the USA with those done in the UK showed doctors and lawyers mentioning different issues. In the UK, there was an emphasis on the medical aspects of asbestosis claims; in the USA people were more likely to discuss the role of the media in encouraging claims, and the state of crisis which the volume of claims had produced. Lawyers had rather different views from doctors. These types of systematic comparison (between countries, or between professional perspectives) are greatly facilitated by the rapid retrieval of coded segments enabled by CAQDAS.

13.2.3 Team research

In addition, Durkin notes its impact in the context of an international, collaborative research project where researchers needed to agree on the meaning of codes and so had to assess inter-rater **reliability**. Some qualitative researchers who claim a separate philosophical position from the majority have suggested that a concern with inter-rater reliability smacks of naive realism (see the review in Armstrong et al. (1997) for more details on this debate), preferring the view that all researchers will see a different reality in a given text. Most, however, feel that for collaborative work to proceed it is necessary to create some sort of shared agreement about the meaning of particular segments of data. Durkin found that CAQDAS helped the team check whether it was interpreting segments in the same way. This was particularly useful as coding moved from the more descriptive and mundane codes to ones that reflected broader theoretical concerns. Researchers could pass coded interviews between them, and compare the results of blind second coding rapidly, using the counting facilities made available by the computer. Lee and Fielding (1995), who have interviewed many researchers about their use of CAQDAS, note that in collaborative projects one of the major impacts has been the encouragement that this gives to agree shared meanings for codes, a matter that is easier to ignore without the discipline imposed by the use of computers.

13.2.4   Sampling

As well as counting, avoidance of anecdotalism and the encouragement of consistent coding of data, CAQDAS has been found helpful in relation to sampling issues. Durkin's project, like most qualitative work, did not involve representative random sampling of the type used to ensure external **generalizability** in statistical work. Instead, the project used snowball and volunteer sampling, as the people involved in the legal and medical networks of asbestosis litigation were mostly known to each other:

> [CAQDAS] made it … easier to keep track of which actors we had spoken to. It was simple enough to compare a list of mentioned names with the interview directory [made available by the CAQDAS program] … . We knew we had reached near closure on the influential actors when the snowball sample question ('who else do we need to interview?') yielded only names of people we had already interviewed. (Durkin, 1997: 97)

I am now going to show you how CAQDAS can help a writer take an idea forward. I am writing about sampling and CAQDAS at the moment. Whenever I read an article or a book, I make notes of what I read in handwriting. Recently, I have been preparing a book on the quality of qualitative research, for which I have read a large number of books and articles over the past few months. First, I studied all my notes about this reading, typing the main ideas I had noted into my word processor, along with relevant code words to indicate the topics concerned. Two of the topics were CAQDAS and sampling issues, for which I have coded, although CAQDAS will not be a major preoccupation of the book and the level of detail I have given on this topic in my typed notes is fairly thin. However, I am now at the point in writing this chapter where I would like to say more about these two subjects. I can half-remember that there are issues about representativeness that someone has written about in relation to CAQDAS, but I cannot remember who it was or what they said. I am going to switch from my word processor into NUD•IST, the CAQDAS program which I have been using for this project. I am going to search for overlaps between the code words *caqdas* and *sample* and see what happens. Then I will show you the result.

   OK, I have done this. I have used the 'copy' command of NUD•IST to paste the results into my word-processing program. The whole thing took 2–3 minutes as I had to load the NUD•IST software. It looks like there are several references, so I will edit the output from NUD•IST to reduce this, showing just one 'hit'.

```
Q.S.R. NUD•IST Power version, revision 3.0 GUI.
Licensee: Clive Seale.

PROJECT: VALREL.PRJ, User Clive, 11:13 am, Jan 19, 1998.

********************************************************
(1 1)                          /auton/IndSysSrch
*** Definition:
Search for (intersect (30) (57))
++++++++++++++++++++++++++++++++++++++++++++++++++++
+++ ON-LINE DOCUMENT: DATA
+++ Retrieval for this document: 11 units out of 1034, = 1.1%

Kelle (1995) 3 — Smith style relat*ivism a waste of time.
                    482
Most research reports contain an implied realism (q). R/I*
Kerlinger a
positiv* ist at other extreme from Smith. Hammersley is in the
middle —
Reals* — though Denzin and Lincoln (postmod*) call him a
post-positivist.
You need to take a fallibilistic approach and try to reduce error,
without going for perfect corrrespondence between text and reality.
Neginst* Caqdas* can help with sample* issues and rel* of
coding.                    483

++++++++++++++++++++++++++++++++++++++++++++++++++++
+++ Total number of text units retrieved = 11
+++ Retrievals in 1 out of 1 documents, = 100%.
+++ The documents with retrievals have a total of 1034 text units,
    so text units retrieved in these documents = 1.1%.
+++ All documents have a total of 1034 text units,
    so text units found in these documents = 1.1%.
++++++++++++++++++++++++++++++++++++++++++++++++++++
```

FIGURE 13.1   AN EXAMPLE OF DATA ANALYSIS USING NUD•IST

Figure 13.1 shows that NUD•IST has given me a lot of extraneous information about the number of segments ('text units') I have found with this search.

This sort of thing might have been useful were I using NUD•IST for analysis of data, but this usage is different — I just want a reference and I don't want to spend hours leafing through my notes to find it. The item of interest is Kelle (1995), an edited book on CAQDAS. The output tells me that on the third page of my notes about this book, Kelle discusses the work of Smith (as in Smith and Heshusius (1986) mentioned earlier), rejecting the relativistic philosophical position of this writer.

As you can see, my summary of the arguments here is pretty brief! If I wanted to see more on this topic, I would go back to the handwritten notes, or look again at the book. Then, there is a summary of the arguments of a number of writers concerning philosophical issues in social research, the topics indicated by the code words with asterisks next to them. Right at the end is 'Caqdas★ can help with sample★ issues' which indicates that this text contains material on these topics, though without specifying the detail of the argument.

Looking now at my handwritten notes I see that this is a reference to a chapter by Kelle and Laurie on 'Computer use in qualitative research and issues of validity' in a book edited by Kelle (1995). Here, they make the point that the rapid retrieval which CAQDAS makes possible can help in dealing with larger samples, so enhancing the confidence with which empirical generalizations are made. However, their main point is that theoretical sampling in qualitative research has a different purpose from random sampling. The aim is not so much to create empirical generalizations through large representative samples, but to develop theory. For example, this can be done by comparing cases where a phenomenon exists with those where it does not, seeing which other conditions appear to be associated with the phenomenon. This is the strategy of constant comparison described in the **grounded theory** approach of Glaser and Strauss (1967) – see Chapter 12. CAQDAS can help with this, say these authors, by ensuring that comparison of cases is systematic rather than impressionistic. If thorough coding has occurred across a number of cases, a CAQDAS program can rapidly indicate which cases show a phenomenon, as well as showing what other conditions are present in each case.

You can see from this example of my use of NUD•IST that as well as using CAQDAS for data analysis, programs can be adapted for other purposes too, often not envisaged by the original software developers. I use NUD•IST as a reference manager too. On the market at present are a number of such managers which promise to produce lists of references in a variety of conventional forms, suitable for the different demands of particular academic journals. These can create searchable databases, very similar to those available at computer terminals in libraries. My problem, though, was that I did not wish to key in afresh several hundred references that I had already in electronic form, from a variety of books and articles I had done over the years. NUD•IST has been helpful here, allowing me to import these files in the rough and ready formats in which they are typed, to which I have added code words for particular topics. When I was asked to write this chapter, my first step was to go to this database and search for a list of articles I had read on the topic of CAQDAS, which I could then retrieve from my paper files and use for a more thorough investigation of the academic literature that is now emerging on this topic.

13.3 LIMITATIONS AND DISADVANTAGES

My computer search tells me, in the objective and balanced way that computers generally do, that I must now restrain my personal enthusiasm for CAQDAS and attend to the documented disadvantages and limitations that have been reported in the literature and which I have found in my personal experience and duly jotted down in the CAQDAS database that now reports them to me. My computer-assisted survey tells me that there are three major sub-topics here:

1 Do specialist CAQDAS packages do anything that cannot be done by a good word processor?
2 Do computers impose a narrowly exclusive approach to the analysis of qualitative data?
3 While clearly of use in analysing large volumes of data, CAQDAS packages are of little help in examining small data extracts, of the sort often examined by **conversation analysts** and some **discourse analysts**.

13.3.1 Using word processors for CAQDAS

Reid (1992) makes the first point, going on to describe ways in which word processors can help the qualitative data analyst. Most CAQDAS programs expect data to have been entered in a word-processing package and this task, along with reading and coding large volumes of data, remains one of the major time-consuming elements of qualitative data analysis, which computers do not remove. The time-saving elements of CAQDAS occur at a later stage of data searching and retrieval. Having said this, data in the typed or printed form used in some qualitative projects (e.g. newspaper articles, reports of political speeches) can be scanned into a computer using optical character recognition software (see Fisher (1997) for an example of this).

Reid is helpful in pointing out a number of analytic tasks feasible with a word processor. For example, it is possible to search for strings of text. This feature can be exploited if the researcher enters code words near particular topics, which can subsequently be retrieved using the string search facility. Reid outlines a 'macro' (a sequence of keystrokes contained in a command file) which will search for paragraphs in which a particular code word (say, 'discipline') is embedded, saving each paragraph which it finds to a separate 'results' file. One can then repeat a similar macro on this results file to search and save only those paragraphs containing a second code word (say 'children'), in which case one will have retrieved data where the two codes ('discipline' and 'children') overlap. The file management capacities of most word processors mean that this can be done for separate files, if need be, so that perhaps one could compare files for male with female interviewees. Not described by Reid, but also valuable for the qualitative data analyst, is a feature known as a 'spike' (available in Microsoft Word, for example). This feature enables a text to be visually inspected and segments of text extracted, to be temporarily stored in a clipboard, then added to by the contents of the next 'spiking' operation. All of the spiked material thus collected can then be copied to a separate document.

Clearly, then, word processors can do some of the things done by specialized packages. However, to an experienced user of CAQDAS programs, the procedures described by Reid appear unnecessarily time consuming. In CAQDAS programs the complex macro-style instructions are already programmed in and available with just a few simple clicks or keystrokes. Additionally, they offer facilities not available on word processors, such as the export of counts to statistical packages, or visualization of conceptual maps. The cost of moving from a word processor is not a strong argument since CAQDAS programs are less expensive than, for example, most statistical software (e.g. SPSS) and, indeed, most commercial word-processing software.

13.3.2 A narrow approach to analysis

The second issue, concerning the possible imposition of a narrowly exclusive approach to analysis, has been raised most intelligently by Coffey and Atkinson (1996). I say 'most intelligently' because I think concerns about the computer imposing a particular analytic logic, alien to the spirit of qualitative research, can be fuelled by the slight paranoia about technology felt by some qualitative researchers, discussed at the start of this chapter. In contrast, Coffey and Atkinson begin with a description of a variety of analytic strategies used by researchers working within different qualitative genres. As well as the conventional and popular code-and-retrieve approach, typical of researchers working within the grounded theory approach, they also describe analysis of the formal structures of **narratives** (see also Riessman, 1993) and what they call 'domain analysis', which involves close examination of actors' use of language, seen through their choice of particular words, phrases and metaphors. Domain analysis involves a fine-grained attention to the way in which language constructs meaning, along the lines of a semiotic or discourse analytic approach (see e.g. Potter and Wetherell, 1994). This contrasts with the code-and-retrieve approach of grounded theory which relies on commonsense interpretations of the meaning of particular segments of text. Coffey and Atkinson's comment therefore reflects a balanced analysis of the extent to which CAQDAS packages support particular forms of analysis, though they do not discuss conversation analysis in any depth.

By now, you should be convinced that CAQDAS supports the code-and-retrieve operations of grounded theorizing adequately. Indeed, two of the leading packages (ETHNOGRAPH and ATLAS) were designed with this methodology in mind. For discourse analysts, concerned to discover how particular speakers use particular words and phrases, the capacity for rapid retrieval of word strings in large bodies of data will be attractive in a preliminary identification of areas of text likely to repay closer analysis. For such researchers it is useful, too, to make comparisons of different settings or speakers, to identify systematic differences in the language chosen. However, for the discourse analyst or semiotician CAQDAS would be pointless for detailed analysis of short data extracts and would not substitute for in-depth consideration of the meaning of particular, telling instances. Barthes (1973) would not have found CAQDAS particularly useful for *Mythologies*.

Coffey and Atkinson (1996) make the point that most CAQDAS software does not support analysis of the formal structure of narratives, but note that one program, ETHNO (Heise, 1988), is devoted to this. Heise shows this by using the software to analyse the formal structure of the Little Red Riding Hood story. The analyst identifies events in narratives and enters them into the computer. For example, there may be a point in most stories where the hero's task is outlined, another point where the first difficulty is overcome, another where good defeats evil, and so on. The computer generates diagrams of such events and allows the user to explore and test logical relationships between events across different narratives, as well as comparing different narrative structures. The formal structure of fairy stories, biographical accounts, observed rituals and so on can all be analysed and compared in this way.

Coffey and Atkinson observe that CAQDAS software 'generally is more valuable for the organization and retrieval of content than the discovery of form or structure' (1996: 176) and Heise's program clearly offers features unavailable in other packages, but it is worth considering how more conventional code-and-retrieve software could support the analysis of narrative form. Clearly, code words can refer to form as well as content. One might code what the wolf said to Red Riding Hood as being about big eyes, or big teeth, or hunger, or sexual terrorism, in which case we would be coding for content (though the last example relies on an underlying theory that might not be obvious or agreed by some readers). On the other hand we could use code words like *springing the trap* or *villain tricks victim* to indicate that a recurrent formal feature of fairy stories occurs at that moment in the text. Retrieval of all *springing the trap* moments in the Brothers Grimm or the Arabian Nights collections could be a part of an analysis of narrative form. Once coded one could search for co-occurring forms (e.g. the presence of saviour figure in a fairy story) in order to test logical propositions about formal structures.

13.3.3 Small data extracts

The point I have been discussing merges with the third limitation of CAQDAS listed at the head of this section: the issue of small data extracts. This is not controversial. It has long been conventional advice to users of statistical packages that there is no point in spending time entering data from a ten-question interview schedule, done with ten people, in order to find out how many people answered 'yes' or 'no' to each question. You can work this out by hand more quickly. This advice also applies to CAQDAS. For the conversation analyst interested in reading and rereading a particular ten-second extract of talk, or the discourse analyst paying close attention to a single paragraph of text, there is no point in using CAQDAS.

Having said this, it is increasingly recognized that these more advanced and theory-driven modes of qualitative analysis have established a body of basic findings that can be extended by the comparative analysis of different data extracts. This can involve quite large bodies of data. For example, Silverman (1997) presents a conversation analytic study of a large number of HIV counselling sessions, drawn from several different clinics. He finds that counselling sessions in this highly focused setting vary, for the most part, between a directive 'information delivery' (ID) format that has the virtue of being brief, but is not designed to elicit or address the particular concerns of clients, and an 'interview' (IV) format which takes longer, is more recognizable as being 'counselling' in the conventional sense implying elicitation of clients' concerns, and has the virtue of resulting in 'recipient-designed' advice. The IV format is effective, in that it is accompanied by overt acknowledgement of the relevance of advice by clients, whereas the ID format sometimes shows clients resisting advice. These findings are based on an unusually large body of data, by comparison with most other CA studies. Clearly, it would be possible to build on these findings by examining data from a variety of other counselling settings, searching and marking transcribed extracts for the formal characteristics of ID or IV formats, perhaps as a part of some broader enterprise searching for the co-occurrence of particular formats and particular outcomes. For a study like this, CAQDAS would have some relevance in storing, retrieving and counting coded segments.

Like narrative analysis, though, the more popular CAQDAS packages are unable to support many of the things conversation analysts wish to do. This is particularly evident when it comes to transcription of talk from sound recordings. Here, it is useful to have software that can store and replay sound records, and time events within talk, such as the length of pauses. A program called CODE-A-TEXT (http://www.codeatext.u-net.com) allows the computer storage and replay of sound recordings. (ATLAS, reviewed in the next section, also allows the storage of audio recordings). In CODE-A-TEXT, hypertext links allow the user to work concurrently with transcript and sound or video. One can also add codes to audio segments without transcription. The transcription system of CODE-A-TEXT has a number of features useful for CA, including the automatic recording of the length of silences and the insertion of this into the transcript, as well as supporting the use of CA transcription symbols (see the Appendix to this book). The program can export counts of words or other letter strings, and counts of code words, to spreadsheets for numerical analysis.

Using CAQDAS is no substitute for thinking hard about the meaning of data. This is often said in response to fears that computer technology will be used uncritically for data analysis. No doubt this fear is partly generated by the perception that just such a process has occurred too often in statistical research. However, experienced quantitative researchers have long been aware of the need to treat computers as instruments for pursuing arguments about data, rather than limiting thought to what the computer can do. Additionally, different packages offer different things, and if you think you want to do something that your package cannot do, search for one that can and you will often find it. I hope the examples of ETHNO and CODE-A-TEXT in this section, neither of which are mainstream CAQDAS packages, will show you that this can result in some welcome finds. I will now give you a brief description of three 'mainstream' packages, before discussing some more advanced analytic strategies supported by CAQDAS.

13.4   MAINSTREAM PACKAGES: ETHNOGRAPH, NUD●IST AND ATLAS

A full account of the range of CAQDAS packages is available in Miles and Weitzman (1995). As I've said, new versions continually emerge, and for the latest versions it is best to explore relevant Internet sites (see later) rather than read books which quickly lose their currency. These sites have the advantage of containing demonstration versions of the commercial packages, and free versions of share-ware. There are also email discussion groups where software developers will engage with issues users raise, as well as allowing users to communicate with each other from around the world. However, a brief review of the features of three mainstream packages is appropriate here in order to show you more about what such packages can support and illustrate the view that different programs suit different needs.

13.4.1   *ETHNOGRAPH*

ETHNOGRAPH (http://www.QualisResearch.com) was one of the first CAQ-DAS programs and in the 1980s was the one most often used by qualitative researchers. Developed initially as a DOS program, it is easy to learn. Because of this I use it to teach CAQDAS to beginners, rather than any other package. The documentation is very explicit, and the continual prompts it offers the user to double-check a chosen action are, while very helpful to beginners, a little irritating after a while. The core is a straightforward code-and-retrieve system. As I write, version 5.0 for Windows is due to be released. This promises a number of welcome new features which will overcome limitations of earlier versions. The number of data files will no longer be limited to eighty, for example, and it will be possible to do on-screen coding with a mouse. For the first time it will be possible to export counts of code words to files which can be read by statistical software.

The program, like all CAQDAS software, requires the user to enter text with another program (either a word processor or optical character recognition). Once imported, lines are numbered. Codes can be attached to the numbers associated with particular segments of text. Memoranda about the meaning of codes can be recorded so that their development is logged, and these and other memos can themselves be incorporated as elements of 'data' during searches (a feature which the developers of NUD●IST would call an instance of 'system closure'). Searching for segments of text has become more sophisticated in successive versions of the program. One can restrict searches to particular files, or to particular features of files recorded on attached 'facesheets' (e.g. male/female interviewee, institutional or community setting, and so on). If data takes the form of a conversation between several people, the capacity to restrict searches to particular speakers, or categories of speaker, is useful. 'Boolean' searches are feasible, so that overlaps of codes, and retrieval of segments coded with one word, but not with another, are supported. A new feature is the capacity automatically to scan data files for code words that were entered along with the data. This can be very useful if the researcher has a robust coding scheme developed before all data has been entered.

13.4.2 NUD•IST

NUDIST (http://www.qsr.com.au) entered the scene somewhat later than ETHNOGRAPH, initially as a Macintosh program, but soon developing a PC Windows version. In recent years the developers of NUD•IST have also created NVivo. NUD•IST offers more features than ETHNOGRAPH, but is a little harder to learn. The documentation is less explicit for the novice, and things that are quite simple in ETHNOGRAPH, such as printing out the results of a search, are made more complex in NUD•IST. As well as enabling just about everything that ETHNOGRAPH can do, NUD•IST offers more complex Boolean searches.

NVivo is a very flexible tool, allowing pictures and sound files to be associated with a project as well as raw text. Coding text involves operations that are very similar to those involved in highlighting text in a word processor. The program allows the user to alter original data files (e.g. the transcript of an interview) after they have been coded. Cutting and pasting between NVivo and word processor windows is straightforward and complex searches are feasible. Additionally, like ATLAS (see later) NVivo has a built-in 'modeller', which allows the user to map out ideas in visual displays whose 'nodes' are linked to the underlying data associated with them (see Figure 13.2 below for an example).

13.4.3 ATLAS

ATLAS (http://www.atlasti.de) was explicitly developed to enable a grounded theory approach, resulting in a program of considerable sophistication. Unlike the other two programs reviewed here, ATLAS allows graphics (pictures and so on) to be used as data. This means that, for example, handwritten documents can be electronically scanned as pictures, sections of which can be marked and coded for later retrieval. ATLAS also offers more extended features for theory development, including the capacity to create conceptual diagrams showing links between emerging ideas. These diagrams are themselves linked to instances of data, meaning that quotations illustrating theoretical statements can be gathered very quickly. This is an advance on the hierarchical structure imposed by NUD•IST's graphical display, although it is possible to export codes from NUD•IST to other conceptual mapping software. The appearance of ATLAS is initially rather complex, containing many buttons whose purpose is not easily apparent. Some users will feel that the ease with which ETHNOGRAPH is learned outweighs the sophisticated advantages offered by ATLAS. Coding and retrieving text segments will be all that many researchers wish to do. Others will find the new analytic possibilities opened up by ATLAS a considerable attraction. At this point it is appropriate to consider some more advanced analytic strategies, involving theory building and testing, which packages like ATLAS are designed to support.

13.5   THEORY BUILDING WITH CAQDAS

Most researchers who use CAQDAS confine their use to coding and retrieval of text segments, using the computer as an electronic filing cabinet (Lee and Fielding, 1995). Theory building is generally done in the mind, or with the aid of paper, if at all. Although in one sense all research studies, indeed all observations, are 'theory driven', not all research studies need to be explicitly 'theorized'. Much qualitative research is, in commonsense parlance, 'descriptive' and does not require the explicit elaboration of conceptual thought generally referred to as theory. However, CAQDAS does support theorizing and examples of this are available in the literature. Additionally, I use the term 'theory building' to incorporate both the generation of theory and its testing. It is in fact hard to discuss one without the other, and an important perception of later researchers responding to the original outline of grounded theory (Glaser and Strauss, 1967) has been that the testing of emerging ideas is important in contributing new theoretical ideas. Indeed, the constant comparative method for generating theory (see Chapter 14) can be understood as involving continual tests of ideas against data. The concept of 'abduction' (see Blaikie, 1993) is a helpful half-way house between the poles of induction and deduction, indicating this understanding of data analysis.

The capacity to map out ideas in diagrams or conceptual networks, supported particularly well by ATLAS and NVivo, has already been mentioned. Software that is exclusively devoted to conceptual mapping is also available (such as Decision Explorer; http://www.banxia.co.uk/banxia). Links between concepts can be visually represented in a variety of forms, so that one type of link can mean 'X causes Y', another 'X is associated with Y', or 'X loves Y', 'X depends on Y', 'X is a property of Y' and so on. Since the network is linked to coded segments of data, instances of X and instances of Y, or instances of X where Y also occurs, or instances of Y where X is not present (and so on) can be generated by the application of Boolean search statements.

Let us imagine, for a moment, that CAQDAS had been available when Glaser and Strauss (1964) generated their grounded theory of social loss, an example of the use of the constant comparative method. These researchers recorded, amongst other things, instances of nurses talking about the care of patients who had died. Let us imagine that they searched through all of these stories, perhaps coded as

Nursetalk, and discovered what, in the 1960s, they found through manual methods, that some of these were instances of 'social loss stories'. These were comments made that indicated the extent to which nurses felt a particular death constituted a serious loss or not. A code (let us imagine that it is called *Socialoss*) might have been attached to these stories, enabling their later retrieval and further analysis.

Glaser and Strauss report that the category 'social loss story' contained some variable examples, whose properties Glaser and Strauss were able to explore by comparing different incidents where nurses spoke about the deaths of patients. Thus, a nurse might regretfully say of a 20-year-old man, 'he was to be a doctor', or of a 30-year-old mother, 'who will look after the children?', or of an 80-year-old widow, 'oh well, she had a good life'. This might have been established by close examination of these stories, retrieved by computer. Such an examination could have involved searches for word strings like 'age' or 'years'. Glaser and Strauss concluded that the age of a patient was a key factor in determining the properties of social loss stories, as well as the educational and occupational class of the person who died. Additionally, they found that nurses' 'composure' (itself a category with variable properties) was often disrupted at moments of high social loss. Thus, relationships between two categories were mapped out. Eventually Glaser and Strauss were to incorporate this into a general theory of relationships between professionals and their clients, suggesting that clients of high social value were more likely to receive rapid attention from professionals.

The conceptual network that might then have helped this developing theory to emerge would have looked like that shown in Figure 13.2 (created with the NVivo modeller). The arrows indicate the features of patients considered in social loss stories, which can have two different outcomes, depending on the content of the story. At each stage, retrievals of data would have supported or refuted the emerging theory. Note too that further refinement is then possible. Glaser and Strauss (1964) suggest, for example, that the properties of social loss stories interact. If an elderly person of high education and social class status died, this would be less likely to result in loss of composure than a situation involving a younger person of high education and social class. Such relationships might be indicated by further arrows indicating the conditions influencing particular outcomes. Other types of diagrams are possible for representing these ideas. For example, the hierarchical tree supported by NUD•IST could look as in Figure 13.3. If the researcher wishes to retrieve instances where the great age of a person was mentioned in a social loss story the 'address' of this 'node' for such a retrieval (to use the terms used in NUD•IST) would be 1, 1, 1. Note, though, that unlike Figure 13.2 the tree structure of 13.3 does not allow lines of supposed influence to be shown, making it hard to distinguish the properties of social loss stories (patients' characteristics) from their consequences (composure outcomes).

This example can also help in understanding the theory-testing capabilities of CAQDAS. Before going into this, though, it is important to distinguish between two broad types of code. It is possible to code material *factually* rather than *heuristically*.

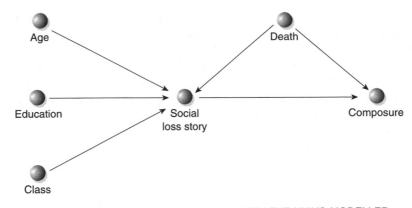

FIGURE 13.2   CONCEPTUAL NETWORK DRAWN WITH THE NVIVO MODELLER

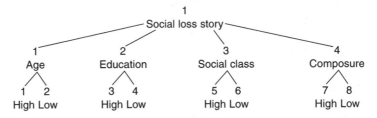

FIGURE 13.3   CONCEPTUAL NETWORK OF THE TYPE SUPPORTED BY NUD•IST

Thus, for example, a segment of text might be described as being about 'composure' or about 'religion' or about 'alienation'. These are examples of heuristic codes, often reflecting the researcher's theoretical **concepts**, useful for retrieving segments of data so that examples of such talk can be thought about more deeply, sub-categorized and so on. However, one might also want to code that composure, in a particular segment, has been retained or lost, that a person is a Catholic or a Protestant, or that someone is alienated or not. These are examples of factual codes. It is necessary to code 'factually' in this way in order to pursue the rigorous hypothesis testing supported by CAQDAS.

Hesse-Biber and Dupuis (1995) give an example of hypothesis testing from a study of the causes of anorexia. Using factual coding with CAQDAS these researchers could test the proposition that weight loss related to certain antecedent conditions. A logical relationship between factual coding categories was written along the following lines: '*If* mother was critical of daughter's body image *and* mother–daughter relationship was strained *and* daughter experiences weight loss *then* count as an example of mother's negative influence on daughter's self image.' Once particular interviews were identified as containing the codes involved, the text could be retrieved for further examination in order to see whether support for this causal interpretation could be justified for each case.

Clearly, the example from Glaser and Strauss could have been treated in a similar fashion. Selecting all examples of the loss of composure, the researchers could have examined to see whether these were accompanied by co-occurrences of codes for high education, class and low age, or particular combinations of these. This strategy would have searched out and retrieved negative instances, thus supporting an approach to data analysis that in, Chapter 14, we describe as analytic induction. Kelle (1995) contains a number of examples of these uses of CAQDAS, as well as references to programs that have been developed to support particular approaches to theory testing, such as AQUAD (Huber and Garcia, 1991).

13.6   HYPERLINKS TO POST-MODERN READINGS OF TEXT

The previous section may have made you feel that some of the fears that computers might take over analytic thought are justified. A technical fantasy seems to have emerged, uncomfortably close to quantitative work, with a language of counting, **hypothesis** testing and causal analysis that is alien to the interpretive freedom supported by qualitative approaches. Perhaps in response to these tendencies, Coffey et al. (1996) have outlined an approach to CAQDAS that is more in line with post-modern sensibilities, where deconstruction of a single authorial voice to enable multiple readings of text and data is enabled (the approach is also described in Coffey and Atkinson, 1996).

This approach makes use of a feature which I have not discussed so far, that of the hypertext link, whereby the analyst of data, or reader of a report, can click on a highlighted word or icon and go instantly to some link which has been previously made. Thus, a click on a code word might lead to an associated segment of text, or to a picture or sound file illustrating the concept. This feature will be familiar to users of the Internet. It has been promoted in certain CAQDAS packages (e.g. HYPERSOFT; Dey, 1993) as avoiding the 'decontextualization' of data that can occur in simple code-and-retrieve approaches, such as those supported by ETHNOGRAPH. This is because the hypertext link does not retrieve the relevant segment, but shows it in its original location, surrounded, for example, by the rest of the interview in which the segment of speech occurs. Additionally, the analyst can attach explanations, interpretations and memos to particular links.

Coffey and Atkinson argue that, as an example, 'we might also attach additional details, such as career details of particular respondents, their family trees, or details about their domestic lives.' (1996: 183). This means that the 'reader' of a research report will in fact interact with a computer rather than a book, with a research 'report' being written to a CD-ROM rather than paper. The reader will be able to explore original data in as much depth as is needed, thereby being free of the need to attend to an overarching and exclusive presentation by a single author.

The presentation of these ideas, like many new and interesting developments in qualitative research, has been couched initially in the form of a critique, to which the use of hypertext in these ways is offered as a solution. It seems that innovators often form their ideas as a response to perceived limitations of the dominant orthodoxy (or perhaps this is a rhetorical ploy to add to the persuasive appeal of the new idea). The ideas of Coffey et al. are presented as emerging in response to the limitations of the dominant grounded theory approach which they perceive to be supported by most CAQDAS software.

This critique has duly received a sophisticated reply from a representative of that approach, namely Kelle (1997), who rejects the simple dichotomizing of hypertext versus coding, post-modernism versus grounded theory. Kelle draws on a learned and interesting discussion of the German **hermeneutic** tradition of Biblical scholarship to show that both approaches can be fruitfully combined.

Here, we are in the realms of advanced methodological debate, a fascinating and somewhat self-sustaining arena of discourse which, however, is a little distanced from the practicalities faced by researchers grappling with particular research tasks. In the spirit of grounding the methodological debate, I would note that the ideas outlined by Coffey et al. seem like good and creative ones that could benefit some researchers in what they want to do. In particular, the authors extend the topic of data analysis by pointing to the intimate links between data, analysis, interpretation and presentation to readers. In one sense, too, they have the potential to address more traditional concerns with reliability and validity, since a CD-ROM can contain a great deal more text and other data than a conventional book. This will enable one of the long-standing problems of qualitative researchers to be addressed, that of anecdotalism, since 'readers' will be able to examine the full corpus of data on which conclusions are based. This would, of course, still be an exhaustive task and it is likely that the single-paragraph abstract of findings will retain a greater appeal for readers concerned to survey a range of studies in order to extract the major research findings of a particular field.

13.7   CONCLUDING REMARKS

In this chapter I have introduced you to some of the basic features of CAQDAS, emphasizing the utility of many such programs for the electronic storage, filing and retrieval of large bodies of textual data.

The time-saving element of this has been stressed, as well as the advantages that are gained in addressing issues of validity and reliability by the simple counting enabled by most such programs. The limitations of CAQDAS have also been discussed, including the issue of whether computer programs are likely to impose a narrowly exclusive approach to qualitative data analysis.

As a result I hope that you will feel able to use CAQDAS for your own ends, rather than have it dictate an analytic strategy to you. There are many such programs available and if you find that a particular one does not support what you want to do, the odds are that another package will contain something more useful if you look hard enough. More elaborate uses of CAQDAS, for theory building and testing, were also described, as well as the more speculative use of hypertext and computer presentations in general, to create research reports that allow readers to engage in interpretive work relatively free from a dominant authorial interpretation.

KEY POINTS

- Specialized computer software (CAQDAS) can speed up the routine tasks of sorting and searching through large quantities of qualitative data. This frees up time for analytic thought.
- Such software also tends to promote certain aspects of rigour. It does not tie the researcher to a particular form of qualitative analysis.
- CAQDAS does not do the thinking for you. It may not be needed where small segments of data are being considered.
- 'Code, search and retrieve' are basic and much used features of the major CAQDAS packages. However, you should not neglect other features designed to facilitate theory-building and innovative approaches to presenting and reading research reports (including visual modelling and hyperlink facilities).

Further reading

Kelle (1995) is a good collection of articles showing a variety of uses of CAQDAS and this author has written thoughtfully on coding for computerized analysis elsewhere (Kelle, 2004). Fielding and Lee (1991) is an edited collection of similar pieces. Richards and Richards (1994), who are the producers of NUD•IST and NVivo, have written an excellent review of the field. Seale (2002) provides a guide to the use of CAQDAS software with interview material. The CAQDAS and NUD•IST web sites listed below contain plentiful advice, and training and self-help tutorials on the subject, as well as links to books and articles:

ETHNOGRAPH (http://www.QualisResearch.Com)
NUD•IST and NVivo (http://www.qsr.com.au)
ATLAS (http://www.atlasti.de)
Sage (http://www.sagepub.co.uk/scolari)
CAQDAS networking project at Surrey University, UK.

Details of how to join user discussion groups are available at the above sites. The Sage Scolari site is included as Sage distributes NUD●IST and ATLAS and contains links to the producers' web sites.

Exercise 13.1

If you have an Internet connection, visit the web sites listed in the 'Further reading' section of this chapter. Download a demonstration version of one of the mainstream programs described in this chapter (i.e. ETHNOGRAPH, NVivo, NUD●IST or ATLAS). When you have spent some time getting to know the package and what it can do, jot down answers to the following questions:

1 How could I use this program to save time on my research project?

2 How could I use this program to improve the rigour of my study?

3 How could I use this program to develop the theoretical aspects of my study?

4 What are the limitations and disadvantages on using this for my study? Would another program overcome these, or should I opt for a 'manual' approach?

Exercise 13.2

Select a published qualitative research project that you already know quite well, which was done without the use of CAQDAS. It could, for example, be an early 'classic' study of Chicago School ethnography, or a well-known study relevant to your research topic. Examine the way in which the researcher appears to have collected and analysed the data and answer the following questions:

1 How might a CAQDAS program have been used to aid data collection on this study?

2 How might a CAQDAS program have been used to develop a coding scheme on this study?

3 How might the use of CAQDAS have improved the quality and rigour of data reporting on this study?

4 What other questions might have been asked of the data in the study, and could a CAQDAS program have helped in answering these?

Quality in Qualitative Research

14.1 INTRODUCTION

Quality has been a continuing theme of this book. Deciding to do qualitative research is not a soft option. Such research demands theoretical sophistication and methodological rigour.

Just because we do not use complicated statistical tests or do much counting does not mean that we can wallow in comforting hot baths of 'empathic' or 'authentic' discussions with respondents. After all, if this is the limit of our ambitions, can we do better than a talk show presenter?

In his excellent book *The Quality of Qualitative Research*, Seale (1999) identifies quality issues with what he calls 'methodological awareness'. As he puts it:

> Methodological awareness involves a commitment to showing as much as possible to the audience of research studies … the procedures and evidence that have led to particular conclusions, always open to the possibility that conclusions may need to be revised in the light of new evidence. (Seale, 1999: x)

It follows that unless you can show your audience the procedures you used to ensure that your methods were reliable and your conclusions valid, there is little point in aiming to conclude a research dissertation. Having good intentions, or the correct political attitude is, unfortunately, never the point. Short of reliable

TABLE 14.1   VALIDITY AND RELIABILITY

Validity

'By validity, I mean truth: interpreted as the extent to which an account
accurately represents the social phenomena to which it refers'.
(Hammersley, 1990: 57)

Reliability

'Reliability refers to the degree of consistency with which instances
are assigned to the same category by different observers or by the
same observer on different occasions. (Hammersley, 1992: 67)

methods and valid conclusions, research descends into a bedlam where the only
battles that are won are by those who shout the loudest.

In Chapter 9, I was able to be reassuring about the scientific status of case
studies based upon small amounts of data. However, I am less tempted to assure
qualitative researchers that they need not be concerned about the reliability of
their data or the quality of their interpretations. The reader has only to refer to
Chapter 15 to see that my concerns about these matters extend to some published
research.

This chapter is the first of two chapters which deal with quality considerations. In this chapter, I will attempt a diagnosis of the problem and suggest some
practical solutions for you to use in your own research. In Chapter 15, I suggest
how you can apply quality rules to evaluate research publications.

But first it is important to be clear about the relevant terms – validity and reliability. For simplicity, I will work with two straightforward definitions set out in
Table 14.1.

Using examples of actual research studies, I review below the pitfalls and
opportunities that the demands of validity and reliability create for the novice
researcher. Let me begin with validity.

14.2   VALIDITY

'Validity' is another word for truth. Sometimes one doubts the validity of an
explanation because the researcher has clearly made no attempt to deal with contrary cases. Or sometimes, the demands of journal editors for shorter and shorter
articles and the word limits attached to university courses mean that the researcher
is reluctantly led only to use 'telling' examples.

Of course, such challenges to validity are not confined to qualitative research.
The same sort of problems can happen in the natural sciences. The demands of
journal editors and university courses are little different in most fields. Nor is the
temptation to exclude contrary cases unique to qualitative research. Moreover, the

large research teams that sometimes collaborate in the natural sciences can unexpectedly threaten the credibility of findings. For instance, laboratory assistants have been shown to select 'perfect' slides for their professor's important lecture, while putting on one side 'slides' about which awkward questions might be asked (see Lynch, 1984).

It also should not be assumed that quantitative researchers have a simple solution to the question of validity. As Fielding and Fielding point out, some interpretation takes place even when using apparently 'hard' quantitative measures:

> ultimately all methods of data collection are analysed 'qualitatively', in so far as the act of analysis is an interpretation, and therefore of necessity a selective rendering. Whether the data collected are quantifiable or qualitative, the issue of the *warrant* for their inferences must be confronted. (1986: 12, my emphasis)

So, as you prepare your qualitative study, you should not be overly defensive. Quantitative researchers have no 'golden key' to validity.

Nonetheless, qualitative researchers, with their in-depth access to single cases, have to overcome a special temptation. How are they to convince themselves (and their audience) that their 'findings' are genuinely based on critical investigation of all their data and do not depend on a few well-chosen 'examples'? This is sometimes known as the problem of **anecdotalism**.

As Mehan (1979) notes, the very strength of ethnographic field studies – its ability to give rich descriptions of social settings – can also be its weakness. Mehan identifies three such weaknesses:

1 Conventional field studies tend to have an anecdotal quality. Research reports include a few *exemplary* instances of the behaviour that the researcher has culled from field notes.
2 Researchers seldom provide the criteria or grounds for including certain instances and not others. As a result, it is difficult to determine the typicality or *representativeness* of instances and findings generated from them.
3 Research reports presented in tabular form do not preserve the materials upon which the analysis was conducted. As the researcher abstracts data from raw materials to produce summarized findings, the original form of the materials is *lost*. Therefore, it is impossible to entertain alternative interpretations of the same materials. (1979: 15, my emphasis)

Some years later, this problem was succinctly expressed by Bryman:

> There is a tendency towards an anecdotal approach to the use of data in relation to conclusions or explanations in qualitative research. Brief conversations, snippets from unstructured interviews ... are used to provide evidence of a particular contention. There are grounds for disquiet in that the representativeness or generality of these fragments are rarely addressed. (1988: 77)

The complaint of anecdotalism questions the validity of much qualitative research. Two common responses to it are to suggest method and data triangulation and/or respondent validation.

Triangulation refers to the attempt to get a 'true' fix on a situation by combining different ways of looking at it or different findings. In Chapter 4, I showed some of the difficulties that novice researchers can get into by attempting such triangulation. In Chapter 9, I discussed in more detail the analytical limitations of this approach.

Broadly, many of the models that underlie qualitative research are simply not compatible with the assumption that 'true' fixes on 'reality' can be obtained separately from particular ways of looking at it. Of course, this does not mean that you should not use different data sets or deploy different methods. The problem only arises when you use such multiplicity as a way of settling validity questions.

Respondent validation suggests that we should go back to the subjects with our tentative results and refine them in the light of our subjects' reactions (Reason and Rowan, 1981). Like triangulation, however, I fear it is a flawed method.

Of course, the subjects we study can, if we ask them, give us an account of the context of their actions. The problem only arises if we attribute a privileged status to that account (see Bloor, 1983; Bryman, 1988: 78–9). As Fielding and Fielding put it:

> there is no reason to assume that members have privileged status as commentators on their actions ... such feedback cannot be taken as direct validation or refutation of the observer's inferences. Rather such processes of so-called 'validation' should be treated as yet another source of data and insight. (1986: 43)

Of course, this leaves on one side the ethics, politics and practicalities of the researcher's relation with subjects in the field (see Chapters 17 and 18). Nonetheless, these latter issues should not be *confused* with the validation of research findings.

If triangulation and respondent validation are fallible paths to validity, what more satisfactory methods remain? I discuss below five interrelated ways of thinking critically about qualitative data analysis in order to aim at more valid findings. These are:

- the refutability principle
- the constant comparative method
- comprehensive data treatment
- deviant-case analysis
- using appropriate tabulations.

14.2.1 The refutability principle

One solution to the problem of anecdotalism is simply for qualitative researchers to seek to refute their initial assumptions about their data in order to achieve objectivity. As Kirk and Miller argue:

> The assumptions underlying the search for objectivity are simple. There is a world of empirical reality out there. The way we perceive and understand that world is largely up to us, but the world does not tolerate all understandings of it equally. (1986: 11)

Following Kirk and Miller, we need to recognize that 'the world does not tolerate all understandings of it equally'. This means that we must overcome the temptation to jump to easy conclusions just because there is some evidence that seems to lead in an interesting direction. Instead, we must subject this evidence to every possible test.

The critical method implied here is close to what Popper (1959) calls 'critical rationalism'. This demands that we must seek to refute assumed relations between phenomena. Then, only if we cannot refute the existence of a certain relationship, are we in a position to speak about 'objective' knowledge. Even then, however, our knowledge is always provisional, subject to a subsequent study which may come up with disconfirming evidence.

Popper puts it this way:

> What characterizes the empirical method is its manner of exposing to falsification, in every conceivable way, the system to be tested. Its aim is not to save the lives of untenable systems but, on the contrary, to select the one which is by comparison the fittest, by exposing them all to the fiercest struggle for survival. (1959: 42)

Of course, qualitative researchers are not alone in taking Popper's critical method seriously. One way in which *quantitative* researchers attempt to satisfy Popper's demand for attempts at 'falsification' is by carefully excluding spurious correlations (see Table 2.3 and associated text in Chapter 2).

To do this, the survey researcher may seek to introduce new variables to produce a form of 'multivariate analysis' which can offer significant, non-spurious correlations (see Mehan, 1979: 21). Through such an attempt to avoid spurious correlations, quantitative social scientists can provide a practical demonstration of their orientation to the spirit of critical enquiry that Popper advocates.

How can qualitative researchers satisfy Popper's criterion? The remaining four methods suggest an interrelated way of thinking critically during data analysis.

14.2.2   *The constant comparative method*

The comparative method means that the qualitative researcher should always attempt to find another case through which to test out a provisional hypothesis. In an early study of the changing perspectives of medical students during their training, Becker and Geer (1960) found that they could test their emerging hypothesis about the influence of career stages upon perceptions by comparing different groups at one time and also comparing one cohort of students with another over the course of training. For instance, it could only be claimed with confidence that beginning medical students tended to be idealists if several cohorts of first-year students all shared this perspective.

Similarly, when I was studying what happened to Down's syndrome children in a heart hospital, I tested out my findings with tape recordings of consultations from the same clinic involving children without the congenital abnormality (Silverman, 1981). And, of course, my attempt to analyse the ceremonial order of private medical practice (Silverman, 1984) was highly dependent on comparative data on public clinics.

However, beginning researchers are unlikely to have the resources to study different cases. Yet this does not mean that comparison is impossible. The constant comparative method involves simply inspecting and comparing all the data fragments that arise in a single case (Glaser and Strauss, 1967).

While such a method may seem attractive, beginning researchers may worry about two practical difficulties involved in implementing it. First, they may lack the resources to assemble all their data in an analysable form. For instance, transcribing a whole data set may be impossibly time consuming – as well as diverting you from data analysis! Second, how are you to compare data when you may have not yet generated a provisional hypothesis or even an initial set of categories?

Fortunately, these objections can be readily overcome. In practice, it usually makes sense to begin analysis on a relatively small part of your data. Then, having generated a set of categories, you can test out emerging hypotheses by steadily expanding your data corpus.

This point has been clearly made by Peräkylä using the example of studies based on tape-recorded data:

> There is a limit to how much data a single researcher or a research team can transcribe and analyse. But on the other hand, a large database has definite advantages ... a large portion of the data can be kept as a resource that is used only when the analysis has progressed so far that the phenomena under study have been specified. At that later stage, short sections from the data in reserve can be transcribed, and thereby, the full variation of the phenomenon can be observed. (2004: 288)

I employed this constant comparative method, moving from small to larger data sets, in my study of AIDS counselling (Silverman, 1997). For instance, having isolated an instance of how a client resisted a counsellor's advice, I trawled through my data to obtain a larger sample of cases where advice resistance was present. This example is discussed in greater detail in Silverman (2001: 244–6).

However, the constant comparative method, because it involves a repeated to and fro between different parts of your data, implies something much bigger. All parts of your data must, at some point, be inspected and analysed. This is part of what is meant by 'comprehensive data treatment'.

14.2.3 *Comprehensive data treatment*

Ten Have notes the complaint that in CA, like other kinds of qualitative research:

> findings ... are based on a subjectively selected, and probably biased, 'sample' of cases that happen to fit the analytic argument. (ten Have, 1998: 135)

This complaint, which amounts to a charge of anecdotalism, can be addressed by what ten Have, following Mehan (1979), calls 'comprehensive data treatment'. This comprehensiveness arises because, in qualitative research, 'all cases of data … [are] incorporated in the analysis' (Mehan, 1979: 21).

Such comprehensiveness goes beyond what is normally demanded in many quantitative methods. For instance, in survey research one is usually satisfied by achieving significant, non-spurious, correlations. So, if nearly all your data supports your hypothesis, your job is largely done.

By contrast, in qualitative research, working with smaller data sets open to repeated inspection, you should not be satisfied until your generalization is able to apply to every single gobbet of relevant data you have collected.

The outcome is a generalization which can be every bit as valid as a statistical correlation. As Mehan puts it:

> The result is an integrated, precise model that comprehensively describes a specific phenomena [*sic*], instead of a simple correlational statement about antecedent and consequent conditions. (1979: 21)

14.2.4   Deviant-case analysis

> What is important in depicting anomalies precisely? If you cannot do it, that shows you do not know your way around the concepts. (Wittgenstein, 1980: 72e)

Comprehensive data treatment implies actively seeking out and addressing anomalies or deviant cases. Again Mehan makes the point:

> The method begins with a small batch of data. A provisional analytic scheme is generated. The scheme is then compared to other data, and modifications made in the scheme as necessary. The provisional analytic scheme is constantly confronted by "negative" or "discrepant" cases until the researcher has derived a small set of recursive rules that incorporate all the data in the analysis. (1979: 21; see also Becker, 1998: 211–12)

Mehan notes that this is very different from the sense of 'deviant-case analysis' in quantitative survey research. Here you turn to deviant cases in two circumstances:

- when the existing variables will not produce sufficiently high statistical correlations
- when good correlations are found but you suspect these might be 'spurious'.

By contrast, the qualitative researcher should not be satisfied by explanations which appear to explain nearly all the variance in their data. Instead, as I have already argued, in qualitative research, every piece of data has to be used until it can be accounted for.

Let me show you two examples which use deviant-case analysis with the aim of a comprehensive data treatment. The first is drawn from an interview study of reports by relatives about family members who had died alone (Seale, 1996; discussed in Seale, 1999: 79–80).

Most relatives reported that a relative dying alone was an unwelcome event and that they would have wanted to be present at the death if they had been able. Seale argued that such accounts worked to display a relative's moral adequacy.

However, in a small minority of cases, people said they had not wanted to be present at such a death. Rather than treat these examples as statistically insignificant, Seale examined them in greater detail to see if his overall argument needed to be modified.

In all these deviant cases, it turned out that respondents offered legitimations for their position. For instance, in one case, a son said that his father's dementia meant that he would have been 'oblivious' if his son had been present. In another case, a husband referred to his own potential distress at being present at the death of his wife. He also added that it 'didn't make any difference as she was in a coma' (Seale, 1999: 79).

Seale concluded that, in his five deviant cases, respondents did not depart from displays of moral adequacy but:

> successfully demonstrated their moral adequacy by alternative means. In doing this, they showed an orientation towards the event [i.e. not being present at the death of a loved one] as deviant from normal behaviour, requiring explanation, so strengthening the general case that accompaniment of dying people is perceived as a generally desirable social norm. (1999: 80)

My second example of deviant-case analysis is drawn from my ethnographic research on paediatric clinics (Silverman,1987). In this research, I compared the heart clinic discussed in Chapter 12 with a clinic treating children born with hare lips and/or cleft palates. The latter is another congenital defect but unlike cardiac anomalies is self-evident and treatable by routine, low-risk, cosmetic surgery usually carried out when the patient is in their teens. In both clinics, I observed and tape recorded what was said. Transcription was for ethnographic purposes and this meant that its level of detail did not follow all the conventions used in CA.

The rationale for delaying cosmetic surgery in the cleft-palate clinic is that, since appearance is a matter of personal judgement, it is best left until somebody is of an age when they can decide for themselves rather than be influenced by the surgeon or their parents. In practice, this reasonable assumption meant that the doctor (D) would ask the young person concerned a question in this general format:

Extract 14.1 [Silverman, 1987: 165]

D: What do you think about your looks Barry?
     (3.0)
B: I don't know
D: You heh heh doesn't worry you a lot.

Barry's answer was common at the clinic. Short of a later self-correction or a persuasive parental intervention (both difficult to engineer), it meant that many such
patients did not get cosmetic surgery.

Drawing upon evidence of this kind, I argued that questioning such young
people about their looks set up the consultation as a psychological interrogation
likely to lead to non-intervention. This was strengthened by the fact that, later
in the consultation, it became clear that Barry, after all, did want cosmetic
surgery. Barry's case and that of others showed that these adolescent patients
had far less difficulty when they were simply asked whether they wanted an
operation.

However, a visit to a clinic in Brisbane, Australia, provided me with the
deviant case shown in Extract 14.2:

Extract 14.2 [Silverman, 1987: 182]

D: Do you worry at all about your appearance?
S: Oh I really notice it but I um if it could be improved, I'd
     Like to get it done. I really worry about it.

In one leap, Simon seems to have overcome the communication difficulties that
a question about your appearance usually generates. He freely admits that he
'notices' and 'worries' about his looks and, consequently, would 'like to get it
done'. What are we to make of this apparently deviant case?

The first thing to report is that, at 18 years of age, Simon is considerably older
than Barry and the other children seen in my English clinic. So reticence to discuss one's appearance may be age related and different medical strategies may be
applied to different age groups.

However, there was something more interesting about Simon's case. This was
how his reports about his worries were treated by doctors in his clinic. Extract 14.3
below is a continuation of 14.2:

Extract 14.3 [Silverman, 1987: 183]

S: I really worry about it.
D: *Really*?
D: Not really but *really*?
S: But *really* yes.

What is going on in Extract 14.3? Why is Simon's apparently straightforward response subject to further questioning? To answer these questions, I noted comments made by a doctor before Simon had entered the room. These are shown in Extract 14.4:

Extract 14.4 [Silverman, 1987: 180]

D: He's er (0.5) it's a matter of deciding whether he should have an
     operation. And, er, what we are concerned about is his degree of
     maturity which it will be very interesting for you [D turns towards me]
     to make a judgement on when he comes in.

We see from Extract 14.4 that, even before Simon enters the room, his 'degree of maturity' will be an issue. We are advised that Simon's answers should not stand alone as expression of his wishes but should be judged as mature or immature and, perhaps, discarded or reinterpreted.

   After Simon leaves, this doctor worries some more about what Simon's answers 'really' mean:

Extract 14.5 [Silverman, 1987: 186]

D: It's very difficult to assess isn't it? Because he's pretty
     sophisticated in some of his comments and it's er (1.0)
     it's just the, you know, continuously sunny nature that's
     troubling me a little bit about the problem as to whether
     it should be done.

Eventually, this doctor concludes that Simon's relaxed manner is merely 'a cover-up' for his self-consciousness about his appearance. Although this is rather an odd conclusion since Simon has freely admitted that he is concerned about his appearance, it generates general consent and all the doctors present agree that Simon is 'motivated' and should have his operation.

   This deviant case considerably added to my understanding of the mechanics of decision making in the cleft-palate clinic. The English data had suggested that asking young people about their appearance tended to set them problems which could lead away from the cosmetic surgery they might want. The Australian data showed that, even where a patient confidently reported their concern about their appearance, this created a further complication. In this case, the doctors worried about how someone so concerned could present themselves in such a confident (or 'sunny') manner.

   A Catch-22 situation was now revealed. The doctors' practical reasoning unintentionally resulted in the following impasse:

1   To get surgery, you needed to complain about your appearance.
2   Those who were most troubled about their appearance would often be the
    least able to complain, so they would not get surgery.

3 Patients who did complain would be viewed as self-confident. Hence their underlying troubles were open to doubt and they too might not get surgery.

The impasse derived from the coupling of the doctors' understandable desire to elicit their patients' own views with psychological versions of the meaning of what their patients actually said.

These two studies show how the identification and further analysis of **deviant cases** can strengthen the **validity** of research. As implied here, it is important to underline the fact that such identification needs to stem from a theoretical approach to the data. Seale's work derived from a way of treating interview responses as moral **narratives**. My own research was based upon an ethnographic interest in the ceremonial order' of the clinic (Strong, 1979).

So pieces of data are never intrinsically 'deviant' but rather become so in relation to the approach used. This theoretically defined approach to analysis should also properly apply to the compilation and inspection of data in tabulated form.

14.2.5 Using appropriate tabulations

A very nice example of how simple tabulations can improve the quality of data analysis is provided by Koppel et al. (2003). Their earlier ethnographic research had revealed that hospital computer-ordering systems were often associated with errors when doctors prescribed patients' medications. A quantitative survey showed that over 75 per cent of doctors had used the computer system incorrectly.

It turned out that the computer display tended to convey a false sense of accuracy to many doctors. For example, by focusing solely on the electronic medication chart, doctors would tend to miss crucial paper stickers attached to the hardcopy case notes. Various features of the computer software also seemed to be associated with these errors. For instance, the display on the screen would show amounts of a medication appropriate for warehousing needs and purchasing decisions. Yet this level might be clinically inappropriate. In addition, it was possible for a doctor to add a new medication without cancelling an existing prescription for something very similar.

Koppel et al.'s survey increased the validity and generalizability of their qualitative study. Using both sets of data, they were able to argue more convincingly about how the computer software could be improved.

However, it is usually mistaken to count simply for the sake of counting. Without a theoretical rationale behind the tabulated categories, counting only gives a spurious validity to research. For instance, in the observation of classroom behaviour, Mehan (1979) suggests that many kinds of quantification have only limited value:

the quantitative approach to classroom observation is useful for certain purposes, namely, for providing the frequency of teacher talk by comparison with student talk … . However, this approach minimizes the contribution of students, neglects the inter-relationship of verbal to non-verbal behavior, obscures the contingent nature of interaction, and ignores the (often multiple) functions of language. (1979: 14)

I do not attempt here to defend quantitative or **positivistic** research *per se*. I am not concerned with research designs which centre on quantitative methods and/ or are indifferent to how participants construct order. Instead, I want to try to demonstrate some uses of quantification in research which is qualitative and inter-pretive in design.

To some extent, the tabulations I developed in my study of cancer clinics (see Chapter 12, Table 12.3) fell foul of Mehan's criticisms. Although my comparison of clinics derived from Strong's (1979) discussion of 'ceremonial orders', the tab-ulation was based upon dubious, commonsense categories. For instance, it is very problematic to count participants' questions when your only data is field notes. Without being able to reinspect a tape recording my category of 'question' has an unknown relation to the participants' orientations.

An alternative is to count members' own categories as used in naturally occur-ring places. For instance, in my analysis of cardiac consultations with Down's syn-drome children (see Chapter 12), I constructed a table, based on a comparison of Down's and non-Down's consultations, showing the different forms of the doctor's questions to parents and the parents' answers. This tabulation showed a strong tendency with Down's children for both the doctor and parents to avoid using the word 'well' about the child and this absence of reference to 'well-ness' proved to be crucial to understanding the subsequent shape of the clinic consultation.

So there is no reason why qualitative researchers should not, where appropri-ate, use quantitative measures. Simple counting techniques, theoretically derived and ideally based on members' own categories, can offer a means to survey the whole corpus of data ordinarily lost in intensive, qualitative research. Instead of taking the researcher's word for it, the reader has a chance to gain a sense of the flavour of the data as a whole. In turn, researchers are able to test and to revise their generalizations, removing nagging doubts about the accuracy of their impressions about the data.

As Kirk and Miller remark:

> By our pragmatic view, qualitative research does imply a commitment to field activities.
> It does not imply a commitment to innumeracy. (1986: 10)

14.3 RELIABILITY

Counting based on members' own categories in the context of comprehensive data treatment is possible because, in principle, the quality of data should be high in qualitative research. By contrast, although quantitative researchers try to claim reliability by using pre-tested measures and scales, they can end up with highly unreliable tabulations. This is not because survey research questions are ambiguously worded but rather because asking and answering any question can never be separated by mutual interpretations which are inherently local and non-standardizable (see Antaki and Rapley, 1996).

By contrast with tabulated figures from survey research interviews, tapes and transcripts are open to further inspection by both researchers and readers. However, this opportunity is not always present in qualitative research. There are many observational studies where the reader has to depend on the researcher's depiction of what was going on. Indeed, perhaps the extended immersion in the 'field', typical of much qualitative research, leads to a certain preciousness about the validity and reliability of the researcher's own interpretation of 'their' tribe or set of interview respondents.

As Bryman notes about such studies:

> field notes or extended transcripts are rarely available; these would be very helpful in order to allow the reader to formulate his or her own hunches about the perspective of the people who have been studied. (1988: 77)

By implication, Bryman is calling for what Seale (1999) calls **low-inference descriptors**. Although, as Seale notes, no act of observation can be free from the underlying assumptions that guide it (see Chapter 7 of this book), detailed data presentations which make minimal inferences are always preferable to researchers' presentation of their own (high-inference) summaries of their data.

Low-inference descriptors involve:

> recording observations in terms that are as concrete as possible, including verbatim accounts of what people say ... rather than researchers' reconstructions of the general sense of what a person said. (Seale, 1999: 148)

I would add that low-inference descriptors also mean providing the reader with long data extracts which include, for instance, the question preceding a respondent's comments as well as the interviewer's 'continuers' (e.g. 'mm hmm') which encourage a respondent to enlarge a comment (see Rapley, 2004).

Earlier in this book, I have discussed two ways of strengthening the reliability of **field** data: field note conventions, and inter-coder agreement (referred to in Chapters 11 and 12). In the remaining part of this chapter, I will concretize this discussion of reliability by looking at an example of how reliability was addressed in the context of one ethnographic study. I will then examine practical issues of reliability in a study which worked with tapes and transcripts of **naturally occurring** interaction.

14.3.1   Reliability in one ethnographic study

In their ethnographic study of adolescent drug users, first discussed in Chapter 11, Glassner and Loughlin carefully tape recorded all their interviews. These tapes were then transcribed and coded by:

> identifying topics, ways of talking, themes, events, actors and so forth ... . Those lists became a catalogue of codes, consisting of 45 topics, each with up to 99 descriptors. (Glassner and Loughlin, 1987: 25)

On the surface, such tabulation appears to involve the counting for the sake of counting found in some quantitative research. However, the authors make clear that their approach to data analysis is different from **positivistic**, survey research studies:

> In more positivistic research designs, coder reliability is assessed in terms of agreement among coders. In qualitative research one is unconcerned with standardizing inter- pretation of data. Rather, our goal in developing this complex cataloguing and retrieval system has been *to retain good access to the words of the subjects*, without relying upon the memory of interviewers or data analysts. (1987: 27, my emphasis)

By retaining this access to subjects' own categories, Glassner and Loughlin satisfy the theoretical orientation of much qualitative research while simultaneously allowing readers to retain some sort of direct access to raw data.

Moreover, Glassner and Loughlin suggest that their analysis fits conventional criteria of reliability. For instance:

● The coding and data analysis was done 'blind' – both the coding staff and the analysts of the data 'conducted their research without knowledge of [the] expectations or hypotheses of the project directors' (1987: 30).
● The computer-assisted recording and analysis of the data meant that one could be more confident that the patterns reported actually existed throughout the data rather than in favourable examples (see Chapter 12).

14.3.2   Reliability in a study of tape-recorded interaction

When people's activities are tape recorded and transcribed, the reliability of the interpretation of transcripts may be gravely weakened by a failure to transcribe apparently trivial, but often crucial, pauses and overlaps. For instance, a recent study of medical consultations was concerned to establish whether cancer patients had understood that their condition was fatal.

In this study (Clavarino et al., 1995), we attempted to examine the basis upon which interpretive judgements were made about the content of a series of audio- taped doctor–patient interviews between three oncologists and their newly referred cancer patients. It was during this interview that the patients were supposedly informed that their cancer was incurable.

Two independent transcriptions were performed. In the first, an attempt was made to transcribe the talk 'verbatim', i.e. without grammatical or other 'tidying up'. Using the first transcription, three independent coders, who had been trained to be consistent, coded the same material. Inter-coder reliability was then estimated. Inconsistencies amongst the coders may have reflected some ambiguity in the data, some overlap between coding categories, or simple coding errors.

The second transcription was informed by the analytic ideas and transcription symbols of CA. This provided additional information on how the parties organized their talk and, we believe, represents a more objective, comprehensive and therefore more reliable recording of the data because of the level of detail given by this method.

By drawing upon the transcription symbols and concepts of CA, we sought to reveal subtle features in the talk, showing how both doctor and patients produced and received hearable ambiguities in the patient's prognosis. This involved a shift of focus from coders' readings to how participants demonstrably monitor each other's talk. Once we pay attention to such detail, judgements can be made that are more convincingly valid. Inevitably, this leads to a resolution of the problem of inter-coder reliability.

For instance, when researchers first listened to tapes of relevant hospital consultations, they sometimes felt that there, was no evidence that the patients had picked up their doctors' often guarded statements about their prognosis. However, when the tapes were retranscribed, it was demonstrated that patients used very soft utterances (like 'yes' or, more usually, 'mm') to mark that they were taking up this information. Equally, doctors would monitor patients' silences and rephrase their prognosis statements.

14.4   CONCLUDING REMARKS

Some social researchers argue that a concern for the reliability and validity of observations arises only within the quantitative research tradition. Because what they call the 'positivist' position sees no difference between the natural and social worlds, reliable and valid measures of social life are only needed by such 'positivists'. Conversely, it is argued, once we treat social reality as always in flux, then it makes no sense to worry about whether our research instruments measure accurately (e.g. Marshall and Rossman, 1989).

Such a position would rule out any systematic research since it implies that we canot assume any stable properties in the social world. However, if we concede the possible existence of such properties, why shouldn't other work replicate these properties?

As Kirk and Miller argue about reliability:

Qualitative researchers can no longer afford to beg the issue of reliability. While the forte of field research will always lie in its capability to sort out the validity of propositions, its results will (reasonably) go ignored minus attention to reliability. For reliability to be calculated, it is incumbent on the scientific investigator to document his or her procedure. (1986: 72)

Of course, exactly the same point may be made about the claims to validity, or truth status, of qualitative research studies. So, to underline the point with which this chapter began, unless you can show your audience the procedures you used to ensure that your methods were reliable and your conclusions valid, there is little point in aiming to conclude a research dissertation.

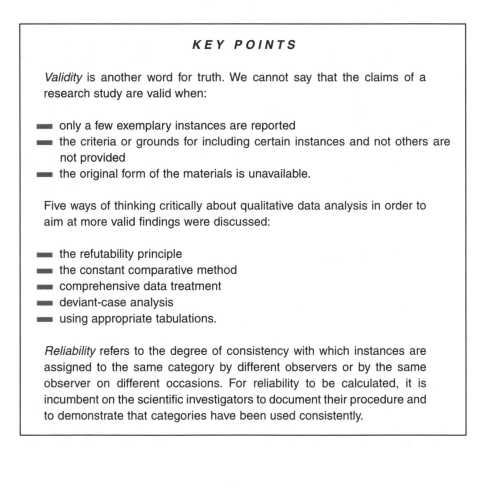

KEY POINTS

Validity is another word for truth. We cannot say that the claims of a research study are valid when:

■ only a few exemplary instances are reported
■ the criteria or grounds for including certain instances and not others are not provided
■ the original form of the materials is unavailable.

Five ways of thinking critically about qualitative data analysis in order to aim at more valid findings were discussed:

■ the refutability principle
■ the constant comparative method
■ comprehensive data treatment
■ deviant-case analysis
■ using appropriate tabulations.

Reliability refers to the degree of consistency with which instances are assigned to the same category by different observers or by the same observer on different occasions. For reliability to be calculated, it is incumbent on the scientific investigators to document their procedure and to demonstrate that categories have been used consistently.

Further reading

Clive Seale's book *The Quality of Qualitative Research* (Sage, 1999) offers an excellent overall treatment of the issues discussed in this chapter. A shorter version of his argument is found in his chapter 'Quality in qualitative research' in Seale et al.'s edited collection *Inside Qualitative Research* (Sage, 2004: 409–19). A more specialized treatment is Peräkylä (2004). For a detailed discussion of deviant-case analysis or 'analytic induction', see Becker (1998: 197–212).

Exercise 14.1

This is an exercise designed to help you think about the validity of your data analysis. It is best attempted when you have already written at least one substantial paper on your findings.

1   Choose any paper you have written on your data.

2   Explain on what grounds you chose those particular data extracts to report.

3   To what extent can you claim that the data was 'typical' or 'representative'?

4   To what extent have you investigated and reported 'deviant' cases?

Exercise 14.2

This exercise is meant to accustom you to the advantages and limitations of simple tabulations.

1   Select one data set from your data corpus (e.g. a particular collection of interviews, observations or transcripts).

2   Count whatever seems to be countable in this data *according to your theoretical orientation.*

3   Assess what this quantitative data tells you about social life in this setting, e.g. what associations can you establish?

4   Identify deviant cases (i.e. items that do not support the associations that you have established). How might you further analyse these deviant cases, using either quantitative or qualitative techniques? What light might that throw on the associations which you have identified?

Exercise 14.3

I reproduce below a quotation from Barry Glassner and Julia Loughlin used earlier in this chapter:

> In more positivistic research designs, coder reliability is assessed in terms of agreement among coders. In qualitative research one is unconcerned with standardizing interpretation of data. Rather, our goal in developing this complex cataloguing and retrieval system has been *to retain good access to the words of the subjects*, without relying upon the memory of interviewers or data analysts. (1987: 27, my emphasis)

Now write a short piece (say 1000 words) explaining how your own data analysis provides the reader with good access to your original data set. Check out this piece with your supervisor and other students. If they think it works, you may be able to use it as part of your final methodology chapter.

Evaluating Qualitative Research

15.1 INTRODUCTION

In Chapter 14, we examined various strategies which can help to improve the quality of your research design and data analysis. Knowledge of such strategies also gives you a powerful set of tools through which to evaluate other people's research. Such evaluation skills are crucial in writing effective literature reviews (see Chapter 21). They will also stand you in good stead in preparing papers for publication (see Chapter 27) and in hallmarking your dissertation as the work of a truly professional researcher (see Chapter 5).

In this chapter, I will review evaluation criteria for qualitative research. As ever, I will use multiple case studies to illustrate what these criteria mean in practice.

I start from the assumption that all social science should base itself on a form of enquiry that is self-critical. This means that, if we wish to establish criteria for evaluating qualitative research, we will need to understand the similar issues faced by any systematic attempt at description and explanation, whether quantitative or qualitative.

15.2 TWO GUIDES FOR EVALUATING RESEARCH

Researchers are not the only people concerned about the quality of published research. Governments and smaller public and private organizations are currently inundated by research reports that seem to have a bearing on policy. How can they assess the quality of such reports?

A very detailed list of evaluative criteria has recently been devised by a team of researchers commissioned by the British Cabinet Office (Spencer et al., 2003). An adapted version of these criteria is set out in Table 15.1.

Another useful set of evaluative criteria is provided in Table 15.2. Like Table 15.1, it can be employed when you are evaluating research publications. It also, of course, suggests a number of tricky questions that you should also address in your own work!

You should now attempt Exercise 15.1.

TABLE 15.1 CRITERIA FOR ASSESSING QUALITATIVE RESEARCH

Appraisal question	Quality indicators
Appropriate research design?	Convincing argument for different features of research design?
Reliable data?	Recording methods? Field note or transcription conventions?
Clear theoretical assumptions?	Discussion of models employed?
Adequate documentation of research process?	Discussion of strengths and weaknesses of data and methods? Documentation of changes made to the research design?
How credible are the findings?	Are the findings supported by data? Clarity of links between data, interpretation and conclusions?
Can the findings be generalized?	Evidence for wider inference?

Source: adapted from Spencer et al. (2003: 9–15)

TABLE 15.2 CRITERIA FOR THE EVALUATION OF RESEARCH

1   Are the methods of research appropriate to the nature of the question being asked?
2   Is the connection to an existing body of knowledge or theory clear?
3   Are there clear accounts of the criteria used for the selection of cases for study, and of the data collection and analysis?
4   Does the sensitivity of the methods match the needs of the research question? Was the data collection and record keeping systematic?
5   Is reference made to accepted procedures for analysis?
6   How systematic is the analysis?
7   Is there adequate discussion of how themes, concepts and categories were derived from the data?
8   Is there adequate discussion of the evidence for and against the researcher's arguments?
9   Is a clear distinction made between the data and its interpretation?

Source: adapted from criteria agreed and adopted by the British Sociological Association Medical Sociology Group, September 1996

TABLE 15.3   FOUR CRITERIA FOR ASSESSING RESEARCH QUALITY

1	How far can we demonstrate that our research has mobilized the conceptual apparatus of our social science disciplines and, thereby, helped to build useful social theories?
2	How far can our data, methods and findings be based on a self-critical approach or, put more crudely, counter the cynic who comments 'Sez you'?
3	To what extent do our preferred research methods reflect careful weighing of the alternatives or simple responses to time and resource constraints or even an unthinking adoption of the current fashions?
4	How can valid, reliable and conceptually defined qualitative studies contribute to practice and policy by revealing something new to practitioners, clients and/or policy-makers?

15.3   FOUR QUALITY CRITERIA

While Tables 15.1 and 15.2 set out a very rigorous set of criteria, they focus on purely methodological issues. By now you will be aware that, in this book, I have been arguing for a more broadly based set of criteria for evaluating qualitative research which weds methodological, theoretical and practical issues. To simplify matters, I limit the discussion to the four aspects of quality set out in Table 15.3.

Using classic case studies, I will now illustrate each of the four quality criteria set out in Table 15.3. My case studies are taken from sociology and anthropology. For a fascinating attempt to apply these criteria to media studies, see Barker (2003).

15.3.1   Building useful theories

My case study here is Douglas's (1975) work on a Central African tribe, the Lele. Since this study has already been discussed in Chapter 7, I can be brief. People in most **cultures** find certain things anomalous. For us, it may be a celebrity who refuses to 'reveal all', rejecting invitations to talk shows and eschewing public performances. For the Lele, it was an animal that seemed to be anomalous.

An anteater, called a pangolin by Western zoology, was seen by the Lele to combine apparently opposite characteristics. The Lele were puzzled by how this pangolin seemed to have some human features – for instance, it tended to have only one offspring at a time. Moreover, while most animals were either land or water creatures, it was both.

Douglas noted how most cultures tend to reject anomalous entities. Since anomaly seems to cast doubt on how we classify the world, it would appear to be dangerous to take it too seriously. However, the Lele are an exception. They celebrate their anomalous pangolin and this suggests that there may be no *universal* propensity to frown upon anomaly.

Douglas moves from this observation to an examination of the forms of social organization which may encourage different responses to perceived anomalies.

In particular, she argues convincingly that successful exchange across borders with other groups may be associated with favourable responses to entities which match such border crossing. Since successful relations with other groups may not be all that common, it is hardly surprising that, in many cultures, anomaly is not tolerated.

Building on an **ethnography** of an obscure tribe, Douglas has developed an important theory about the relation between cultural categories and social organization. In doing so, she reveals how a simple qualitative case study can build social theory.

15.3.2   Using a self-critical approach

Dalton (1959) carried out an early case study of an American factory. He was particularly interested in eliciting the perspectives of middle managers.

He reports that he was very pleased that, in the early stages of his research, he was approached by several managers prepared to tell him their stories. However, he then started to reflect on what these early informants shared in common and compared it with the background information he could gather on other managers. It turned out that the keen informants tended to be managers whose position and prospects within the firm were the most marginal. In brief, they were keen to talk to Dalton because nobody else wanted to hear their stories!

Dalton used this insight to study the resources which gave different managers leverage at the firm. He began to see that power worked through a clique structure in which groups of managers with similar access to resources used collective tactics to oppose (or bring about) particular changes which favoured their own clique.

Dalton's study reveals the benefits of a self-critical approach. Rather than treat the accounts of willing informants as 'inside dope' on what was really going on at the firm, Dalton reflected on their motivation and, as a consequence, obtained a much broader understanding of the links between control over resources and managers' behaviour. In doing so, like Douglas, he made a theoretical contribution (in Dalton's case, a theory about how cliques work within management).

15.3.3   Thinking about appropriate research methods

Like Douglas, Moerman is an anthropologist interested in how a people categorized their world. Moerman (1974) studied the Lue tribe of Northern Thailand.

First, Moerman learnt the local language and then he started to interview Lue people. Like many Western ethnographers, he was interested in how his people saw themselves and how they distinguished themselves from other peoples. As a result of his interviews, Moerman assembled a set of traits which seemed to describe the Lue.

At this stage, like Dalton, he thought critically about the status of his data. Put in its simplest terms, what does it mean when you answer the questions of a visiting ethnographer? Imagine someone coming to your town and asking you to identify your 'group'. You could certainly do it but it would be an unusual activity of self-reflection. Surely most of the time we manage to live our lives without unduly worrying about our identities? As Moerman put it:

> To the extent that answering an ethnographer's question is an unusual situation for natives, one cannot reason from a native's answer to his *normal* categories or ascriptions. (1974: 66, my emphasis)

Moerman now started to see that perhaps he had been asking the wrong kind of questions. He had been using interviews to answer the question: 'Who are the Lue?' But a more interesting question was when, if at all, the people being studied actually invoke ethnic identities.

So Moerman changed his research question to: 'When are the Lue?' This meant abandoning interviews and using observation and audio recording of the people in question engaged in 'ordinary' events like going to market. In such **naturally occurring** contexts, one could observe when (and with what consequences) people living in these Thai villages actually invoked ethnic identification labels.

By thinking critically about the relation between his research methods and research problems, Moerman rightly moved away from a conventional ethnographic research design.

15.3.4 *Making a practical contribution*

Unlike the three earlier studies, Suchman (1987) gathered data through a VCR. However, like Moerman, her method was entirely appropriate to her research problem.

Suchman was interested in the highly practical issue of how people use photocopying machines. Her video recordings revealed that most people's behaviour bore little relation to the user's manual provided by the manufacturer. This was seen most clearly in the troubles that many users had in effectively responding when an order to the machine had produced an unexpected response and the user wanted to abort or repair an activity in which the machine had engaged. People's behaviour could exhibit a variety of actions which from the user's perspective turned out to be ineffective. However, from a design point of view, the machine was acting quite properly.

Suchman's study has clear practical implications. It suggests the constructive role of users' troubles in system design. As she notes, based on this kind of research, expert systems may seek not to eliminate users' errors but 'to make them accessible to the user, and therefore instructive' (Suchman, 1987: 184).

Having cited a number of classic studies, I now want to present a more critical evaluation of some more recent research. As before, however, my evaluation will be based on the four criteria set out in Table 15.3.

15.4 APPLYING QUALITY CRITERIA

For convenience, I have simply selected the four papers reporting research studies in the last two 1996 issues of the US journal *Qualitative Health Research* (QHR). The Editor of QHR, Janice Morse, has a nursing background and many of its contributors are in university nursing departments. This nursing focus distinguishes QHR from other journals like *Sociology of Health and Illness* and *Social Science & Medicine*, although its explicit concern with practice has a parallel with *Social Sciences in Health*.

The contents of these papers can, therefore, only offer a taste of the kind of work that counts as qualitative health research, let alone qualitative research in general. Furthermore, such a 'taste' does not allow inspection of the deviant cases that I recommend below as a feature of good research practice. However, these papers allow me to develop a coherent focus with implications which extend well beyond health research.

15.4.1 *Women's process of recovery from depression*

Schreiber (1996) describes an interview study with a snowball sample of twenty-one women who identified themselves as having recovered from depression. She sets out to establish an account of the depression experience which, she claims, is 'grounded in the real world of the participant' (1996: 471). This 'real world', we are told, contains six 'phases' of '(re)defining the self', each with between three and five 'properties' or 'dimensions'.

Schreiber's discussion of her methodology shows some concern for the quality of her research. Like many researchers with an academic appointment in nursing, she holds up Glaser and Strauss's (1967) account of **grounded theory** as a *sine qua non* of good qualitative research (see Chapter 7). Indeed, three of the four papers I am considering here mentioned grounded theory at some point – usually as a central reference.

Following the logic of grounded theory, Schreiber searched her data for subjects' categories and only stopped when her analysis became 'saturated' because no new information about the emerging theory was forthcoming (1996: 472). These findings were then fed back to the participants and revised accordingly.

However, in my view, a number of problems remain with what we are told about this research and I set these out below:

1   This was a retrospective study. This problem is recognized by the researcher who comments that the first phase ('My Self Before') 'is only seen upon

reflection' (Schreiber, 1996: 474). Such recognition might have led her to abandon her claim to access the depression experience.[1] But instead Schreiber is satisfied with the rather glib assertion that 'there is merit in hearing the women's understandings of the people they were at the time' (ibid.). What merit, we might ask? Moreover, despite the fragile status of her data, she has no hesitation in setting out to search for external causes of these accounts (1996: 489).

2   Schreiber presents extracts from her data. But, in place of analysis, we are simply presented with a commonsense précis of what each respondent said followed by an apparently arbitrary label. This gives the paper an anecdotal feel and makes this reviewer wonder why one needs social science skills to write this kind of report.

3   Of course, it is not difficult to find instances that fit a given set of categories. Despite this, this paper does not report deviant cases although such reporting and subsequent analysis is a central feature of grounded theory.

4   I am uncertain from where Schreiber is claiming her categories (phases and dimensions) derive. It is unclear whether these are the women's categories ('the recovery process was described by the women in this study as ...' (1996: 473)) or the researcher's. If the latter, the author gives no hint of the relevant social science theories from which her categories might derive (e.g. a theory of self-definition). If the former, then one wonders at the lack of analytic nerve which treats research as simply reporting what respondents tell you (see my comments in Chapter 4 on 'going beyond a list' and Gilbert and Mulkay, 1983).

15.4.2   Urban healers

Engebretson (1996) reports a participant observation and interview study of three groups of healers who 'heal' through the laying on of hands. She locates her findings in terms of three 'dimensions' (setting, interaction and cognitive process) and finds, unsurprisingly, that such healing differed from biomedicine on each of these dimensions.

Although she mentions no explicit theory and, unlike Schreiber, has no explicit quality controls, Engebretson does strengthen the **reliability** of her account by detailed ethnographic description. Through it, we learn about the setting, how healing was organized and how the sessions were opened and closed. All of this description has at least the potential to suggest practical relevance. However, three problems remain with the observational data presented:

1   No data extracts are given (presumably what occurred was not taped and, for some reason, the researcher's field notes are not made available). This means that the reader has no basis to contest the researcher's account.

2   No mention is made of the system used for recording field notes and its impact on the reliability of her data (see Chapter 14).

3   Like Schreiber's study, the account of the data is presented just as a simple description. Without a discussion of the analytic basis for the researcher's account, her report once more can only have a journalistic status.[2]

Again, like Schreiber, Engebretson groups her interview respondents' accounts into a number of categories (in this case, physical sensations, emotional experiences and visual images). But there is nothing to suggest that these are anything but *ad hoc* labels without a clear analytical basis (see the discussion in Chapter 13 of using categories in **CAQDAS**). Again the chosen extracts simply illustrate her argument and no deviant cases are provided or explored.

15.4.3   Quality care in the hospital

Irurita (1996) describes semi-structured interviews with a sample of ten patients (1–2 weeks after discharge) and ten nurses from the same hospital wards. Respondents were asked about what they saw as the nature and causes of 'quality care'.

According to the author, patients saw themselves as 'vulnerable' and described what they and the nurses did to preserve patient 'integrity'. Nurses described the time and resource constraints which limited them providing such care.

Like Schreiber, Irurita locates her research within the approach of grounded theory, particularly through her attempt at the constant comparative method. Like many interview researchers, she reports the use of a qualitative software program (in her case ETHNOGRAPH). Moreover, she argues that an important quality control was the separation of the studies of nurses and patients and because theory was built as 'an ongoing process' (Irurita, 1996: 346). Nonetheless, in my view, three serious quality problems remain:

1   Is 'quality care' a normative or a participants' category? Irurita's account of her research findings is unclear about this but her abstract implies that she accepts a **normative** category without question.[3]
2   The interview protocol is not provided and, unlike Schreiber, no extracts from the interviews are given. Hence the reader is in no position to know how 'quality care' was investigated nor how the researchers analysed data.
3   No analytic basis behind the researcher's selection of categories is given (e.g. 'preserving integrity' is presented as a simple description of what respondents said, not, for instance, in relation to Goffman's (1961) account of identity in total institutions). Hence the findings appear, once more, to be journalistic.

15.4.4   Perinatal cocaine crack-users

Pursley-Crotteau and Stern (1996) report a longitudinal interview study with nine female crack-users during and after their pregnancies. The longitudinal

TABLE 15.4   SOME DEFECTS IN SELECTED QUALITATIVE STUDIES

They tend to be atheoretical:

- categories are usually participants' own or are *ad hoc* and commonsensical,
  i.e. journalistic
- **normative** concepts are sometimes accepted unproblematically

They use unreliable data:

- only tidied-up data extracts are given (no interviewers' questions, no indication of
  how far a particular answer had to be extracted from a respondent, e.g. after a pause
  or a monosyllabic initial response)
- data extracts are sometimes replaced by researchers' 'summaries'

The analysis can be of doubtful validity:

- no deviant cases
- some accounts are retrospective

research design allows a solution to the problem of retrospective accounts not found in Schreiber's study.

Moreover, these researchers make a real attempt to establish an analytic framework (based upon 'four dimensions of temperance') with which to make sense of how such women struggle with addiction.[4] Thus, unlike the other three studies, this paper does not simply offer lists of (commonsense) categories but combines them into an analytic scheme which holds out the possibility of generating **formal theories** of the kind that Glaser and Strauss (1967) recommend and which may well have practical relevance.

Unfortunately, Pursley-Crotteau and Stern (1996) do not, in my view, avoid some of the defects of the other studies. In particular:

1   Data extracts are treated as having a self-evident meaning and no **deviant cases** are discussed (see Chapter 14).
2   The question(s) which provoked the interviewee's response are not given.
3   An atheoretical reading of grounded theory is offered. For instance, the researchers suggest that grounded theory 'is used to discover the problem from the point of view of the actors' (1996: 352). But if this is all that research does, how is it different from 'human interest' journalism or indeed Oprah Winfrey?

Obviously, from my own perspective, I have found many defects, as well as some good points, in these examples of qualitative research. Table 15.4 summarizes my criticisms.

Having given these examples of the failings (and successes) of several qualitative research studies, the rest of this chapter will contain some positive proposals about each of the four 'quality' issues identified earlier.

15.5 FOUR QUALITY ISSUES REVISITED

15.5.1 *Analytic Depth*

> How far can we demonstrate that our research has mobilized the conceptual apparatus of our social science disciplines and, thereby, helped to build useful social theories?

A continuing theme of my critiques above was that these researchers tended to describe their data in terms of sets of categories which either reproduced participants' categories or put a commonsense gloss upon them. Although it is arguable that this is a proper first-stage procedure within grounded theory, Glaser and Strauss (1967) make clear that such description cannot itself build theories. To do so, we need to move beyond *ad hoc* labels and redefine our data within a well-articulated analytic scheme.

As we saw above, one of the strengths of Pursley-Crotteau and Stern's (1996) account of pregnant crack-users is precisely that it attempts to establish an analytic framework (based upon 'four dimensions of temperance') with which to make sense of how such women struggle with addiction. In this way, categories are combined into an analytic scheme in order to generate what Glaser and Strauss (1967) would call a 'formal' theory.

As I argue in Chapter 7, a theory is best understood as a set of concepts used to define and/or explain some phenomenon. A criterion for adopting a theory is its usefulness.

The following examples illustrate this sense of theory in sociology and anthropology:

- Using an **interactionist** theory concerned with 'labelling', awareness of dying is related to a set of 'awareness contexts' (Glaser and Strauss, 1968).
- Using a **structuralist** theory of the nature of binary oppositions, an African tribe's favourable response to an anteater is used to build a theory about the relation between perceived 'anomalies' and the experience of crossing boundaries (Douglas, 1975).
- Using a **discourse analytic** theory of the active use of language, scientists' accounts of their work are shown to function in local contexts (Gilbert and Mulkay, 1983).
- Using an **ethnomethodological** theory of accounting practices, the 'cause' of 'suicide' is to be found in the commonsense judgments of coroners (Atkinson, 1978).

Without the active employment of these and other theories, we are bound to lapse into *ad hoc* use of commonsense interpretations and may, like Irurita's (1996) appeal to the label 'quality care', even smuggle **normative** concepts into our data analysis. However, like many other people researching issues that affect our daily lives, health researchers may have two particular difficulties in thinking theoretically. First, their preference for the study of 'people' rather than, say, **variables** may lead to the pursuit of a kind of 'empathy' which does not permit sufficient distance. Second, if you research an area like health, which generates so many pressing social problems, it may sometimes be difficult to look beyond what your commonsense knowledge tells you about the 'meaning' of social situations.

How, then, can we aid our sluggish imaginations to think theoretically about data? In Chapter 6, I discussed how social science theory building can benefit from four types of sensitivity: historical, cultural, political and contextual. I shall return to the question of whether such theoretically guided research can have a greater practical relevance as well as building a better social science. For the moment, I will turn to my second 'quality' issue.

15.5.2 Why should we believe qualitative research?

How far can our data, methods and findings satisfy the criteria of reliability and validity or, put more crudely, counter the cynic who comments 'Sez you'?

If we argue for the pre-eminence of analytic issues in research, the implication might follow that the sole requirement for any research study is analytic integrity. This would mean that the **validity** of a piece of qualitative research could be settled simply by asserting its pristine, theoretical roots.

Along these lines, it is sometimes suggested that the assessment of the quality of qualitative data should transcend the conventional methodological approaches. The quality of qualitative research, it is argued:

cannot be determined by following prescribed formulas. Rather its quality lies in the power of its language to display a picture of the world in which we discover something about ourselves and our common humanity. (Buchanan, 1992: 133)

If Buchanan is saying that the main question in field research is the quality of the analysis rather than the recruitment of the sample or, say, the format of the interview, then I would agree (see Mitchell, 1983). However, Buchanan's opposition to 'prescribed formulas' can amount to something which might be called 'methodological anarchy' (see Clavarino et al., 1995).

How far do you want to go with such anarchism? First, does it make sense to argue that all knowledge and feelings are of equal weight and value? Even in everyday life, we readily sort 'fact' from 'fancy'. Why, therefore, should science be any different? Second, methodological anarchy offers a clearly negative message to research-funding agencies: that is, don't fund qualitative research because even its proponents have given up claims to reliability and validity. Moreover, in such an environment, can we wonder that qualitative research's potential audiences (e.g. the medical professions, corporations, trade unions) take its 'findings' less than seriously?

TABLE 15.5   TYPE OF RESEARCH METHOD (QHR)

	Articles	
	Number	**% of total**
Qualitative interviews	65	71
Other methods	26	29

Source: Qualitative data articles in *Qualitative Health Research*, 1991–6; $n = 91$

The reliability of our data should be a central concern of any research. Attempts to bypass this issue by appealing to the different philosophical position of qualitative research (e.g. Marshall and Rossman, 1989) are unconvincing. As others have recently pointed out:

> Qualitative researchers can no longer afford to beg the issue of reliability. While the forte of field research will always lie in its capability to sort out the validity of propositions, its results will (reasonably) go ignored minus attention to reliability. For reliability to be calculated, it is incumbent on the scientific investigator to document his or her procedure. (Kirk and Miller, 1986: 72)

In Chapter 14, I examined in detail methods for improving the validity, reliability and generalizability of qualitative research. I now turn to my third 'quality' issue.

15.5.3   *Only interviews?*

> To what extent do our preferred research methods reflect careful weighing of the alternatives or simple responses to time and resource constraints or even an unthinking adoption of the current fashions?

In 1996, while writing a paper for a methodology conference, I did a crude survey of recently published research-based articles which used qualitative methods. In my own sub-specialty, the sociology of health, the preference for the open-ended interview was overwhelming. Table 15.5 is based on articles in QHR.

Table 15.5 is consistent with the four non-randomly selected health research articles discussed above, all of which used interviews as their sole (or main) method. The skewing towards qualitative interviews in QHR probably reflects the fact, already noted, that many of the authors are in nursing where the open-ended interview is regarded as both an appropriate research technique and a preferred model of communicating with the patient.

Of course, we should not make too much of findings based on such a tiny and perhaps unrepresentative data set. Nonetheless, Table 15.5 may not be strikingly out of line with the preference for interview-based qualitative research found in the articles published in the more mainstream journals.

TABLE 15.6   TYPE OF RESEARCH METHOD (*SOCIOLOGY*)

	Articles	
	Number	**% of total**
Qualitative interviews	27	55
Other methods	22	45

Source: Qualitative data articles in *Sociology*, 1991–6; *n* = 49

To test out this hypothesis, I turned to the journal of the British Sociological Association called *Sociology*. My findings are set out in Table 15.6.

Table 15.6 shows a preference for the use of the interview method in qualitative papers published in *Sociology*. Although the proportion is only 55:45 per cent given that the category 'other methods' lumps together every other non-interview-based qualitative method, the interview method clearly predominates as the single most preferred method.

Other social sciences may vary in the extent of use made of the interview method. Anthropologists, for instance, may pay relatively more attention to observational methods (but see my discussion of Moerman's study above). However, I suspect that the choice of the open-ended interview as the gold standard of qualitative research is pretty widely spread. For example, information systems (IS) is a discipline which studies the human consequences of information technology. In preparing a recent talk to an IS conference, I surveyed the methodologies chosen in research articles published in a number of recent IS journals. Of the six qualitative research articles, five were derived from interviews.

I have discussed elsewhere the possible cultural roots of this phenomenon in the context of an **interview society** (Atkinson and Silverman, 1997). At the present, I am more concerned with its methodological impact.

In interviews, as Heritage puts it, the mistake is to treat the verbal formulations of subjects 'as an appropriate substitute for the observation of actual behaviour' (1984, 236). Drew and Heritage (1992) show how this has a direct impact on the kind of data we think are relevant. Most qualitative researchers use such data as interviews, focus groups and diaries. They thus attempt 'to get inside the "black box" of social institutions to gain access to their interior processes and practices' (1992: 5). However, such studies may suffer from two problems:

- the assumption of a stable reality or context (e.g. the 'organization') to which people respond
- the gap between beliefs and action and between what people say and what they do (Webb and Stimson, 1976; Gilbert and Mulkay, 1983).

Qualitative researchers' preference for interview studies ironically respects a division of labour preferred by quantitative researchers. According to this division, while quantitative research focuses on objective structures, it falls to qualitative researchers to give 'insight' into people's subjective states.

The unfortunate consequence of this division of labour is that *both* approaches neglect a great deal about how people interact. Put more strongly, both kinds of research are fundamentally concerned with the environment around the phenomenon rather than the phenomenon itself.

Moreover, we need to question the argument that observational or other naturally occurring data is 'unavailable' in the supposedly 'private' sphere of human interaction (e.g. in domestic life).

As Gubrium and Holstein have noted:

> The formulations of domestic order that we hear outside households are treated as authentic as are those heard within them. … . As a practical matter, this means that the analyst would treat *private* and *public* as experiential categories – constructed and oriented to by interacting persons – not actual geographic or social locations … . [This implies that] methodologically, we should not take for granted that privacy implies privileged access – that those occupying the private sphere are taken to be experts on its description, the final arbiters of its meaning. (Gubrium and Holstein, 1995: 205)

Such a situation suggests that we need to look twice at the unthinking identification of the open-ended interview as the 'gold standard' of qualitative research (see my discussion of naturally occurring data in Chapter 8). Note that this is not to reject each and every interview study. I merely suggest that the choice of any research instrument needs to be defended and that the pursuit of people's 'experience' by no means constitutes an adequate defence for the use of the open-ended interview.

I now turn to my final 'quality' point.

15.5.4   *Research and practitioners*

> How can valid, reliable and conceptually-defined studies of health care processes contribute to practice and policy by revealing something new to practitioners, clients and/or policy-makers?

Research instruments, like interviews, focus groups and questionnaires, which ask respondents to provide facts, attitudes or experiences, have an important part to play in areas like health which affect us all. In particular, they can give policy-makers a reasonable sense how, at one moment of time, their clients are responding to a particular service (see Chapters 17 and 28). Moreover, unlike observational or **conversation analytic** studies, interview studies can be completed relatively quickly and, in this sense, can give rapid 'answers'.

Unfortunately, as I have already suggested, some qualitative interview studies may lack the analytic imagination to provide anything more than anecdotal 'insights'. When there are also legitimate doubts about the rigour of the data analysis, then I suggest that policy-makers and practitioners should doubt the quality of the 'answers' such research provides.

One response might be to return to purely quantitative research, given the serious attention it usually pays to issues of reliability and validity. Indeed, if the only alternative was *impressionistic* qualitative research, I would certainly always back quantitative studies such as well-designed questionnaires or randomized control trials.

However, this is not the only alternative. As already suggested, both the 'in-depth' accounts apparently provided by the 'open-ended' interview and the seemingly unequivocal measures of information retention, attitude and behaviour that we obtain via laboratory or questionnaire methods have a tenuous basis in what people may be saying and doing in everyday contexts.

Take the case of general practice consultations. In an interview study of patients involved in fifty British GP consultations, Webb and Stimson (1976) noted how doctors were routinely portrayed as acting insensitively or with poor judgement. By contrast, patients presented themselves as having acted rationally and sensibly.

As Webb and Stimson (1976) imply, we only get into difficulties if we treat patients' responses as standing in a one-to-one account with what happened in the actual consultation. This is not to suggest that these patients were lying. Rather, by telling 'atrocity stories', Webb and Stimson suggest that patients were able to give vent to thoughts which had gone unvoiced at the time of the consultation, to redress a real or perceived inequality between doctor and patient and to highlight the teller's own rationality. Equally, atrocity stories have a dramatic form which captures the hearer's attention – a point of which qualitative researchers become aware when asked to give brief accounts of their findings.

As I have commented elsewhere:

> Stimson and Webb are rejecting the assumption that lay accounts can do the work of sociological explanations. [They do not] want to take the actor's point of view as an explanation because this would be to equate commonsense with sociology – a recipe for the lazy field researcher. Only when such a researcher moves beyond the gaze of the tourist, bemused with a sense of bizarre cultural practices ('Goodness, you do things differently here'), do the interesting analytic questions begin. (Silverman, 2001: 289)

To underline my earlier point, this is not to suggest that interview studies of patient satisfaction have *no* place in health research. Rather, it implies that such studies must be supplemented by data on what actually happens in the consultation itself. Fortunately, from the pioneering work of Byrne and Long (1976) through to Heath's (2004) precise analysis of videos of the consultation, this is what we now possess. Because of this work, practitioners and clients can be informed of interactional skills they did not know they possessed and of communication dilemmas of which they may have been unaware (see also Silverman, 1987: Chapter 8). Moreover, policy-makers can make decisions on far fuller evidence than provided by simple records of respondents' 'opinions' or 'attitudes'.

A further bonus of studying communication *in situ* is that both findings and raw data can be valuable resources in training practitioners. Although the researcher cannot tell practitioners how they should behave, understanding the intended and unintended consequences of actions can provide the basis for a fruitful dialogue.

15.6 CONCLUDING REMARKS

The ability to evaluate published research is a key skill which will help you to locate gaps in the field which can inspire your own research and to write your literature review (see Chapter 21). In this chapter, I have critically assessed four published qualitative research articles using four criteria of 'quality':

1 How far can we demonstrate that our research has mobilized the conceptual apparatus of our social science disciplines and, thereby, helped to build useful social theories?
2 How far can our data, methods and findings satisfy the criteria of reliability and validity or, put more crudely, counter the cynic who comments 'Sez you'?
3 To what extent do our preferred research methods reflect careful weighing of the alternatives or simple responses to time and resource constraints or even an unthinking adoption of the current fashions?
4 How can valid, reliable and conceptually defined studies of health care processes contribute to practice and policy by revealing something new to practitioners, clients and/or policy-makers?

KEY POINTS

Good-quality research satisfies the following criteria:

- It thinks theoretically through and with data.
- It develops empirically sound, reliable and valid findings.
- It uses methods which are demonstrably appropriate to the research problem.
- Where possible, it contributes to practice and policy.

NOTES

1   Abandoning the claim that interview accounts directly represent 'experience' need not be disastrous to interview research, as I show elsewhere (Silverman, 2001: 110–14). As Gubrium and Holstein (1997) point out, we can say analytically and practically interesting things about interviews analysed as locally structured narrative forms.

2   This is not to criticize journalism which, at its best, can be highly illuminating. It is simply intended to distinguish between journalism and social science.

3   Note how 'quality care' gets defined is not treated as problematic in the following sentence: 'The delivery of quality care, although acknowledged as being vital to health care systems, is a complex, poorly understood phenomenon' (Irurita, 1996: 331).

4

<table>
<tr><td></td><td></td><td colspan="2" align="center">HAVING DESIRE</td></tr>
<tr><td></td><td></td><td align="center">+</td><td align="center">–</td></tr>
<tr><td rowspan="2">HAVING
STRUCTURE</td><td align="center">+</td><td>HOLDING ONTO
THE LIFELINE</td><td>MESSIN' UP</td></tr>
<tr><td align="center">–</td><td>GOIN' IT ALONE</td><td>DANCIN' WITH
THE DEVIL</td></tr>
</table>

FIGURE 15.1   FOUR DIMENSIONS OF TEMPERANCE

Source: adapted from Pursley-Crotteau and Stern (1996: 360)

Further reading

State-of-the-art accounts of qualitative research which fit the criteria discussed in this chapter are to be found in David Silverman's (ed.) *Qualitative Research: Theory, Method and Practice* (Sage, 2004). Martin Barker's recent paper 'Assessing the "quality" in qualitative research: the case of text-audience relations' (*European Journal of Communication*, 18 (3), 315–35, 2003) applies the criteria set out in Table 15.3 to research in cultural studies. Good treatments of theoretically inspired but rigorous qualitative research are: Pertti Alasuutari's *Researching Culture: Qualitative Method and Cultural Studies* (Sage, 1995); Jennifer Mason's *Qualitative Researching* (Sage, 1996); Amanda Coffey and Paul Atkinson's *Making Sense of Qualitative Data* (Sage, 1996); and Anselm Strauss and Juliet Corbin's *Basics of Qualitative Research* (Sage, 1990). The various theoretical traditions that comprise qualitative research are skilfully dissected in Jaber Gubrium and James Holstein's *The New Language of Qualitative Method* (Oxford University Press, 1997). Gary Marx's paper, 'Of methods and manners for aspiring sociologists: 37 moral imperatives' (*The American Sociologist*, Spring 1997, 102–25), is a lively and extremely helpful short guide for the apprentice researcher.

Exercise 15.1

Select a qualitative research study in your own area. Now go through the following steps:

1   Review the study in terms of the quality criteria set out in Table 15.3 (if you prefer, you may use the criteria in Table 15.1 or 15.2).

2   If the study fails to satisfy all these criteria, consider how it could have been improved to satisfy them.

3   Consider to what extent these criteria are appropriate to your area. Are there additional or different criteria which you would choose?

Keeping in Touch

In Part Four, I address ways of keeping in touch with your data, with subjects 'in the field' and with your university department. In four chapters, I discuss record keeping (including a research diary), relations in the field (including ethical issues), making good use of your supervisor and how to get feedback about your research.

Keeping a Record

16.1 INTRODUCTION

Record keeping seems like a very dull activity. It may conjure up a picture of boring account books or even of Dickensian clerks with wing collars poring over ledgers in a gloomy nineteenth-century office.

In this short chapter, I will try to convince you that good record keeping is not a dull and lonely activity but a fruitful, even enjoyable, way of establishing a dialogue with other people. It should be noted that these other people include yourself and your thoughts as they were a few years, months or even days ago.

The two principal areas of record keeping discussed below are:

- a record of your reading
- a research diary.

16.2 RECORDING YOUR READING

By the time you begin a research degree, it is likely that you will have learned the habit of keeping your reading notes in a word-processed file, organized in terms of (emerging) topics. I stress 'reading notes' because it is important from the start that you do *not* simply collate books or photocopies of articles for 'later' reading but read as you go. Equally, your notes should not just consist of chunks of written or scanned extracts from the original sources but represent your ideas on the *relevance* of what you are reading for your (emerging) research problem.

So read critically. Don't just copy chunks of material. Strauss and Corbin (1990: 50–3, adapted here) suggest that the existing literature can be used for five purposes in qualitative research:

1 *To stimulate theoretical sensitivity* 'providing concepts and relationships that (can be) checked out against (your) actual data'.
2 *To provide secondary sources of data* to be used for initial trial runs of your own concepts and topics.
3 *To stimulate questions during data gathering and data analysis.*
4 *To direct theoretical sampling* to 'give you ideas about where you might go to uncover phenomena important to the development of your theory'.
5 *To be used as supplementary validation* to explain why your findings support or differ from the existing literature.

Following Strauss and Corbin, you should always approach any publication with a set of questions, for instance:

● What are the relevant findings?
● What are the relevant methodologies?
● What are the relevant theories?
● What are the relevant hypotheses?
● What are the relevant samples?
● What is the relevance to how I now see my research problem?
● What possible new directions for my research are implied?

Exercise 16.1 gives you an opportunity to test out your skills in using the existing literature to help you in your own research. It emphasizes that we should never read such literature without having formulated some prior set of questions.

It goes without saying that you should use a consistent system for referencing authors and other details of the material you are reading. The Harvard method of referencing is usually the system chosen. This involves entering an author's surname, followed by date of publication and any page reference in your main text as below:

Abrams (1984: 2); Agar (1986: 84)

By using this method, you can save footnotes for substantial asides rather than for (boring) references. Detailed references are then appended in a bibliography with the form set out below:

Abrams, P. (1984) 'Evaluating soft findings: some problems of measuring informal care', *Research Policy and Planning*, 2 (2), 1–8.
Agar, M. (1986) *Speaking of Ethnography*, Qualitative Research Methods Series, Vol. 2, London: Sage.

In Chapter 21, I discuss how such records of your reading can be integrated into the literature review chapter of your thesis. When you come to write that chapter, ideally towards the *end* of your research, you will have all the relevant material on file. But, just as important, you will also have a record of your changing thoughts about the literature and its relevance to your emerging research topic.

16.3 RESEARCH DIARIES

We commonly find the sense of the past in the present. Such **rewriting of history** (Garfinkel, 1967) means that, unless you are careful, you may forget important aspects of your early thinking about your research which may be crucial to your readers' understanding. One way to ensure that you spell out your reasoning is to keep a research diary.

This will avoid presenting the reader with an apparently 'seamless web' of ideas which conceals the development of your thinking with all its setbacks and dead ends. In this way:

> the text can be like a detective story, where one presents these kinds of "false leads" until they are revealed to be dead-ends. (Alasuutari, 1995: 192)

Another danger with the 'seamless web' picture of research is that it can conceal various tricks, sleights of hand and simple mistakes through which you reach your conclusions. Keeping proper records, including a research diary, helps to make your reasoning transparent – to yourself as well as to your readers. In this spirit, Huberman and Miles call for:

> careful retention, in easily retrievable form, of all study materials, from raw field notes through data displays and final report text. (1994: 439)

Keeping such careful records means that you will be amassing material that can form a substantial part of the methodology chapter of your thesis (see Chapter 22). It also implies an open-minded and critical approach to your research. This is what Huberman and Miles mean by 'a reflexive stance'. It involves:

> regular, ongoing, self-conscious documentation – of successive versions of coding schemes, of conceptual arguments of analysis … episodes – both successful ones and dead ends. (ibid.)

In Table 16.1 I summarize the uses of a research diary.

As an example of the kind of material that can be put into a research diary, here is an extract from the diary of Vicki Taylor who completed her PhD under my supervision:

TABLE 16.1   WHY KEEP A RESEARCH DIARY?

1	To show the reader the development of your thinking
2	As an aid to reflection
3	To help improve your time management
4	To provide ideas for the future direction of your work
5	To use in the methodology chapter of your thesis

Source: adapted in part from Cryer (1996: 73)

VICKI'S RESEARCH DIARY

JANUARY–MAY 96
Solid progress
Continued transcribing extracts. Also wrote chapter on natural history of the research process (to date), chapter on HIV counselling, chapter on offers sent to DS for comments.

MAY 96
Disaster
Hard disc crashed – lost 2 chapters and some data files that were not backed up!! Also lost draft chapter prepared on offers.

JULY 1–5 96
Conference
Went to 4th international social science methodology conference at Essex university. Set out framework for overall PhD and timetable.

SEPTEMBER 19–21 96
Workshop
Went to CA weekend data workshop organized by Sarah Collins. This was a good experience for me. I came away feeling very confident about my data and the direction of my research.

OCTOBER 96
Despair
Time spent trying to recover data and get transcript back to where had been 6 months previously – disheartened!!

OCTOBER 96 – JANUARY 97
Time out
I felt I had achieved next to nothing since my hard disk crashed in May. I took time out and went to Australia to visit my sick brother,

JANUARY–MAY 97
Starting up again
Transcribed new data – transcripts 10/14/15 and identified other transcripts
for transcription and identified extracts within these. Became interested in
how doctors' clients responded to the offer to see the health adviser. Key
themes: offers of screening tests for other STDs; offers to see the Health
Advisor and offers by doctors/health advisors.

This extract from Vicki's diary covers most of what a research diary should
contain. That is (adapted in part from Cryer, 1996: 74):

- your research activities with dates
- your reading (see below)
- details of data collected
- directions of data analysis including 'special achievements, dead-ends and surprises'
- your own personal reactions
- your supervisor's reactions and suggestions.

It is also possible to write a research diary in a more structured form. For instance,
in ethnographic research it may make sense to distinguish data analysis from the
data itself, using square brackets for analytic observations (Hammersley and
Atkinson, 1983: 164).

In a still more formalized approach, following Glaser and Strauss (1967),
Richardson (2000: 923–49) has suggested that you organize your notes into four
different categories:

1 *Observation notes (ON)* 'fairly accurate renditions of what I see, hear, feel, taste,
   and so on'.
2 *Methodological notes (MN)* 'messages to myself regarding how to collect data'.
3 *Theoretical notes (TN)* 'hunches, hypotheses … critiques of what I am doing/
   thinking/seeing'.
4 *Personal notes (PN)* 'feeling statements about the research, the people I am
   talking to … my doubts, my anxieties, my pleasures'. (2000: 941)

The truism that 'there is no one right method' applies to the keeping of research
diaries as to so many other aspects of research. Whether you use a more or less
structured method of diary keeping, the most important thing about keeping a
research diary is that it will encourage you to be *meticulous* in record keeping and
reflective about your data. As Hammersley and Atkinson comment:

> The construction of such notes … constitutes precisely the sort of internal dialogue,
> or thinking aloud, that is the essence of reflexive ethnography … . Rather than coming

to take one's understanding on trust, one is forced to question *what* one knows, *how* such knowledge has been acquired, the *degree of certainty* of such knowledge, and what further lines of inquiry are implied. (1983: 165)

16.4 CONCLUDING REMARKS

Keeping a record should involve both making an ordered record of your reading and keeping a research diary. In a research diary, you can show your readers the development of your thinking; help your own reflection; improve your time management; and provide ideas for the future direction of your work. As we see in Chapter 22, by keeping a research diary, you also can produce a substantial part of the methodology chapter of your thesis.

KEY POINTS

■ Making notes on your reading should be an active and critical process.
■ Always keep a research diary because what happens to you in the field is a vital source of data.

Further reading

On keeping a record of your reading, see Anselm Strauss and Juliet Corbin's *Basics of Qualitative Research* (Sage, 1990), Chapter 4. Pat Cryer's *The Research Student's Guide to Success* (Open University Press,1996), Chapter 7, is a useful account of why and how to keep a research diary. On keeping more specialized notes about your data, see Richardson (2000) and Strauss and Corbin, Chapter 12.

Exercise 16.1

Below is an extract of around 300 words from my book *Discourses of Counselling: HIV Counselling as Social Interaction.*

1 Read the passage and make notes from it (no more than 200 words) appropriate to a thesis on the nature of professional–client communication.

2 Now repeat the process on the assumption that your thesis topic is 'effective AIDS counselling'.

3   What relevance, if any, does this extract have to your own research? Note that such relevance can be methodological and theoretical as well as substantive. This means that a reading can be useful even if your substantive topic is very different.

Three major points have emerged from this discussion of a small number of post-test counselling interviews. First, following Peräkylä (1995), 'cautiousness' is seen, once more, to be a major feature of HIV counselling. This is true of the activities of both counsellors and clients. Thus, these counsellors seek to align their clients to the disclosure of their test-result, while clients, to whom the character of counselling is presumably 'opaque', often demur at taking any action which might demand an immediate telling of their test-result (or indeed, many other activities, like directly demanding clarification of the validity of HIV-tests) even when, as here, given the right to decide the agenda of their counselling interview. However, these agenda-offers, unlike the alignment strategies discussed by Maynard (1991) and Bergmann (1992), are being used in an environment where the upcoming diagnosis is likely to be heard as 'good'.

Second, we have seen how, when clients respond to agenda-offers by introducing other topics than the test-result (e.g. volunteering statements about themselves or asking, usually indirectly, about the validity of the HIV-test), they seem to 'kick in' standard counselling responses (e.g. information and requests for specification). While such responses are consonant with normative standards of good counselling practice, they are, once again, produced in an environment in which their positioning (prior to the telling of the test-result) may be problematic.

Finally, we have demonstrated that, for at least one client, this delay in telling is problematic. As Ex 7 (and its continuations) showed, this client analysed the delay in the delivery of his test-result as implying that C was about to deliver a 'positive' result – by referring to 'support groups' for HIV-positive people.

This apparent lack of fit between a delayed delivery of the test-result and its content (i.e. as HIV-negative) leads directly into some fairly clear practical implications. (Silverman, 1997: 106)

Relations in the Field

17.1 INTRODUCTION

Qualitative researchers prefer to get close to the people and situations they are studying. What should you make of the weeks and months you spend 'in the field'? How should you respond to the challenges you will find there – are they just irritating troubles or can they be valuable sources of data?

In trying to answer these questions, we find ourselves, somewhat surprisingly, deep in a theoretical minefield. The very meaning of 'relations in the field' will vary according to the model of social research with which you are operating. For instance, as Gubrium and Holstein (1997) point out, while **naturalists** seek to understand the field as 'it really is', **post-modernists** would argue that 'the field' is itself a **narrative** construction, produced by various ways of writing (see Turner, 1989).

The obvious implication is that 'relations in the field' cannot simply be a technical issue to be resolved by technical means. Nevertheless, for ease of presentation, I will begin with some more practical questions, returning to the crucial analytic issues at the end of this chapter.

The following four practical questions are often asked about field research:

- What is involved in obtaining access to a field site?
- What ethical issues lie in wait for me?

- Is feedback to research subjects necessary and/or useful?
- Can I learn anything from relations with subjects in the field?

I discuss below each of these questions. Each question will lead on to the discussion of possible 'solutions' and several case studies will be used for illustration.

17.2 SETTINGS AND ACCESS

Textbook chapters (e.g. Hornsby-Smith, 1993: 53; Walsh, 1998: 224–5) usually distinguish two kinds of research setting:

1 'Closed' or 'private' settings (organizations, deviant groups) where access is controlled by **gatekeepers**.
2 'Open' or 'public' settings (e.g. vulnerable minorities, public records or settings) where access is freely available but not always without difficulty either practical (e.g. finding a role for the researcher in a public setting) or ethical (e.g. should we be intruding upon vulnerable minorities?).

Depending on the contingencies of the setting (and the research problem chosen) two kinds of research access may be obtained:

- 'covert' access without subjects' knowledge
- 'overt' access based on informing subjects and getting their agreement often through gatekeepers.

The impression you give may be very important in deciding whether you get overt access:

> Whether or not people have knowledge of social research, they are often more concerned with what kind of *person* the researcher is than with the research itself. They will try to gauge how far he or she can be trusted, what he or she might be able to offer as an acquaintance or a friend, and perhaps also how easily he or she could be manipulated or exploited. (Hammersley and Atkinson, 1983: 78)

Five ways of securing and maintaining overt access have been noted, as follows.

Impression management
Impression management is to do with the 'fronts' that we present to others (see Goffman, 1959). It involves avoiding giving an impression that might pose an obstacle to access, while more positively conveying an impression appropriate to the situation (see Hammersley and Atkinson, 1983: 78–88). For instance, I have failed to gain access, despite initial expressions of interest, in two settings. In a paediatric clinic in the early 1980s, a very conservatively dressed physician, spotting my

leather jacket, said I was being 'disrespectful of his patients' and threw me out! Fifteen years before that, as a novice researcher, I let slip over lunch that I was thinking of moving from the UK to North America when I had completed my PhD. This attitude was apparently viewed as improperly 'instrumental' by my host organization and the promised access was subsequently refused. The implication of this latter incident is that there is no 'time out' in field relations and that the most apparently informal occasions are times when you will often be judged.

Obtaining 'bottom-up' access

This can sometimes be forgotten at great cost. For instance, in the early 1970s, the access granted by the head of personnel at a large local government organization was put in danger by the fact that I had not explained my aims properly to his subordinates. This underlines the point that access should not be regarded as a once and for all situation.

Being non-judgemental

Being 'non-judgemental' is often a key to acceptance in many settings including informal sub-cultures and practitioners of a particular trade or profession. While the **relativist** tendencies of many social sciences may allow the researcher sincerely to profess non-judgementality on particular groups' values and practices, this is not always the case when you are studying certain forms of professional practice. Indeed to the researchers who think they know something about 'professional dominance' or even just basic communication skills it is very easy to appear judgemental. However, this not only endangers field relations but also espouses a dangerous orthodoxy.

The divine orthodoxy is that people are 'dopes' (see Silverman, 1997: 23-6). Interview respondents' knowledge is assumed to be imperfect; indeed they may even lie to us. In the same way, practitioners (like doctors or counsellors) are assumed always to depart from normative standards of good practice.

Under the remit of the divine orthodoxy, the social scientist is transformed into a philosopher–king (or queen) who can always see through people's claims and know better than they do. Of course, this assumption of superiority to others usually guarantees that access will not be obtained or, if obtained, will be unsuccessful!

Offering feedback

Some research subjects will actually want your judgements – providing they are of an 'acceptable' kind. For instance, business organizations will expect some 'payoff' from giving you access. I discuss what this might involve shortly.

Establishing a contract

Establishing a contract with the people researched may vary from an information sheet, read and agreed by an individual, to a full-blown contract (but see Punch (1986) on post-contract problems).

I have so far avoided discussing 'covert' access, i.e. access obtained without subjects' knowledge. We should not assume that 'covert' access always involves possible offence. For instance, on a course I used to teach, students were asked to observe people exchanging glances in an everyday setting (see Sacks: 1992, Vol. 1: 81–94). Providing the students are reasonably sensitive about this and refrain from staring at others, I do not envisage any problems arising.

However, in other cases, covert observation can lead to severe ethical problems as well as physical danger to the researcher. For instance, Fielding (1982) obtained permission to research a far-right British political party but still felt it necessary to supplement official access with covert observation (see also Back, 2004). In this new situation, he put himself at some potential risk as well as creating ethical dilemmas relating to how much he revealed to his subjects and to outside authorities. It is such ethical issues which I will discuss in the next section.

17.3 ETHICS IN QUALITATIVE RESEARCH

As the German sociologist Weber (1946) pointed out nearly a century ago, all research is contaminated to some extent by the values of the researcher. Only through those values do certain problems get identified and studied in particular ways. Even the commitment to scientific (or rigorous) method is itself, as Weber emphasizes, a value. Finally, the conclusions and implications to be drawn from a study are, Weber stresses, largely grounded in the moral and political beliefs of the researcher.

From an ethical point of view, Weber was fortunate in that much of his empirical research was based on documents and texts that were already in the public sphere. In many other kinds of social science research, ethical issues are much more to the fore. For instance, both qualitative and quantitative researchers studying human subjects ponder over the dilemma of wanting to give full information to subjects but not 'contaminating' their research by informing subjects too specifically about the research question to be studied.

Moreover, when you are studying people's behaviour or asking them questions, not only the values of the researcher but also the researcher's responsibilities to those studied have to be faced.

Mason (1996: 166–7) discusses two ways in which such ethical issues impinge upon the qualitative researcher:

1   The rich and detailed character of much qualitative research can mean intimate engagement with the public and private lives of individuals.
2   The changing directions of interest and access during a qualitative study mean that new and unexpected ethical dilemmas are likely to arise during the course of your research.

TABLE 17.1   WHAT IS INFORMED CONSENT?

- Giving information about the research which is relevant to subjects' decisions about whether to participate
- Making sure that subjects understand that information (e.g. by providing information sheets written in subjects' language)
- Ensuring that participation is voluntary (e.g. by requiring written consent)
- Where subjects are not competent to agree (e.g. small children), obtaining consent by proxy (e.g. from their parents).

Source: adapted from Kent, (1996: 19–20)

Mason suggests that one way to confront these problems is to try to clarify your intentions while you are formulating your research problem. Three ways of doing this are to:

1   Decide what is the purpose(s) of your research, e.g. self-advancement, political advocacy, etc.
2   Examine which individuals or groups might be interested or affected by your research topic.
3   Consider what are the implications for these parties of framing your research topic in the way you have done. (Mason, 1996: 29–30)

Ethical procedures can also be clarified by consulting the ethical guidelines of one's professional association. All such guidelines stress the importance of 'informed consent' where possible (see Punch, 1994: 88–94). The nature of 'informed consent' is set out in Table 17.1.

However, initial consent may not be enough, particularly where you are making a recording. In such cases, it often is proper to obtain further consent to how the data may be used (see Table 17.2).

I have now responded to two of the five questions with which I began, namely:

- What is involved in obtaining access to a field site?
- What ethical issues lie in wait for me?

However, so far, I have provided fairly general answers to these questions. I now want to slow the pace down and give an example of a case study. I hope this will 'flesh out the bare bones' of these important issues.

TABLE 17.2 A SAMPLE CONSENT FORM FOR STUDIES OF LANGUAGE USE

As part of this project, we have made a photographic, audio and/or video recording of you … .
We would like you to indicate below what uses of these records you are willing to consent to.
This is completely up to you. We will only use the records in ways that you agree to.
In any use of these records, names will not be identified.

1 The records can be studied by the research team for use in the research project.
2 The records can be used for scientific publications and/or meetings.
3 The written transcript and/or records can be used by other researchers.
4 The records can be shown in public presentations to non-scientific groups.
5 The records can be used on television or radio.

Source: adapted from ten Have (1998: Appendix C) based on a form developed by Susan Ervin-Tripp, Psychology Department, University of California at Berkeley

17.4 CASE STUDY I

This case study is drawn from my work on HIV counselling (Silverman, 1997: 226–8). It illustrates the changing trajectory of one qualitative research project according to the nature and kind of access and funding and my relations with people 'in the field'.

In 1987, I was given permission to sit in at a weekly clinic held at the Genito-Urinary Department of an English inner-city hospital (Silverman, 1989). The clinic's purpose was to monitor the progress of HIV-positive patients who were taking the drug AZT (Retrovir). AZT, which seems able to slow down the rate at which the virus reproduces itself, was then at an experimental stage of its development.

Like any observational study, the aim was to gather first-hand information about social processes in a **naturally occurring** context. No attempt was made to interview the individuals concerned because the focus was upon what they actually did in the clinic rather than upon what they thought about what they did. The researcher was present in the consulting room at a side-angle to both doctors and patient.

I set out below some of the things that happened during this research using indicative headings.

Making concessions

Patients' consent for the researcher's presence was obtained by the senior doctor who preferred to do it this way (this was effective but was it ethical?). Given the presumed sensitivity of the occasion, tape recording was not attempted. Instead, detailed handwritten notes were kept, using a separate sheet for each consultation. Because observational methods were rare in this area, the study was essentially exploratory.

Giving feedback

Along the way, I also discovered how an ethos of 'positive thinking' was central to many patients' accounts and how doctors systematically concentrated on the 'bodies' rather than the 'minds' of their patients. This led on to some practical questions about the division of labour between doctors and counsellors.

Good luck

About the time I was writing up this research, Kaye Wellings, who then was working for the publicly funded Health Education Authority (HEA), approached me about the possibility of extending my research to HIV counselling. Until that time, the HEA had been funding research on the effectiveness of 'safer sex' messages carried in the mass media. In the light of the explosion in the number of HIV tests in the UK in the late 1980s, Kaye thought it might be useful to take a longer look at the effectiveness of the health promotion messages being delivered in counselling people around the HIV antibody test.

I was interested in such a study for two reasons. First, it was the logical development of my study of medical interviews with AIDS patients. Second, it offered the opportunity to pursue my interest in looking at how communication between professionals and their clients worked out in practice – as opposed to the injunctions of textbooks and training manuals. Consequently, I submitted a research proposal and received funding from the HEA for thirty months beginning in late 1988.

Troubles with access

As it turned out, receiving the funding was only the first part of what became a battle to recruit HIV-testing centres for the research. It must be remembered that the late 1980s were a time when AIDS health workers were being flooded with patients and by requests from researchers anxious to study AIDS care. Apart from such overload, two other factors complicated access. First, obviously, there were the multiple ethical issues involved in studying consultations where patients were asked to reveal the most intimate aspects of their behaviour. Second, extra patients and government worries about the AIDS 'pandemic' had brought sudden huge increases in resources to the previously 'Cinderella' branch of medicine treating patients with sexually transmitted diseases. Following the usual pattern, these resource changes produced 'turf' battles between different professions and different centres involved in the AIDS field (see Silverman, 1990).

All this meant that many months were taken in obtaining research access. One leading British centre turned me down, offering the understandable reason that it was already overloaded with researchers. At another such centre, a doctor gave me access but the counsellors subsequently proved very resistant to my observing or tape recording their HIV consultations. Eventually, a compromise was reached whereby I myself was required to request patients to agree to participate in the research. Predictably, very few agreed in these circumstances.

More luck

Just as I thought that I had been funded for a study that I could never carry out, my luck began to turn. Riva Miller and Robert Bor agreed to offer me access to their counselling work with respectively haemophiliacs and the general population at the Royal Free Hospital (RFH) in London. This was a major breakthrough in two respects. First, Miller and Bor had just produced a major book (Miller and Bor, 1988) on using 'systemic' method in AIDS counselling. Second, Miller and Bor had a video archive of the work of their clinics going back to the early 1980s.

On the basis of my access at the RFH, a major pharmaceuticals company, Glaxo Holdings plc (now GSK) agreed to fund a two-year study (subsequently increased to three years) of the video archive. I was then lucky enough to recruit Anssi Peräkylä from Finland as Glaxo Research Fellow to work on this archive. Anssi had already conducted distinguished ethnographic work in hospital settings. Following his appointment, he more or less taught himself **conversation analysis (CA)** and had finished his PhD on the RFH data in three years, as well as publishing many articles both jointly with me and/or Bor and on his own. Gradually, other centres joined the project and data was also obtained directly from centres in the USA and Trinidad, as well as from Douglas Maynard's US HIV-counselling materials.

Ethical issues again

As the research started to take off, great attention had to be paid to the ethical issues involved. We ended up with a method of recruitment whereby counsellors themselves explained the research to patients (often with the aid of written materials) and invited them to participate. Consent was sought on the understanding that the anonymity of all patients would be strictly protected by concealing their names (and other identifying information) in reports or publications. In addition, only Peräkylä, myself and a limited number of trained researchers and transcribers would have access to the audiotapes. The RFH videotapes were given additional protection – Peräkylä himself transcribed them, so access to them was limited to the two of us and the videos were never to be publicly shown or indeed to leave the premises of the RFH.

The contingency of methodology

In a multiple centre study, I could not, as in my earlier work, be physically present as all the data was gathered. Instead, the audiotapes were simply sent to me by each of the centres for analysis. Soon we were inundated by data to be passed on to our main transcriber, Dr David Greatbatch, himself a distinguished CA researcher.

However, given the high quality of transcription required and our limited resources, it became totally impractical to transcribe all the tapes. Instead, a few interviews were transcribed from each centre. On this basis, what I can best call 'candidate hypotheses' were developed about particular features in the talk, for instance how health advice was delivered and received. Peräkylä and I would then transcribe multiple instances from many more interviews where relevant phenomena seemed to occur.

In this way, the initial hypotheses were refined and subject to the test of **deviant cases** which we actively sought out in our data. Overall, our method had much in common with the method of deviant-case analysis commonly used by anthropologists and ethnographers (see Chapter 13).

Let us now return to the two remaining questions:

● Is feedback to research subjects necessary and/or useful?
● Can I learn anything from relations with subjects in the field?

As we shall see, my case study bears on both these questions.

17.5   FEEDBACK IN CASE STUDIES

> The bottom line for practitioners is always, "So what?" A qualitative researcher's efforts to convey nonjudgemental objectivity is likely to be perceived instead as a typical academic cop-out. (Wolcott, 1990: 59)

In order to address practitioners' 'So what?' question, during and after the research described above, I held many workshops for AIDS counsellors – including many who had not participated in the study. To give some idea of the extent of this 'feedback', between 1989 and 1994 I ran four workshops on the research for counsellors in London (two at hospitals, one at Goldsmiths College and one at The Royal Society of Medicine), as well as three workshops in Australian centres, three in Trinidad and Tobago, and one each in the USA, Finland and Sweden. In addition, each participating centre was given a detailed report of our findings.

At these workshops, we did not shield behind a posture of scientific neutrality. But neither did we seek to instruct counsellors about their presumed 'failings'. Instead, we spoke about the ways in which our data showed that all communication formats and techniques had mixed consequences. We then invited our audience to discuss, in the light of their own priorities and resources, the implications for their practice. Moreover, when asked, we were not afraid to suggest possible practical options.

In my judgement, these meetings were successful, not least because our detailed transcripts showed features of counselling of which the practitioners themselves were often unaware. Often such features revealed how these people were cleverer than they had realized in following their own theoretical precepts and achieving their desired goals.

However, less experienced researchers may be more hesitant to offer feedback to practitioners and organizations. In this case, Wolcott (1990) offers three ideas set out in Table 17.3.

TABLE 17.3 GIVING FEEDBACK TO SERVICE PROVIDERS

1	Ask for the kind of additional information required for you to make a recommendation (e.g. what exactly is the organization trying to accomplish?)
2	Identify seeming paradoxes in the pursuit of goals (e.g. doctors who encourage their patients to communicate and to make choices may be the most autocratic – see below)
3	Identify alternatives to current practices and offer to assess these

Source: Wolcott (1990: 60)

Of course, not all qualitative research is concerned with service providers such as organizations or professional practitioners. What kind of feedback is possible when you are studying non-work-related activities?

It is important that you try to offer feedback to all parties that are under study. So, if your target is, say, the activities of counsellors or doctors, then you have not finished your task without offering some degree of feedback to their clients or patients. One way to do this is to utilize already existing networks, e.g. patients' or community groups. So during my work on paediatric clinics in the early 1980s, I spoke to parents' groups at heart and diabetic clinics. For instance, I used my clinic data to show mothers of diabetic adolescents that their feelings of inadequacy were common and probably inevitable given the guilt-provoking character of diabetic control and the usual rebelliousness of teenagers.

Where it is difficult to find such community groups, you may well find that participants in a study welcome receiving their own transcript of relevant data. For instance, a transcript of your own medical interview may work as a useful reminder of what the doctor said. And a transcript of a life-history interview may give a respondent a tangible autobiographical record.

I now want to move from ethical and practical matters to the methodological issue suggested by my final question:

● Can I learn anything from relations with subjects in the field?

One way of answering this question is to think through how your own identity was viewed by the participants. As the earlier case study showed, my identity and aims as a researcher were viewed differently, in various contexts, by different professionals such as counsellors and doctors and by research funding bodies. However, this was viewed not just as a 'trouble' for the smooth running of the research but also as a source of data about how organizations worked (see also Peräkylä, 1989).

I now want to use the example of gender to examine further what we can learn from our relationships with our subjects. Following some general observations, I will offer a second case study.

17.6   GENDER IN CASE STUDY RESEARCH

Almost all the 'classics' of the Chicago School were written by men, as were those researchers who rose up the academic hierarchy to become full professors (see Warren, 1988: 11). Increasingly, the gender of fieldworkers themselves was seen to play a crucial factor in observational research. Informants were shown to say different things to male and female researchers. For instance, in a study of a nude beach, when approached by someone of a different gender, people emphasized their interest in 'freedom and naturalism'. Conversely, where the researcher was the same gender as the informant, people were far more likely to discuss their sexual interests (Warren and Rasmussen, 1977, reported by Warren, 1988).

In studies which involved extended stays in 'the field', people have also been shown to make assumptions based upon the gender of the researcher. For instance, particularly in rural communities, young, single women may be precluded from participating in many activities or asking many questions. Conversely, female gender may sometimes accord privileged access. For instance, Oboler (1986) reports that her pregnancy increased her rapport with her Kenyan informants, while Warren (1988: 18) suggests that women fieldworkers can make use of the sexist assumption that only men engage in 'important business' by treating their 'invisibility' as a resource. Equally, male fieldworkers may be excluded or exclude themselves from contact with female respondents in certain kinds of situation (see McKeganey and Bloor, 1991).

One danger in all this, particularly in the past, was that fieldworkers failed to report or reflect upon the influence of gender in their fieldwork. For instance, in a study of a large local government organization, we discussed but did not report the different kinds of situations to which the male and female researchers gained easy access (Silverman and Jones, 1976). Moreover, even as the role of doing fieldwork as a woman has become more addressed, hardly any attention has been paid by researchers to questions of male gender (McKeganey and Bloor, 1991: 198).

Nonetheless, as fashions change, it is possible to swing too far and accord gender issues too much importance. As McKeganey and Bloor (1991: 195–6) argue, there are two important issues relevant to the significance of gender in fieldwork. First, the influence of gender may be negotiable with respondents and not simply ascribed. Second, we should resist 'the tendency to employ gender as an explanatory catch-all' (1991: 196).

For instance, McKeganey and Bloor suggest other variables than gender, like age and social class, may also be important in fieldwork. Equally, I would argue, following Schegloff (1991), that we need to demonstrate that participants are actually attending to gender in what they are doing, rather than just work with our intuitions or even with statistical correlations. None of this should imply that it would be correct to swing full circle and, like an earlier generation, ignore gender issues in research. It is incumbent upon fieldworkers to reflect upon the basis and status of their observations. Clearly, how the researcher and the community studied respond to their gender can provide crucial insights into field realities. Indeed, we would do well to become conscious that even taken for granted assumptions may be culturally and historically specific. For instance, Warren suggests that:

> The focal gender *myth* of field research is the greater communicative skills and less threatening nature of the female fieldworker. (1988: 64, my emphasis)

As Warren notes, the important thing is to resist treating such assumptions as 'revealed truths' but as 'accounts' which are historically situated.

The second case study below provides one example of how gender can be relevant to field research.

17.7   CASE STUDY II: GENDER IN EAST AFRICAN FIELDWORK

Using observation coupled with face-to-face and email interviews, Ryen (2004) has been doing fieldwork on East African businesses. In part, she is interested in the activities and identities of entrepreneurs of Asian origin.

Ryen's work involves crossing boundaries in three senses:

- doing fieldwork in different cultures and countries
- studying entrepreneurs whose freewheeling activities do not fit within a 'Western' organizational model
- working as a female researcher with male businessmen who regularly seek to test the boundaries of the relationship.

Extract 17.1 below, from Ryen's field notes, shows how delicate issues can arise in such a context:

Extract 17.1

[We ended a day by a three hour talk in my informant's office. Here is an extract from our conversation]

Mahid: I have some American Rotarian visitors here. We are going out for dinner tonight. May I invite you to the dinner?

Anne: Thank you that would be very nice.

Mahid: Let me pick you up at your hotel.

Anne: Thanks but we have a car and a driver.
[At dinner, Anne finds herself seated next to Mahid. He leans towards her and says softly]

Mahid: Can I invite you out to the disco tomorrow?

Anne: Oh, I have never been to a disco in this region. That would be fun but unfortunately we are leaving tomorrow afternoon.

Ryen reports that such invitations are much more frequent when she is doing fieldwork in East Africa than when studying Western businessmen. Considered purely instrumentally, they represent great opportunities for further ethnographic data and so she is reluctant to dismiss them. At the same time, with the kind of quick footwork seen in Extract 17.1, she establishes clear boundaries, finding 'good' reasons not to accept activities that might categorize a meeting as a 'date'.

When such invitations move towards more explicit 'flirting', matters can become still more delicate as Extract 17.2 from an interview with an Asian businessman (Patel) suggests:

Extract 17.2

Patel: You are like a Sony radio. You know Sony radio?
A: Yes, we had one years back
Patel: I still have it, and you turn it on, and I get turned on (6.0) and then it comes to fine tuning, ohhhhh (4.0) that is exceptionally good (8.0)
A: that is a compliment
Patel: that is exceptionally good
A: even when I am interviewing, eh? (3.0)
Patel: yeah. The fault does not lie with the other party whom you are interviewing. The fault lies in you
A: Oh really? Tell me more
Patel: no, it is not that you do it deliberately. Ah I find you very attractive (3.0)
Patel: alright?
A: thank you. You made my day …
Patel: that's my style. These guys who have probably seen women different ways, they look at you, they probably consider you the goddess
A: (smiling) so you think I should charge them?
Patel: you could actually
A: yes, that's a good idea

Ryen (2004) characterizes what is going on here as 'a light hearted flirt'. By co-operating with Patel's flirtation, Anne turns it into a playful game of mutual responses in rhythm with each other. In doing so, she argues that she can maintain her relationship with her informant in a relaxed, joyful and mutually interesting way.

Ryen's data shows how the researcher needs to work at balancing the closeness and distance present in ethnographic fieldwork. In a sense, she is engaged in 'emotion work'. Such work may not produce 'better' data but may give more data if the result is to prolong the relationship and also give access to data collection in a wider variety of contexts. So this second case study shows how gender may help you learn something from relations with subjects in the field.

Another way in which researchers have attempted to use field relations as data is by seeking and responding to comments made by participants about research conducted upon them. Returning to an issue I first raised in Chapter 14, can responses to feedback be used as a means of validating your research findings?

17.8 FEEDBACK AS A VALIDATION EXERCISE?

Reason and Rowan (1981) criticize researchers who are fearful of 'contaminating their data with the experience of the subject'. On the contrary, they argue, good research goes back to the subjects with the tentative results, and refines them in the light of the subjects' reactions.

This is just what Bloor (1978, 1983) attempted in his research on doctors' decision making. Bloor (1978) discusses three procedures which attempt respondent validation:

1   The researcher seeks to predict members' classifications in actual situations of their use (see Frake, 1964).
2   The researcher prepares hypothetical cases and predicts respondents' responses to them (see also Frake, 1964).
3   The researcher provides respondents with a research report and records their reactions to it.

In his study of doctors' decision making in tonsillectomy cases, Bloor used method 3. However, he had reservations about his surgeons' reactions to his report. It was not clear that they were very interested in findings that were not focused on their day-to-day concerns. Bloor's worries have been very effectively taken up by Fielding and Fielding (1986) (respondent validation is also criticized by Bryman, 1988: 78-9). The Fieldings concede that subjects being studied may   have additional knowledge, especially about the context of their actions. However:

> there is no reason to assume that members have privileged status as commentators on their actions ... such feedback cannot be taken as direct validation or refutation of the observer's inferences. Rather such processes of so–called "validation" should be treated as yet another source of data and insight. (1986: 43)

I can only add that, if feedback is a highly problematic part of validating research, this does *not* mean that it should be ignored as a way of maintaining contact with subjects in the field. However, this issue should not be *confused* with the validation of research findings.

Moreover, as Bloor points out, the problematic research status of this activity need not mean than attempts at respondents' validation have *no* value. They do generate further data which, while not validating the research report, often suggests interesting paths for further analysis (Bloor, 1983: 172).

17.9   CONCLUDING REMARKS

By referring to the function of respondent 'accounts', we are implying a **constructionist** model of how social reality operates. By contrast, **positivists** would be more concerned with how far any account was biased, while **emotionalists** might treat such feedback as adding to the authenticity of the research's findings. This is because, as noted at the outset of this chapter, the issue of 'relations in the field' is riddled with theoretical assumptions.

So the message of this chapter is to treat your forays into 'the field' as a rare opportunity to come to analytic grips with the nitty-gritty of human interaction. This is not merely an exciting (or boring) escape from the rhythms of academic life but a crucial opportunity to discover if your years of education can offer a useful prism through which to re-view what the rest of the world is up to.

KEY POINTS

In this chapter, I discussed how to respond to *four* practical questions in doing fieldwork:

- What is involved in obtaining access to a field site?
- What ethical issues lie in wait for you?
- What can you learn from relations in the field?
- Is feedback to research subjects necessary and/or useful?

Throughout, I emphasized that 'relations in the field' are theoretically saturated. This cannot, therefore, be simply a technical issue to be resolved by technical means.

Further reading

Hammersley and Atkinson (1983: 54–76) provide a useful discussion of the practicalities of obtaining access to individuals, groups and organizations. A more introductory account of these issues, appropriate to the undergraduate researcher, is found in Walsh (2004). Fielding (1982), Ryen (2004) and Back (2004) provide very interesting accounts of the perils of field research in tricky settings. Issues of ethics in qualitative research are well discussed in Jennifer Mason's *Qualitative Researching* (Sage, 1996), Chapters 2, 4 and 8. Peräkylä (1989) and McKeganey and Bloor (1991) provide revealing accounts of the negotiation of identity in fieldwork. Before you contemplate taking your findings back to your subjects, you should read Bloor (1978, 1983).

Exercise 17.1

Consult your research notes on your contacts 'in the field'. Now answer the following questions:

1   What 'successes' and 'troubles' have occurred during your fieldwork?

2   How can you treat such events as data?

3   What theoretical ideas can you use to help you (if you need help, consult Peräkylä, 1989; McKeganey and Bloor, 1991; or Ryen, 2004)?

Exercise 17.2

Make a list of the ethical problems that you have detected in your research. Now explain how you have resolved them.

Then give your account, together with your research diary, to your supervisor or a fellow student. Ask them whether they are satisfied with how you have (a) identified and (b) handled ethical issues.

Making Good Use of Your Supervisor

18.1 INTRODUCTION

Over the past thirty years, around twenty-five students have completed their PhDs under my supervision. I don't know the exact number because the hard disk on my PC crashed not long ago and I lost my CV (a lesson to all of us about the need to back up files!).

I am sure that some students have been happier than others about my supervision. Equally, the enjoyment I derived from the supervision experience varied. In the best cases, the student's work would so stimulate me that I seemed to come up with lots of bright ideas and sparks would fly. On other occasions, I felt quite stupid, bereft of good ideas, maybe, I have to admit, a little bored.

I like to think that the quality of my supervisions improved over the years as I became more experienced and also more selective about which students I chose to supervise. Towards the end of my career, I simply refused to take on anybody whom I had not supervised for their MA. That way, I could ensure that my new PhD students had already learned the way I liked (them) to work.

Now my supervisions are limited to one-off meetings during my PhD workshops, usually in Scandinavian universities with business, sociology and social policy students. The students simply send me a brief summary of their research and a few questions which I try to answer. I hope to stimulate them but, of course, a lot will depend on whether any new ideas will work (or even be appropriate) in their home university and discipline. In this chapter, I want to put my experience to work for you.

The chapter is organized in the following sections:

- supervision horror stories (it may be good to frighten you at the start!)
- student and supervisor expectations
- early stages of supervision
- later stages of supervision
- standards of good practice.

18.2 SUPERVISION HORROR STORIES

The British academic and novelist Malcolm Bradbury has written about 'the three-meeting supervisor' (Bradbury, 1988). The first meeting is when this character informs you about which topic you will study. Three years pass before the next meeting which happens when you deliver your dissertation. The third and final meeting takes place after a telephone call from your supervisor to tell you that he has lost your thesis!

Of course, this story has a farcical element. However, like all good farce, there is an element of truth in it. Back in the 1960s, PhD supervision in many British universities had something of this feel about it – as my own experience as a student demonstrates.

Unfortunately, even today, all is not sweetness and light in the supervision stakes. In Table 18.1, you will find a few recent horror stories adapted from the higher education section of the *Guardian*, a British newspaper, between 2000 and 2003.

I hope that these horror stories do not accord with even the slightest aspect of your own experience. If you are just starting out, let me reassure you that, at least at the present time, such happenings are exceptional, not least because supervisors are usually better trained and are monitored by their departments.

Such stories do, however, underline an important point: when writing a dissertation, a bad outcome usually indicates bad supervision.

Later we will consider standards of good practice. But first let us consider what students and supervisors expect of each other.

18.3 STUDENT AND SUPERVISOR EXPECTATIONS

Estelle Phillips chose as her PhD topic the PhD as a learning process. Some of her findings are reported in Phillips and Pugh (1994). Although her data was obtained in the UK, I have no reason to think that it does not, in general terms, apply elsewhere.

Table 18.2 sets out Phillips' findings about the expectations of PhD students.

All the student expectations shown in Table 18.2 seem quite reasonable to me. If you do not feel that your supervisor is meeting such expectations, it is worth raising your concerns at an early stage.

TABLE 18.1   SUPERVISION HORROR STORIES

- Everything that could possibly have gone wrong, has gone wrong. My supervisor was a bully and I quarrelled with him. We eventually fell out over working arrangements: I was chastised for arriving late in the mornings, though I often worked till 9 pm. I began to suffer from anxiety and depression. I took time off which only made matters worse.
- I was within sight of finishing my PhD when my supervisor changed universities. I was isolated and left to plough on alone with my research. Not that I now saw much less of my supervisor. We had not been on speaking terms for some time and I can't even remember the last time we had a supervision.
- Our department has a very high staff turnover, with most professors leaving in a year or two. I went through three supervisors, each one worse than the last. After my second supervisor left, during my third year, I got someone who knew nothing about my research area. All three supervisors have tried to steer my research towards a topic that they were personally interested in. With each change, there were miscommunications and political manoeuvring to ensure they would not be blamed for lack of progress on my part.
- My supervisor encouraged me to undertake teaching responsibilities, and I ended up leading some of his courses. Off the record, he was sympathetic to my heavy teaching load, but during progress committee meetings he would blame me for too much time spent preparing lectures when I should have been concentrating on research.
- My worst experience, and the one that caused me to leave the university, was a personal one. I got engaged and my supervisor said I could return home to get married if I handed in a first draft of my thesis by April. But then my supervisor changed and my next one refused to give me a leave of absence. I was told the decision was 'in my best interests'.
- I told my supervisor I wanted to complain about his supervision, only to be told: 'You can make a complaint but you won't have a future in science.'
- The department's idea was, if you are not brilliant, get out.
- My experience has taught me that most academics have forgotten what it is like to wonder if one would ever actually do research, or to wonder just how research is done, or not to appreciate how large a contribution needs to be so as to be judged original and how one may go about doing it.
- My supervisor restricted his written comments to 'super', 'well done' and 'perhaps re-work this paragraph'.

Source: adapted from the *Guardian* (Education Section), 25 September 2001, 23 October 2001 and 18 March 2003

However, you should also know that your supervisor will have certain expectations about you. A good guide to how the land lies in this area is found in Table 18.3.

I suspect that Table 18.3 will contain some items that you may never have thought about. But, yes, it is true that supervisors expect you to be fun to be with. Most want to be stimulated by and, indeed, to learn from their students. Such expectations may, of course, be quite different from your experience. I now consider how your expectations can be converted into (good) practice.

TABLE 18.2 STUDENTS' EXPECTATIONS

- to be supervised
- to have their work read well in advance
- supervisors to be available when needed
- to be friendly, open and supportive
- to be constructively critical
- to have a good knowledge of your research area
- to be interested/excited by your topic
- to help you get a good job afterwards

Source: adapted from Phillips and Pugh (1994: Chapter 11)

TABLE 18.3 SUPERVISORS' EXPECTATIONS

- the student will work independently
- first drafts will not usually be submitted
- the student will be available for 'regular' meetings
- (s)he will be honest about their progress
- (s)he will follow advice
- (s)he will be excited about their work
- the student will be able to surprise them
- (s)he will be fun to be with

Source: Phillips and Pugh (1994: Chapter 8)

18.4 THE EARLY STAGES

The first few months of working towards a PhD are crucial. If you fail to make a good start, it may be very difficult to retrieve the situation at a later point. Here are some points to think about:

- *Choosing a supervisor*: ideally, you should choose someone whose approach and interests gel with your own. This may be someone whose work you have read or, better still, whose courses you have taken. Alternatively, try to get a look at completed dissertations supervised by this person. Try to avoid simply being allocated a supervisor. Also try to establish beforehand whether your potential supervisor is planning any long trips abroad or other career moves.
- *Do you need joint supervision?*: where your work covers more than one area, it can make sense to have two supervisors. However, tread warily! Not infrequently, joint supervision means that each supervisor will assume that the other is taking care of you. So make sure that there is planning so that you don't fall between the cracks.
- *Combining the PhD with being an RA or TA*: sometimes you will be expected to do some research for your supervisor or teaching within your department.

If so, again make sure that there is a clear agreement about the extent of this work and the support that you can expect.

● *Getting early direction*: in the early stages, you should expect a lot of support. You should not be fobbed off with a reading list and an appointment in three months' time! Instead, you might expect weekly meetings, based on small tasks, to build your confidence and give you a sense of direction.

● *Being informed*: right at the start of your studies, you should expect to be properly inducted with regard to your department's research training programme and to your rights and responsibilities as a student.

18.5 THE LATER STAGES

After the first crucial three to six months, your supervisor should gradually wean you from total dependence. As you become more confident and independent, your supervisor should encourage you to believe that you know more about your topic than they do. At these later stages, the following issues become important:

● *Shaping your writing in a professional manner*: your supervisor should help you move your style of writing to the kind expected in journals in your field. For instance, this may mean encouraging you to cut down the kind of tedious literature reviews you wrote as an undergraduate and to use concepts 'economically'. A few concepts (even just one) applied to your data are generally much more productive than data analysis that is all over the place.

● *Self-confidence*: to be economical in this way you need self-confidence and this is what your supervisor should provide. Where appropriate, you should also be told that your work is 'up to standard' for the degree you are seeking.

● *Setting deadlines*: deadlines and targets can be a source of neurosis for students. However, without them, I guarantee you will be lost. Therefore, at the end of each supervision, you should expect to set a reasonable target and agree a date by which it can be reached.

● *Working with other students*: you should not be confined to your relationship with your supervisor. Expect to be advised about relevant conferences and web sites. You will also meet other students during your research training. Find out which ones have similar topics to yours or are working with similar concepts and/or data. Then organize discussions with them. Even better, ask your supervisor to set up data sessions with other students that they are supervising.

● *Learning 'tricks'*: based on a long career of supervision, the American ethnographer Howard Becker has suggested a number of useful 'tricks' that supervisors can employ for your benefit. As he puts it: 'a trick is a specific operation that shows a way around some common difficulty, suggests a procedure that solves relatively easily what would otherwise seem an intractable and persistent problem' (Becker, 1998: 4) (for some of these tricks, try Exercise 18.1).

- *Advising on publications*: towards the later stages of your work, your supervisor should be a good source of advice about which journals are appropriate for submission of some of your work and about how to organize your presentation for such a setting (see Chapter 27).
- *Giving you a 'mock' viva*: finally, it is entirely reasonable to expect your supervisor to provide a practice dry run for your oral examination (see Chapter 25).

Much of the support that your supervisor can give you should be facilitated by an institutional structure within your department which encourages good practice. I conclude this chapter by discussing such practice.

18.6   STANDARDS OF GOOD PRACTICE

As a research student, you have a right to expect the following institutional structures. Although different formats will apply in different disciplines and countries, what follows seems to me to be a minimum requirement:

- An induction session when research training is explained and you get to meet new and existing research students.
- A graduate committee with an identified and accessible chairperson.
- A handbook of expected practice for the supervision and training of research students. This handbook should set out training requirements and the rights and responsibilities of research students. It should also explain what to do if you want to change supervisors or if you have a problem that you cannot sort out between you.
- Written memos to be agreed after each supervision.
- Annual reports agreed between supervisor and student. These to be submitted for review by the graduate committee of your department.

18.7   CONCLUDING REMARKS

The number of students registered for courses involving a research dissertation has increased hugely over the past few decades. One good consequence of this has been that supervision has increasingly become recognized as a professional skill which requires proper training and monitoring.

Of course, getting a PhD, or even an MA, should never be achieved via any methods resembling factory mass production. I hope that there will always be a place for inspiration and lateral thinking. But such features of intellectual achievement should not be a substitute for an institutional structure that offers proper student support and guidance. Let us hope that Bradbury's three-meeting supervisor is a thing of the past!

KEY POINTS

- Some students have terrible experiences of supervision. By understanding what produced these 'horror stories', you can try to avoid them happening in your case.
- It is not unreasonable to have a set of clear expectations about the support and advice which your supervisor can offer (and to know what to do if these expectations are not met).
- Supervisors have a set of expectations about you too. Know what they are and try to meet them.
- Your department should have structures of training and of monitoring supervision which offer you the support you need.

Further reading

Estelle Phillips and Derek Pugh's *How To Get a PhD* (2nd edn, Open University Press, 1994) is a goldmine of practical advice. For an American guide, see Kjell Rudestam and Rae Newton's *Surviving Your Dissertation* (Sage, 1992). Howard S. Becker's book *Tricks of the Trade* (University of Chicago Press, 1998) is a beautifully written account of a lifetime of helping research students to think critically.

Exercise 18.1

Here are a few activities which you might ask your supervisor to think about offering you:

1   Offering a snap characterization of your work which you can, if you wish, deny and thereby be helped to get a better understanding of what you *are* doing.

2   Challenging any generalization that you come up with by asking 'or else what?' You will then probably find that something you thought impossible (about your topic) happens all the time.

3   Cutting through purely theoretical characterizations of your work by giving you a limited task which asks you to begin from one situation or data and then to theorize through it. (adapted from Becker, 1998)

Getting Feedback

19.1 INTRODUCTION

Analysing research data and writing up our findings are never solitary activities – although this is certainly how they can seem as we labour in front of our PC screens in the small hours. In practice, researching involves entering a series of social relationships. These include supervisor–supervisee, student–student, student–members of the wider academic community and student researcher–research subjects in the **field**.

As we saw in the previous chapter, such relationships need not just be viewed as potential or real sources of 'trouble'. Instead, they can and should be treated as important sources of insight into how well we are practising our research skills. Effective feedback is an essential resource for effective research. As two psychologists have put it:

> Adults learn best in situations where they can practise and receive feedback, in a controlled, non-threatening environment. So a good principle to aim for is: no procedure, technique, skill, etc., which is relevant for your thesis project should be exercised by you there for the first time. (Phillips and Pugh, 1994: 52)

Non-threatening feedback can also work if your writing seems to have dried up. 'Writer's block' is something we all experience from time to time. So don't despair. If you can't face feedback, I have found that a complete break for a week or two usually works (for more discussion of writer's block, including solutions, see Ward, 2002: 96–100).

In this chapter, I will discuss two means of obtaining feedback on your research:

● writing draft papers
● giving oral presentations.

19.2   WRITING

Delivering papers on agreed topics at regular intervals to your supervisor is the standard university method of working towards a final piece of assessed research. Constructive feedback from your supervisor can encourage you to scale new heights. By contrast, where that feedback is minimal or even destructive, your whole enterprise may be threatened.

So, if your supervisor is very critical of a paper you have submitted, you should expect to be told how you can improve your work and to be offered practical suggestions rather than woolly generalities. For instance, being told to think 'more critically' or to 'be more rigorous' is unlikely to be helpful. By contrast, specific advice about a new topic or a different way of pursuing one of your existing topics should give you some useful impetus (see Chapter 18).

But your supervisor is not the only person who can give you useful feedback on your work. Your fellow students, particularly those working in similar areas, should be delighted to provide feedback. In return, they will learn about related work and have the opportunity to test their ideas out on you.

Sometimes you will need to take the initiative to form such a student support group. Sometimes, as I do with my own research students, your supervisor will organize workshops for students working on similar topics or using similar methods to present and discuss their data. In either case, you will gain the opportunity to test out preliminary ideas in a non-threatening environment.

Writing for your peers or speaking to them is wonderful practice at getting the correct level for your thesis. The great temptation in writing up what may be your first piece of serious research is to try to achieve an exalted level of technical language in order to impress your supervisor. Unfortunately, this attempt often leads to clumsy jargon which clouds your real line of argument and confuses your readers.

In discussing writing a thesis, Wolcott wisely addresses this issue of the level at which you write:

> Write for your peers. Pitch the level of discussion to an audience of readers who do *not* know what you are talking about. Write your dissertation with fellow graduate students in mind, not your learned committee members. Address your subsequent studies to the many who do not know, not the few who do. (1990: 47)

Contrary to appearances, Wolcott's injunction 'write for your peers' is *not* a cop-out. For many researchers, the most difficult thing to do is to write with such clarity that their work can be understood and enjoyed by non-specialists. Indeed, for some researchers, the hardest thing to grasp is that writing should always be tailored for as big an audience as possible. This means thinking about what that audience may know already and expect from you. Naturally, the same applies to oral presentations.

19.3 SPEAKING

Take every opportunity to present your research at any setting that arises from an informal meeting of fellow students, to interested laypeople, to a scientific conference in your field. Watch out for 'calls for papers' and regularly inspect the sites where they are posted.

When you speak, tailor what you say for your audience. Early on in my academic career, I was invited to talk about my research at a seminar at another university. I had already grasped the need to tailor my remarks to a particular audience and so had prepared two different talks on my research. One was highly specialist, the other was non-technical. Unfortunately, on that day, I had misjudged my audience and brought with me what turned out to be the 'wrong' talk. Faced with a heavyweight group of specialists, I was insufficiently experienced to improvise and was forced to present the 'Mickey Mouse' version of my research!

I still cringe when I think of this experience. However, although I failed embarrassingly on this occasion, I had at least been partially correct in my method: I had attempted to prepare a talk with an audience in mind (see Cryer, 1996: 133). Just as we design our ordinary conversation for particular recipients (children, colleagues, etc.) so **recipient design** should always go into your oral presentations. As Marx comments:

> Try to remember who you are talking to, and the differential stake you and your audience have in your topic. Gear your talk to your audience. (1997: 107)

Following Marx, you will clearly want to give different kinds of talks to experts in your field, participants in your research or to general but non-specialist academic audiences. For each audience, you should choose a particular focus (e.g. theory, method, substance) and an appropriate vocabulary (see Strauss and Corbin, 1990: 226–9).

However, such recipient design is insufficient. Many have had the experience of speakers who only have time to get through a small part of their material or who overrun and then use up the time for questions. Good time management is a quality possessed by effective speakers. If you think you will not have the confidence to improvise to beat the clock, then it is wise to try out your talk beforehand with a watch nearby.

The usual experience is that it takes far longer to get through your material than you expect. So take the minimum of material in one file and, if necessary, bring a 'comfort blanket' of additional material in another file to use in the unlikely event that you need it. Bear in mind the wise advice below if time runs out:

> If you find that you are running out of time, do not speed up. The best approach is normally to abort the presentation of your findings … and move straight to your conclusion. (Watts and White, 2000: 445)

Finally, never read out a talk (see Watts and White, 2000: 444). I know having your full script is a source of comfort. As Marx puts it:

> The fact that you get only one chance with a live audience may engender anxiety and the written word is a safety net. But it has a pre-determined, even stultifying quality, which denies the fluid and interactive nature of live presentations. (1997: 107)

But think back to all those boring talks you have attended in which the speaker had his head buried in his script. Do you really want to inflict that on your audience? More positively: 'You will never know what verbal riffs lie buried in your consciousness if you always cling to the security of the page' (ibid.). Instead, try to present your points through uncluttered visual aids (PowerPoint slides, overhead projector transparencies). Where you need to provide extensive material (e.g. long transcripts or tables), then distribute handouts.

Above all, try to grab your audience's attention at the outset. There are many tactics you can use at the start of your talk:

● begin with a puzzle, as in a detective novel
● start with an interesting data extract
● start with a personal anecdote about how you became interested in your topic
● if you are not the first speaker, try to relate what you have to say to what has gone before
● tell an apposite witty story (but only if this comes naturally!).

Finally, remember that both you and your audience need to get something out of your talk. Avoid the temptation just to give talks based on finished chapters approved by your supervisor. If the chapter is really finished, what will you gain from audience feedback? A much better strategy is to send such a chapter to a journal (see Chapter 27).

Instead, try to use early work or working papers. Here the responses of your audience may well help you to see a way ahead. As Watts and White suggest:

> In giving … conference papers from your project … present incomplete work. In this way, you can seek guidance from your audience and receive stimulus for thinking

about the next stage of your work … . In your paper you can direct the discussion towards particular issues on which you would like other people's opinions by drawing attention to them. (2000: 443)

Let me now illustrate these suggestions by some examples.

19.4   THE ART OF PRESENTING RESEARCH

You will have gathered already that, in my view, even the most astounding research can sound dull if not properly presented. Unfortunately, this does not mean that poor research can be retrieved if you are a witty and effective speaker because you will eventually be found out! But effective presentation of good research should be your aim.

To flesh out the bare bones of my argument, I have taken extracts from my reports on presentations by research students completing their first year in my own department. Naturally, to protect the innocent, I have given these students false names.

Each student was allowed up to fifteen minutes to make a presentation to their fellow students on their progress during their first year and their plans for further work; 10–15 minutes were allowed for questions.

Just as we tend to preface 'bad' news by 'good' news when giving information in everyday life, let me begin by some reports of 'good' practice. Below are some extracts from my reports.

19.4.1   *Good practice*

Pat's talk was lively and clear, making good use of overhead transparencies. She responded well to questions. This was a well-focused presentation, lively and interesting. The handouts were helpful and the video data was fascinating.

Derek gave a lively and relatively clear talk, making good use of his overheads. He spoke with some humour, gave an 'agenda' to his audience and explained the difficulties of his project.

This was highly professional with good use of overheads and handouts. She used her limited time well, managing to accommodate her talk to the fifteen minutes available. Her answers to questions were most effective, giving me the impression that she is already in control of her topic.

This was a well-focused presentation, lively and interesting. Sasha's answers to questions were good. Overall, I felt this was an excellent presentation based upon a piece of highly professional research. My views seem to be shared by the students present, one of whom remarked that she hoped her own work would be up to this standard in a year or two's time. Congratulations are due to Sasha and her supervisor.

This was a well-focused presentation, lively and interesting and improvised rather than read. The audience's attention was held throughout. Ray's answers to questions were thoughtful and helpful. In particular, he was able to establish a dialogue with students from a range of backgrounds and was at home responding to theoretical and practical issues. I especially liked Ray's attempt to derive methodological issues from the data analysis. There were time problems from which Ray will have learned something. Overall, I felt this was an excellent presentation based upon a piece of highly professional research.

Summary

I list below the qualities that impressed me in these presentations:

- liveliness
- not reading out a prepared text
- recipient design for the audience
- clarity
- effective visual aids
- humour
- explaining the agenda
- not minimizing the difficulties
- good time management
- good response to questions.

Now for the 'bad' news!

19.4.2 Bad practice

John was hampered by lack of preparation. His extempore presentation may have confused the audience by introducing too many topics and using too many examples which were not fully explained. His habit of turning his back on the audience to address the (empty) blackboard was unfortunate and, I am afraid, added to the impression of a non-user-friendly talk. This is disappointing given John's breadth of reading and excellent understanding. I think the only solution is to work harder on trying to relate his concerns to the interests and knowledge of particular audiences.

This was an interesting presentation. However, Bruce made things a little difficult for his audience by offering no initial agenda, not using overheads and by having only one copy of some data extracts. He also ran into time problems which better planning could have obviated. This presentation will have given him the opportunity in future talks to think through his objectives and to offer more user-friendly methods.

This was probably too specialized for a mixed audience, although Larry responded clearly to questions. The talk came to life when Larry departed from his script and gave an example (about record production) which brought to life the abstract concepts he was using. I strongly suggest that, in future, for such an audience, he uses more overheads and then talks around them, using such helpful examples.

Summary

The following qualities concerned me in this group of presentations:

- lack of preparation
- too much material
- not looking at the audience
- lack of recipient design
- no agenda
- no visual aids
- poor time planning.

Most presentations fell between these extremes. I will conclude with some 'mixed' examples.

19.4.3   Mixed practice

Maurice gave a clear presentation using handouts and overheads. His delivery was good and appropriately recipient designed. My only suggestion is that he should try to type overheads and put less material on each sheet.

Stan had taken the trouble to prepare handouts. However, it was disappointing that, perhaps because of time limitations, he did not have time to analyse the data provided. I would also have preferred him not to read out a paper. It is important to practise the art of talking using only a few props, like overheads, if you want to keep the audience's attention. Nonetheless, Stan's talk was well organized and timed and he offered interesting responses to questions, showing a pleasing ability to admit when he was unsure about a point.

As in an earlier talk, this was very professional, combining good overheads with helpful illustrations from video- and audiotape. My only suggestion is that it might be helpful to give more guidance to the audience about the issues to look for before offering data.

Mary gave a confident, well-prepared talk based on a handout. She responded well to questions. My only suggestion is that, in future, she works more on integrating any handout with her talk so that her audience are not confused about what they should be attending to at any one time.

Yoko had thoughtfully prepared overheads but these were not as clearly related to her talk as they might have been. Although it is always very difficult to speak in one's second language, it is difficult to keep the audience's attention when a paper is read. In my view, it is worth Yoko practising at giving presentations simply by talking around her overheads. One way to do this would be to focus on the nice examples of texts and images that she presented and to pull out her analytic and methodological points from them rather than to attempt to read a rather abstract paper.

Julia gave an engaging, lively presentation which held her audience throughout. I liked her explanation of the personal reasons behind her research and admired her ability to speak without notes. Her overheads were useful. Some minor suggestions for future talks: remember to avoid turning away from the audience to look at the screen; think about using other information sources as well as overheads (handouts of definitions would have been useful); try out a talk beforehand so as to avoid time problems.

This was an interesting talk which carefully explained the issues involved for a non-specialist audience. Jane's account of how her interest in the topic 'coalesced' was very useful as were her overhead transparencies (although, in future, she should note that these can be most effectively used by covering up parts of each slide until she gets to them). She ran into some time difficulties and this is also something to watch in future. Overall, a good account of a fascinating topic.

Luigi made a good attempt to explain a difficult topic to a non-specialist audience. I particularly liked his account of his intellectual and personal background. In future, he will need to pay more attention to explaining his concepts and to time constraints.

Summary

The following were the 'good' and 'bad' news about these presentations:

- using visual aids *but* these are poorly prepared
- well organized *but* reading out a prepared text
- giving examples of data *but* not explaining what to look for
- using handouts *but* not integrating them in the talk
- explaining the background *but* not explaining the concepts
- using overheads *but* turning away to look at them or having too much material on the screen.

19.4.4   Good and bad presentations

> Take your oral presentations as seriously as you do your writing. Speak to your audience with clarity, logic, vigour, and examples that will grab them. (Marx, 1997: 107)

In Table 19.1, I set out what we have learnt about making an effective oral presentation of your research.

TABLE 19.1 GIVING A TALK: PROBLEMS AND SOLUTIONS

Problem	Solution
Losing your audience	Recipient design
Overrunning	Don't prepare too much material
Boring your audience	Use visual aids – don't read out a talk

19.5 CONCLUDING REMARKS

Why does feedback matter? There are two reasons why student researchers write papers and give talks:

- to pass some internal assessment
- to get feedback on their work.

Unfortunately, in our assessment-obsessed university culture, students tend to forget that feedback from peers and advanced scholars serves both normative and instrumental ends.

In a normative sense, offering material for feedback recognizes the community of scholars to which scientific work aspires. Instrumentally, such feedback will undoubtedly help improve your thesis. If you have long-term academic ambitions, it will also help you to improve your teaching skills and, perhaps, to plant the seeds of future journal articles!

So never think of this as 'mere' presentation or the 'boring' bit that has to be got through in order to get your degree. If we cannot use our research to engage others in dialogue, maybe we are in the wrong business!

KEY POINTS

Effective feedback is an essential resource for effective research. This chapter has discussed two means of obtaining feedback on your research:

- by writing draft papers
- by giving oral presentations.

Writing should always be tailored for as big an audience as possible and this means thinking about what that audience may know already and expect from you. So get feedback from fellow students as well as your supervisor.

Attempt to give a talk on your research before you write a final version for your thesis. In this talk, avoid losing your audience (recipient design your presentation); set a time limit and never overrun; and use visual aids to avoid boring your audience.

Further reading

Harry Wolcott's little book, *Writing Up Qualitative Research* (Sage, 1990) covers feedback as well as many other practical matters. Pat Cryer's *The Research Student's Guide to Success* (Open University Press, 1996), Chapter 13, and the chapter by Watts and White in Dawn Potter's edited book *Research Training for Social Scientists* (Sage, 2000: 437–55) discuss giving presentations on your work. Gary Marx's paper, 'Of methods and manners for aspiring sociologists: 37 moral imperatives' (*The American Sociologist*, Spring 1997: 102–25), is a lively and extremely helpful guide for the apprentice researcher.

Exercise 19.1

Select two articles in your area of research from two different journals or books. Work out the audience(s) at which the journal or book is aimed by reading the journal's 'Instructions to Contributors' or a book's introductory editorial chapter. Then go through the steps below:

1   In what way does each article attempt to reach its appropriate audience(s)?

2   How successful is it in doing so?

3   How could it be improved to appeal more to its target audience(s)?

Exercise 19.2

Get invited to give a talk on your research and make sure that somebody attends who is prepared to give you good feedback. Plan the talk to reach the audience (e.g. students, staff, laypeople or a mixture). Having given your talk, ask the attending person for feedback on the success of your talk. Then consider how you could have improved the talk to appeal more to its target audience.

PART FIVE

Writing Up

Alasuutari describes writing a thesis as rather like learning to ride a bicycle through gradually adjusting your balance:

> Writing is first and foremost analyzing, revising and polishing the text. The idea that one can produce ready-made text right away is just about as senseless as the cyclist who has never had to restore his or her balance. (1995: 178)

Alasuutari reminds us that 'writing up' should never be something left to the end of your research. Instead, writing should be a continuous process, learning as you go from your supervisor, your peers and from your own mistakes.

In the following five chapters, we will examine how this writing up can be accomplished efficiently if rarely painlessly. The five chapters address the following topics: how to begin your research report; how to write an effective literature review and methodology chapters; how to write up your data chapters and what to put in your concluding chapter.

The First Few Pages

CHAPTER OBJECTIVES

By the end of this chapter, you will be able to:

- Recognize why the first few pages of your thesis are very important.
- Construct a title, abstract, list of contents and introduction which are appropriate, informative and attention grabbing.

20.1 INTRODUCTION

Nearly all dissertations begin with four elements:

- a title
- an abstract
- a list of contents
- an introduction.

If you follow my advice and devote most attention to your data–analysis chapters, then you may tend to treat these beginnings as routine matters, speedily disposed of. However, the impression you create at the start of your dissertation is very important and the writing of the first few pages should never be regarded as 'busy work', i.e. as a triviality.

In this short chapter, I offer some practical advice about each of these beginning sections of your dissertation.

20.2 THE TITLE

In the early stages, you will probably be asked to give a short title to your research for administrative purposes. You will almost certainly change this title before long, so do not attach too much importance to it. However, as Wolcott suggests, it is a good idea to be thinking about an effective final title and to keep notes about your ideas (1990: 70–1).

Titles should catch the readers' attention while properly informing them about the main focus of your research. My own preference is for a two-part title: a snappy main title often using a present participle to indicate activity. The sub-title can then be more descriptive. For illustration, two of my books were entitled:

> *Reading Castaneda: A Prologue to the Social Sciences*
> *Interpreting Qualitative Data: Methods for Analysing Talk, Text and Interaction.*

Among my papers, you will find the following titles:

> 'Describing sexual activities in HIV counselling: the co-operative management of the moral order'
> 'Unfixing the subject: viewing "bad timing"'
> 'Policing the lying patient: surveillance and self-regulation in consultations with adolescent diabetics'

Of course, using a present participle in the main title is merely my preference, intended to stress the *active* nature of your research as well as the fact that I study people's *activities*. Nor do I always follow my own rule. For instance, my 1997 book on AIDS counselling was entitled *Discourses of Counselling: HIV Counselling as Social Interaction*.

But titles do matter and need careful thought as any marketing person will tell you. So give this matter thought and discuss it with your supervisor. Then try Exercise 20.1.

20.3 THE ABSTRACT

This should succinctly cover the following:

- your research problem
- why that problem is important and worth studying
- your data and methods
- your main findings
- their implications in the light of other research.

There is usually a word limit for abstracts (100 words is common). So, as Punch points out: 'abstract writing is the skill of saying as much as possible in as few words as possible' (1998: 276). Within the word limitations, try to make your abstract as lively and informative as possible.

Read the abstracts of other dissertations in your area and try out drafts on other students and see if they find your abstract clear and pithy. Know what your audience are likely to be most interested in and 'emphasize your problem and content, not your fieldwork techniques' (Wolcott, 1990: 81).

Wolcott also nicely sums up what makes a good abstract:

> An abstract can offer a valuable opportunity to inform a wide audience, to capture potential readers, and to expand your own interactive professional network. Whether others will pursue their reading may depend largely on their assessment of your abstract, including its style. (1990: 81)

20.4 THE LIST OF CONTENTS

You may think this is a very trivial matter. Not so! A scrappy or uninformative table of contents (or, worse still, none at all) will create a terrible impression.

In order to be user-friendly, recipient design this list to achieve two ends:

1 To demonstrate that you are a logical thinker, able to write a dissertation with a transparently clear organization.
2 To allow your readers to see this at once, to find their way easily between different parts of the dissertation and to pinpoint matters in which they have most interest.

One useful device which helps to achieve these two things is to use a double numbering system. So, for instance, a review of the literature chapter may be listed as:

CHAPTER 3 REVIEW OF THE LITERATURE

3.1 The background studies
3.2 The core readings
3.3 The study closest to my own

Of course, this is only an illustration. More detailed discussion of what a literature review should contain is provided in the next chapter of this volume.

20.5 THE INTRODUCTION

Murcott (1997: 1) says that the point of an introduction is to answer the question: what is this thesis about? She suggests that you answer this question in four ways by explaining:

1 Why you have chosen this topic rather than any other, e.g. either because it has been neglected or because it is much discussed but not properly or fully.
2 Why this topic interests you.
3 The kind of research approach or academic discipline you will utilize.
4 Your research questions or problems.

Like this chapter, there is no reason why your introduction should be any longer than two or three pages, particularly if your methodology chapter covers the natural history of your research (see Chapter 22). The role of the introduction, like your abstract, is to orientate your readers. This is best done clearly and succinctly.

20.6 CONCLUDING REMARKS

The impression you create at the start of your dissertation is very important. Your title should catch the readers' attention while properly informing them about the main focus of your research.

An abstract should describe your research problem; why that problem is important and worth studying; your data and methods; your main findings and their implications in the light of other research.

Your list of contents should allow your readers to find their way easily between different parts of the dissertation and to pinpoint matters in which they have most interest. Your introduction should explain why you have chosen this topic rather than any other; why this topic interests you; the kind of research approach or academic discipline you will utilize; and your research questions or problems.

KEY POINTS

- The first few pages of your thesis are very important.
- Your title, abstract, list of contents and introduction should be appropriate, informative and attention grabbing.

Further reading

Harry Wolcott's *Writing Up Qualitative Research* (Sage, 1990: 70–82) has an excellent discussion of how to present student dissertations. A further useful source is Pat Cryer's *The Research Student's Guide to Success* (Open University Press: 1996), Chapter 12.

Exercise 20.1

This is an exercise to encourage you to find a good title and abstract for your dissertation.

1   Make a list of three or four possible titles for your dissertation. Try to make the main title intriguing and the sub-title descriptive.

2   Now reverse the order, putting the sub-title first. Which works best? Why?

3   Try out your titles on students working in similar areas or using similar methods or data. Which do they think works best? Why?

4   Now try out two different abstracts in the same way.

Exercise 20.2

Show the introduction to your dissertation to a range of fellow students. Encourage them to tell you whether they feel tempted to read more. If not, why not? If so, why?
    Now use their response to revise your introduction.

The Literature Review Chapter

21.1   INTRODUCTION

There are four common misconceptions of the literature review chapter:

● It is done just to display that 'you know the area'.
● It is easier to do than your data analysis chapters.
● It is boring to read (and to write).
● It is best 'got out of the way' at the start of your research.

Later in this chapter, all these assertions will be questioned. By contrast I will argue that a literature review:

● should combine knowledge with critical thought
● involves hard work but can be exciting to read
● should mainly be written *after* you have completed your data analysis.

I will begin, however, by trying to answer some practical questions about writing a literature review: What should it contain? Where will you find what you need to read? How should you read?

TABLE 21.1 CONTENTS OF A LITERATURE REVIEW

- What do we already know about the topic?
- What do you have to say critically about what is already known?
- Has anyone else ever done anything exactly the same?
- Has anyone else done anything that is related?
- Where does your work fit in with what has gone before?
- Why is your research worth doing in the light of what has already been done?

Source: adapted from Murcott (1997)

21.2 PRACTICAL QUESTIONS

21.2.1 *What should a literature review contain?*

In part, a literature review should be used to display your scholarly skills and credentials. In this sense, you should use it:

> To demonstrate skills in library searching; to show command of the subject area and understanding of the problem; to justify the research topic, design and methodology. (Hart, 1998: 13)

Such justification also means, as I remarked in Chapter 6, that any literature review connected with a piece of research has as much to do with the issue of **generalizability** as with displaying your academic credentials. This involves addressing the questions set out in Table 21.1.

Once you start to see your literature review as dialogic rather than a mere replication of other people's writing, you are going in the right direction. Conceived as an answer to a set of questions, your reading can immediately become more directed and your writing more engaging and relevant.

21.2.2 *Preparing a literature search*

As Hart (2001: 24) points out, it helps to do some preliminary thinking about what you are doing before you begin the search itself. Below are some issues to think about (drawn from Hart, 2001: 24):

- What discipline(s) relate to my main topic?
- How can I focus my topic to make my search more precise?
- What are the main indexes and abstracts relevant to my topic?
- What means of recording will be most efficient for many tasks such as cross-referencing? (Hart points out that index cards are useful.)

21.2.3   Where will I find the literature?

Once you are prepared, it is time to review the many potential sources of information about what literature you need to read and where to find it:

- your supervisor
- the subject librarian in your university library
- bibliographies in the literature you read
- online searches on the World Wide Web
- the social sciences citation index
- newsgroups on the Internet
- your fellow students (past and present).

There is no need to worry about admitting your lack of knowledge. Indeed the American sociologist Gary Marx recommends taking 'short cuts': 'learn how to use computer searches, encyclopedias, review articles. Ask experts for help' (1997: 106).

Once you start looking, you will speedily find that you do not have a problem with too little literature but of too much!. Getting away from the books and towards your data is a leap that most of us need to make as early as possible. As Marx cautions: 'Don't become a bibliophile unless it suits you' (1997: 106).

21.2.4   There's so much; how will I find the time?

Before you panic, you need to remember that you would not have reached this stage of your academic career without learning the tricks of the reading trade. These tricks go beyond the skills of speed reading (although these help) but also mean that your aim is usually to 'fillet' a publication in terms of your own agenda (not the author's!).

Again, Marx makes the point well:

> Sample! Learn how to read by skimming, attending to the first and last sentence, paragraph or chapter. Read conclusions first, then decide if you want the rest. Most social science books probably shouldn't be books; they have only a few main (or at least original) ideas. (1997: 106)

If these are some answers to the usual 'nuts and bolts' questions, we still need to tackle the underlying principles behind a literature review. As my earlier discussion of 'misconceptions' suggested, these principles are not always obvious or clear cut.

21.3   PRINCIPLES

This is how the best recent book on the topic defines a literature review:

The selection of available documents (both published and unpublished) on the topic, which contain information, ideas, data and evidence written from a particular stand-point to fulfil certain aims or express certain views on the nature of the topic and how it is to be investigated, and the effective evaluation of these documents in relation to the research being proposed. (Hart, 1998: 13)

Hart's term 'effective evaluation' means, I believe, attending to the following principles.

21.3.1   Show respect for the literature

Your single-minded pursuit of your (ideally) narrow research topic should not lead you to show disrespect for earlier research or to disconnect your work from the wider debate in which it figures. Your dissertation will be assessed in terms of its scholarship and being 'scholarly' means showing 'respect' as well as striking out on your own. In Marx's words:

Even producers of literature must know the literature, and a major criterion for evalu-ating work is whether or not it is put in a context of prior scholarship. We are not only creators of new knowledge, but protectors and transmitters of old knowledge. Our inheritance is the astounding richness of the work of prior scholars. Beyond that, one has a strategic interest in the peer reciprocity inherent in the citing system. (1997: 106)

21.3.2   Be focused and critical

Respect can only get you so far. Scholarship also means advancing knowledge – although the level of that advance required will vary according to the degree at which you are aiming. Such advance involves a strict focus and a critical perspective on what you read:

After some initial grovelling, know what you are looking for. Approach the literature with questions and remember that your goal is to advance it, not simply to marvel at its wonders. Seek an appropriate balance between appreciation and advancement of the literature. (Marx, 1997: 106)

21.3.3   Avoid mere description

Any academic has horror stories of literature reviews which were tediously and irrelevantly descriptive. Rudestam and Newton characterize well such failing reviews:

[they consist of] a laundry list of previous studies, with sentences or paragraphs begin-ning with the words, "Smith found …", "Jones concluded …", "Anderson stated…", and so on. (1992: 46)

In this vein, Marx recommends avoiding writing 'a literature summary without an incisive critique that will help your peers to view the world differently' (1997: 106). Instead, you need to focus on those studies that are relevant for defining *your* research problem. By the end of the literature review:

> the reader should be able to conclude that, "Yes, of course, this is the exact study that needs to be done at this time to move knowledge in this field a little further along." (Rudestam and Newton, 1992: 47)

This entails giving different amounts of attention to what you read according to how central they are to your topic. Background literature can just be described in a sentence. By contrast, the most relevant studies 'need to be critiqued rather than reported' (1992: 49). Such critique can focus on failings of theory or method (see Chapter 15).

21.3.4 Write up after your other chapters

The common version of a student research trajectory suggests that a major early aim is to complete a literature review. This version is supported in the 'Time Checklist' provided by British Research Councils for PhD students. This includes the following recommendation: 'First year ... student to complete a literature survey' (British Research Councils, 1996). Elsewhere the same publication gives less dogmatic advice:

> In some subjects a *literature survey* forms an important starting portion of the work, and this should be carried out in the early stages. Before the end of the first year, the student should have a good idea of relevant work carried out by others, but it will be necessary to keep up with new literature throughout the period, so that the thesis takes account of the latest developments in its subject area.

This more considered advice hints at the problems of completing your literature review at an early stage. These problems may include:

● Completing the literature survey in year 1 and writing it up can mean a lot of wasted effort – until you have done your data analysis, you do not know what stuff will be relevant.

● You may be tempted to regard the literature review as a relatively easy task. Since it tests skills you have already learned in your undergraduate career, it may become potential 'busy work'. If so, it only will delay getting down to the data analysis on which you should be judged.

● As I asked in Chapter 6, can you ever get out of the library in order to write your thesis? One book will surely have a list of further 'crucial' references and so on, *ad infinitum*. Anybody who thinks a library PhD is a 'quick fix' would be well advised to ponder whether they have the will-power to stop reading.

These considerations mean that the bulk of your reading is usually best done in and around your data collection and analysis. In the end, this will save you the time involved in drafting your literature review chapter before you can know which literature will be most relevant to your treatment of your topic. It will also force you out of the library. As Marx comments: 'searching the literature must not become an end in itself or a convenient way to avoid the blank page' (1997: 106).

So: read as you do the analyses. By all means write notes on your reading but don't attempt to write your literature review chapter early on in your research.

However, as researchers, we should be critical and innovative. In this regard, how far is the literature review chapter simply an unthought relic of an out-of-date version of scholarship? Do you need such a chapter?

21.4   DO YOU NEED A LITERATURE REVIEW CHAPTER?

The major unorthodox figure here is the American ethnographer Harry Wolcott. He argues that student researchers often mistakenly assume a need to defend qualitative research in general as well as the particular approach or method they are using. But, as he suggests after a century of qualitative research (and several decades of more specific qualitative approaches):

> There is no longer a call for each researcher to discover and defend [qualitative methods] anew, nor a need to provide an exhaustive review of the literature about such standard procedures as participant observation or interviewing. Instead of having to describe and defend qualitative approaches, as we once felt obligated to do, it is often difficult to say anything new or startling about them. Neophyte researchers who only recently have experienced these approaches first-hand need to recognize that their audiences probably do not share a comparable sense of excitement about hearing them described once again. (1990: 26)

Wolcott also points to some positive gains of avoiding the statutory review chapter. As he puts it:

> I expect my students to know the relevant literature, but I do not want them to lump (dump?) it all into a chapter that remains unconnected to the rest of the study. I want them to draw upon the literature selectively and appropriately as needed in the telling of their story. (1990: 17)

This means that you can bring in appropriate literature as you need it, not in a separate chapter but in the course of your data analysis:

> Ordinarily this calls for introducing related research toward the end of a study rather than at the beginning, except for the necessary "nesting" of the problem in the introduction. (1990: 17)

Wolcott's radical suggestion is, no doubt, too radical for most students (and their supervisors!). Nevertheless, even if you decide to write the conventional literature review chapter, what he has to say is a salutary reminder that, in writing a research dissertation, you should cite other literature only in order to connect your narrow research topic to the directly relevant concerns of the broader research community. Making wider links should properly be left to your final chapter (see Chapter 24).

21.5 CONCLUDING REMARKS

In this chapter, I have argued that a literature review should combine knowledge with critical thought. It should involve hard work but be exciting to read and should mainly be written *after* you have completed your data analysis.

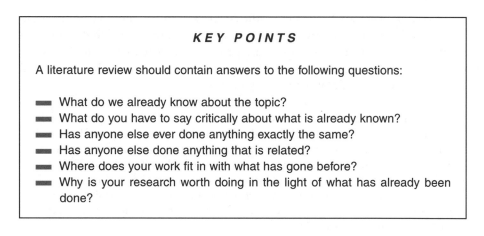

KEY POINTS

A literature review should contain answers to the following questions:

- What do we already know about the topic?
- What do you have to say critically about what is already known?
- Has anyone else ever done anything exactly the same?
- Has anyone else done anything that is related?
- Where does your work fit in with what has gone before?
- Why is your research worth doing in the light of what has already been done?

Further reading

The essential book on this topic is Chris Hart's *Doing a Literature Review: Releasing the Social Science Imagination* (Sage, 1998). This covers in detail all the issues discussed in this brief chapter as well as addressing the different requirements of literature reviews for BA, MA and PhD dissertations. Hart's later book, *Doing a Literature Search* (Sage, 2001), is a helpful guide to planning and executing a literature search. For shorter, lively discussions see Harry Wolcott's *Writing Up Qualitative Research* (Sage, 1990) and Gary Marx's paper, 'Of methods and manners for aspiring sociologists: 37 moral imperatives' (*The American Sociologist*, Spring 1997, 102–25).

Exercise 21.1

Select what you regard as the two or three most relevant pieces of literature. Now:

1   Make notes on each, attempting to use each one to answer the questions found in Table 21.1.

2   Incorporate these notes in a short literature review chapter which only refers to these two or three works.

3   Discuss this review with your supervisor.

Exercise 21.1

When you complete each data-analysis chapter, look back over the literature you have discussed. Now ask yourself these questions:

1   Is there sufficient discussion of each reference to render further discussion (in a literature review chapter) redundant?

2   If not, practise writing about these references in a way that adds to how you have described them in your data-analysis chapters. Again, you may use Table 21.1 as a guide.

The Methodology Chapter

22.1 INTRODUCTION

We can distinguish three different kinds of student dissertation: theoretical, methodological and empirical. Each of these demands different discussion of 'methods'.

1 *Theoretical*: here you claim to develop some theoretical insights by means of a critical review of a body of literature. In the theoretical dissertation, your methodology chapter will need to discuss your rationale for selecting your corpus of literature and any illustrative examples. It will also need to show how you have attempted to produce a systematic analysis, e.g. by considering the arguments for positions that you reject.

2 *Methodological*: here you may be mainly concerned to develop a method (e.g. focus groups or textual analysis) or to compare and contrast the use of several different methods. Here the whole thesis may be devoted to methodological matters and so a separate chapter called 'methodology' may be redundant or simply devoted to explaining why you have chosen certain methods to compare and/or which data you choose to use for this exercise.

3 *Empirical*: in this, the most common form of research report or dissertation, you will analyse some body of data. Here you will be expected to show that

you understand the strengths and weaknesses of your research strategy, design and methods.

This chapter focuses on empirically based research reports. It argues for openness and clarity about what actually happened during your research. It argues that a bland account in the passive voice is an entirely inappropriate format for your methodology chapter.

Qualitative researchers are often interested in the narratives or stories that people tell one another (and researchers). Indeed, our data-analysis chapters tell (structured) stories about our data. It is only natural, then, that our readers should expect to be told how we gathered our data, what data we ended up with and how we analysed it.

This is why all research reports seem to have a methodology chapter or at least a section devoted to 'data and methods'. Within that rubric, however, as I show later in this chapter, there are many different (non-bland) formats we can use to give an account of our data and methods. First, however, we need to clear the ground about the issues you need to cover in your methods chapter.

22.2   WHAT SHOULD THE METHODOLOGY CHAPTER CONTAIN?

In a quantitative study, there is a simple answer to this question. You will have a chapter usually entitled 'Data and Methods'. As Table 22.1 shows, this chapter will typically contain four elements.

The straightforward character of a quantitative methods chapter unfortunately does not spill over into qualitative research reports. At first sight, this simply is a matter of different language. So, in reporting qualitative studies, typically we do not talk about 'statistical analysis' or 'research instruments'. These linguistic differences also reflect broader practical and theoretical differences between quantitative and qualitative research.

More particularly, in writing up qualitative research, we need to recognize:

- the (contested) theoretical underpinnings of methodologies
- the (often) contingent nature of the data chosen
- the (likely) non-random character of cases studied
- the reasons why the research took the path it did (both analytic and chance factors).

Each of these four features raises issues which should not be concealed or generate guilt. Your research training courses and your reading should have made you aware of the theories on which your methods rest. So the rule here, in writing your methods chapter, is simply: *spell out your theoretical assumptions.*

Everybody realizes that contingent events related to personal interest, access or even simply being in the right (wrong) place at the right (wrong) time often

TABLE 22.1   THE METHODS CHAPTER IN A
QUANTITATIVE THESIS

1   Subjects studied
2   Research instruments used
3   Procedures used in applying these instruments to these subjects
4   Statistical analysis

Source: adapted from Rudestam and Newton (1992: 61)

determine which data you are able to work upon. So be straightforward: *spell out the (sometimes contingent) factors that made you choose to work with your particular data.*

Finally, everybody knows that qualitative researchers can work fruitfully with very small bodies of data that have not been randomly assembled. If this is the case, *explain how you can still generalize from your analysis.* For example, in Chapter 9, I discussed four different but positive answers to this question of how we can obtain generalizability:

● combining qualitative research with quantitative measures of populations
● purposive sampling guided by time and resources
● theoretical sampling
● using an analytic model which assumes that generalizability is present in the existence of *any* case.

So, when writing your methodology chapter, avoid over-defensiveness. Many great researchers will have used similar methods with few qualms. So draw from their strength.

On the other hand, self-confidence should not mean lack of appropriate self-criticism. Your literature review chapter will already have considered other studies in terms of 'the strengths and limitations of different research designs and techniques of data collection, handling and analysis' (Murcott, 1997: 2).

Treat your methodology chapter in the same way – as a set of cautious answers to questions that another researcher might have asked you about your work (e.g. why did you use these methods; how did you come to these conclusions?). This means that your methods chapter should aim to *document* the rationale behind your research design and data analysis.

Spencer et al. (2003) argue that this documentation process requires transparency about your methods. In other words, you should anticipate and answer reasonable questions about your research. Table 22.2 sets out the issues involved here.

Another way of putting these kinds of matters has been suggested by Murcott (1997). Table 22.3 shows how we can use our methods chapter to answer a set of questions.

TABLE 22.2   HOW TO DOCUMENT YOUR RESEARCH TRANSPARENTLY

- Give an honest account of the conduct of the research
- Provide full descriptions of what was actually done in regard to choosing your case(s) to study, choosing your method(s), collecting and analysing data
- Explain and justify each of your decisions
- Discuss the strengths and weaknesses of what you did
- Be open about what helped you and held you back

Source: adapted from Spencer et al. (2003: 76)

TABLE 22.3   QUESTIONS FOR A QUALITATIVE METHODS CHAPTER

1   How did you go about your research?
2   What overall strategy did you adopt and why?
3   What design and techniques did you use?
4   Why these and not others?

Source: Murcott (1997)

To answer the questions in Table 22.3 will usually mean describing the following:

- the data you have studied
- how you obtained that data (e.g. issues of access and consent)
- what claims you are making about the data (e.g. as representative of some population or as a single case study)
- the methods you have used to gather the data
- why you have chosen these methods
- how you have analysed your data
- the advantages and limitations of using your method of data analysis.

22.3   A NATURAL HISTORY CHAPTER?

To answer Murcott's four questions in Table 22.3, in the context of my elaborations above, may now look to be a pretty tall order, particularly if you feel you have to devote a long section to each of these issues.

However, the methodology chapter of a qualitative study can be a much more lively, interesting affair than this suggests. In this context, there are three issues to bear in mind. First, a highly formal chapter can be dull to read as well as to write. Many is the time I have ploughed through a desperately boring methodology chapter, usually written in the passive voice. I often get the feeling that the chapter is there for purely formal purposes. In the words of a British song about war, 'because we're here, because we're here, because we're here'! In such cases, I can hardly wait to get on to the (more lively) heart of the study.

Second, 'methodology' has a more flexible meaning in qualitative research than its quantitative sister. In Chapter 7, I defined 'methodology' as 'a general approach to studying research topics'. As such, your readers will be more interested in a methodological discussion in which you explain the actual course of your decision making rather than a series of blunt assertions in the passive voice (e.g. 'the method chosen was …').

Third, a research study submitted for a university degree, even up to the PhD level, is principally evaluated in terms of how far you can demonstrate that you have the makings of a competent researcher. Hence your examiners will be interested to know something about the history of your research, including your response to the various difficulties and dead ends that we all experience.

As Alasuutari argues, false leads and dead ends are just as worth reporting as the method eventually chosen:

> It is precisely for this reason that taking 'field notes' about the development of one's thinking is needed … . The text can be like a detective story, where one presents these 'false leads' until they are revealed to be dead-ends. (1995: 192)

Alasuutari's version of the history of research as a 'detective story' is incompatible with a formal methodology chapter in the passive voice. Instead of a formal, impersonal chapter, one offers the reader 'field notes about the developments of one's thinking'. One way to do this is to rename the 'methodology' chapter 'The natural history of my research'.

In Chapter 3, we saw how some of my research students used their field diaries to write lively natural histories. These informed the reader, among other things, about:

● the personal context of the students' research topic
● the reasons for their research design
● how they developed their research through trial and error
● the methodological lessons they learned.

Examples of how these topics can be treated in your 'natural history' chapter are set out in Table 22.4.

The more informal 'natural history' style of methodology chapter that I recommend should not be taken to mean that 'anything goes'. On the contrary, by asking readers to engage with your thinking *in process*, they are in a far better position to assess the degree to which you were self-critical. Moreover, an autobiographical style is only appropriate to the extent that it allows you to address

TABLE 22.4   TOPICS FOR A NATURAL HISTORY CHAPTER

The personal context

By the end of my period of undergraduate study, I was greatly vexed by issues surrounding the tendency within the various schools of sociology towards using 'social structure' too loosely as a way of accounting for data. (Simon)

The micro-analysis of social interaction seemed to me to be a valuable way of understanding some of the health issues and problems I had encountered in my experience working in clinical health settings as a psychiatric nurse and as a research nurse. Many of these problems appeared to hinge on the interactive practices and skills of the various parties involved. (Moira)

Like Silverman's (1987) experience of gaining access to the field of paediatric cardiology, my entry to the field of mental health casework was a chance happening. I met up with a former colleague in a local supermarket. After recounting my difficulty in negotiating access to an in-patient area, he invited me to meet the community team with whom he worked. (Sally)

Reasons for research design

I chose to collect data in the way that I did because it was appropriate to the study of situated action. Audio tapes provide detailed recorded talk which field notes alone cannot provide, while preparing transcripts is itself a research activity. (Sally)

Many qualitative research studies set out clear aims and objectives at the start of a project. These may often refer to collecting and analysing data on a particular topic, such as describing the views of patients about a particular type of illness experience. The aims of ethnomethodological studies such as this one tend to be quite general, centring on the examination of some data. Decisions therefore need to be made about objectives for particular pieces of analysis at each stage. (Moira)

Developing through trial and error

I had initially intended to undertake separate analyses of instances of criticisms of self and of the dead spouse. However, I decided a more constructive tack would be to conduct a closer analysis of members' practices in producing the accounts. This would involve taking a step back in order to take a closer look. (Moira)

To undertake a case study of 'single homelessness' in the context of full-time employment makes heavy demands on the researcher in terms of personal resources and operational constraints. The field is so vast and the nature of subjects' lives so dispersed that I elected to observe professional caseworkers rather than service users. For practical reasons then, I became a participant-observer at weekly case conferences. (Sally)

Methodological lessons I have learned

I was attempting to describe something that I knew was going on but could not see at the start. The need to refrain from introducing my own categorizations *before* producing the description of members' practices that I was aiming for has not been easy. However, I believe that the fine grained analysis of the practices adopted by interview participants has enabled me to contribute new insights to the sociology of health and illness. (Moira)

(Continued)

TABLE 22.4   CONTINUED

With hindsight, I might use more conventional transcription devices if I were to do the transcripts again. This would save the 'creative' work of devising my own. (Sally)

How, then, should this research be seen in terms of both sampling variety and external validity? I believe the answer lies in seeing this research not as an attempt to provide categorical 'truths' about all parents' evenings in general, but as an attempt to raise questions about such meetings by looking at a single case in detail. This study can therefore be seen as being *exploratory* rather *definitive*, examining the achievement of routine by a single individual in a specific setting in such a way that further analytical possibilities are opened up. (Simon)

properly the kind of crucial methodological questions set out in Tables 22.2 and 22.3. Clearly, your readers will not want to hear needlessly and endlessly about how your personal life impinged upon the process of obtaining your degree!

22.4   CONCLUDING REMARKS

Some universities (like some academic journals) still have a pretty fixed idea of what a methodology chapter (or section) should contain. Therefore, it is probably worth discussing with your teachers whether a 'natural history' format is appropriate to describe the methodology that you have chosen. But even if you do not write your chapter in this way, you will still gain by keeping dated field notes about the trajectory of your project.

However, if you do write a 'natural history' chapter, it is much more likely that you will avoid boring your readers (and yourself). It is also more likely that you will overcome the common problem of failing to explicate to the reader what is now 'obvious' to you. As Alasuutari puts it: 'Researchers always become more or less blind to their texts and thoughts, so that they do not notice that they have failed in spelling out certain premises or starting points without which an outsider has a hard time understanding the text' (ibid.). A 'natural history' chapter, based on contemporary field notes, will be more likely to make your readers 'insiders' and to avoid you being an 'outsider' in relation to your own text.

KEY POINTS

All research reports have a methodology chapter or at least a section devoted to 'data and methods'. In it, you will be expected to show that you understand the strengths and weaknesses of your research strategy, design and methods. In this chapter you should explain:

- your theoretical assumptions
- the factors that made you choose to work with your particular data
- how you can generalize from your analysis.

However, a highly formal methodology chapter can be dull to read as well as to write. Instead, it is often right to offer the reader field notes about the developments of one's thinking called 'The natural history of my research'.

Further reading

The most helpful comments on writing a methodology chapter are to be found in Pertti Alasuutari's *Researching Culture: Qualitative Method and Cultural Studies* (Sage, 1995), Chapters 13 and 14.

Exercise 22.1

Assemble the various memos you have written during your research. Now write 500 words on each of the following topics related to your research:

1   The main things that have helped you finish and the main things that have held you back.

2   What you have learned about your research topic.

3   How you have improved your knowledge of (a) methodology and (b) theory.

4   What lessons your research has for other students at your level.

Note: If you have not finished your research yet, do Exercise 2.1 instead.

Writing your Data Chapters

23.1 INTRODUCTION

As we have already seen, many supervisors and funding bodies suggest that doing a research study falls into three equal phases. These phases are commonly defined as:

- reviewing the literature
- gathering your data
- analysing your data.

Faced with this convention, it may be necessary to restate the obvious. Assuming that you are writing an empirically based study, your data-analysis chapters are (or should be) the key basis on which your dissertation will be judged. Unlike course-work essays, where knowledge of the literature and an ability to analyse it critically will stand you in good stead, dissertations that involve research count as nothing without good data analysis. Moreover, as I have said several times already, there are usually no brownie points awarded for successfully gathering your data. Whether or not such data gathering involves discomfort, danger or the need to learn another language is, ultimately, neither here nor there. In the final assessment, everything comes down to what you *do* with your data.

This situation implies two clear messages. First, as I have stressed throughout this book, you cannot begin too early in your data analysis. Second, when you write up data, you need to develop the skills to present your analysis clearly and cogently to your readers.

This is why, as Jay Gubrium (personal correspondence) has commented, students need advice on the actual writing up of their data analysis. They need to understand 'what to say first, next, where to place things, how to introduce extracts and what to say in relation to them, how to draw conclusions'. In this chapter, I offer advice addressed to the issues that Gubrium raises.

It will be useful at once to make a distinction between how you write up your analysis of particular sets of data and how you craft your overall argument. Alasuutari (1995) calls the former area the 'microstructure' of a thesis and the latter its 'macrostructure'. This is how he explains the difference between the two levels:

> The difference between the two could be compared to different dimensions of the architecture of a house. At the macrolevel one thinks how the rooms and different activities are placed in relation to each other, whereas at the microlevel one considers the furnishing and interior decoration of different rooms. (Alasuutari, 1995: 179)

This is a helpful distinction because, as Alasuutari suggests, different issues arise in relation to the organization of individual chapters (the 'microstructure') and the overall organization of your thesis ('the macrostructure'). In the rest of this chapter, I will consider each structure separately and then go on to explain how to make a final check that everything is in place before you tighten up the structure (Wolcott, 1990: 47).

23.2   THE MACROSTRUCTURE

> The macrostructure is how the investigation proceeds from one chapter to another so that it forms a logical and sound whole. (Alasuutari, 1995: 179)

How do you ensure that your data-analysis chapters form 'a logical and sound whole'? I discuss below two answers to this question:

- Plan your table of contents at an early stage and continually revise it.
- In the final write-up, decide the form of the 'story' you want to tell about your research.

23.2.1   *Early planning of table of contents*

Plan what you may put into your data chapters as early as you can and then keep revising your list. As Wolcott suggests, projecting a table of contents provides for:

> an orderly progression, a clear identification of major points and subordinate ones, and an overview ... to assess whether the structure I have designed accommodates

the data to be presented and provides an appropriate sequence for the presentation. (1990: 18)

By such early planning of the structure of your thesis you can help to clarify your research design and identify upcoming problems:

> Insurmountable problems in finding a sound macrostructure may be a sign of weaknesses in the research design: problems which have to be sorted out first. (Alasuutari, 1995: 179)

Alasuutari gives the example of a set of chapters which veer unpredictably between different themes – a good indication of an unclear research design. This means that, if you have difficulty in working out your table of contents, then you are exhibiting symptoms of a confused research design.

To show you how tables of contents can be projected, I set out below examples from two of my research students: Sally Hunt and Kay Fensom. In each case, these research students started to project a table of contents at an early stage.

Sally gathered audio recordings of case conferences of a community health team seeking to house mentally ill, homeless people. Her work, which was discussed in Chapter 2, is ethnographic in focus. Example 23.1 shows her draft table of contents prepared while she was still writing her data chapters.

EXAMPLE 23.1   Sally's draft table of contents

'Producing single homelessness: descriptive practice in community mental casework'

1	Introduction: aims of the study
2	Natural history of the research
3	Literature used in the analysis
4–6	The ethnographic context
7	Constructing the case
8	Constructing the client
9	Gender as an interpretive framework
10	Constructing the mental health team
11	Conclusion: limitations and implications

In the final version of her thesis, Sally reorganized most of her thesis into two parts: an introduction (which included Chapters 1–3 above) and data analysis (Chapters 7–10). Sally recognized that her projected chapters on the ethnographic context were peripheral to her main argument. So her draft Chapters 4–6 were vastly shortened and incorporated in her introduction.

Kay analysed crime stories in local newspapers in London and Northern Ireland. To do this, she used Harvey Sacks's **membership categorization device** analysis (see Chapter 11, in relation to the story about the navy pilot). Example 23.2 shows her early ideas about the organization of her thesis.

EXAMPLE 23.2 Kay's draft table of contents

'Locating newsworthiness in newspaper headlines: reading inference and "motive"'

1 Natural history: stages, directions and influences
2 Theoretical framework
3 The media, 'newsworthiness' and the activity of reading
4–7 Data chapters (each on a separate crime headline)
8 Dealing with critiques of MCD analysis
9 Conclusions: what has the analysis achieved?

By the time Kay submitted her PhD, she had one extra data chapter. She now felt that two of her draft chapters were based on literature reviews which were not distinctively original. So Chapters 3 and 8 disappeared from the final version of her thesis although parts of each were used elsewhere. Kay's title also changed to: 'Crime, locality and morality: membership categorization and "newsworthiness" in local newspapers'. This improved title nicely reflected (what had turned out to be) Kay's key concepts and database.

Sally and Kay's redrafting carries three important implications about how you should think about the structure of your thesis:

● Work out what main message and findings you want your data chapters to contain.
● Ensure that the structure of your thesis underlines that message.
● Strip out or minimize draft chapters that are peripheral to your argument.

Deleting or shortening chapters over which you have toiled requires a degree of ruthlessness on your part. Seek the guidance of your supervisor about whether such chapters might find a better home in, say, a conference paper or journal article (see Chapter 27).

More than a year before Sally and Kay finished their dissertations, they were already planning a draft table of contents. Planning is important because your research dissertation will probably be the longest piece of writing you have ever done. BA or MA research essays are commonly 10,000 words and PhDs are usually between 70,000 and 100,000 words long. However, it is important not to focus upon your own difficulties at writing at this length for I guarantee that, in nearly every case, you will find you have too *little* space.

Instead, think of how the reader needs a guide to follow a long story. Provide that guide at the start and repeat it, as appropriate, in every chapter (see Alasuutari, 1995: 180). This will mean giving regular 'signposts' to help the reader understand what you are going to do (or have done) and how these relate to your overall theme. It also means planning the form of the 'story' you wish to tell.

23.2.2   Planning your story

There are at least three models to choose from in working out the macrostructure of your thesis:

- the hypothesis story
- the analytic story
- the mystery story.

Each is discussed briefly below.[1]

The hypothesis story

This is how many journals require you to organize your paper. It follows a standard three-part way of writing up research reports derived from quantitative studies:

1   State your **hypotheses**.
2   Test them.
3   Discuss the implications.

As Alasuutari (1995: 181) points out, there are two reasons why you are unlikely to want to use this model for writing up your qualitative dissertation. First, you may well be proceeding inductively, developing and testing hypotheses in the course of your data analysis. If so, then clearly you cannot state a prior hypothesis. Second, however, there are reasons to be suspicious of the hypothesis story because, even in quantitative studies, it often represents not the 'actual' logic of the research but a reconstructed logic fitted to how your cross-tabulations of variables actually worked out (see Alasuutari, 1995: 181–3).

The analytic story

The hypothesis story usually demands a passive voice format (e.g. 'it was hypothesized that …' or 'the findings were …') which can be difficult to write and still more painful to read! Telling an analytic story is a more conversational way of writing. It involves deciding 'the main analytic story line that you wish to tell' (Strauss and Corbin, 1990: 230). As they put it:

think intently about the *analytic logic* that informs the story. Every research monograph, indeed every research paper, will have such a logic … . In a sense the entire thesis or monograph will represent a spelling out of this analytic story. (ibid.)

To write this story, you need to ask yourself questions like:

- What are the key concepts that I have used in this study?
- How do my 'findings' shed light on these concepts and, through them, on the substantive topics I studied?
- What, therefore, has become of my original research problem and the literature regarding it?

Rather than hope that the reader will eventually find out these matters, telling an analytic story lays everything out on a plate at the outset.

There is much to be said for this model for it helps the readers to settle back knowing what they will find in the rest of your thesis. Some readers, however, may actually want to be surprised. Such surprises can be planned rather than the mere outcome of sloppy design. This is where the mystery story comes in.

The mystery story

Alasuutari refers to an approach to writing that 'proceeds by pointing out mysteries and by gradually developing questions and answers'. In this approach, one:

starts directly from **empirical** examples, develops the questions by discussing them, and gradually leads the reader to interpretations of the material and to more general implications of the results. (Alasuutari, 1995: 183, bold added)

Beginning one's data analysis in the form of a mystery story has at least two advantages. First, it may well capture your readers' attention as, like the readers of detective stories, they want to stay with you in order to find 'whodunnit'. Second, it more accurately mirrors the inductive form of much qualitative research where findings (and even topics) are only gradually revealed.

Set against this, you must remember that writing a mystery story requires many craft skills. Should you fail, you will certainly lose your readers' interest. So, in practice, many writers of good qualitative dissertations follow Strauss and Corbin's idea of telling an analytic story to lead their readers through the data-analysis chapters.

In a sense, whichever story form you choose can be safely left to personal choice. More important is whether you are telling *some* coherent story. For, despite their differences, all three models share one important feature in common: they give the study focus and point. This means that the structure of your thesis should only rarely flow from the chronological order in which you happened to find out things. As Cryer puts it: 'the final version of the thesis should be written, with hindsight, knowing where one has been' (1996: 178).

So, if you just remember one lesson from this chapter it is this: *avoid telling your story in the order which you found things out or wrote them up.* Such a story is only appropriate for a natural history chapter (see Chapter 22). If the overall structure of your thesis just reflects the order in which you discovered things, then your examiners are unlikely to praise you for your verisimilitude. They are much more likely to criticize you for being too lazy to work out a coherent structure for your argument.

As Alasuutari puts it, returning to the motif of a 'mystery story':

> A good investigation is indeed like a murder mystery in that it does not contain much irrelevant text: themes or details that have nothing to do with the solution revealed in the end ... . One could talk about the *economy principle* of a study: everything included must be related and tied in with the argumentation developed and presented in the investigation. (1995: 186, my emphasis)

Now attempt Exercise 23.1.

23.3 THE MICROSTRUCTURE

With a clear 'macrostructure', you are well set up to write well-organized and well-argued data chapters. Whether it is a matter of setting out an overall argument (the macrostructure) or developing an analysis of a particular topic (the microstructure), you should always write in a way that helps the reader. As Jay Gubrium (personal communication) notes, this is not always something that comes easily to inexperienced researchers:

> many students 'don't take their readers into account; they don't know how to "teach" their readers what they should be reading into the empirical material present. Many just throw stuff into the text and expect the reader to get the point.'

Thinking about your reader(s) turns out to be an excellent way of answering perennial problems that arise when you first write up a qualitative study. For instance, you may ask yourself: how much depth is needed in my data analysis? How much is enough?

Strauss and Corbin suggest a good way of answering such questions:

> The answer is first that you must know what your main analytic message will be. Then you must give enough conceptual detail to convey this to readers. The actual form of your central chapters should be consonant with the analytic message and its components. (1990: 232–3)

So the answer to these questions is found in how you have depicted the main message of your thesis (the macrostructure). The point here is: know your message and stick to it!

Normally, each data-analysis chapter will have three sections:

- an introduction, in which you explain what you are going to do in advance
- the main section, in which you work through your data in terms of what you have already said
- a conclusion, in which you summarize what you have shown and connect to the next chapter.

I set out below some suggestions for writing each of these sections with an audience in mind.

23.3.1 Introduction

Never spring anything on your readers. Even if you have decided to tell a mystery story (see above), your audience should always know what the mystery is about and what kind of 'clues' they should be looking for. As Becker has cautioned:

> Many social scientists … think they are actually doing a good thing by beginning evasively. They reveal items of evidence one at a time, like clues in a detective story, expecting readers to keep everything straight until they produce the dramatic concluding paragraph …
>
> I often suggest to these would-be Conan Doyles that they simply put their last triumphant paragraph first, telling readers where the argument is going and what all this material will finally demonstrate. (1986: 51–2)

So at the outset, preface each data-analysis chapter with an explanation of how its topic relates to your thesis as a whole and how the chapter will be organized. As a broad rule, no sub-heading should ever appear in a chapter without it having received a prior explanation of its nature and logical place in your argument.

Along these lines, Pat Cryer suggests four components of a good introduction to a chapter. These are set out in Table 23.1.

23.3.2 Main section

Now that your readers know the areas that this chapter will discuss, it is important that you initially pull apart these areas and discuss each one separately. The golden rule for writing data analysis is:

- Make one point at a time.

So, if you find yourself veering off in another direction, cut out the offending material and put it in another section. Sometimes this will mean returning to the same data but from a different perspective. Sometimes it will mean getting rid of some data altogether.

TABLE 23.1 COMPONENTS OF A DATA CHAPTER INTRODUCTION

1	Scene-setting for the chapter, i.e. explaining the general area(s) that the chapter considers
2	Locating the gap in knowledge which the chapter addresses
3	Explaining how the chapter fills that gap
4	Providing a brief overview of what is in the chapter

Source: adapted from Cryer (1996: 182)

Your readers will find their lives much easier if they are not distracted by too many different arguments. And it is also much more likely that you will be able to recognize holes in your argument if it is stripped to the bone.

If you are making just one point at a time, it is, of course, crucial that your readers should immediately grasp what that point is. Therefore, a second rule is:

● 'Top and tail' each data extract.

This means writing a sentence or two before every extract to context it in your argument. This way your readers will know what to look for while they read it.

Follow that up with a more detailed analysis of the extract in terms of the single point you are using it to make. If the extract is inconclusive, then admit to it. So, a third rule is:

● Always show that you understand the limitations of both your data and your analysis of it.

For your readers to be able to follow your analysis, they will need to be able to locate the extract(s) to which you are referring and where to find the relevant part of that extract. So a fourth rule is:

● Always number your extracts.

One effective way to do this is to give each extract two identifying numbers: the first will be the chapter number in which it appears and the second the order in which it is placed in the chapter. So the first data extract in Chapter 3 of your thesis should be numbered Extract 3.1.

Line numbers should also be used for any extracts over two lines in length. In this way, for instance, you can refer to Extract 3.1, lines 5–7, without having to reprint the passage.

A fifth rule is:

● Convince the reader.

TABLE 23.2 COMPONENTS OF A DATA CHAPTER
CONCLUSION

1	Explain what the chapter has done
2	Describe the new questions the chapter has identified
3	Explain where these questions will be addressed (e.g. in the next chapter or in the overall conclusions)

Source: adapted from Cryer (1996: 183)

Not only must your readers be able to see why you interpreted your data in the way you did, but also they must be convinced by your interpretation. As Murcott suggests: 'the basis for saying that the data say "x" rather than "y" has to be made apparent' (1997: 2).

Murcott also suggests that the way to display that your analysis has this kind of critical component is to: 'discuss candidate interpretations and make the case for judging, and so discarding, alternatives as inferior or inadequate' (1997: 2).[2]

23.3.3 Conclusion

When you reach the end of a tight piece of data analysis, you may feel that nothing further needs to be done. Not so! You owe it to your readers to tie the whole chapter together again. Not only will this remind them of what you (and they) have learnt in the preceding pages, but it will also prepare them for the chapter(s) to follow.

Table 23.2 sets out what the conclusion of a data chapter might contain.

It is worth remembering that it is unlikely that you will achieve a well-argued, reader-friendly thesis at one go. I conclude this chapter, therefore, with some suggestions about moving to a final draft or what Wolcott calls 'tightening up' (1990: 47).

23.4 TIGHTENING UP

Make sure all parts are properly in place before tightening. (directions for assembling a new wheelbarrow, reported by Wolcott, 1990: 47)

Wolcott's analogy of assembling a wheelbarrow reminds us that no subtle change of detail will work if the macrostructure of your thesis is not properly in place. As he puts it:

Before you start tightening, take a look at how the whole thing is coming together. Do you have everything you need? (And do you need everything you have? Remember, you're only supposed to be tightening up that wheelbarrow, not filling it!). (1990: 48)

You are likely to be too close to your work to tell easily whether everything is properly in place. As Cryer suggests, the author of a thesis:

will know it inside and out and back to front. So the link between its components may be clear to you, while not being as clear to those who have met your work only recently. (1996: 186)

There are two ways of giving yourself the critical distance necessary to see whether all the parts of your thesis are in place. First, if time allows, put it to one side for a while. After a time on the back burner, Wolcott notes:

> I do a better job of strengthening the interpretation, spotting discrepancies and repetitions, locating irregularities in sequence or logic, and discovering overworked words, phrases, and patterns after periods of benign neglect. (1990: 52)

Locating what Wolcott calls 'irregularities' can mean deleting particular points to which you may have become attached but which detract from your overall argument (Clive Seale, personal correspondence).

A second strategy to obtain distance is to give a talk on your research during the writing-up stage or to find:

> someone new to your work who will listen to you explaining it or will read the draft thesis and tell you where they have trouble following. (Cryer, 1996: 186)

Once the macrostructure is in place, it is time to tighten up the microstructure. Among the things to look at here are:

- unclear or infelicitous language
- over-large claims about your data or analysis
- needless repetition
- insufficient detail (see Wolcott, 1990: 49–50).

When you have done all of these things, you must recognize that the tightening-up period is nearly over. Certainly, you can ask yourself: 'Have I really got the last details in? Got them right?' (Strauss and Corbin, 1990: 235).

To check this out, you can ask your supervisor and/or fellow students to have one final read and then respond to their comments. But remember: the revision process is potentially endless! The real cop-out is not submitting a less than perfect thesis but being stuck in a process of endless revisions:

> Part of an increasing maturity as a research-writer is to understand that no manuscript is ever finished. (Strauss and Corbin, 1990: 235)

Just as parents eventually realize that their children have become adults and will leave home, now is the time to make the break with your manuscript. Like 'empty nest' parents, you should be ready to strike out in new directions. But first you must 'let go'.

23.5 CONCLUDING REMARKS

Your data-analysis chapters are (or should be) the key basis on which your dissertation will be judged. However, different issues arise in relation to the organization of individual chapters ('the microstructure') and the overall organization of your thesis ('the macrostructure').

Good overall organization is based upon planning your table of contents at an early stage and continually revising it. You also need to decide the form of the 'story' you want to tell about your research and structure your data chapters accordingly. Each data chapter should have a microstructure based on three sections: an introduction in which you explain what you are going to do in advance; the main section in which you work through your data in terms of what you have already said; and, finally, a conclusion in which you summarize what you have shown and connect to the next chapter.

KEY POINTS

In planning the overall (macro)structure of your thesis:

- Work out what main message and findings you want your data chapters to contain.
- Ensure that the structure of your thesis underlines that message.
- Strip out or minimize draft chapters that are peripheral to your argument.

When writing data chapters, it is wise to consider the following instructions:

- Make one point at a time.
- Context each data extract in your argument.
- Show that you understand the limitations of your analysis.
- Always number your data extracts.
- Realize that the reader will need to be convinced and that what is obvious to you will not always be so clear to others.

NOTES

1   As we shall see, the idea of the hypothesis story and the mystery story derives from Alasuutari (1995).
2   See Chapter 14 for a discussion of these issues in terms of 'validity' and 'reliability' and Chapter 12 for an explanation of how diagrams and charts may illustrate your rigorous thinking. On this latter point, see also Mason (1996: 131–3) and Strauss and Corbin (1990: 131–7).

Further reading

Harry Wolcott's *Writing Up Qualitative Research* (Sage, 1990) is a marvellous account of how to write up data. Useful, shorter treatments are: Pat Cryer's *The Research Student's Guide to Success* (Open University Press, 1996), Chapter 18; Pertti Alasuutari's *Researching Culture: Qualitative Method and Cultural Studies* (Sage, 1995), Chapter 14; and Anselm Strauss and Juliet Corbin's *Basics of Qualitative Research* (Sage, 1990), Chapter 13.

Exercise 23.1

Try organizing your data analysis into two chapters. Don't do this arbitrarily but find a logical way to do it. Now try reordering this material into five shorter chapters with a different logic. Consider which format works best and why.

Exercise 23.2

Select a coherent piece of your data analysis which might become a chapter. Give the chapter a title that fits what you are trying to do there. Using Tables 23.1 and 23.2, now:

1   Write an introduction for this chapter.

2   Write a conclusion.

3   Add in your data analysis and show the whole chapter to a colleague. Ask them to what extent your introduction and conclusion helped them to see what you were getting at. If so, why? If not, why not?

4   Now revise and repeat the process.

The Final Chapter

24.1 INTRODUCTION

In the previous chapter, I concluded with the recommendation to 'let go'. However, since all research reports (including dissertations) seem to end with a set of 'conclusions', you cannot finally let go until your concluding chapter is written. Having cycled painfully to the top of the hill, the great temptation at this point is to relax and freewheel down to the finish. In practice, such relaxation of effort is reflected in the all too common 'summaries' found in the final chapter of dissertations.

Although summaries are often quite useful devices at the end of data-analysis chapters, I suggest that you should never write a summary as your concluding chapter. If your readers need a summary at this point, then your 'macrostructure' (Alasuutari's concept discussed in the previous chapter) is not in place. If it is in place, then what you have said should already be crystal clear. So resist the temptations of a final downhill freewheel.

But does this mean that do you even need a concluding chapter? Cannot your thesis stop after you have finished your data analysis?

Take a musical example. Classical symphonies typically end with a fast movement marked 'allegro' or 'presto'. Rather than a mere recapitulation of earlier themes, they take them up and develop them still more. As such, they seem designed to provide listeners with some of the most stimulating material in the composition. So your final chapter is, indeed, necessary. But it should function to stimulate your readers by demonstrating how your research has stimulated you.

This chapter begins by showing you the interesting and liberating functions of a concluding chapter. It then provides some practical suggestions about what this chapter should contain and reviews the balance between confessing to your errors and proclaiming your achievements. I go on to show how your concluding chapter should reconnect your data analysis to the basic analytic questions that have inspired you and should think through what your research can offer to a range of different audiences. Finally, I demonstrate why writing your final chapter can be fun.

24.2   THE FINAL CHAPTER AS MUTUAL STIMULATION

Your final chapter should be stimulating for you to write. If this is the case, it is likely to stimulate your readers. Part of that stimulation arises in linking the particularities of your own research back to the more general issues that arise within (your part) of your discipline. As the authors of the standard British text on PhDs comment:

> You are not doing some research for its own sake; you are doing it in order to demonstrate that you are a fully professional researcher, with a good grasp of what is happening in your field and capable of evaluating the impact of new contributions to it – your own as well as others. (Phillips and Pugh, 1994: 60)

Your contribution is what you must set out to demonstrate in your final chapter:

> It is here that you underline the significance [to your discipline] of your analysis, point out the limitations in your material, suggest what new work is appropriate, and so on. (1994: 59)

Phillips and Pugh's remarks suggest part of the answer to the practical question: what exactly should your final chapter contain?

24.3   WHAT EXACTLY SHOULD YOUR FINAL CHAPTER CONTAIN?

> In the most general terms it [your final chapter] is a discussion as to why and in what way ... the theory that you started with [is] now different as a result of your research work. Thus your successors (who include, of course, yourself) now face a different situation when determining what their research work should be since they now have to take account of your work. (Phillips and Pugh, 1994: 59–60)

TABLE 24.1 SUGGESTED CONTENTS FOR YOUR FINAL CHAPTER

- The relation between the work done, the original research questions, previous work discussed in the literature review chapter and any new work appearing since the study began
- Some answer to the classic examiner's question: 'if you were doing this study all over again is there anything you would do differently? Why so?; that is, the lessons to be learned from the conduct of the study
- Any implications for policy and practice
- Further research that might follow from your findings, methods or concepts used

Source: adapted from Murcott (1997: 3)

A helpful way of looking at this is in terms of Murcott's question: 'What does the candidate want the reader to make of all this?' (1997: 3). As Table 24.1 shows, the final chapter offers you the opportunity to give your own twist to the wider implications of your research. Such implications must, of course, reflect your own critical sense of what is good and not so good in your own research. Always remember: unless you define your own sense of the limitations (and implications) of your work, your readers will do it for you!

You can, however, go too far in focusing solely on the limitations of your work. Research reports should not just be confessions! In the next section, I discuss the balance between owning up to where you feel you went wrong and blowing your own trumpet about your achievements.

24.4 CONFESSIONS AND TRUMPETS

As Wolcott notes, in assessing your thesis your examiners will recognize that chance happenings as well as your research design have limited (as well as improved) your research. Be upfront about these matters. So, in your final chapter, write:

> a broad disclaimer in which (you) make quite clear (your) recognition of all the limitations of the study (e.g. that it occurred in a particular place, at a particular time, and under particular circumstances; that certain factors render the study atypical; that limited generalization is warranted; etc). (1990: 30)

However, what Wolcott calls 'this litany of limitations' should be coupled with a stress on what you believe you have achieved. So, as in life, be realistic but don't undersell yourself! This can be in the form of:

> a conservative closing statement that reviews succinctly what has been attempted, what has been learned, and what new questions have been raised. (1990: 56)

Wolcott's helpful suggestion is, in my view, somewhat undermined by his use of the adjective 'conservative'. Beware of employing so much caution that you bore the reader! If you can effectively show why you have been stimulated, then you are much more likely to stimulate your audience.

Stimulation requires an active imagination. And, in science, it is theory which feeds the imagination.

Theory has been extensively discussed in the first three parts of this volume. Here, I want to suggest a practical sense of theorizing which can help in writing an effective final chapter.

24.5 THEORIZING AS THINKING THROUGH DATA

An imaginative conclusion will move on from the careful description and analysis of your earlier chapters to a stimulating but critical view of the overall implications of your research. Without this, your research may amount to no more than a set of descriptions of data achieved by some mechanical use of a method.

Since much qualitative research works inductively, generating and testing hypotheses during data analysis, your final chapter is often the best place to present theoretical linkages and speculations. As Alasuutari comments, in qualitative data analysis:

> One preferably starts directly from empirical examples, develops the questions by discussing them, and gradually leads the reader into interpretations of the material and to more general implications of the results. If one feels like discussing and constructing them, the best position for grand theoretical models is *in the final pages*. (1995: 183, my emphasis)

Grounded theory is a term used to describe a way of inducing theoretically based generalizations from qualitative data. However, it is crucial that, if grounded theory is your 'thing', you use it imaginatively rather than as a label to dress up a largely pedestrian study.

As I argue in Chapter 15, some grounded theory studies fall short of imagination. This possibility is recognized in a leading text on grounded theory:

> It is entirely possible to complete a grounded theory study, or any study, yet not produce findings that are significant. If the researcher simply follows the grounded theory procedures/canons without imagination or insight into what the data are reflecting – because he or she fails to see what they are really saying except in terms of trivial or well-known phenomena – then the published findings can be judged as failing on this criterion [i.e. of being significant]. (Strauss and Corbin, 1990: 256)

The final chapter is likely to be the place where your examiners will discover whether your theoretical pretensions are, as implied by Strauss and Corbin, merely mechanical. But, if theory must never be mere window dressing, this does not mean that theory is ultimately more important than research. Theory without data is empty; data without theory says nothing. This reciprocal relationship between theory and data is well captured by Coffey and Atkinson. As they put it:

> Data are there to think with and to think about … . We should bring to them the full range of intellectual resources, derived from theoretical perspectives, substantive traditions, research literature and other sources … [this means] that methods of data collection and data analysis do not make sense when treated in an intellectual vacuum and divorced from more general and fundamental disciplinary frameworks. (1996: 153)

The problem is that you may become so immersed in your highly specific research topic that you are ill-prepared to step back and to think about what Coffey and Atkinson call 'more general and fundamental disciplinary frameworks'. You can give your research this broader perspective by forcing yourself to think about how what you have discovered may relate to broader issues than your original research topic. In this way, a very narrow topic may be related to much broader social processes. As we saw in Chapter 15, this was how Mary Douglas's anthropological study of an African tribe took us from a very narrow issue (how the Lele perceive the pangolin) to a very broad social process (how societies respond to anomalous entities). In this way, argue Coffey and Atkinson:

> qualitative data, analyzed with close attention to detail, understood in terms of their internal patterns and forms, should be used to develop theoretical ideas about social processes and cultural forms that have relevance *beyond these data themselves*. (1996: 163, my emphasis)

24.6 WRITING FOR AUDIENCES

A continuing message of this book is that, like any form of writing, writing a research report should always be framed for particular audiences. Drawing on this insight, many of my PhD students have organized their concluding chapters in terms of the different audiences who might be interested in their research.

Take the case of Moira Kelly's research on how her respondents describe the death of a spouse (discussed in Chapter 3). Her concluding chapter describes what her findings imply for four different audiences: methodologists, theorists, people with a substantive interest in the sociology of health and illness, and health policy-makers.

One useful exercise to get you thinking about how to proceed in this way is simply to list all the possible audiences for your research. When I used this exercise recently with students doing business PhDs at the Helsinki School of Economics, the following audiences were noted:

- disciplinary (e.g. management, organization studies, marketing)
- methodological (e.g. case study researchers, interviewers, etc.)
- practitioners (e.g. managers, entrepreneurs, marketers, etc.)
- the general public (clients, consumers, politicians, etc.).

Such a list of your likely audiences should give you a good idea of how you could structure an effective concluding chapter. But don't just guess what will most interest your audiences! Show your findings to groups drawn from each audience and find out what is relevant to them (see Chapter 28 for further discussion of audiences for research).

24.7   WHY YOUR FINAL CHAPTER CAN BE FUN

It may surprise you to think that writing your concluding chapter can be fun. Having struggled to reach the end of your data chapters, you may already be exhausted and tempted to try to get away with a short concluding summary. After all you feel, what more can you add?

I have good news for you! Until your final chapter, you have had to be highly disciplined. Not only have you had to stick to the point, you also (I hope) have had to stick closely to your data. Your only respite has been your footnotes. Used properly, footnotes are the place for asides and barbed comments (never the place for references).

But, if footnotes can be fun, so can your concluding chapter. For this is the place where caution temporarily should go out of the window and lateral thinking should rule. Here is the place to make broader links, eschewing the narrow focus found in the rest of your thesis. Here 'off the wall' comments ('from left field' as they say in baseball) are not only allowable but welcome. At last, perhaps, here is a space for you to reveal your true colours – providing that you recognize that such self-expression has always to be recipient designed for an audience.

24.8   CONCLUDING REMARKS

Let me make an obvious point: when you have finished your final chapter, it is time to submit your thesis. Yes I know research reports can always be improved and the beauty of word processing is that the mechanical aspects of revision are quite simple. But how long do you want to stay a student? Providing your supervisor is supportive, isn't it better to submit right now? Even if your examiners require changes, at least your rewrites will have a pragmatic focus.

Being a perfectionist sounds like a nice identity. As Becker has commented:

> Getting it out the door is not the only thing people value. A lot of important work in a lot of fields has been done with little regard for whether it ever got out the door.

Scholars and artists, especially, believe that if they wait long enough they may find a more comprehensive and logical way to say what they think. (1986: 123)

However, Becker also makes us aware that rewriting can also be the alibi for the persistent waverer. By contrast, he tells us:

I like to get it out the door. Although I like to rewrite and tinker with organization and wording, I soon either put work aside as not ready to be written or get it into a form to go out the door. (1986: 124)

After a long period of study, do you really want to 'put work aside'? Follow your supervisor's advice (providing the supervisor is not a ditherer!) and get your work 'out the door'!

KEY POINTS

You should never write a summary as your concluding chapter. Instead, your final chapter must help the reader to decide what to make of your dissertation. This should explain:

- The relation between the work done, the original research questions, previous work discussed in the literature review chapter and any new work appearing since the study began.
- Anything you would do differently now.
- Implications for policy and practice.
- Further research that might follow from your findings, methods or concepts used.
- The limitations of your own study.

Above all, your final chapter should stimulate your readers by:

- Showing how theories have helped you think through your data.
- Addressing each of the audiences who might be interested in your work.

Further reading

Estelle Phillips and Derek Pugh's *How To Get a PhD* (2nd edn, Open University Press, 1994), Chapter 6, is the best British account of the practical issues involved in concluding a research dissertation. On using theory to develop your conclusions, see: Pertti Alasuutari's *Researching Culture:*

Qualitative Method and Cultural Studies (Sage, 1995), Chapter 13; Anselm Strauss and Juliet Corbin's *Basics of Qualitative Research* (Sage, 1990), Chapters 1–4; Jennifer Mason's *Qualitative Researching* (Sage, 1996), Chapter 7; Amanda Coffey and Paul Atkinson's *Making Sense of Qualitative Data* (Sage, 1996), Chapter 6.

Exercise 24.1

Get into the habit of keeping files on each of the issues below (taken from Table 24.1):

● the relation between your present work and your original research questions

● anything you would do differently now

● implications for policy and practice

● further research that might follow from your findings, methods or concepts

● the limitations of your own study.

At regular intervals, attempt to write a summary of what you can currently say about each of these issues.

Exercise 24.2

As this chapter has argued:

Data are there to think with and to think about ... [this means] that methods of data collection and data analysis do not make sense when treated in an intellectual vacuum and divorced from more general and fundamental disciplinary frameworks. (Coffey and Atkinson, 1996: 153)

Find one or two recent journal articles which you think are important and, following Coffey and Atkinson, show why your dissertation does not exist 'in an intellectual vacuum'.

Exercise 24.3

Make a list of the different audiences who might be interested in your research (e.g. disciplinary, methodological, practitioners, general public).

Now work out how you could write a chapter which framed the contribution of your research for each of these audiences.

The PhD Examination

For PhD students, the oral or viva is a crucial and much feared part
of the process. It may also seem to be shrouded in mystery, like
some weird Masonic ritual! Part Six attempts to demystify the
PhD examination.

25 Surviving a PhD Oral

25.1 INTRODUCTION

When you have finished a BA or MA thesis, your task is done. Your research paper will now be marked but its grading will be out of your hands. However, if you are working for a PhD, one further task awaits you – your oral examination or 'viva'. Here you will be expected to 'defend' your dissertation and your performance will have an impact on the outcome. For instance, in the UK, your dissertation may pass but you may be required to retake your viva if your performance is weak.

How this viva is conducted will vary between different universities and countries. In the UK, a specialist external examiner will be appointed from outside your university and will take the lead in questioning you. Further questions will come from an internal examiner who may be rather less of a specialist in your area.

In other countries, many more academics may be able to question you. In the Nordic countries, for instance, an 'opponent' will be appointed from outside your university to interrogate you. The viva will be a public affair with members of the audience able to ask questions.

In Scandinavia, your faculty committee are usually passive observers of the dialogue between the opponent and candidate. By contrast, in North America, you will face a faculty committee all of whom may ask you questions. The character of this dialogue can vary considerably as an American text points out:

> The defense ranges from a congenial ritual in which the student publicly presents his or her findings to an assemblage of receptive "colleagues," to a more excruciating examination of the quality of the dissertation and grilling of the candidate by an unsympathetic faculty committee. (Rudestam and Newton, 1992: 142)

To use Rudestam and Newton's word, what can a 'grilling' look like? In this chapter, I set out to prepare you for a PhD oral examination, reviewing the mechanics of the oral and its possible outcomes (including the subsequent revisions to your thesis that your examiners may require).

This chapter seeks to offer sensible reassurance. As I will later demonstrate, the viva is not usually quite as awful as you may suspect. However, to prepare you for the worst, I begin with some 'horror' stories.

25.2 VIVA HORROR STORIES

One student reported a common fear about an impending viva: 'When I went into that room, I was scared – what if they ask me something I do not know, what if they said: this a PhD, you have got to be joking?' Such fears are normal; terrible experiences are much rarer. Murray (2003: 2) provides four examples of pretty nasty vivas:

● A nine-hour viva.
● Aggressive examiners who seem to want to break down the candidate.
● The candidate forgetting everything she knew ('blank mind syndrome').
● Examiner(s) deciding that you have made a serious error; but this is based on a misunderstanding about what you have said and you don't have the confidence to correct them.

I have a horror story of my own to add. Back in the 1960s, I felt confident about submitting my thesis because of the praise it had received from my PhD supervisors. I was totally unprepared when the external examiner was very critical of what I had written. Indeed, I later learned that it was only my strong defence at the viva that saved me from being failed! Fortunately, the external examiner gave me several pages of suggestions and I managed to put together a revised version which was passed twelve months later.

By now, you may be thoroughly scared. But take comfort. Supervision is much better monitored nowadays and is usually much more effective than the example of the three-meeting supervisor described in Chapter 19. There are also a number of practical steps you can take beforehand to prepare for your examination.

25.3 PREPARING FOR YOUR ORAL

Examiners need time to read your dissertation. They also have busy diaries. So you will probably have between one to three months between submission of your dissertation and your oral examination. How should you spend this time?

TABLE 25.1 PREPARING FOR A PHD ORAL EXAMINATION

- Revise your thesis, particularly the concluding chapter
- Prepare a list of points you want to get across
- Be ready to explain and to defend any changes to your original research question
- Read up recent work in your field
- Find out about your external/internal examiners' work
- Practise with others in a mock viva

In the immediate weeks after submission, with the viva some way away, you deserve some time off after your exertions – although a break is usually an unavailable luxury to students in full-time employment. However, as your viva approaches, some preparation is very useful. This preparation can take a number of forms, as set out in Table 25.1.

Following Table 25.1, Phillips and Pugh (1994) suggest that summarizing in a sentence each page of your finished thesis can be a very effective way of revising your thesis so that you will be fully in touch with it on the big day. You should then use this summary as a basis for deciding which points you want to try to get across at the examination.

Now is a good time to research your examiners' own work. Reading their latest papers may well inform you about the likely slant of their questions and, perhaps, allow you to look for any links between your work and theirs – although you should first consult your supervisor about whether this is appropriate.

Finally, try to find some fellow students or some friendly faculty members prepared to simulate an oral examination.

25.4 DOING THE ORAL

Remember that, as a result of your research, you are now a specialist. This probably means that you now know more about your topic than your examiners. As Rudestam and Newton put it:

> In the best of cases, the oral defense is an opportunity to think about and articulate the implications of your study [for] your own discipline and to be challenged by your committee to claim your right to sit among them as an acknowledged expert in your field of study. (1992: 142)

Being 'an acknowledged expert' is not a licence to wallow in jargon. By contrast, part of one's expertise is the ability to explain your work in a straightforward way and to make links with the work of others.

So, at the viva, be ready to summarize your main research problem, the contribution of your research and how you would do anything differently. Remember

TABLE 25.2   TIPS FOR THE ORAL EXAMINATION

- Always say if you have not understood a question; if so, ask for more clarification
- Avoid one-word/sentence answers even if the question is a 'closed' one. Use the questions as opportunities to get your point across by making links between the questions and the things you want to say
- Avoid overlong answers which drift very far from the original question
- Ask if you are on the right track and if your examiners want to know more
- Refer to the list of points you want to get across when your examiners ask whether there is anything they have not covered
- Ask your supervisor to make notes of questions and answers. This will be of considerable use if you have to revise your thesis and/or intend to publish any of it.

Source: adapted in part from (Clive Seale, personal correspondence)

that the oral examination is not a test of memory, so you will be allowed to refer to the text of your thesis as necessary.

In order to add more substance to these points, I have appended at the end of this chapter some details of a Swedish PhD dissertation that I examined in September 1998. While the questions I asked, as the opponent, were, of course, tied to that particular dissertation, I believe that they can give you some flavour of the kind of concerns, both specific and general, that examiners raise at PhD vivas.

As Clive Seale (personal correspondence) has pointed out, the skills you need at an oral examination are not dissimilar to those you need at a job interview (see Chapter 29). In both situations, it helps to be fairly assertive while respecting the knowledge and experience of your interviewer. Table 25.2 offers some tips for your oral along these lines.

25.5   OUTCOMES

In most British universities, the possible outcomes of a PhD viva are as follows (see also Phillips and Pugh, 1994: 142–5):

- The immediate award of the PhD – often subject to certain minor corrections or amendments.
- The requirement that you put right some weaknesses identified in writing by the examiners (the 'Yes, but …' result as Phillips and Pugh (1994: 143) put it) and a given time period (up to two years) to do this.
- A pass on the dissertation but a fail on the viva with an opportunity to resit the latter after a period of up to a year.
- The examiners deem your dissertation inadequate and cannot see any way in which it can be successfully revised but offer you the lower award of an MPhil degree.
- An outright fail with no possibility of resubmission and no offer of any lower degree.

Despite your worse fears, an outright fail is rare. This is less to do with the goodwill of your examiners than with the fact that your supervisor(s) are unlikely to recommend submission unless they believe that your work has a reasonable chance of passing – although the recent punitive policy of the British Economic and Social Research Council on departments whose funded students take more than four years to submit may change this.

If you are passed, remember to ask for advice about what parts of your thesis might be publishable, how you should revise or shorten them and which journals might be the best place to submit them. Now go out and celebrate!

25.6 REVISING YOUR THESIS AFTER THE ORAL

In the UK, it is common practice for examiners to require some rewriting of your thesis before they will pass it. After discussion with your supervisor, they will allow you a certain period to undertake such revision – normally between six and eighteen months.

Following Clive Seale (personal correspondence), I suggest below some tips to follow when you are revising a thesis for re-examination:

- Make a list of the main criticisms.
- Make sure your revisions address all of these criticisms.
- Resubmit your thesis together with a separate sheet of paper identifying what you understand the criticisms to have been, how you have addressed them and the page numbers where this has been done.

25.7 A CASE STUDY

One example of an actual PhD oral may be helpful. Vesa Leppanen completed his thesis at the Department of Sociology at Lund University in Sweden. I was appointed his opponent because Vesa's work was related to mine analytically (we both use **conversation analysis** – CA) and substantively (we both had studied communication between health care professionals and patients).

25.7.1 A brief summary of the dissertation

Vesa had researched encounters between Swedish district nurses and their elderly patients. These encounters may take place in the patient's home or at a clinic. Their primary clinical purpose is to perform routine tasks like measuring blood pressure or giving injections. Naturally, in the course of these encounters, other matters arise – from the patient raising a problem to the nurse giving advice. A sample of thirty-two consultations provided just over ten hours of videotaped and transcribed nurse–patient interaction – half at primary care centres, half in patients' homes (pp. 56–7). Standard CA notation was used on the audio. Non-verbal activities were reported by descriptions placed immediately above the place in the transcript where they occurred.

Four principal topics were studied:

- the interactional achievement of tests and treatments
- patients' presentations of their concerns
- the delivery of test results to patients
- advice-giving about health behaviours.

The dissertation concludes with a summary of the research findings, a practical recommendation that such data is highly appropriate in training nurses (and many other practitioners) and some general implications for future research. Its call for the study of apparently non-problematic research settings and data is a useful reminder of Sacks's (1992) call, three decades ago, to discover the extraordinary in the ordinary.

25.7.2 My questions

What do you see as the main contribution of your research?

Would you do anything differently now?

Chapter 4 on tests and treatments reads as very 'descriptive' based on one extended case. Would you agree?

On p. 88, you explain that this chapter serves as a background to the other three data chapters. But can you say anything more, e.g. do you ever meet resistance to tests? Do nurses ever have to work at getting permission?

(Several detailed questions on the data analysis follow. Now come some more general points.)

Your data is equally drawn from home and clinic. Why did you decide not to systematically compare these different environments? Don't clinic and home provide very different resources? (I mention one of my past PhDs, by Maura Hunt, who had looked at the problems that community nurses may face in beginning their work in the patient's home as well as the work of Anssi Peräkylä on doctors' use of X-rays and scans in the clinic to 'prove' diagnoses to patients.)

Your use of the video material. I remember us talking about your video data on nurses touching patients when I visited Lund in March 1996. Yet the only detailed treatment is on pp. 213–18 where you use the video to show how the nurse underlines advice by abandoning other tasks, gazing at the patient and waving a pill bottle. Why is there relatively little use of the video data elsewhere?

(I discuss various possible uses of the video data that might have strengthened the dissertation.)

Have you never given feedback to the nurses you studied? Why not?

Your only practical conclusion is about the relevance of this kind of detailed research for professional training. I entirely agree about this but isn't there more that you can say?

Your discussion of the analytic implications of your research is not very specific. How does your work advance other well-known [named] studies and findings?

25.7.3 My concluding remarks

This is a fascinating, detailed and orderly study of great analytic interest. I learned a lot from reading it. It is also an exemplary case from which nurses and beginning researchers could learn a great deal about the value of the analytic mentality of CA.

The highlights for me were:

1   Various parts of Ch.5. First, the most detailed treatment on institutional data about the positioning and functioning of the question: 'how are you?' Second, the discussion in Ch.5 about how pts achieve recipiency for the statement of their concerns.
2   Parts of Ch.7. In particular, nurses finding the right position to deliver advice.
3   An unusually lively methods (or procedures) chapter. This provides a nice natural history of your research and a lovely account of the ethnographic work that preceded it.
4   Throughout, I liked your non-partisan spirit and open-mindedness, particularly towards the judicious combination of CA and **ethnography** (e.g. p. 44).

Of course, as you show, bad news is usually delayed. So, in this case too. But I really have only two reservations. First, is your somewhat limited use of your video data. Second, is your underplaying of the practical relevance of your research.

But, in the context of such a well-crafted dissertation, these are quibbles. I eagerly encourage you to turn parts of thesis into journal articles. In particular:

● Your excellent summary and critique of much nursing research (pp. 21–7) is highly relevant in a field riddled by crude **positivism** and **emotionalism**.
● Your account of patients' skills in positioning their statement of their concerns is highly original and publishable (pp. 110–28). Perhaps it could be combined with your comparison (pp. 130–1) with Jefferson on everyday troubles-telling or perhaps the latter could be a separate article.
● Parts of Ch.7 where you compare your findings with other [named] research on advice-giving and advice-reception are also highly publishable.

25.7.4   The outcome

I am pleased to say Vesa was awarded his PhD by his local committee. When I last heard, Dr Leppanen had a teaching position at a Swedish university and his supervisor, Professor Ann-Mari Sellerberg, had obtained a substantial research grant for the two of them to study telephone counselling by community nurses.

25.7.5   General implications

1   My two first questions are pretty standard for PhD vivas:

   'What do you see as the main contribution of your research?'
   'Would you do anything differently now?'

   It pays to prepare your answers to such questions!

2   Prepare for constructive criticism of your analysis, e.g. 'Chapter 4 on tests and treatments reads as very "descriptive" based on one extended case. Would you agree?' (This is a nice example of a question where a one-word answer would have been inappropriate. The right strategy here might be to agree in part but point to counter-evidence elsewhere.)

3   Prepare to defend your methods and selection of cases, e.g. 'Your data is equally drawn from home and clinic. Why did you decide not to systematically compare these different environments?' (If possible, explain the advantages of not making such a comparison.)

4   Be ready to discuss further the contribution of your research to your discipline and (where relevant) to practitioners and policy-makers.

5   Expect your examiners to offer advice about which parts of your thesis may be publishable (see my concluding remarks).

25.8   CONCLUDING REMARKS

Although the prospect of a PhD oral is intimidating, horror stories are actually quite rare. Use your revision period to prepare a list of points you want to get across at the examination. Now is also the time to find out about your examiners' own published work. In addition, try to get some practice with others in a mock viva.

At the oral examination, always say if you have not understood a question and, if so, ask for more clarification. Avoid one-word/sentence answers even if the question is a 'closed' one. Use the questions as opportunities to get your point across by making links between the questions and the things you want to say. But avoid overlong answers which drift very far from the original question. Finally, refer to the list of points you want to get across when your examiners ask whether there is anything they have not covered.

It is also a good idea to ask your supervisor to make notes of questions and answers. This will be of considerable use if you have to revise your thesis and/or intend to publish any of it.

KEY POINTS

There are many ways to prepare for your oral. You can:

- Revise your thesis, particularly the concluding chapter.
- Prepare a list of points you want to get across.
- Be ready to explain and to defend any changes to your original research question.
- Read up recent work in your field.
- Find out about your external/internal examiners' work.
- Practise with others in a mock viva.

At the oral itself:

- Always say if you have not understood a question; if so, ask for more clarification.
- Avoid one-word/sentence answers even if the question is a 'closed' one. Use the questions as opportunities to get your point across by making links between the questions and the things you want to say.
- Avoid overlong answers which drift very far from the original question.
- Ask if you are on the right track and if your examiners want to know more.

Further reading

The most useful guides to preparing for oral examinations are Pat Cryer's *The Research Student's Guide to Success* (Open University Press,1996), Chapter 19, and Estelle Phillips and Derek Pugh's *How To Get a PhD* (2nd edn, Open University Press, 1994), Chapter 10. For an American guide, see Kjell Rudestam and Rae Newton's *Surviving Your Dissertation* (Sage, 1992), Chapter 8. A useful web link is: http://www.cs.man.ac.uk/infobank/broada/cs/cs710/viva.html

Exercise 25.1

To find out about your examiners' own published work, read at least one book or journal article by each of them. As you read, make notes about the following points:

1   What **model** of social research (see Chapter 7) is being used? How far does it differ or complement your own? What useful lessons can you learn from these differences or similarities?

2   Are there any theoretical developments, methodological innovations or substantive findings that relate to your own work? If so, how can you bring these out in the oral? If not, how can you demonstrate respect for your examiner's approach while standing up for your own?

3   Examine the writing style in this material. How different is it from your own? What can you learn from these differences (or similarities)? For example, do these simply reflect the differing demands of (say) a scholarly journal and a research dissertation or are there basic differences of temperament and outlook?

Exercise 25.2

When you have completed your revision, ask your supervisor or a couple of your fellow students who are familiar with your research to give you a mock oral examination. Following Table 25.2 and using your prepared list of points that you want to get across, try out your skills in answering their questions.

PART SEVEN

Review

This part of the book contains just one chapter. It sums up
many of the themes discussed in this work by seeking
to describe how to do 'effective' qualitative research.

Effective Qualitative Research

26.1 INTRODUCTION

In this chapter, I want to pull together the different threads that have run through this book. Throughout, I have encouraged you to distinguish relatively easy activities from the really tough ones and to concentrate your efforts on the latter. For instance, writing a literature review should be relatively easy for any graduate student (see Chapter 21). Equally, obtaining your data does not need to be too difficult if you follow some of my suggestions in Chapter 11.

By contrast, the really tough issues tend to concern data analysis. This area is discussed in detail in Part Three of this book. In this short chapter, I want to provide a snapshot of the issues involved in the form of four rules to encourage effective qualitative research. Here are the rules:

- Keep it simple.
- Take advantage of using qualitative data.
- Avoid 'drowning in data'.
- Avoid 'journalistic' questions and answers.

I will now review each rule in turn. But one word of warning: none of us can escape our intellectual biography. I have been influenced in more ways than I can realize by my training and experience as (one kind of) a sociologist. Therefore, if any of my rules look a little odd in the light of your own discipline, please discuss it further with your supervisor. Even if you differ, at least you will have a point of departure!

26.2   KEEP IT SIMPLE

In Chapter 6, I identified a 'kitchen sink' mentality. Kitchen-sinkers attempt to study very broad problems, using many concepts and methods as well as large sets of data. Unfortunately, such a wide-ranging approach is unlikely to impress examiners and often will prevent you finishing your study.

In doing student research, simplicity is not a drawback but a necessity. Here are some ways to keep it simple:

● Narrow down your research problem (Chapter 6 offers a number of ways to do this).
● Use one **model** only.
● Use concepts which fit your model.
● Avoid multiple methods or, if you must use them, make sure they fit your model and research problem.
● Analyse a small data set (you can always add comparative data later – if you have time).
● Recognize that the comparative method can be used within a small data set (see Table 12.1).

26.3   TAKE ADVANTAGE OF USING QUALITATIVE DATA

Sometimes students elect to use qualitative methods because (they feel) they are not very good at statistics. This is not unreasonable (assuming they are right). However, qualitative methods are not appropriate for every research problem. In Chapter 2, I illustrated this point with one example of a study concerned with how 'psycho-social adversity' is related to asthma morbidity and care. I suggested that this study's focus on the relation between a set of **variables** could most effectively be researched using quantitative rather than qualitative methods. The former approach could employ **reliable**, standardized **operational definitions** of the variables studied. It could also work effectively with large data sets to establish correlations between these variables. By contrast, 'psycho-social adversity' is a very slippery concept within most qualitative research models. For instance, we can effectively study if participants themselves use such a concept, when and how they do so and with what local consequences. These are interesting research issues but they take us on a very different path to that envisaged by the original formulation of the research problem.

Considerations of this nature suggest that, if we want to do qualitative research, there are a set of strategies to *avoid*:

● Beginning with variables that you wish to relate.
● Beginning with problems that are already defined by members of society (e.g. social or administrative problems).

- Making assumptions about where things take place (e.g. is 'psycho-social adversity' a state of mind, a set of behaviours or a commonsense category employed in many different ways?).
- Searching for explanations: 'why' questions are usually best answered by quantitative methods.
- Working with **normative** assumptions (e.g. what is 'effective' communication?) and with prior versions of policy outputs.

However, we do not need to be entirely negative. Taking advantage of qualitative data means using some or all of the following strategies:

- Asking 'how', 'what' and 'when' and delaying (or avoiding) 'why' questions.
- Wherever possible (and it usually is possible) working with **naturally occurring** data (see Chapter 8).
- Studying the categories actually employed by participants (and when and how they are used – and with what effect).
- Studying what is unremarkable, the routine and the 'ordinary'.
- Recognizing the interconnectedness of subjects' categories and of their activities so that we always study how each is laminated upon another (see Chapter 4).

26.4 AVOID DROWNING IN DATA

A continuing argument of this book is that, if you delay your data analysis until your final year of study, you are courting disaster. By contrast, I have suggested:

- Start data analysis from day 1 – if you have no data then work with other people's data or use other publicly available material, e.g. texts of all kinds (see Chapter 11).
- One case is usually enough, providing you use internal comparisons (see Chapter 9); delay other cases and then try to sample theoretically.
- Keep to small targets – recognize that the student researcher is usually an apprentice and that learning from your mistakes is a key to success.
- Write above your PC the following motto: 'the point of qualitative research is to say a lot about a little'!

26.5 AVOID JOURNALISM

Journalism is a trade which, like any other, has good and bad features. In suggesting that you should avoid journalism, I do not mean to disparage what journalists do but simply to underline that qualitative research should not be the same thing as journalism.

Given the daily nature of most newspapers, journalists tend to focus on unusual, out of the ordinary events which often involve 'celebrities'. When they describe public rather than private issues, the journalistic focus, quite understandably, is on social problems as generally conceived, e.g. the economy, health policy, international relations.

My message to student researchers is: let journalists get on with what they do best. Your job is somewhat different. Now is the time to display the skills which you have learnt through years of training. As an apprentice qualitative researcher, your research will differ from most journalism in the following ways:

- How you formulate a problem, e.g. you will not begin from a social problem but will often seek to study something that is quite unremarkable, even 'obvious' to participants.
- Your data analysis will not rely on identifying gripping or spectacular stories; instead it will reveal the various ways in which apparently 'obvious' phenomena are put together.
- You will not rush to conclusions even when you have some compelling instances; instead, you will carefully sift all the evidence, actively seeking out **deviant cases**.
- You will employ the analytical resources of your discipline, working with your data in the context of a coherent model and set of concepts.
- You will unashamedly theorize about situations and events, but this will not serve as mere window-dressing (see Chapter 7); instead you will theorize with your data and build new theories.

26.6   CONCLUDING REMARKS

This book has been written to offer you practical ways to cope with some of the doubts that affect most novice qualitative researchers. Apart from what I can offer, I suggest that you turn to your fellow students. If you do so, I guarantee that nearly all of them will have been through many of the same doubts about their research and their capacity to do it.

If you remain worried that you do not have enough data, my message has been that you probably have too much! If you believe that your work is not particularly original, I ask: 'who is?' Just turning to some of the more pedestrian journal articles in your field should convince you of my argument.

As I suggest in Chapter 5, success in student qualitative research can be achieved by demonstrating that you are a 'professional'. We all know that professions contain people with varying capacities. So the bar you face is really quite low. However, I hope you will aspire to something higher!

KEY POINTS

Effective qualitative research can be undertaken on the basis of following these four rules:

- Keep it simple.
- Take advantage of what qualitative data can offer.
- Avoid drowning in data.
- Avoid 'journalistic' questions and answers.

Further reading

A longer version of this chapter is provided in David Silverman's *Interpreting Qualitative Data* (2nd edn, Sage, 2001), Chapter 10.

Exercise 26.1

Select any qualitative research report in your field. Now proceed as follows:

1 Apply to it the four rules discussed in this chapter.

2 Consider how well it stands in relation to each.

3 How could the research be improved?.

4 Do any of the rules need to be modified or overturned in the light of your example?

The Aftermath

The three chapters in Part Eight consider the aftermath of a finished piece of research. Depending on the level of your work, this may involve the possibility of getting your research published and, perhaps, getting a job. Whatever its level, a good research report always is designed for a particular audience.

Getting Published

27.1 INTRODUCTION

When you have finished your research study, you usually want its readership to extend beyond your supervisor and examiners. Don't expect that any more than a handful of people will borrow it from your university library. So, if you want your work to be disseminated, you must publish it.

Of course, there are less altruistic reasons involved here. 'Publish or perish' has, for many years, been the injunction that rings in the ears of most established academics. But at least such people have already succeeded in climbing upon the greasy pole. If you aspire to a university career as a teacher or researcher, you still need to work out how to clamber up onto the foot of that pole.

The most discouraging news is that, in these competitive times, it is unlikely that an MA or even a PhD will get you a university post. Certainly, a good reference from your supervisor and other examiners will help. And any teaching experience you have gained is also a plus mark if you are seeking a regular academic post. However, if you have not yet made it into print, faced with people with PhDs and several publications, you may not even make it on to the shortlist – at least at prestigious institutions.

Obviously, your desire to publish is only the first part of the battle. If you want to be successful, you need to think through a number of strategic choices which are outlined in the next section of this chapter. This is followed by a discussion of what kinds of paper appeal to academic journals and some suggestions about how to write an effective journal article.

27.2   STRATEGIC CHOICES

There are three sets of issues here: the medium of publication (usually a book or journal article), the particular outlet chosen (publisher or journal) and the kinds of material that obtain publication. Each of these issues are discussed below.

27.2.1   *Books*

You may have plans to publish your PhD as a book. But don't count on it! PhDs can be written for a tiny audience – effectively composed of your supervisor, committee or examiners. Before a publisher will even consider publication, they will usually want to know how you plan to revise your thesis to reach a wider audience.

The other thing is that publishers in the new millennium are not actually standing in line to publish (even revised) PhDs. Unless you can find a kind university press, you will discover that publishers are driven by the commercial need to find books that will sell upwards of 5000 copies. And the sad fact is that even a good research monograph will be unlikely to sell more than 1000 – an amount that probably will mean that its publisher will actually lose money.

In 1990, it was this situation that made Wolcott (1990) write about how difficult it can be to get your PhD published in entirety. A decade or more later, things are still tougher. Most social science publishers will now only rarely publish research monographs – even by established scholars. So, for most researchers, the answer is to be realistic! Pick out a promising data chapter and rewrite it for a journal.

27.2.2   *Choosing a journal*

The moral of this story is to plan ahead. So, if your supervisor likes, say, one of your data chapters, discuss with the supervisor whether it might not be worth sending it to a journal.

Of course, it is important to find the journal which is likely to be most sympathetic to what you have to say because its audience shares your interests and its editorial policy is favourable to your kinds of ideas and/or data.

For example, qualitative researchers should be cautious about journals that expect papers to be written in the standard form of introduction, methods, results and discussion. As Alasuutari points out, this format is likely to be inappropriate to non-quantitative, inductive studies (1995: 180–1). Again, not all qualitative journals have the same policy about legitimate approaches and/or adequate datasets. For instance, a paper submitted by one of my students was unexpectedly turned down on the grounds that 'it did not have a big enough data set'.

So find the right journal. Seek guidance from established academics and look at recent editions of journals they mention. Look out for statements of policy printed in most journals and note changes of editor and of editorial policy.

27.2.3 Responding to editors' decisions

Once submitted, don't be discouraged by a rejection. Most journal articles are rejected or returned with a request for substantial revision. So treat the outcome as a learning experience.

The great thing is that, in return for a submission, you are very likely to get a set of (often detailed) referees' comments. Treat these as gold dust. However biased you might think they are, they inform you, in practical detail, of the external audience outside (what may be) your cosy relationship with your supervisor. So now you can see what might be required to make your way in the academic world. If your resubmission is not much better received, you probably have only yourself to blame.

27.2.4 Recognizing the format for a journal article

Above all, bear in mind that journal articles (usually around 6000 words) are often much shorter than data chapters from a PhD. This can make things very difficult for you since, in a shorter space, you must fill in your audience about the overall orientation of your research. So, in writing a journal article, you must, at one and the same time, be highly focused but also provide a proper context.

Easier said than done! How do you write a paper that is likely to be published? And how do you cope with such strict word limits? Don't you need more rather than fewer words to explain the context of your research?

There are four quick solutions to these dilemmas:

- Select a topic which will be the most intriguing to readers of this journal.
- Ensure that this topic can be handled with a limited amount of data extracts.
- Provide the *appropriate* context for your work – for instance, your audience will not need to be reminded about the basic assumptions of research in their area.
- Stick rigidly to the point throughout.

The rest of this chapter will expand upon this advice. Shortly, I will discuss how to focus a journal article within the required word length. Such focus, of course,

TABLE 27.1 EVALUATION OF QUALITATIVE ARTICLES

1	Goodness of fit between the **model** chosen and what is actually delivered
2	Internal coherence
3	Showing something 'new' when compared with past work
4	Speaking to the interests of the journal's target audience
5	Clear presentation

Source: adapted from Loseke and Cahill (2004)

requires that you have a good sense of what journal editors are looking for. So now I will look in more detail at the criteria used by academic journals to make their decisions.

27.3 WHAT JOURNALS ARE LOOKING FOR

The policy of academic journals may vary by their focus, discipline or audience. As I have already noted, many quantitatively oriented journals expect their articles to have a standard format which assumes that all research has an initial hypothesis and that some form of random sampling will be employed. Equally, journals that seek to appeal to practitioners and other non-specialists will be particularly interested in looking for papers that set out to have this wider appeal.

Despite this degree of variation, my experience suggests that there are several criteria that recur in referees' comments in the kind of qualitative journals to which you might submit a paper. These criteria are set out in Table 27.1.

The table indicates what to do if you want your submitted piece to have a reasonable chance of success. It, therefore, implies a series of 'don't's:

- don't cite models or approaches if they are mere window-dressing
- don't vary the format; announce a clear structure at the start and stick to it
- don't forget that your paper should contribute to an ongoing conversation of scholars in your area
- don't defend approaches already familiar to readers of this journal.

27.4 REVIEWERS' COMMENTS

As well as these general points, it is also useful to have advance warning of the specific kinds of criticisms that reviewers make about the submissions they see. Since other people may be quite sensitive about showing you the critical reviews they have received, I have set out below extracts from some of my (usually anonymous) reviews during the past few years. Naturally, I've tried to delete any references that might identify the paper or the author. No doubt I am still going to make myself very unpopular by giving these examples!

To help you follow these comments, I have grouped them as 'good news' and 'bad news'. Each section contains portions of comments about many papers.

27.4.1 Good news

A fascinating topic with some nice data.

This is an interesting paper, using theoretically generated analysis on a practically relevant topic.

This paper deals with an important issue. As presently written, it is highly accessible to practitioners and patients.

The paper is based on an apparently well-transcribed piece of data.

The data chosen is very manageable.

This is a carefully done study and brings out some important practical issues.

This is a highly ambitious methodological paper. Its claim to originality, I take it, is that several different methods can be combined to shed more light on a text than any one alone.

There is considerable insight in the way in which these methods are used.

This paper discusses some potentially interesting data. It uses an approach which, I presume, will be relatively unfamiliar to readers of the journal. Quite correctly, therefore, the author(s) take up a fair bit of space explaining the approach used.

27.4.2 Bad news

I have grouped these 'bad news' comments under several headings.

I hope that my present readers will not be intimidated by these comments. Please treat them as providing guidance about practices best avoided. However, I try never to be merely negative. In the following section are some suggestions I have made to authors.

Over-ambition

I think it currently tries to do too much.

Unfortunately, the abstract promises much more than is ever delivered.

There are so many issues that are raised that it is difficult for any to be developed properly. Each would make a separate paper. Given so many issues, it is not surprising that the data analysis is rather thin and not really linked to the literature review.

Over-generality

The broad brush approach adopted here I found frustrating. There is no attempt to ground the argument in a piece of data.

Unanalytic

For the most part, the observations on the data strike me as commonsensical. To develop this paper further, much more use needs to be made of the vast literature on this subject based on transcripts of this kind.

The final sentence of the abstract is trite and unnewsworthy. The analysis of data only begins more than half-way through the paper and is very thin.

It hardly analyses its data at all and should be rejected. The paper works by assertion. For instance, it simply isn't always the case that [X follows Y].

Unfortunately, the data analysis is very thin indeed, barely rising above descriptions which are sometimes banal.

Inconsistency

Methodologically, the approach does not fit the issues that the author wants to address.

Methodological failings

I found the citation of 'cases' less than convincing. While space constraints always limit the number of data extracts one can use, the paper fails to give any sense that deviant cases were analysed and that prior assumptions were in any way tested by the data.

Lack of originality

The paper discusses a contentious methodological issue. It is also an issue that has been discussed in a mountain of publications over the last ten years. Therefore, it is particularly hard to say anything fresh about the topic.

Lack of clarity

I am unclear about the relevance of the approach used; the presence of several traditional assumptions which sit uneasily with it and the issue of practical relevance.

I don't understand the first sentence of the abstract.

Lack of recipient design

The section on theory is, I feel, inappropriate. Readers who know about this already will be bored and readers who do not will not want to cope with a theoretical discussion before they get to the data. Much better, then, to introduce the required elements of theory in the course of the data analysis.

You may lose your international audience by going straight into issues relating to one small country.

27.4.3 Suggestions

I would like the paper to be revised to become sharper in focus and to take account of other relevant work.

You need an introduction setting out the *general* themes. Then an early data extract would whet the reader's appetite.

I suggest that you submit your revised draft to a native English speaker. Currently, there are multiple infelicities.

If space allowed, the analysis would also benefit from comparison with one more case.

The present conclusion combines analytic *descriptions* of the findings and practical recommendations. Instead, I would like to see the practical conclusions separated and the paper's analytic *contribution* clarified.

27.4.4 Implication

It may be the case that my own reviewing methods are idiosyncratic and even unfair! If so, I hope you never come across me as a reviewer! However, every reviewer is likely to attend to the word limits of the journal. I now turn to the art of writing a short journal article.

27.5 HOW TO WRITE A SHORT JOURNAL ARTICLE

As already noted, most journals nowadays cap papers at around 6000 words. Yet no doubt you want to context your research but you have so much data and so many findings. How can you present your research in such a small frame?

There are three ways to shorten a paper:

- Stick rigidly to the point (e.g. one topic, one case, one theory, one model, one method).
- If you are working within an existing approach or model, don't waste time defending it (reinventing the wheel).
- Consider whether you need all your footnotes; if they are not worthy of being in your main text, do you need them at all? At this level, you should not need extensive footnotes to demonstrate your academic respectability.

By shortening your paper through such techniques, you can create space to enlarge on what matters. For example:

- focusing on a topic that will intrigue readers of this journal (e.g. one relating to a recent debate)
- demonstrating credibility by combining intensive and extensive methods (e.g. short data extracts and simple tabulations)
- writing a conclusion that displays lateral thinking, for instance by relating your substantive account to a broader area.

Finally, if your paper is still too long, consider splitting it up into different topics appropriate for several journals. Working the same material in a number of different ways is what Gary Marx has called **leverage**. Marx's idea is discussed in the following chapter.

27.6   CONCLUDING REMARKS

Publications are good for academic careers. They also can provide an outlet for your key data chapters as well as for beloved draft chapters that you decided were too peripheral to be included in the final version of your thesis (see Chapter 24).

Getting published depends upon making a number of strategic choices (e.g. book or journal article? Which journal to select?). There are several ways of improving your chance of getting your paper accepted by a journal. First, 'decide on what you wish to focus. What is your theoretical story?' (Strauss and Corbin, 1990: 246). Second, you need to ask yourself:

> Do I need this detail in order to maximize the clarity of the analytic discussion, and/or to achieve maximum substantive understanding? (1990: 247)

Remember that your audience are both bigger and very different to the small audience for your thesis. So ruthlessly strip out inappropriate references and material and recontext your work. As Wolcott (1990: 51) puts it, when writing a journal article: 'dedissertationalize' your work. Don't expect to get your paper accepted as is. Make use of the referees' comments as helpful encouragements to rewrite a better article!

Finally, you should try to write a compelling argument. Jay Gubrium (personal communication) has suggested that much qualitative data is 'inherently' interesting. Take advantage of this and use the interest that the reader may have in your material to your advantage. Tease, entice and puzzle your readers.

KEY POINTS

There are at least five ways of improving your chances of getting a paper accepted by a journal:

- ▬ Find a focus.
- ▬ Avoid too much detail.
- ▬ Redefine your audience.
- ▬ Expect an initial rejection and make use of referees' comments in a second submission.
- ▬ Make a compelling case.

Further reading

The four best sources on this topic are: Donna Loseke and Spencer Cahill's chapter 'Publishing qualitative manuscripts' in C. Seale et al. (eds) *Qualitative Research Practice* (Sage, 2004); Harry Wolcott's little book, *Writing Up Qualitative Research* (Sage, 1990), Chapter 6; Anselm Strauss and Juliet Corbin's *Basics of Qualitative Research* (Sage, 1990), Chapter 13; and Nigel Gilbert's chapter 'Writing about social research' in N. Gilbert (ed.) *Researching Social Life* (Sage, 1993a: 328–44).

Exercise 27.1

Gilbert (1993a) suggests choosing a journal article written by someone else and writing a review of it as if you were the referee. If you need guidance on what to look for, use some of the 'good news' and 'bad news' lines of approach found in this chapter.

Now ask your supervisor to read your review. Use the feedback you get to:

1 Think critically about how you might publish your own work.

2 Invite your supervisor to ask book review editors to send books to you for review in journals (this is one way to get a first step on the publications ladder!).

Audiences

28.1 INTRODUCTION

As I suggested in the previous chapter, getting published is all about designing your writing for a particular audience. In this way, we attempt to tailor our writing for the likely sense-making priorities of our audience. As Coffey and Atkinson put it:

> Reading is an active process, and no text can have a completely fixed meaning. When we write – and hence inscribe certain preferred interpretations in our books, dissertations and papers – we do so with an implied audience of readers. (1996: 118)

In this sense, fellow academics are only one of several potential audiences, including policy-makers, practitioners and lay audiences. Each group will only want to hear about your work if it relates to their needs. These four audiences and their likely expectations are set out in Table 28.1.

The expectations of academic audiences about both written work and oral presentations have already been discussed at length in this book. However, the range of other audiences, shown in Table 28.1, may tend to induce despair about the amount of work required to meet their separate expectations and needs. However, it contains a simple, easy-to-follow message: good communication requires focus and yet more focus.

The trick is to combine a recognition of the expectations and needs of such audiences with our own active shaping of our materials. The good news is that a

TABLE 28.1   AUDIENCES AND THEIR EXPECTATIONS

Audience	Expectation
Academic colleagues	Theoretical, factual, or methodological insights
Policy-makers	Practical information relevant to current policy issues
Practitioners	A theoretical framework for understanding clients better; information; practical suggestions for better procedures; reform of existing practices
Lay audiences	New facts; ideas for reform of current practices or policies; guidelines for how to manage better or get better service from practitioners or institutions; assurances that others share their own experience of particular problems in life

Source: adapted from Strauss and Corbin (1990: 242–3)

little practice may make you adept at working the same material in a range of different ways. In this context, Marx's concept of 'leverage' is very useful. As he puts it:

> Try to leverage your work. The sociological equivalent of a bases-loaded homerun is to take material prepared for a class lecture, deliver it at a professional meeting, publish it in a refereed journal, have it reprinted in an edited collection, use it in a book you write, publish foreign versions and a more popular version and have the work inform a documentary. (1997: 115)

Marx reminds us of the range of audiences that await the qualitative researcher. In the rest of this chapter, I consider the three non-academic audiences listed in Table 28.1: policy-makers, practitioners and lay audiences. How do you fashion what Marx calls 'a popular version' for such audiences?

28.2   THE POLICY-MAKING AUDIENCE

The idea that social research might influence public policy provides an inspiration for many young social scientists. In most English-speaking countries, the sad truth is that things have never worked in this way.

Qualitative research has rarely had much appeal to civil servants and administrators geared to focus on numbers and the 'bottom line'. The one possible exception, Goffman's (1961) account of the dehumanizing consequences of 'total institutions' in his book *Asylums*, appears merely to have legitimated the cost-cutting frenzy known as 'community care'.

Moreover, it is arguable that number-crunching researchers have fared little better. As Hadley (1987: 100) has pointed out, 'not being heard' is the common experience of Anglo-American social researchers who attempt to influence public policy. Among the reasons for this, Hadley suggests that:

- Research is often commissioned to buy time in the face of public scandal or criticism. This means that: 'the customer's motives for commissioning a research project may not necessarily be directly related to an interest in the topic concerned' (1987: 101).
- The time lag between commissioning a study and receiving a report may mean that the customer's interests have shifted (see my discussion in Chapter 17 of the failure of the funding body to implement my findings about HIV counselling).
- Academic researchers who produce unpalatable conclusions can be written off as 'unrealistic' (1987: 102).

Of course, fashions change. At the time of writing, there is some evidence that public bodies may be starting to take qualitative research more seriously. **Focus groups**, in particular, seem to be 'the flavour of the month', mainly, I think, because they are relatively cheap and quick and give nice 'sound-bites' for politicians and advertisers. However, such changes in fashion do little to affect the natural tendency of policy-makers to redefine the meaning of research 'findings'.

However, as Bloor (2004) has noted, the policy community is not the sole audience for social research.

28.3   THE PRACTITIONER AUDIENCE

> the real opportunities for sociological influence lie closer to the coalface than they do to head office … [they] lie in relations with practitioners, not with the managers of practice. (Bloor, 2004: 318)

Taking the example of the sociology of health and illness, Bloor argues that practitioners rather than policy-makers are the most reliable and eager audience for social research:

> Sociologists who have conducted research on sociological aspects of health and medicine … have long been aware that there is a role for sociologists as participants in debates on public policy, but that there are also other audiences for social research, notably audiences of patients and practitioners (clinicians, nurses and other professionals). (2004: 307)

Bloor suggests that qualitative social researchers have a twofold advantage in influencing practitioners. First, they can build upon their research relationships with practitioners in order to discuss practical implications. As he puts it:

> In respect of practitioners who are research subjects, qualitative researchers can call upon their pre-existing research relationships with their research subjects as a resource for ensuring an attentive and even sympathetic response to their research

findings. A close personal and working relationship, based on lengthy social contact and built up over weeks and months, is likely to ensure that, not only will practitioner research subjects have a particular interest in the findings (because of the identity of the researcher as much as a particular interest in the research topic), but also they may be willing to devote an unusual amount of time and effort to discussions of the findings. (2004: 320–1)

Second, even if you have no research relationship with them, the detail and transparency of some qualitative data has an appeal to many practitioners:

the qualitative researcher has the advantage that the research methods allow rich descriptions of everyday practice which allow practitioner audiences imaginatively to juxtapose their own everyday practices with the research description. There is therefore an opportunity for practitioners to make evaluative judgments about their own practices and experiment with the adoption of new approaches described in the research findings. (ibid.)

Bloor's argument resonates with my own recent experience with AIDS counsellors. Like most practitioners, counsellors will be suspicious that outside researchers intend to be judgemental. It helps to reassure them that you do not believe in any normative, decontextualized theory of *good* communication. For further discussion of how to approach such practitioner audiences, refer back to Chapter 17 and see Silverman (2001: 294–7).

28.4 THE LAY AUDIENCE

There are at least four reasons why qualitative researchers may become involved in reporting back to lay audiences:

1 to answer questions asked by your respondents
2 to 'check' provisional findings
3 to provide 'feedback' to organizations and relevant groups
4 to provide information for the media.

Points 1 and 2 have been considered in Chapter 17. In particular, you should refer to the section on 'open and covert access' for point 1 and the section on feedback as a validation exercise for point 2.

Feedback to lay audiences is usually set up because of your own desire to 'give something back' to the general public. The format should vary according to whether your audience are members of an established organization or simply just a group of people with similar interests or concerns.

As an example, following my own research on hospital clinics for children, I gave a talk to the Parents' Association at one of the hospitals I had studied. In this talk, following Table 28.1, I discussed new facts from my research about doctor–parent communication. I also examined the implications of my findings for reform of current hospital practices. Subsequently, I was invited to write a short piece on my research for the newsletter of a British organization called the Patients' Association. In this article, I covered much the same ground as well as adding guidelines for how to manage better or get better service from hospitals that treat sick children. Finally, I spoke at a meeting of parents of children with diabetes. My aim here was to stress what my research had revealed about the painful dilemmas experienced by such parents. In this way, I sought to assure them that others share their own experience and that there is no need for them to reproach themselves.

It is most unlikely, however, that you will be able to reach a general audience through the mass media. Nearly all social science goes unreported by such media. Needless to say, this is even more true of student research.

However, perhaps your research has provided you with a story that you want to tell to the general public. How should you go about this?

Perhaps a journalist approaches you after a talk you have given. More likely, a media contact will begin after you have studied the kind of topics covered by broadcast programmes and by particular journalists and approached the 'right' person.

For example, when my book on communication in hospital clinics was published (Silverman, 1987), I rang the medical correspondent of a national newspaper. He was very interested in some of my findings and, by the next day, I had a reporter at my house.

At this point, I panicked! I started to worry that the reporter might sensationalize my research and, thereby, upset the medical staff who had supported it. To try to avoid this, I got the reporter to agree for me to tape-record her interview and for me to have a sight of her copy before it was published.

My cautiousness had an unforeseen and unfortunate consequence. The 'story' that followed ended up being so bland that it was never printed.

This experience highlights the dilemma that researchers have in seeking to get their work more widely known. The cautious way in which researchers are taught to write about their findings runs up against the media's need to pull in audience with sensational stories. So it is always a question of balance between the media's sense of what is 'newsworthy' and your own desire for an accurate, unsensationalized account of your research.

28.5   CONCLUDING REMARKS

It is appropriate that towards the end of this book we are reflecting on 'audiences'. Too often, qualitative research is written up in an intellectual and social vacuum in which one writes for just oneself or, at best, for one supervisor. Sometimes, this partial approach can succeed in getting you the degree you require. More frequently, in the absence of actual or imagined audiences, it will lead to writer's block and consequent failure to complete.

In the final analysis, if you want to succeed in your research and beyond, you will have to be responsive to the various audiences who might be prepared to listen to what you have to say. As in so many other aspects of life, people who complain about the 'cruel world' are often the very people who disdain the occasionally difficult but generally rewarding business of listening to what others are saying.

KEY POINTS

Communication should always be designed for a particular audience:

- Academic colleagues will expect theoretical, factual or methodological insights.
- Policy-makers will want practical information relevant to current policy issues.
- Practitioners will expect a theoretical framework for understanding clients better; factual information; practical suggestions for better procedures; reform of existing practices.
- The general public wants new facts; ideas for reform of current practices or policies; guidelines for how to manage better or get better service from practitioners or institutions; and assurances that others share their own experience of particular problems in life.

If you want to communicate effectively, you must focus upon your audience's concerns and recipient design your output accordingly.

Further reading

Anselm Strauss and Juliet Corbin's *Basics of Qualitative Research* (Sage, 1990), Chapter 13, covers both written and oral presentations of your research for different audiences. Gary Marx's paper, 'Of methods and manners for aspiring sociologists: 37 moral imperatives' (*The American Sociologist*, Spring 1997, 102–25), is a lively and extremely helpful guide for the apprentice researcher desiring to make links with a range of audiences. Roger Hadley's chapter 'Publish and be ignored: proselytise and be damned' in G.C. Wenger (ed.), *The Research Relationship: Practice and Politics in Social Policy Research* (Allen & Unwin, 1987: 98–110) is a lively account of the pitfalls of trying to reach a policy audience. Practitioner audiences are very well discussed in Michael Bloor's chapter 'Addressing social problems through qualitative research' in D. Silverman (ed.), *Qualitative Research: Theory, Method and Practice*, 2nd edn (Sage, 2004).

Exercise 28.1

Refer back to Gary Marx's comments, cited in this chapter, about 'leveraging' your work. Now take any chapter of your dissertation and outline how you might write it up for as many as possible of the following audiences:

1   a specialist academic journal

2   a non-specialist social science audience

3   policy-makers

4   practitioners

5   the general public.

Now try out these different versions with their intended audiences.

Finding a Job

> ## *CHAPTER OBJECTIVES*
>
> By the end of this chapter, you will be able to:
>
> ▬ Work out ways of getting on a shortlist.
> ▬ Devise strategies that improve how you present yourself at job interviews.
> ▬ Respond appropriately to job offers and rejections.

29.1 INTRODUCTION

Another, more forbidding, audience await most of us – the employer. There are three stages in this process:

1 Learning about appropriate vacancies.
2 Getting on a shortlist.
3 Succeeding at a job interview.

In this final chapter, I will deal with each stage in turn.

29.2 LEARNING ABOUT VACANCIES

There are two main information channels about jobs: formal and informal. The formal channels consist of job advertisements in the general press and in more specialist, professional publications, as well as the job markets that may be set up at career fairs and meetings of professional associations. For instance, the annual meetings of the American Sociological Association provide a venue for university employers to meet with potential recruits.

The informal channels work through the guidance and information you can get from people on 'the inside'. Here the most likely contacts will be your supervisor(s) and, perhaps, the academics who examined your thesis.

Whatever channels you use, it is worth making an inventory of the skills you possess and then relating them to the skills demanded by likely employers. This should be done well before you complete your degree so that you can seek to give yourself the best chances on the job market.

Your research should have given you the useful qualities of being able to express yourself clearly, to work independently and to meet deadlines. It will also have probably provided you with substantive knowledge of a particular area relevant to university and non-university employers.

Other kinds of marketable skills that you can pick up during your university courses are:

● information technology skills
● knowledge of basic statistical packages
● teaching experience
● administrative skills (for instance, gained by serving as a student representative).

So plan for the future: find out where the job openings are and gain the skills that will be most likely to fit you for them.

29.3 GETTING ON A SHORTLIST

Of course, before you get a job interview, you have to be shortlisted. My experience as candidate and selector tells me that there are several things that may tilt the balance in your favour. For instance:

● Write a curriculum vitae that embodies the capacity for logical, organized thought that your employer will be looking for. Spelling mistakes and hasty corrections are complete 'no-nos'! Don't undersell yourself. Recipient design your CV for different employers having worked out which features are most likely to interest that employer.
● Choose referees that cover the different aspects of your life in which a particular employer is likely to be interested. Try to ensure that you are getting the 'right kind' of references. At interview, try to elicit information about how helpful your references were and/or ask referees if you can have sight of an old reference they wrote for you. If a possible referee does not seem highly enthusiastic about agreeing to write a reference for you, find somebody else.
● Always write an accompanying letter with your CV in which you explain why your experience is right for this job and your provisional thoughts of what fresh ideas you can bring to the tasks involved.

Shortlisting committees will generally assess your application in terms of agreed criteria. For instance, many years ago, I was asked to write a report for a university making a senior academic appointment in the field of medical sociology. I used the following criteria in my assessment of the candidates:

1 breadth of interests
2 quality of published work
3 research productivity
4 international research contacts
5 overall standing as a sociologist.

I then attached a letter grade to these criteria for each candidate.

This gives you an idea of some of the criteria that selectors may use when they scan your CV. Of course, how they will use these criteria is an open question. As my own research on selection interviews suggests, such criteria generally operate to rationalise decisions that are already made rather than to cause these decisions (Silverman and Jones, 1976).

29.4   THE JOB INTERVIEW

Job selection interviews are one of the most intimidating experiences that we have to go through. Part of the reason for this is that we know that employers will treat our answers as a way of evaluating our qualities. This is, of course, very different from question–answer sequences in ordinary conversation where no such hidden agenda may be present.

For instance, as Button (1992) points out, in ordinary conversation, where an answerer seems to have misunderstood a question, the questioner will repair the understanding. This is shown in Extract 29.1:

Extract 29.1 [Button, 1992]

Mandy: There should be 'bout twuny or so people
Tina: I hope- will Chris be coming?
Mandy: If she can:[: get
Tina: [No you ninny Christopher

Button (1992) compares the extract above with data from a job interview for the post of head of an arts faculty in an English comprehensive (or high) school. Extract 29.2 occurs during this interview:

Extract 29.2 [IV=interviewer, IE=interviewee; Button, 1992, adapted]

IV: Huhrm (.) What sort of sty::le do you see (.) yourself as-
        as a le::ader of- of (.) a- a team of teachers.
        (0.5)
IE: D'you mean how w'd I get other people to do it.
→   (1.5)
IE: Well er:: (0.5) I think there are two ways of approaching
        tea::m teaching

TABLE 29.1 GETTING THROUGH JOB INTERVIEWS

- *Research*: find out what the job entails in order to relate your own experience to the duties involved. Check the employer's web site and talk to anybody listed on the job advertisement
- *Rehearsal*: compose half-a-dozen sentences to cover: how your background fits the job description; why you want to work here; and what you hope to be doing in five years' time. Practise these out loud so they are easy to say
- *Interview*: Goldilocks found the porridge either too hot or too cold. By contrast, don't say too much in any answer but ask the panel if you have covered what they wanted. If you are worried about saying too little ('drying up'), use a written note of some key sentences as a prompt
- *Afterwards*: before accepting a job, negotiate the terms and conditions; if you are turned down, don't take it personally – there is always a lottery element in any appointment and you will have gained experience for your next interview

Source: adapted from Bradby (2003)

Although, as Button suggests, IV's question is hearable as about person management, IE chooses to hear it as about a teaching style ('team teaching') and the selectors do not take up the opportunity he gives to correct him. Later, however, the selectors noted that the candidate's answer 'does not answer the question'.

As Button points out, unlike the Mandy–Tina extract, where Tina corrected Mandy's understanding of her question:

> the interviewers never undertook this sort of correction on occasions where understanding problems may have been possibly relevant. Interviewers not only did not start to speak at first possible places where a transfer of speakership could be co-ordinated [e.g. arrowed pause in extract above – but note that IV might have nodded at this point], they neither, without request from the candidate, intervened in the course of an answer. (1992: 217)

Button's data makes clear that you can expect few favours at job interviews. Preparation and planning will help you to present yourself in the best light. Some ideas about what such preparation can involve are set out in Table 29.1.

As at your university oral examination, your job interview is the time to sell yourself while respecting the knowledge and experience of your assessors. So refer back to Table 29.1 and follow the tips there about self-presentation.

29.5 CONCLUDING REMARKS

As with policy-makers, selection committees have their own agendas. For instance, in the shortlisting example discussed earlier, the appointing committee chose not to follow my advice.

Nonetheless, this is a game that has to be played and which can be played well or badly. So go to it!

KEY POINTS

There are two main information channels about jobs:

- formal channels (job advertisements and job markets)
- informal channels which work through the guidance and information you can get from people on 'the inside'.

Whatever channels you use, make an inventory of the skills you possess and then relate them to the skills demanded by likely employers.
To improve your chances of getting a job, you should:

- Write a model curriculum vitae showing logical, organized thought.
- Redesign your CV for the needs of different employers.
- Choose referees that cover the different aspects of your life in which a particular employer is likely to be interested.
- Try to ensure that you are getting the 'right kind' of references.
- Always write an accompanying letter with your CV geared to what you can bring to this particular opening.
Prepare yourself for the job interview and check with the selectors before making any one answer very long.

Further reading

For research on job selection interviews, see David Silverman and Jill Jones's *Organizational Work: The Language of Grading/The Grading of Language* (Collier-Macmillan, 1976) and Graham Button's chapter 'Answers as interactional products: two sequential practices used in job interviews', in P. Drew and J.C. Heritage (eds), *Talk at Work* (Cambridge University Press, 1992: 212–34).

Exercise 29.1

Collect job advertisements for positions that interest you. Now make a list of the skills you possess and then relate them to the skills demanded by likely employers.

Appendix

Appendix: Simplified transcription symbols

[	C2: quite a [while Mo: [yea	Left brackets indicate the point at which a current speaker's talk is overlapped by another's talk.
=	W: that I'm aware of = C: = Yes. Would you confirm that?	Equal signs, one at the end of a line and one at the beginning, indicate no gap between the two lines.
(.4)	Yes (.2) yeah	Numbers in parentheses indicate elapsed time in silence in tenths of a second.
(.)	to get (.) treatment	A dot in parentheses indicates a tiny gap, probably no more than one-tenth of a second.
_____	What's up?	Underscoring indicates some form of stress, via pitch and/or amplitude.
::	O: kay?	Colons indicate prolongation of the immediately prior sound. The length of the row of colons indicates the length of the prolongation.
WORD	I've got ENOUGH TO WORRY ABOUT	Capitals, except at the beginnings of lines, indicate especially loud sounds relative to the surrounding talk.
.hhhh	I feel that (.2) .hhh	A row of h's prefixed by a dot indicates an inbreath; without a dot, an outbreath. The length of the row of h's indicates the length of the in- or outbreath.
( )	future risks and ( ) and life ( )	Empty parentheses indicate the transcriber's inability to hear what was said.
(word)	Would you see (there) anything positive	Parenthesized words are possible hearings.
(( ))	confirm that ((continues))	Double parentheses contain author's descriptions rather than transcriptions.
. , ?	What do you think?	Indicate speaker's intonation (. = falling intonation; , = flat or slightly rising intonation)
>	>What do you think?	Indicates data later discussed

Glossary

Adjacency pairs
Consecutive actions which are grouped in pairs and constrain what the next speaker may do (e.g. questions and answers).

Anecdotalism
Found where research reports appear to tell entertaining stories or anecdotes but fail to convince the reader of their scientific credibility.

CAQDAS
Computer-assisted analysis of qualitative data.

Coding
Putting data into theoretically defined categories in order to analyse it.

Concepts
Clearly specified ideas deriving from a particular *model*.

Constructionism
A *model* which encourages researchers to focus upon how particular phenomena are put together through the close study of particular behaviours.

Content analysis
Data analysis, usually of texts, using a systematic approach that involves sampling, *coding* and quantification.

Continuer
An utterance which signals to a listener that what they have just said has been understood and that they should now continue.

Control group
A group not given some stimulus provided to another group; a control group is used for comparative purposes.

Conversation analysis (CA)
A qualitative approach based on an attempt to describe people's methods for producing orderly talk-in-interaction. It derives from the work of Sacks (1992).

Credibility
The extent to which any research claim has been shown to be based on evidence.

Culture
A common set of beliefs, values and behaviours.

Deviant-case analysis
In qualitative research involves testing provisional hypotheses by 'negative' or 'discrepant' cases until all the data can be incorporated in your explanation.

Discourse analysis
The study of 'the way versions of the world, of society, events, and inner psychological worlds are produced in discourse' (J. Potter, 2004: 202).

Emotionalism
A model of social research in which the primary issue is to generate data which gives an authentic insight into people's experiences. Emotionalists tend to favour open-ended interviews (see Gubrium and Holstein: 1997).

GLOSSARY

Empirical
Based on evidence through trial or experiment.

Empiricism
An approach which believes that evidence about the world does not depend upon *models* or *concepts*.

Ethnography
Puts together two different words: 'ethno' means 'folk' while 'graph' derives from 'writing'. Ethnography refers, then, to social scientific writing about particular folks.

Ethnomethodology
The study of folk – or *members*' – methods. It seeks to describe methods persons use in doing social life. Ethnomethodology is not a methodology but a theoretical *model*.

Field
The setting or place where *ethnographic* research takes place.

Focus groups
Group discussions usually based upon stimuli (topics, visual aids) provided by the researcher.

Formal theories
Theories which relate findings from one setting to many situations or settings.

Frames
Following Goffman (1974), how people treat what is currently relevant and irrelevant defines the frame through which a setting is constituted.

Gatekeeper
Someone who is able to grant or refuse access to the *field*.

Genealogical
Following Foucault (1977, 1979), the study of the ways in which *discourses* have been structured at different historical points.

Generalizability
The extent to which a finding in one setting can be applied more generally.

Grand theory
A term used by Mills (1959) to describe highly abstract speculation which has little or no use in research.

Grounded theory
A term used by Glaser and Strauss (1967) to describe a way of inducing theoretically based generalizations from qualitative data.

Hermeneutics
An approach concerned with interpretation (originally derived from the study of biblical texts).

Hypotheses
Testable propositions often based on educated guesses.

Idioms
A term used by Gubrium and Holstein (1997) to describe a set of analytical preferences for particular *concepts*, styles of research and ways of writing (*see model*).

Inductive
Based on the study of particular cases rather than just derived from a theory.

Interactionism
A theory, commonly used in qualitative sociological research, which assumes that our behaviour and perceptions derive from processes of interaction with other people.

Intervening variable
A *variable* which is influenced by a prior factor and then goes on to influence another. Commonly used in quantitative research to work out which statistical association may be spurious.

Interview society
A term used by Atkinson and Silverman (1997) to point out the ways in which interviews have become a central medium for understanding who we are.

Leverage
Used by Marx (1997) to describe ways of finding multiple publishing outlets for one piece of research.

Low-inference descriptors
Recording observations 'in terms that are as concrete as possible, including verbatim accounts of what people say, for example, rather than researchers' reconstructions of the general sense of what a person said, which would allow researchers' personal perspectives to influence the reporting' (Seale, 1999: 148) (*see reliability*).

Member
Used by Garfinkel (1967) to refer to participants in society. It is a shorthand term for 'collectivity member' (*see ethnomethodology*).

Membership categorization device
A collection of categories (e.g. baby, mommy, father = family; male, female = gender) and some rules about how to apply these categories.

Methodology
Refers to the choices we make about cases to study, methods of data, gathering, forms of data analysis etc., in planning and executing a research study.

Models
Provide an overall framework for how we look at reality. They tell us what reality is like and the basic elements it contains ('ontology') and what is the nature and status of knowledge ('epistemology'). *See also idioms*.

Narratives
The organization of stories (e.g. beginning, middle and end; plots and characters) which makes stories meaningful or coherent in a form appropriate to the needs of a particular occasion.

Naturalism
A model of research which seeks to minimize presuppositions in order to witness subjects' worlds in their own terms (Gubrium and Holstein, 1997).

Naturally occurring data
Data which derives from situations which exist independently of the researcher's intervention.

Normative
Pertaining to a norm or value; prescriptive.

Operational definitions
Working definitions which allow the measurement of some *variable*.

Paradigm
A conceptual framework (*see model*).

Paradigmatic
A term used in structuralism to indicate a polar set of *concepts* or activities where the presence of one denies the existence of the other (e.g. a red traffic light).

Participant–observation
A method that assumes that, in order to understand the world 'first hand', you must participate yourself rather than just observe at a distance. This method was championed by the early anthropologists but is shared by some *ethnographers*.

Positivism
A model of the research process which treats 'social facts' as existing independently of the activities of both participants and researchers.

Post-modern theory
An interdisciplinary movement based on the critique of all *concepts* and *paradigms*.

Preference organization
A concept derived from *CA* which suggests that recipients of actions recognize a preference for what they should do next.

Recipient design
Work that is designed for a particular audience (the term derives from *CA* where it is used to describe how all actions are implicitly designed in this way).

Reflexivity
A term deriving from *ethnomethodology* where it is used to describe the self-organizing character of all interaction so that any action provides for its own context. Mistakenly used to refer to self-questioning by a researcher.

GLOSSARY

Relativism
A value position where we resist taking a position because we believe that, since everything is relative to its particular context, it should not be criticized.

Reliability
'The degree of consistency with which instances are assigned to the same category by different observers or by the same observer on different occasions' (Hammersley, 1992: 67) (*see validity*).

Rewriting of history
A term used by Garfinkel (1967) to refer to the way in which any account retrospectively finds reasons for any past event.

Sample, sampling A statistical procedure for finding cases to study. Sampling has two functions: it allows you to feel confident about the representativeness of your sample and such representativeness allows you to make broader inferences.

Semiotics
The study of signs (from speech, to fashion to Morse code).

Social constructionism
See constructionism.

Social structure
A term used in sociology and anthropology to describe the institutional arrangements of a particular society or group (e.g. family and class structures).

Social survey
A quantitative method involving the study of large numbers of people often through the use of questionnaires.

Structuralism
A *model* used in anthropology which aims to show how single cases relate to general social forms. Structural anthropologists draw upon French social and linguistic theory of the early twentieth century, notably Ferdinand de Saussure and Emile Durkheim. They view behaviour as the expression of a 'society' which works as a 'hidden hand' constraining and forming human action.

Sub-culture
A set of beliefs, values and behaviours shared by a particular group.

Substantive theory
A theory about a particular situation or group. Can be used to develop *formal theory*.

Syntagmatic
A term used within *semiotics* to denote the order in which related elements occur (e.g. how colours follow one another in traffic lights).

Theories
Arrange sets of concepts to define and explain some phenomenon.

Triangulation
The comparison of different kinds of data (e.g. quantitative and qualitative) and different methods (e.g. observation and interviews) to see whether they corroborate one another.

Turn-taking
The sequential organization of speech acts (*see CA*).

Validity
'The extent to which an account accurately represents the social phenomena to which it refers' (Hammersley, 1990: 57). Researchers respond to validity concerns by describing 'the warrant for their inferences' (Fielding and Fielding, 1986: 12) (*see reliability*).

Variables
Factors which are isolated from one another in order to measure their relationship; usually described in quantitative research.

References

Acourt, P. (1997) 'Progress, utopia and intellectual practice: arguments for the resurrection of the future, unpublished PhD thesis, University of London, Goldsmiths College.

Alasuutari, P. (1995) *Researching Culture: Qualitative Method and Cultural Studies*, London: Sage.

Antaki, C. and Rapley, M. (1996) '"Quality of life" talk: the liberal paradox of psychological testing', *Discourse and Society*, 7 (3), 293–316.

Arber, S. (1993) 'The research process', in N. Gilbert (ed.), *Researching Social Life*, London: Sage, 32–50.

Armstrong, D., Gosling, A., Weinman, J. and Marteau, T. (1997) 'The place of interrater reliability in qualitative research: an empirical study', *Sociology*, 31 (3), 597–606.

Atkinson, J.M. (1978) *Discovering Suicide*, London: Macmillan.

Atkinson, J.M. and Heritage, J.C. (eds) (1984) *Structures of Social Action*, Cambridge: Cambridge University Press.

Atkinson, P. (1992) 'The ethnography of a medical setting: reading, writing and rhetoric', *Qualitative Health Research*, 2 (4), 451–74.

Atkinson, P. and Coffey, A. (2004) 'Analysing documentary realities', in D. Silverman (ed.), *Qualitative Research*, 2nd edn, London: Sage, 56–75.

Atkinson, P. and Silverman, D. (1997) 'Kundera's *Immortality*: the interview society and the invention of self', *Qualitative Inquiry*, 3 (3), 324–45.

Avis, M., Bond, M. and Arthur, A. (1997) 'Questioning patient satisfaction: an empirical investigation in two outpatient clinics', *Social Science and Medicine*, 44 (1), 85–92.

Back, L. (2004) 'Politics, research and understanding', in Seale C., Gobo, G., Gubrium, J.F. and Silverman, D. (eds), *Qualitative Research Practice*, London: Sage, 261–75.

Baker, C. (2002) 'Ethnomethodological analysis of interviews', in J. Gubrium and J. Holstein (eds), *Handbook of Interview Research,* Thousand Oaks, CA: Sage, 777–96.

Baker, C. and Keogh, J. (1995) 'Accounting for achievement in parent-teacher interviews', *Human Studies*, 18 (2/3), 263–300.

Barker, M. (2003) 'Assessing the "quality" in qualitative research: the case of text-audience relations', *European Journal of Communication*, 18 (3), 315–35.

Barthes, R. (1973) *Mythologies*, London: Paladin.

Baruch, G. (1981) 'Moral tales: parents' stories of encounters with the health profession', *Social Health and Illness*, 3 (3), 275–96.

Becker, H. (1963) *Outsiders – Studies in the Sociology of Deviance*, New York: Free Press.

Becker, H. (1986) *Writing for Social Scientists*, Chicago: University of Chicago Press.

Becker, H. (1998) *Tricks of the Trade: How to Think about Your Research while Doing It,* Chicago and London: University of Chicago Press.

REFERENCES

Becker, H. and Geer, B. (1960) 'Participant observation: the analysis of qualitative field data', in R. Adams and J. Preiss (eds), *Human Organization Research: Field Relation and Techniques*, Homewood, IL: Dorsey.

Bell, J. (1993) *Doing Your Research Project*, 2nd edn, Buckingham: Open University Press.

Berelson, B. (1952) *Content Analysis in Communicative Research*, New York: Free Press.

Bergmann, J. (1992) 'Veiled morality: notes on discretion in psychiatry', in P. Drew and J. Heritage (eds), *Talk at work,* Cambridge: Cambridge University Press, 137–62.

Blaikie, N. (1993) *Approaches to Social Enquiry,* Cambridge: Polity.

Bloor, M. (1978) 'On the analysis of observational data: a discussion of the worth and uses of inductive techniques and respondent validation', *Sociology*, 12 (3), 545–57.

Bloor, M. (1983) 'Notes on member validation', in R. Emerson (ed.), *Contemporary Field Research: a Collection of Readings,* Boston: Little, Brown.

Bloor, M. (2004) 'Addressing social problems through qualitative research', in D. Silverman (ed.), *Qualitative Research: Theory, Method and Practice,* 2nd edn, London: Sage, 304–23.

Blumer, H. (1969) *Symbolic Interactionism*, Englewood Cliffs, NJ: Prentice Hall.

Boden, D. and Zimmerman, D.H. (eds) (1991) *Talk and Social Structure: Studies in Ethno-Methodology and Conversation Analysis*, Cambridge: Polity, 44–71.

Bradbury, M. (1988) *Unsent Letters,* London: Andre Deutsch.

Bradby, H. (2003) 'Getting through employment interviews', in *Network,* Durham: British Sociological Association.

British Research Councils (1996) *Priorities News*, Spring, Swindon: ESRC, http://www.pparc.ac.uk/work/supervis/intro.ht

Brown, P. and Levinson, S. (1987) *Politeness: Some Universals in Language Usage,* Cambridge: Cambridge University Press.

Bryman, A. (1988) *Quantity and Quality in Social Research*, London: Unwin Hyman.

Buchanan, D.R. (1992) 'An uneasy alliance: combining qualitative and quantitative research methods', *Health Education Quarterly*, 117–35.

Bulmer, M. (1984) *The Chicago School of Sociology*, Chicago: Chicago University Press.

Burton, D. (ed.) (2000) *Research Training for Social Scientists*, London: Sage.

Button, G. (1992) 'Answers as interactional products: two sequential practices used in job interviews', in P. Drew and J.C. Heritage (eds), *Talk at Work*, Cambridge: Cambridge University Press, 212–34.

Byrne, P. and Long, B. (1976) *Doctors Talking to Patients*, London: HMSO.

Chapman, G. (1987) 'Talk, text and discourse: nurses' talk in a therapeutic community', PhD thesis, University of London, Goldsmiths College.

Cicourel, A. (1968) *The Social Organization of Juvenile Justice,* New York: Wiley.

Clavarino, A., Najman, J. and Silverman, D. (1995) 'Assessing the quality of qualitative data', *Qualitative Inquiry*, 1 (2), 223–42.

Coffey, A. and Atkinson, P. (1996) *Making Sense of Qualitative Data*, London: Sage.

Coffey, A., Holbrook, B. and Atkinson, P. (1996) 'Qualitative data analysis: technologies and representations', *Sociological Research Online*, 1 (1). http://www.soc.surrey.ac.uk/socresonline/1/1/4.html

Cohen, S. (1980) *Folk Devils and Moral Panics – The Creation of The Mods and Rockers*, Oxford: Martin Robertson.

Cohen, S. and Young, J. (1973) *The Manufacture of News*, London: Constable.

Cornwell, J. (1981) *Hard Earned Lives*, London: Tavistock.

Cryer, P. (1996) *The Research Student's Guide to Success*, Buckingham: Open University Press.

Curtis, S., Gesler, W., Smith, G. and Washburn, S. (2000) 'Approaches to sampling and case selection in qualitative research: examples in the geography of health', *Social Science and Medicine*, 50, 1000–14.

Dalton, M. (1959) *Men Who Manage*, New York: Wiley.

Denzin, N. (1997) *Interpretive Ethnography: Ethnographic Practices for the 21st Century*, Thousand Oaks, CA: Sage.

Denzin, N. and Lincoln, Y. (eds) (1994) *Handbook of Qualitative Research*, Thousand Oaks, CA: Sage.

Denzin, N. and Lincoln, Y. (eds) (2000) *Handbook of Qualitative Research,* 2nd edn, Thousand Oaks, CA: Sage.

Dey, I. (1993) *Qualitative Data Analysis: a User-Friendly Guide for Social Scientists*, London: Routledge.

Dingwall, R. and Murray, T. (1983) 'Categorization in accident departments: "good" patients, "bad" patients and children', *Sociology of Health and Illness*, 5 (12), 121–48.

Douglas, M. (1975) 'Self-evidence', in M. Douglas, *Implicit Meanings,* London: Routledge.

Drew, P. (2001) 'Spotlight on the patient', *Text*, 21 (1/2), 261–8.

Drew, P. and Heritage, J.C. (1992) 'Analysing talk at work: an introduction', in P. Drew and J.C. Heritage (eds), *Talk at Work*, Cambridge: Cambridge University Press, 3–65.

Durkheim, E. (1951) *Suicide*, New York: Free Press.

Durkin, T. (1997) 'Using computers in strategic qualitative research', in G. Miller and R. Dingwall (eds), *Context and Method in Qualitative Research*, London: Sage, 92–105.

Emerson, R.M., Fretz, R.I. and Shaw, L.L. (1995) *Writing Ethnographic Fieldnotes*, Chicago: University of Chicago Press.

Emmison, M. and Smith, P. (2000) *Researching the Visual*, Introducing Qualitative Methods Series, London: Sage.

Engebretson, J. (1996) 'Urban healers: an experiential description of American healing touch groups', *Qualitative Health Research*, 6 (4), 526–41.

Fielding, N. (1982) 'Observational research on the National Front', in M. Bulmer (ed.), *Social Research Ethics: An Examination of the Merits of Covert Participant Observation*, London: Macmillan.

Fielding, N. and Fielding, J. (1986) *Linking Data*, London Sage.

Fielding, N. and Lee, R. (eds) (1991) *Using Computers in Qualitative Research*, Newbury Park, CA: Sage.

Fisher, M. (1997) 'Qualitative computing: using software for qualitative data analysis', Cardiff Papers in Qualitative Research, Aldershot: Ashgate.

Foucault, M. (1977) *Discipline and Punish*, Harmondsworth: Penguin.

Foucault, M. (1979) *The History of Sexuality*, Vol. 1, Harmondsworth: Penguin.

Frake, C. (1964) 'Notes on queries in ethnography', *American Anthropologist*, 66,132–45.

Fraser, M. (1995) 'The history of the child: 1905–1989', PhD thesis, University of London, Goldsmiths College.

Garfinkel, H. (1967) *Studies in Ethnomethodology*, Englewood Cliffs, NJ: Prentice Hall.

Gilbert, N. (1993a) 'Writing about social research', in N. Gilbert (ed.), *Researching Social Life*, London: Sage, 328–44.

Gilbert, N. (ed.) (1993b) *Researching Social Life*, London: Sage.

Gilbert, N. and Mulkay, M. (1983) 'In search of the action', in N. Gilbert and P. Abell (eds), *Accounts and Action*, Aldershot: Gower.

Glaser, B. and Strauss, A. (1964) 'The social loss of dying patients', *American Journal of Nursing*, 64 (6), 119–21.

Glaser, B. and Strauss, A. (1967) *The Discovery of Grounded Theory*, Chicago: Aldine.

Glaser, B. and Strauss, A. (1968) *Time for Dying*, Chicago: Aldine.

Glassner, B. and Loughlin, J. (1987) *Drugs in Adolescent Worlds: Burnouts to Straights*, New York: St Martin's Press.

Goffman, E. (1959) *The Presentation of Self in Everyday Life*, New York: Doubleday Anchor.

Goffman, E. (1961) *Asylums*, New York: Doubleday Anchor.

Goffman, E. (1974) *Frame Analysis*, New York: Harper and Row.

Gouldner, A. (1954) *Patterns of Industrial Bureaucracy*, Glencoe, IL: Free Press.

Gubrium, J. (1988) *Analyzing Field Reality*, Newbury Park, CA: Sage.

Gubrium, J. (1992) *Out of Control: Family Therapy and Domestic Disorder*, London: Sage.

Gubrium, J. (1997) *Living and Dying in Murray Manor*, Charlottesville, VA: University Press of Virginia.

Gubrium, J. and Buckholdt, D. (1982) *Describing Care: Image and Practice in Rehabilitation*, Cambridge, MA: Oelschlager, Gunn and Hain.

Gubrium, J. and Holstein, J. (1987) 'The private image: experiential location and method in family studies', *Journal of Marriage and the Family*, 49, 773–86.

Gubrium, J. and Holstein, J. (1995) 'Qualitative inquiry and the deprivatization of experience', *Qualitative Inquiry*, 1 (2), 204–22.

Gubrium, J. and Holstein, J. (1997) *The New Language of Qualitative Method*, New York: Oxford University Press.

Hadley, R. (1987) 'Publish and be ignored: proselytise and be damned', in G.C Wenger (ed.), *The Research Relationship: Practice and Politics in Social Policy Research*, London: Allen and Unwin, 98–110.

Hammersley, M. (1990) *Reading Ethnographic Research: A Critical Guide*, London: Longmans.

Hammersley, M. (1992) *What's Wrong with Ethnography? Methodological Explorations*, London: Routledge.

Hammersley, M. and Atkinson, P. (1983) *Ethnography: Principles in Practice*, London: Tavistock.

Handy, C. and Aitken, A. (1994) 'The organisation of the primary school', in A. Pollard and J. Bourne (eds), *Teaching and Learning in the Primary School*, London: Routledge, 239–49.

Hart, C. (1998) *Doing a Literature Review: Releasing the Social Science Imagination*, London: Sage.

Hart, C. (2001) *Doing a Literature Search*, London: Sage.

Heath, C. (2004) 'Analysing face-to-face interaction: video and the visual and the material', in D. Silverman (ed.), *Qualitative Research: Theory, Method and Practice*, 2nd edn, London: Sage, 265–81.

Hill, C.E. et al. (1988) *Therapist Techniques and Client Outcomes*, London: Sage.

Heaton, J.M. (1979) 'Theory in psychotherapy', in N. Bolton (ed.), *Philosophical Problems in Psychology*, London: Methuen, 179–98.

Heise, D. (1988) 'Computer analysis of cultural structures', *Social Science Computer Review*, 6, 183–96.

Heritage, J. (1984) *Garfinkel and Ethnomethodology*, Cambridge: Polity.

Heritage, J. and Sefi, S. (1992) 'Dilemmas of advice: aspects of the delivery and reception of advice in interactions between health visitors and first time mothers', in P. Drew and J. Heritage (eds), *Talk at Work*, Cambridge: Cambridge University Press, 359–417.

Hesse-Biber, S. and Dupuis, P. (1995) 'Hypothesis testing in computer-aided qualitative data analysis', in U. Kelle (ed.), *Computer Aided Qualitative Data Analysis: Theory, Methods and Practice*, London: Sage, 129–35.

Hindess, B. (1973) *The Use of Official Statistics in Sociology*, London: Macmillan.

Holstein, J.A. (1992) 'Producing people: descriptive practice in human service work', *Current Research on Occupations and Professions*, 7, 23–9.

Holstein, J. and Gubrium, J. (1995) *The Active Interview*, Thousand Oaks, CA: Sage.

Hornsby-Smith, M. (1993) 'Gaining access', in N. Gilbert (ed.), *Researching Social Life*, London: Sage, 52–67.

Houtkoop-Steenstra, H. (1991) 'Opening sequences in Dutch telephone conversations', in D. Boden and D.H. Zimmerman (eds), *Talk and Social Structure: Studies in Ethno-methodology and Conversation Analysis*, Cambridge: Polity, 232–50.

Huber, G.L. and Garcia, C.M. (1991) 'Computer assistance for testing hypotheses about qualitative data: the software package AQUAD 3.0', *Qualitative Sociology*, 14 (4), 325–48.

Huberman, A.M. and Miles, M.B. (1994) 'Data management and analysis methods', in N. Denzin and Y. Lincoln (eds), *Handbook of Qualitative Research*, Thousand Oaks, CA: Sage, 413–27.

Hughes, E.C. (1984) *The Sociological Eye*, New Brunswick, NJ: Transaction Books.

Irurita, V. (1996) 'Hidden dimensions revealed: progressive grounded theory study of quality care in the hospital', *Qualitative Health Research*, 6 (3), 331–49.

Jeffery, R. (1979) 'Normal rubbish: deviant patients in casualty departments', *Sociology of Health and Illness*, 1 (1), 90–107.

Kafka, F. (1961) 'Investigations of a dog', in *Metamorphosis and Other Stories*, Harmondsworth: Penguin.

Kelle, U. (ed.) (1995) *Computer Aided Qualitative Data Analysis: Theory, Methods and Practice*, London: Sage.

Kelle, U. (1997) 'Theory building in qualitative research and computer programs for the management of textual data', *Sociological Research Online*, 2 (2), http://www.socresonline.org.uk/socresonline/2/2/1.html

Kelle, U. (2004) 'Computer assisted qualitative data analysis', in C. Seale, G. Gobo, J.F. Gubrium and D. Silverman (eds), *Qualitative Research Practice,* London: Sage, 473–89.

Kelle, U. and Laurie, H. (1995) 'Computer use in qualitative research and issues of validity', in U. Kelle (ed.), *Computer Aided Qualitative Data Analysis: Theory, Methods and Practice*, London: Sage, 19–28.

Kelly, M. (1998) 'Writing a research proposal', in C. Seale (ed.), *Researching Society and Culture*, London: Sage, 111–22.

Kelly, M. (2004) 'Research design and proposals', in C. Seale (ed.), *Researching Society and Culture*, 2nd edn, London: Sage, 129–42.

Kendall, G. and Wickham, G. (1998) *Using Foucault's Methods*, London: Sage.

Kent, G. (1996) 'Informed consent', in 'The principled researcher', unpublished manuscript, Social Science Division, The Graduate School, University of Sheffield, 18–24.

Kirk, J. and Miller, M. (1986) *Reliability and Validity in Qualitative Research*, London: Sage.

Kitzinger, C. and Wilkinson, S. (1997) 'Validating women's experience? Dilemmas in feminist research, *Feminism and Psychology*, 7 (4), 566–74.

Koppel, R., Cohen, A. and Abaluck, B. (2003) 'Physicians' perceptions of medication error using differing research methods', Conference paper, *European Sociological Association* (Qualitative Methods Group), Murcia, Spain.

Kuhn, T.S. (1970) *The Structure of Scientific Revolutions*, 2nd edn, Chicago: University of Chicago Press.

Lee, R.M. and Fielding, N.G. (1995) 'Users' experiences of qualitative data analysis software', in U. Kelle (ed.), *Computer Aided Qualitative Data Analysis: Theory, Methods and Practice*, London: Sage, 29–140.

Lincoln, Y. and Guba, E. (2000) 'Paradigmatic controversies contradictions and emerging influences, in N. Denzin and Y. Lincoln (eds), *Handbook of Qualitative Research*, 2nd edn. Thousand Oaks, CA: Sage, 162–88.

Lindström, A. (1994) 'Identification and recognition in Swedish telephone conversation openings', *Language in Society*, 23 (2), 231–52.

Lipset, S.M., Trow, M. and Coleman, J. (1962) *Union Democracy*, Garden City NY: Anchor Doubleday.

Livingston, E. (1987) *Making Sense of Ethnomethodology*, London: Routledge.

Loseke, D. (1989) 'Creating clients: social problems' work in a shelter for battered women', *Perspectives on Social Problems*, 1, 173–93.

Loseke, D. and Cahill, S. (2004) 'Publishing qualitative manuscripts: lessons learned', in C. Seale, G. Gobo, J.F. Gubrium and D. Silverman (eds), *Qualitative Research Practice*, London: Sage, 576–91.

Lynch, M. (1984) *Art and Artifact in Laboratory Science*, London: Routledge.

Malinowski, B. (1922) *Argonauts of the Western Pacific*, London: Routledge.

Marsh, C. (1982) *The Survey Method*, London: Allen and Unwin.

Marshall, C. and Rossman, G. (1989) *Designing Qualitative Research*, London: Sage.

Marx, G. (1997) 'Of methods and manners for aspiring sociologists: 37 moral imperatives', *The American Sociologist*, Spring, 102–25.

Mason, J. (1996) *Qualitative Researching*, London: Sage.

Maynard, D.W. (1991) 'Interaction and asymmetry in clinical discourse', *American Journal of Sociology*, 97 (2), 448–95.

McKeganey, N. and Bloor, M. (1991) 'Spotting the invisible man: the influence of male gender on fieldwork relations', *British Journal of Sociology*, 42 (2), 195–210.

McLeod, J. (1994) *Doing Counselling Research*, London: Sage.

Mehan, H. (1979) *Learning Lessons: Social Organization in the Classroom*, Cambridge, MA: Harvard University Press.

Mercer, K. (1990) 'Powellism as a political discourse', PhD thesis, University of London, Goldsmiths College.

Mergenthaler, E. (1996) 'Emotion-abstraction patterns in verbatim protocols: a new way of describing psychotherapeutic process', *Journal of Consulting and Clinical Psychology*, 64 (6), 1306–15.

Miall, D.S. (ed.) (1990) *Humanities and the Computer: New Directions*, Oxford: Clarendon.

Miles, M. and Huberman, A. (1984) *Qualitative Data Analysis*, London: Sage.

Miles, M. and Weitzman, E. (1995) *Computer Programs for Qualitative Data Analysis*, Beverly Hills, CA: Sage.

Miller, G. and Silverman, D. (1995) 'Troubles talk and counseling discourse: a comparative study', *The Sociological Quarterly*, 36 (4), 725–47.

Miller, J. (1996) 'Female gang involvement in the Midwest: a two-city comparison', doctoral dissertation, Department of Sociology, University of Southern California.

Miller, J. and Glassner, B. (2004) 'The inside and the outside: finding realities in interviews', in D. Silverman (ed.), *Qualitative Research: Theory, Method and Practice*, 2nd edn, London: Sage, 125–39.

Miller, R. and Bor, R. (1988) *AIDS: a Guide to Clinical Counselling*, London: Science Press.

Mills, C.W. (1959) *The Sociological Imagination*, New York: Oxford University Press.

Mitchell, J.C. (1983) 'Case and situational analysis', *Sociological Review*, 31 (2), 187–211.

Moerman, M. (1974) ''Accomplishing ethnicity', in R. Turner (ed.), *Ethnomethodology*, Harmondsworth: Penguin, 34–68.

Morse, J.M. (1994) 'Designing funded qualitative research', in N. Denzin and Y. Lincoln (eds), *Handbook of Qualitative Research*, Thousand Oaks, CA: Sage, 220–35.

Mulkay, M. (1984) 'The ultimate compliment: a sociological analysis of ceremonial discourse', *Sociology*, 18, 531–49.

Murcott, A. (1997) 'The PhD: some informal notes', unpublished paper, School of Health and Social Care, South Bank University, London.

Murray, R. (2003) 'Survive your viva', *Guardian Education*, 16 September.

O'Brien, M. (1993) 'Social research and sociology', in N. Gilbert (ed.), *Researching Social Life*, London: Sage, 1–17.

Oboler, R. (1986) 'For better or for worse: anthropologists and husbands in the field', in T. Whitehead and M. Conway (eds), *Self, Sex and Gender in Cross-Cultural Fieldwork*, Urbana, IL: University of Illinois Press, 28–51.

Peräkylä, A. (1989) 'Appealing to the experience of the patient in the care of the dying', *Sociology of Health and Illness*, 11 (2), 117–34.

Peräkylä, A. (1995) *AIDS Counselling*. Cambridge: Cambridge University Press.

Peräkylä, A. (2004) 'Reliability and validity in research based upon transcripts', in D. Silverman (ed.), *Qualitative Research: Theory, Method and Practice*, 2nd edn, London: Sage, 282–303.

Phillips, E. and Pugh, D. (1994) *How To Get a PhD*, 2nd edn, Buckingham: Open University Press.

Popper, K. (1959) *The Logic of Scientific Discovery*, New York: Basic Books.

Potter, J. (2002) 'Two kinds of natural', *Discourse Studies*, 4 (4), 539–42.

Potter, J. (2004) 'Discourse analysis as a way of analysing naturally-occurring talk', in D. Silverman (ed.), *Qualitative Research: Theory, Method and Practice*, 2nd edn, London: Sage, 200–21.

Potter, J. and Wetherell, M. (1987) *Discourse and Social Psychology: Beyond Attitudes and Behaviour*, London: Sage.

Potter, J. and Wetherell, M. (1994) 'Analysing discourse', in A. Bryman and R.G. Burgess (eds), *Analysing Qualitative Data*, London: Routledge, 47–66.

Potter, S. (2002) (ed.) *Doing Postgraduate Research*, London: Sage.

Propp, V.I. (1968) *Morphology of the Folktale*, 2nd rev. edn, ed. L.A. Wagner, Austin and London: University of Texas Press.

Psathas, G. (1990) *Interaction Competence*, Washington, DC: University Press of America.

Punch, K. (1998) *Introduction to Social Research: Quantitative and Qualitative Approaches*, London: Sage.

Punch, K. (2000) *Developing Effective Research Proposals*, London: Sage.

Punch, M. (1986) *The Politics and Ethics of Fieldwork*, Beverly Hills, CA: Sage.

Punch, M. (1994) 'Politics and ethics in fieldwork', in N. Denzin and Y. Lincoln (eds), *Handbook of Qualitative Research*, Thousand Oaks, CA: Sage, 83–97.

Pursley-Crotteau, S. and Stern, P. (1996) 'Creating a new life: dimensions of temperance in perinatal cocaine crack users', *Qualitative Health Research*, 6 (3), 350–67.

Radcliffe-Brown, A.R. (1948) *The Andaman Islanders*, Glencoe, IL: Free Press.

Rapley, T. (2004) 'Interviews', in C. Seale, G. Gobo, J.F. Gubrium and D. Silverman (eds), *Qualitative Research Practice*, London: Sage, 15–33.

Reason, P. and Rowan, J. (1981) *Human Inquiry: a Sourcebook of New Paradigm Research*, Chichester: Wiley.

Reid, A.O. (1992) 'Computer management strategies for text data', in B.F. Crabtree and W.L. Miller (eds), *Doing Qualitative Research*, Newbury Park, CA: Sage, 125–45.

Richards, L. and Richards, T. (1994) 'Using computers in qualitative analysis', in N. Denzin and Y. Lincoln (eds), *Handbook of Qualitative Research*, Thousand Oaks, CA: Sage, 445–62.

Richardson, L. (1990) *Writing Strategies: Reaching Diverse Audiences*, Newbury Park, CA: Sage.

Richardson, L. (2000) 'Writing: a method of inquiry', in N. Denzin and Y. Lincoln (eds), *Handbook of Qualitative Research*, 2nd edn, Thousand Oaks, CA: Sage, 923–49.

Riessman, C.K. (1993) *Narrative Analysis*, Newbury Park, CA: Sage.

Rudestam, K. and Newton, R. (1992) *Surviving Your Dissertation*, Newbury Park, CA: Sage.

Ryen, A. (2004) 'Ethical issues', in C. Seale, G. Gobo, J.F. Gubrium and D. Silverman (eds), *Qualitative Research Practice*, London: Sage.

Sacks, H. (1974) 'On the analysability of stories by children', in R. Turner (ed.), *Ethnomethodology*, Harmondsworth: Penguin.

Sacks, H. (1984a) 'On doing "being ordinary"', in J.M. Atkinson and J. Heritage (eds), *Structures of Social Action: Studies in Conversation Analysis*, Cambridge: Cambridge University Press, 513–29.

Sacks, H. (1984b) 'Notes on methodology' in J.M. Atkinson and J. Heritage (eds), *Structures of Social Action: Studies in Conversation Analysis*, Cambridge: Cambridge University Press, 21–7.

Sacks, H. (1992) *Lectures on Conversation*, Vols 1 and 2, ed. Gail Jefferson with introduction by Emmanuel Schegloff, Oxford: Blackwell.

Sacks, H., Schegloff, E.A. and Jefferson, G. (1974) 'A simplest systematics for the organization of turn-taking in conversation', *Language*, 50 (4), 696–735.

Schegloff, E. (1986) 'The routine as achievement', *Human Studies*, 9, 111–51.

Schegloff, E. (1991) 'Reflections on talk and social structure', in D. Boden and D. Zimmerman (eds), *Talk and Social Structure: Studies in Ethnomethodology and Conversation Analysis*, Cambridge: Polity, 44–70.

Schreiber, R. (1996) '(Re)defining my self: women's process of recovery from depression', *Qualitative Health Research*, 6 (4), 469–91.

Schwartz, H. and Jacobs, J. (1979) *Qualitative Sociology: A Method to the Madness*, New York: Free Press.

Seale, C. (1996) 'Living alone towards the end of life', *Ageing and Society*, 16, 75–91.

Seale, C. (1999) *The Quality of Qualitative Research*, London: Sage.

Seale, C.F. (2002) 'Computer-assisted analysis of qualitative interview data' in J. Gubrium and J. Holstein (eds), *Handbook of Interview Research*, Thousand Oaks, CA: Sage, 651–70.

Seale, C. (ed.) (2004) *Researching Society and Culture*, 2nd edn, London: Sage.

Seale, C., Gobo, G., Gubrium, J.F. and Silverman, D. (eds) (2004) *Qualitative Research Practice*, London: Sage.

Sharples, M., Davison, L., Thomas, G. and Rudman, P. (2003) 'Children as photographers: an analysis of children's photographic behaviour and intentions at three age levels', *Visual Communication*, 2 (3), 303–30.

Silverman, D. (1981) 'The child as a social object: Down's syndrome children in a paediatric cardiology clinic', *Sociology of Health and Illness*, 3 (3), 254–74.

Silverman, D. (1983) 'The clinical subject: adolescents in a cleft palate clinic', *Sociology of Health and Illness*, (5) 3, 253–74.

Silverman, D. (1984) 'Going private: ceremonial forms in a private oncology clinic', *Sociology*, 18, 191–202.

Silverman, D. (1985) *Qualitative Methodology and Sociology: Describing the Social World*, Aldershot: Gower.

Silverman, D. (1987) *Communication and Medical Practice: Social Relations in the Clinic*, London: Sage.

Silverman, D. (1989) 'Making sense of a precipice: constituting identity in an HIV clinic', in P. Aggleton, G. Hart and P. Davies (eds), *AIDS: Social Representations, Social Practices*, Lewes: Falmer.

Silverman, D. (1990) 'The social organization of HIV counselling', in P. Aggleton, G. Hart and P. Davies (eds), *AIDS: Individual, Cultural and Policy Perspectives*, Lewes: Falmer, 191–211.

Silverman, D. (1997) *Discourses of Counselling: HIV Counselling as Social Interaction*, London: Sage.

Silverman, D. (1998) *Harvey Sacks: Social Science and Conversation Analysis*, Cambridge: Polity, New York: Oxford University Press.

Silverman, D. (2001) *Interpreting Qualitative Data: Methods for Analysing Text, Talk and Interaction,* 2nd edn, London: Sage.

Silverman, D. (2004) 'Analysing conversation', in C. Seale (ed.), *Researching Society and Culture*, 2nd edn, London: Sage, 261–74.

Silverman, D. (ed.) (2004) *Qualitative Research: Theory, Method and Practice,* 2nd edn, London: Sage.

Silverman, D. and Bloor, M. (1989) 'Patient-centred medicine: some sociological observations on its constitution, penetration and cultural assonance', in G.L. Albrecht (ed.), *Advances in Medical Sociology*, Greenwich, CT: JAI Press, 3–26.

Silverman, D. and Gubrium, J. (1994) 'Competing strategies for analyzing the contexts of social interaction', *Sociological Inquiry*, 64 (2), 179–98.

Silverman, D. and Jones, J. (1976) *Organizational Work: The Language of Grading/the Grading of Language*, London: Collier-Macmillan.

Silverman, D., Baker, C. and Keogh, J. (1997) 'Advice-giving and advice-reception in parent–teacher interviews', in I. Hutchby and J. Moran-Ellis (eds), *Children and Social Competence*, London: Falmer, 220–40.

Singleton, R., Straits, B., Straits, M. and McAllister, R. (1988) *Approaches to Social Research*, Oxford: Oxford University Press.

Smith, J.K. and Heshusius, L. (1986) 'Closing down the conversation: the end of the qualitative–quantitative debate among educational enquirers', *Educational Researcher*, 15, 4–12.

Sontag, S. (1979) *Illness as Metaphor*, Harmondsworth: Penguin.

Speer, S. (2002) '"Natural" and "contrived" data: a sustainable distinction?', *Discourse Studies*, 4 (4), 511–25.

Spencer, L., Ritchie, J., Lewis, J. and Dillon, J. (2003) *Quality in Qualitative Evaluation: a framework for assessing research evidence*, London: Government Chief Social Researcher's Office.

Spradley, J.P. (1979) *The Ethnographic Interview*, New York; Holt, Rinehart and Winston.

Stake, R. (2000) 'Case studies', in N. Denzin and Y. Lincoln (eds), *Handbook of Qualitative Research,* 2nd edn, Thousand Oaks, CA: Sage, 435–54.

Stimson, G. (1986) 'Place and space in sociological fieldwork', *Sociological Review,* 34 (3), 641–56.

Strauss, A. and Corbin, J. (1990) *Basics of Qualitative Research*, Thousand Oaks, CA: Sage.

Strauss, A. and Corbin, J.(1994) 'Grounded theory methodology: an overview', in N. Denzin and Y. Lincoln (eds), *Handbook of Qualitative Research*, Thousand Oaks, CA: Sage, 262–72.

Strong, P. (1979) *The Ceremonial Order of the Clinic*, London: Routledge.

Suchman, L. (1987) *Plans and Situated Actions: The Problem of Human–Machine Communication*, Cambridge: Cambridge University Press.

Sudnow, D. (1968a) *Passing On: the Social Organization of Dying*, Englewood Cliffs, NJ: Prentice Hall.

Sudnow, D. (1968b) 'Normal crimes', in E. Rubington and M. Weinberg (eds), *Deviance: The Interactionist Perspective*, New York: Macmillan.

ten Have, P. (1998) *Doing Conversation Analysis: A Practical Guide*, London: Sage.

Turner, R. (1989) 'Deconstructing the field', in J.F. Gubrium and D. Silverman (eds), *The Politics of Field Research*, London: Sage, 30–48.

Tyler, S.A. (1986) 'Post-modern ethnography: from document of the occult to occult document', in J. Clifford and G. Marcus (eds), *Writing Culture: the Poetics and Politics of Ethnography*, Los Angeles: University of California Press, 122–40.

Walsh, D. (1998) 'Doing ethnography', in C. Seale (ed.), *Researching Society and Culture*, London: Sage, 225–38.

Ward, A. (2002) 'The writing process', in S. Potter (ed.), *Doing Postgraduate Research*, London: Sage, 71–116.

Warren, A. (1988) *Gender Issues in Field Research*, Newbury Park, CA: Sage.

Warren, A. and Rasmussen, P. (1977) 'Sex and gender in fieldwork research', *Urban Life*, 6, 359–69.

Watts, H.D. and White, P. (2000) 'Presentation skills', in D. Burton (ed.), *Research Training for Social Scientists*, London: Sage.

Webb, B. and Stimson, G. (1976) 'People's accounts of medical encounters', in M. Wadsworth (ed.), *Everyday Medical Life*, London: Martin Robertson.

Weber, M. (1946) 'Science as a vocation', in H. Gerth and C.W. Mills (eds), *From Max Weber*, New York: Oxford University Press.

Weber, M. (1949) *Methodology of the Social Sciences*, New York: Free Press.

Whyte, W.F. (1949) 'The social structure of the restaurant', *American Journal of Sociology*, 54, 302–10.

Wield, D. (2002) 'Planning and organizing a research project', in S. Potter (ed.), *Doing Postgraduate Research*, London: Sage, 35–70.

Wilkinson, S. (2004) 'Focus group research', in D. Silverman (ed.), *Qualitative Research: Theory, Method and Practice*, 2nd edn, London: Sage, 177–99.

Wilkinson, S. and Kitzinger, C. (2000) 'Thinking differently about thinking positive: a discursive approach to cancer patients' talk', *Social Science and Medicine*, 50, 797–811.

Wittgenstein, L. (1980) *Culture and Value*, trans. P. Winch, Oxford: Basil Blackwell.

Wolcott, H. (1990) *Writing Up Qualitative Research*, Newbury Park, CA: Sage.

Author Index

Subject Index